El diccionario del español chicano

The Dictionary of Chicano Spanish

Compiled by
Roberto A. Galván, Southwest Texas State University
Richard V. Teschner, University of Texas at El Paso

INSTITUTE OF MODERN LANGUAGES, INC.
SILVER SPRING, MARYLAND

Publicado por el
Institute of Modern Languages, Inc.
The Language People
2622-24 Pittman Drive
Silver Spring, Maryland 20910
U.S.A.

Impreso en los Estado Unidos de Norteamérica

ISBN 0-88499-146-6

* * * * *

Published by
Institute of Modern Languages, Inc.
The Language People
2622-24 Pittman Drive
Silver Spring, Maryland 20910

Printed in the United States of America

ISBN 0-88499-146-6

Índice de materias/Table of Contents

Abreviaturas usadas en este diccionario/List of Abbreviations

abbrev.	abbreviation / abreviatura
adj.	adjective / adjetivo
adv.	adverb / adverbio
Ang.	Anglicism (word or phrase historically Spanish but altered in meaning through Eng. influence) / anglicismo (palabra o frase de origen castellano pero que se alteró luego por influencia del inglés)
ant.	antiquated / anticuado -da
aut.	automotive, automobile / automovilístico -ca, carro
cf.	compare / compárese
coll.	colloquial / coloquial
conj.	conjunction / conjunción
dim.	diminutive / diminutivo
e.g.	for example / por ejemplo
Eng.	word from English borrowed into Spanish / palabra prestada del inglés al español (cf. Ang.)
esp.	especially / especialmente
et al.	and others / y otros -tras
euph.	euphemism, euphemistic / eufemismo, eufemístico -ca
fam.	familiar / familiar
f.	feminine / femenino -na
fig.	figurative / figurado -da
fpl.	f. plural / plural f.
fsg.	f. singular / singular f.
ger.	gerund / gerundio
hum.	humorous(ly) / festivo -va
id.	identical (to) / lo mismo (que)
i.e.	that is to say / es decir
imperf.	imperfect tense / tiempo imperfecto
ind.	indicative (mode) / (modo) indicativo
infra	below / abajo
interj.	interjection / exclamación
iron.	irony, ironic / ironía, irónico -ca
m.	masculine / masculino -na
mf.	either m. or f. according to sex of human referent / m. o f. según el sexo
m. & f.	word taking either gender/ palabra de ambos géneros
mfsg.	singular (either m. or f.) singular (o m. o f.)
mpl.	m. plural / plural m.
msg.	m. singular / singular m.
n. place	no place of publication indicated / no se indica el lugar de imprenta
orthog.	orthographic / ortográfico -ca
pej.	pejorative / peyorativo -va
pers.	person (e.g., 1st person sg. = <u>yo</u>) / persona (e.g., 1ª persona de sg. = <u>yo</u>)
pl.	plural
poss.	possible / posible
pr.	pronounced / se pronuncia
pres.	present tense / tiempo presente
ppart.	past participle / participio pasado
pret.	preterite tense / tiempo pretérito
prob.	probably / probablemente
pron.	pronoun / pronombre
q.v.	which see / véase
ref.	reference, refer(s) / referencia, se refiere(n)
resp.	respectively / respectivamente
rus.	rustic, rural or small town / rústico -ca, de pueblo chico
s.	see / véase
sg.	singular
Std.	standard Spanish, normative usage / español normativo
subj.	subjunctive mode / subjuntivo
supra	above / arriba
underw.	underworld / del hampa
va.	active (transitive) verb / verbo activo (transitivo)
var.	variant / variante
vn.	neutral (intransitive) verb / verbo intransitivo
vr.	reflexive verb / verbo reflexivo
vulg.	vulgar, obscene / obsceno -na, ordinario -ria

Guía al lector

Cualquier forma nominativa o adjetival que termina en *o* es de considerarse masculina si no se indica lo contrario; asimismo se considera de género femenino cualquier forma terminada en *a*, de no indicarse que sea masculina. De igual manera se consideran m. y f., respectivamente, las parejas que terminan en *ÓN* y *ONA* si no se indica lo contrario.

Como el español se escribe como se pronuncia, por regla general, no se ofrecen aquí pronunciaciones "figuradas" al lado de los casi 8,000 artículos de este diccionario.

User's Guide

Nouns or adjectives not marked for gender and ending in *o* and *a* are assumed to be masculine and feminine, respectively, unless otherwise indicated. Likewise m. and f., respectively, are pairs which end in -*ÓN*, -*ONA* unless otherwise indicated.

Since Spanish is, for the most part, "pronounced as written," this dictionary does not give figured pronunciation for its nearly 8,000 entries.

Prefacio a la 1ª edición

La presente obra es un diccionario suplemental del español que se usa en el estado de Tejas. Los dos millones y medio (más o menos) de méxicoamericanos o chicanos que lo emplean, representan aproximadamente un veintitrés por ciento de la población de dicha área. Esta última cifra constituye, a su vez, cerca de treinta y ocho por ciento de los seis millones y pico de personas de apellidos españoles que se hallan en los Estados Unidos sudoccidentales (California, Arizona, Nuevo México, Colorado y Tejas).

Al usar el vocablo que denominamos "suplemental" queremos dar a entender que nuestro diccionario consigna, define en inglés y--cuando es necesario--ejemplifica en contexto conversacional de carácter verosímil todas aquellas palabras y frases que se usan en el español de Tejas, pero que aún no se han catalogado en los diccionarios de consulta más asequibles. Los siete mil artículos que integran nuestra obra representan, pues, las expresiones que no se hallan en los diccionarios monolingües (español) y bilingües (inglés-español/español-inglés) de extensa diseminación. (Para títulos véase el párrafo siguiente.) Hacemos constar de antemano para el lector, pues, que el Diccionario del español de Tejas (DET) viene siendo un léxico de tipo suplementario porque no incorpora el voluminoso vocabulario normativo del español general--los 100.000 artículos, o más, que aparecen en los diccionarios monolingües o bilingües a que acabamos de aludir. En consecuencia, hemos tenido a bien advertir al público que nuestro trabajo debe utilizarse principalmente para llenar la laguna de aquéllos en lo que toca al vocabulario tejano.

En nuestro esfuerzo por recoger un léxico bastante completo, fue alfabetizado mediante su elaboración en computadora electrónica todo aquel material tomado de fuentes secundarias en que se apunta o se examina el léxico español de Tejas. (Véase el Apéndice C para una lista de dichas fuentes.) Eliminamos de esta lista todas las expresiones que se hallan con formas y acepciones idénticas en uno o más de los diccionarios populares que citamos a continuación: University of Chicago Spanish (/English) Dictionary, 2ª ed., 1972; Collins Spanish-English English-Spanish Dictionary, 1971; Nuevo Diccionario Cuyás Inglés-Español y Español-Inglés (5ª ed.,

Preface to the 1st Edition

This is a supplementary dictionary of the Spanish spoken in the state of Texas by approximately two and a half million Mexican-Americans or Chicanos, representing about 23 per cent of the population of that state, and constituting roughly 38 per cent of the ca. 6,540,000 persons of Spanish surname in the five-state area of the United States Southwest (California, Arizona, New Mexico and Colorado, in addition to Texas).

By "supplementary" we mean that this dictionary lists, defines in English and, when necessary, exemplifies through citations of likely conversational usage all those words and phrases used in Texas Spanish but not included, as yet, in the more readily available reference lexicons. Our nearly 7,000 entries represent, then, the words and phrases one cannot locate in the widely-distributed monolingual-Spanish or bilingual Spanish-English dictionaries. (See below for reference to these.) The user is advised aforehand that the Diccionario del español de Tejas (DET) is not a "full-length" dictionary for the simple reason that it does not give items which form part of "standard" Spanish as defined by the several canons of inclusion of those monolingual and bilingual dictionaries which aim at omnivorous coverage and whose total entries, in consequence, run somewhere in the neighborhood of 100,000. Our dictionary, then, is intended for use "alongside" a full-length lexicon.

To insure maximum coverage, all secondary literature which listed or otherwise examined the vocabulary of Texas Spanish (see Appendix C for citations) was processed by computer into an alphabetized master-list. Subsequently discarded were all those items which were already to be found in one or more of the following widely-distributed dictionaries: University of Chicago Spanish (/English) Dictionary, 2nd ed., 1972; Collins Spanish-English English-Spanish Dictionary, 1971; Nuevo Diccionario Cuyás Inglés-Español y Español-Inglés (5th ed., 1966); Pequeño Larousse Ilustrado (1966); Simon and Schuster's International Dictionary, English-Spanish/Spanish-English (1973); and The Williams Spanish & English Dictionary, Expanded Edition (1963).

To the several thousand entries thus derived, the compilers of this dictionary added several thousand

1966); Pequeño Larousse Ilustrado (1966); Simon and Schuster's International Dictionary, English-Spanish/Spanish-English (1973); y The Williams Spanish & English Dictionary, Expanded Edition (1963).

A los miles de artículos que hallamos para nuestra compilación al utilizar el susodicho proceso, añadimos miles más tomados del tarjetero del profesor Galván, cuyas investigaciones en su dialecto nativo empiezan ya en las postrimerías de la década de los cuarenta. Por otro lado, suprimimos de nuestras fuentes secundarias varios artículos que desconoce el coleccionista mayoritario, el profesor Galván, y que tampoco hemos podido hallar en los diccionario autoritativos del español del mexicano (Francisco J. Santamaría, Diccionario de mejicanismos, 1959, en particular, o en otros de semejante categoría); en otras palabras, el léxico que incorporamos en nuestro DET ha sido comprobado personalmente por el profesor Galván como parte del vocabulario que integra el español vigente en Tejas.

La mayor parte de las expresiones que se hallan en las fuentes secundarias (cincuenta, más o menos) que consultamos no llevan designación geográfica. Este hecho nos ha impedido señalar ciertas observaciones del tipo, que por regla general, se hacen en los "atlas lingüísticos"; por ende, legamos a los investigadores interesados en el campo la tarea de compilar un "atlas lexicográfico" del español de Tejas. Por otro lado, sí nos fue posible señalar el nivel social de nuestro léxico, gracias a los conocimientos del profesor Galván respecto de todas las esferas sociales (media y baja) del hispanohablante que reside en las ciudades, en los pueblos pequeños y en las regiones campestres de Tejas. A base de estos conocimientos el profesor pudo asimismo fijar el grado de aceptación que el pueblo tejano hispanohablante concede a sus vocablos, v. gr., voces jergales, coloquiales, hampescas, vulgares, eufemísticas, rústicas (rurales y de pueblos pequeños).

Hacemos constar que todas las expresiones que hemos incorporado en nuestro DET se emplean actualmente en el español de Tejas, a no ser que las hayamos catalogado como arcaísmos. Por otro lado, no mantenemos que tal o cual vocablo de nuestro léxico es "peculiar" al español de la región hispanohablante que estudiamos; pues; no queremos dar a entender que el vocablo en cuestión sea desconocido o more from the card files of Prof. Galván, the senior compiler, whose fieldwork in the lexicon of his native dialect dates back to the late 1940's. On the other hand, several dozen items appearing in the various secondary sources but unknown to Prof. Galván and furthermore not traceable through any of the standard lexicons of Mexican Spanish (chiefly Francisco J. Santamaría, Diccionario de mejicanismos, 1959) or else verifiable elsewhere were deliberately discarded; this is to say that all items appearing in the DET have been personally attested to by Prof. Galván as forming part of the lexicon of Texas Spanish.

Thanks in large part to the nearly total lack of geographical labeling of lexical items in the fifty-some secondary sourceworks consulted, we were forced to foreswear certain "linguistic atlas" features we would otherwise have liked to incorporate; we will thus leave to future investigators the task of compiling a word atlas of Texas Spanish. But while geographical labeling was not possible, the description of many items according to their level of social use and acceptability was vastly facilitated by Prof. Galván's thorough-going knowledge of all strata of Texas Mexican-American society-lower- and middle-class, urban, small-town and rural alike. Thus all socially marked items are labeled according to the consideration in which they are generally held, whether as slang, as colloquial, as criminal (underworld), as vulgar, as euphemistic, as rustic (rural/small-town), etc.

While we do not hesitate to assert that all DET entries are currently in use in the Spanish of Texas (unless, of course, they are marked as antiquated), we do not claim that the entries in our lexicon are "peculiar to" the Spanish of this particular Spanish-speaking region and thus, by inference, unknown or else accepted solely as foreignisms "elsewhere" throughout the Hispanic world. It is the authors' firmly-held belief that until a complete conflation is attempted of all secondary sources of Hispanic "regional" lexicon (thereby providing the would-be collector of "-ismos" with a baseline against which to measure the distribution of a particular form), any claim that an item is unique to a given region must be viewed at best with a coldly-cast eye.

que se acepte únicamente como extranjerismo en otras comarcas del mundo hispanohablante. Creemos firmemente que hasta hacerse una compilación completa del léxico regional que se halla en todas las fuentes secundarias disponibles, tendremos que sospechar de toda aquella aseveración que señale tal o cual vocablo como localismo exclusivo. Una colección completa dará al compilador la oportunidad de llevar a efecto un estudio comparativo que le permita hallar los giros y dicciones de carácter locativo.

Al arreglar cada artículo y sus partes hemos hecho un esfuerzo especial a fin de producir una obra de referencia de máxima utilidad. Para realizar dicha meta y para eliminar los problemas que la pronunciación regional pueda ocasionarle al lego, hemos incluido las variantes fonéticas que se han venido efectuando como consecuencia de ciertos fenómenos evolutivos: (1) por supresión de consonante: ll o y> Ø, v. gr. bolillo> bolío; (2) por elevación de vocal: así, encontramos espeletiar al lado de espeletear (véase el Apéndice B para un modelo completo de conjugación que muestra el intercambio de los verbos que terminan en -ear e -iar). Los fenómenos de esta clase, así como otras variantes regionales, tales como güe- o bue- por hue-, j por h, etc., se deletrean cada vez más según y conforme se pronuncian en la literatura chicana cuyo vigor y contenido viene aumentándose a pasos agigantados. Las variantes que referimos se apuntan por separado alfabéticamente o en el mismo artículo en que aparece la forma principal de que son variantes aquéllas. No hemos creído necesario incluir los casos en que se suprime la d final (bondá = bondad) o medial de los participios pasivos de los verbos de la primera conjugación (v. gr. hablao = hablado), ya que dicha variación aparece al final o hacia el final de las palabras en cuestión, y que por tanto, no le sería difícil al lector dar con ellas en nuestro diccionario o en otros.

El criterio que empleamos para escoger los proverbios del español de Tejas a que damos cabida en el Apéndice A de nuestra obra ha sido menos exigente que el que nos guió al seleccionar los vocablos que consignamos en la parte principal del DET. Ello se debe al hecho de no

Maximum utility has been our guideword throughout the compilation of the DET. To insure that utility, and to guarantee that the non-specialist user is not stumped by the problems frequently brought about by "regional" pronunciations, we have not hesitated to include as separate entries or, when alphabetically feasible, as coordinate entries the various phonetically "variant" forms whose distinctiveness derives from consonant supression (thus the many instances of ll or y> Ø, e.g., bolillo> bolío), from vowel raising (thus espeletiar alongside espeletear--see Appendix B for the complete conjugation of a model -ear/-iar interchanging verb), and so forth. Words containing these and other "regional" variations such as güe- or bue- for hue-, j for h, etc., are increasingly spelled "as pronounced" in the growing and vigorous body of Chicano literature, and to avoid at least a quick reference to such forms would do a considerable disservice to users of the DET. Only in the case of the suppression of the d in word-final position (e.g., bondá = bondad) or in the close-to-word-final position, as in the past participles of first conjugation verbs (e.g., hablao = hablado), have we failed to give separate listing to regional pronunciations and spellings; our logic here is that since the variation comes close to the end of the word, user frustration in locating the appropriate entry in this or any other dictionary will be minimal at most.

Since there appears to exist no widely-distributed, up-to-date compendium of Spanish-language proverbs, our criterion for admitting these to Appendix A ("Proverbs and Sayings"/ "Proverbios y Refranes") has been, thus, considerably more liberal than was the case with lexical entries: if the proverb is heard in Texas we include it in our Appendix.

The DET does not purport to be an etymological dictionary, though infrequent etymologies are given. For those in search of a painstaking etymological study of caló ("slang") terms in Chicano Spanish we can recommend a recently-completed unpublished doctoral dissertation: John Terrance Webb. "A Lexical Study of Caló and Non-Standard Spanish in the Southwest," PhD Diss., University of California, Berkeley, (Dec.) 1975.

haber un compendio actualizado de los proverbios de la lengua española.

Aunque aventuramos esporádicamente algunas etimologías, no nos hemos propuesto escribir un diccionario etimológico. Recomendamos dos obras capitales a todo aquel que se interese en este aspecto de nuestro material: (1) para el caló o voces jergales del español chicano: John Terrance Webb, "A Lexical Study of Caló and Non-Standard Spanish in the Southwest," PhD Diss., Univ. de California, Berkeley, (dic.) 1975; (2) para las voces del español general: J. Corominas, Diccionario etimológico del español, 4 vols., Madrid: Gredos, 1954.

For a complete general etymological dictionary one naturally turns to the J. Corominas Diccionario etimológico del español, 4 vols., Madrid: Gredos, 1954.

Roberto A. Galván, San Marcos, Texas
Richard V. Teschner, Iowa City, Iowa

September, 1975

Prefacio a la edición revisada

En el presente volumen acrecentamos a 8.000 artículos lo que llegó a casi 7.000 en nuestra primera edición, El diccionario del español de Tejas/The Dictionary of the Spanish of Texas (Silver Spring MD: IML, 1975, vii, 102 pp.). La extensión que agregamos a la difusión geográfica, y los vocablos y acepciones que añadimos al presente trabajo (a nuestra segunda edición hemos incorporado artículos recogidos de estudios lingüísticos realizados en California, Arizona, Nuevo México, la Florida y Tejas; para documentar el habla de esta última región utilizamos una bibliografía corriente y más amplia que la de la primera edición) han ocasionado el cambio de título que hemos efectuado: ... de Tejas > El diccionario del español chicano.

He aquí cuatro palabras sobre las adiciones que hemos asignado a la distribución geográfica. Creemos que la presente edición representa, en forma fidedigna y en lo que toca a todo el sudoeste de los Estados Unidos y sus extensiones (así como lo representa la primera edición para Tejas), una colección completa de las voces y frases chicanas que, por regla general, no se catalogan en los diccionarios monolingües y bilingües de carácter normativo. Sin embargo, sería una impropiedad de nuestra parte no indicar que el núcleo lexicográfico de nuestra obra (proveniente en forma directa del material que nos proporcionaron nuestros informantes) sigue describiendo, en lo esencial, el español de Tejas (nos referimos aquí a ambas variedades: las que se hablan más allá de Pecos y las de San Antonio y sus comarcas circumvecinas). Debemos señalar asimismo que, por regla general, hemos tenido que valernos de los hallazgos de otros investigadores respecto del léxico chicano y de su difusión geográfica cuando este se halla más allá del estado de Tejas, es decir en el resto de los Estados Unidos sudoccidentales y en otros parajes en donde se usa el susodicho dialecto de Aztlán. El hecho de que existe, en lo esencial, una unidad lexicográfica dentro del español chicano, nos fue evidente a medida que buscábamos voces adicionales en las obras de consulta que se registran a continuación (también examinamos otros trabajos a fin de actualizar nuestros hallazgos en la presente edición, pero sólo los que consignamos aquí nos proporcionaron más de un

Preface to the Revised Edition

The present volume brings to 8,000 the nearly 7,000 items found in its parent lexicon, El diccionario del español de Tejas/The Dictionary of the Spanish of Texas (Silver Spring, MD: IML, 1975, vii, 102 pp.). An expansion of geographical as well as lexical coverage (our second edition has included items from sources based on research undertaken in California, Arizona, New Mexico, Colorado, and Florida, as well as an expansion and up-date of the original work's Texas lexical base) has brought about a change in title from ... de Tejas to the present El diccionario del español chicano.

A word about our expanded geographical coverage. While we are confident that the present work faithfully represents, for the entire Southwest and its extensions (as did the original work, for Texas), a complete compilation of Chicano words and phrases not typically found in standard home-reference dictionaries both monolingual and bilingual, it would be unscrupulous of us not to note that the first-hand, field-work-based core lexicon remains essentially Texas (in both its trans-Pecos and circum-San Antonio varieties), and that in the main we have had to rely on other people's work for information about the Chicano lexicon of ultrasolosellarian Aztlán. That there exists within Chicano Spanish an essential unity of vocabulary, however, was apparent to us as we sought out neoteric items in the following sourceworks (others were also consulted for the present edition, but only the following provided us with more than a small handful of new words and phrases): Aranda, Charles, comp. Dichos: Proverbs and Sayings from the Spanish. Santa Fe, NM: Sunstone Press, 1975, 69 pp. Beltramo, Anthony Fred. "Lexical and Morphological Aspects of Linguistic Acculturation by Mexican Americans in San José, California." PhD Diss., Stanford Univ., 1972, vii, 324 pp., DAI 33/08-A, p. 4379. Blanco S., Antonio. La lengua española en la historia de California. Madrid: Ediciones Cultura Hispánica, 1971, 827 pp. Domínguez, Domingo. "A Theoretical Model for Classifying Dialectal Variations of Oral New Mexican Spanish." PhD Diss., Univ. of New Mexico, 1975, 107 pp., DAI 35/09-A, p. 5674. Fuentes, Dagoberto and José A. López. Barrio Language

manojo de nuevas expresiones): Aranda, Charles, comp. Dichos: Proverbs and Sayings from the Spanish. Santa Fe NM: Sunstone Press, 1975, 69 pp. Beltramo, Anthony Fred. "Lexical and Morphological Aspects of Linguistic Acculturation by Mexican Americans in San José, California." PhD Diss., Stanford Univ., 1972, vii, 324 pp., DAI 33/08-A, p. 4379. Blanco S., Antonio. La lengua española en la historia de California. Madrid: Ediciones Cultura Hispánica, 1971, 827 pp. Domínguez, Domingo. "A Theoretical Model for Classifying Dialectal Variations of Oral New Mexican Spanish." PhD Diss., Univ. of New Mexico, 1975, 107 pp., DAI 35/09-A, p. 5674. Fuentes, Dagoberto and José A. López. Barrio Language Dictionary: First [sic] Dictionary of Caló. Los Angeles/La Puente CA: Southland Press/El Barrio Publications and Lubbock TX: Trucha Publications, 1974, vii, 160 pp. Gross, Stuart Murray. "A Vocabulary of New Mexican Spanish." MA Thesis, Stanford Univ., 1935, vi, 78 pp. (=una compilación de los lexemas que se hallan en la obra total neomexicéntrica de Aurelio M. Espinosa, padre, publicada antes de 1934.). Kay, Margarita Artschwager, John D. Meredith, Wendy Redlinger and Alicia Quiroz Raymond. Southwestern Medical Dictionary: Spanish-English/English-Spanish, Tucson AZ: Univ. of Arizona Press, 1977, xvi, 217 pp. Riegelhaupt-Barkin, Florence. "The Influence of English on the Spanish of Bilingual Mexican Migrants in Florida." PhD Diss., SUNY-Buffalo, 1976, 249 pp., DAI 37/05-A, pp. 2834-35. Ross, Lyle Ronald. "La lengua castellana en San Luis, Colorado." PhD Diss., Univ. of Colorado, 1975, 192 pp., DAI 36/L8-A, pp. 5264-65. Serrano, Rodolfo G. Dictionary of Pachuco Terms. Bakersfield CA: Sierra Printers, 1976, v, 66 pp.

Consideraciones imprevistas de espacio nos obligan a omitir una versión acrecentada de la bibliografía desarrollada a base de fuentes primarias y secundarias que lleva nuestra obra en su primera edición. No obstante, todo aquel que desee una guía completa de lo que se ha escrito sobre el español del Chicano (y el de otros hispanohablantes que residen en los EE.UU.) podrá consultar el trabajo de Richard V. Teschner, Garland D. Bills and Jerry R. Craddock (eds.), Spanish and English of United States Hispanos: A Critical, Annotated, Linguistic

Dictionary: First [sic] Dictionary of Caló. Los Angeles/La Puente CA: Southland Press/El Barrio Publications and Lubbock TX: Trucha Publications, 1974, vii, 160 pp. Gross, Stuart Murray. "A Vocabulary of New Mexican Spanish." MA Thesis, Stanford Univ., 1935, vi, 78 pp. (=a compilation of lexemes found in all pre-1934 neomexocentric publications of Aurelio M. Espinosa, Sr.). Kay, Margarita Artschwager, John D. Meredith, Wendy Redlinger and Alicia Quiroz Raymond Southwestern Medical Dictionary: Spanish-English/English-Spanish Tucson AZ: Univ. of Arizona Press, 1977, xvi, 217 pp. Riegelhaupt-Barkin, Florence. "The Influence of English on the Spanish of Bilingual Mexican American Migrants in Florida." PhD Diss., SUNY-Buffalo, 1976, 249 pp., DAI 37/05-A, pp. 2834-35. Ross, Lyle Ronald. "La lengua castellana en San Luis, Colorado." PhD Diss., Univ. of Colorado, 1975, 192 pp., DAI 36/L8-A, pp. 5264-65. Serrano, Rodolfo G. Dictionary of Pachuco Terms. Bakersfield CA: Sierra Printers, 1976, v, 66 pp.

Unforeseen considerations of space have obliged us to do without an expanded version of the full-fledged bibliography of secondary and primary sources which accompanied the present work's first edition (pp. 99-102). However, readers interested in a complete guide to writings on Chicano (and other U.S.) Spanish need only consult Richard V. Teschner, Garland D. Bills and Jerry R. Craddock (eds.), Spanish and English of United States Hispanos: A Critical, Annotated, Linguistic Bibliography (Arlington VA: Center for Applied Linguistics, 1975, xxii, 352 pp.) and the same authors' enumerative supplement to that work, "Current Research on the Language(s) of U.S. Hispanos," Hispania 60.347-358 (1977).

Bibliography (Arlington VA: Center for Applied Linguistics, 1975, xxii, 352 pp.), así como el suplemento enumerativo a dicha obra compilado por los mismos autores: "Current Research on the Language(s) of U.S. Hispanos," *Hispania* 60.347-358 (1977).

Roberto A. Galván, San Marcos, Texas
Richard V. Teschner, El Paso, Texas

August, 1977

El diccionario del español chicano

A

A: A CA (var. of a casa de): "Voy a ca mamá" 'I'm going over to mom's house'; A CARRILLA hurriedly, rapidly; A CAS DE (var. of) a casa de: "Voy a cas de Chucho" 'I'm going to Chucho's house'; A CAS E (var. of a casa de); A COMO DÉ LUGAR one way or another, any way it can be done: "¿Cómo piensan hacerlo?-- A como dé lugar;" A FUERZA QUE SÍ most likely, in all likelihood, more likely than not: "¿Tendrán frío los gatos?-- A fuerza que sí" 'Are the cats cold?--More likely than not.'; A HUEVO by force, forcibly; A LA BRAVA seriously; genuinely; A LA BUENA voluntarily, willingly; A LA BUENA O A LA MALA willingly or else: "Lo haces a la buena o a la mala" 'You'll do it willingly or else'; A LA HORA DE LA HORA/A L'HORA DEL HORA when it comes right down to it, at the moment of truth, when all is said and done; A LA MALA by force (cf. A LA BUENA); A LA MEJOR probably, likely as not (cf. Std. a lo mejor); AL NO SER QUE (var. of a no ser que); A MANOS tied (in a sports competition); even, all paid up; A PATIN on foot; A PESPUNTE (slang) on foot; A PINCEL (slang) on foot; A PLATA LIMPIA innocent, blameless; A POCO perhaps (often used as interj.: 'You don't say!' --used when the speaker dares a braggard to make good a threat; also used to register surprise or incredulity); A POCO RATO shortly, soon thereafter; A RAIZ (said of a person dressed too sparingly for the weather); A RATO afterwards, in a while; A TIRO DE QUE although, despite; A TODA FUERZA in full swing: "El baile estaba a toda fuerza" 'The dance was in full swing'; A TODA MADRE super, great, tremendous (etc.); rapidly, quickly; A TODA MÁQUINA very fast, rapidly; A TODO DAR very good, tremendous, great, super (etc.); A TODO ESTO while we're speaking about that, while we're on the subject: "Bueno, y a todo esto, ¿qué hiciste con el reloj?" 'Well, while we're on the subject, what did you do with the watch?'; A TODOS TIROS always; A TODO TREN very good, excellent, super (etc.); ¡A VOLAR! (interj.) Get out of here!, Beat it! (coll.); ¡A VOLAR CON ALAS! Beat it! Scram!; AL RATÓN (var. of) al rato 'in a short while'

ABANICAR EL AIRE (slang) vn. to strike out (baseball)

ABANICO (slang) easy out (ref., in baseball, to person who strikes out easily)

ABARROTES mpl. groceries; groceries and other items sold at grocery stores

ABOCANADO -DA running wild (ref. to horses); (ref. to persons, hum.) footloose, wild, fancy-free

ABOCANAR vr. to rear up and run wild (said of horses and, hum., of persons)

ABOLIADO -DA (see ABOLILLADO -DA)

ABOLIAR (see ABOLILLAR)

ABOLILLADO -DA (coll.) gringo-like, gringoized (see also BOLILLO-LLA)

ABOLILLAR va. to cause to become like a gringo, gringoize; vr. to act like a gringo

ABRELIO (var. of) Aurelio (proper name)

ABREMOS (var. of) abrimos (1st pers. pl. pres. ind. of abrir)

ABRICIAS (var. of) albricias

ABRIDERO -DA act of opening a door, a container, a drawer, etc., repeatedly: "Siempre anda con esa abridera de puerta" 'He just keeps on opening and closing the door'

ABRIDO -DA (var. of) abierto -ta (ppart. of abrir)
ABRIDURA act of repeatedly opening a door, a container, etc. (cf. ABRIDERO -RA)
ABRILES (usually mpl.) (coll.) years, years old: "¿Cuántos abriles tienes?" 'How old are you?'
ABRORA (var. of) aurora 'dawn'
ABRORA (var. of) Aurora (proper name)
ABRUJA (var. of) aguja
ABUELITO -TA (slang) friend
ABUJA (slang, underw.) joint of a narcotic cigarette; injection (of a narcotic substance), fix (slang); (also: var. of aguja)
ABUJAZO (slang, underw.) injection of a narcotic substance, fix (slang) (cf. ABUJA)
ABUJERADO -DA (var. of) agujerado-da
ABUJERAR (var. of) agujerar
ABUJERO (var. of) agujero
ABURI (var. of) bure et al. (see also DE ABURI et al.)
ABUSADO -DA bully; clever person; wealthy person; miser
ABUSAR vr. to be alert; to become alert
ABUSÓN -SONA abusive, bully-like
ACÁ: ¿DE CUÁNDO ACÁ? Since when?, What do you mean by that? (statements indicating incredulity and often intended as a form of challenge to the speaker); ACÁ GARCÍA (see GARCÍA, IR ACÁ GARCÍA); ACÁ LA MADRE DE LOS BURROS/ACÁ LA MADRE DE LOS CABALLOS (fig.) a long way away, half way to hell and gone (slang)
ACABADO -DA old, worn out
ACABAR va. to age, wear down, fatigue: "Me estás acabando con tus pleitos"; vr. to wear oneself down, become run down; to die
ACAPRICHAR (var. of) encaprichar
ACARREAR vn. to spread tales, bear rumors
ACARTONADO -DA lean, thin (ref. to persons)
ACARRIAR (var. of) acarrear
ACE (Eng.) mf. ace (person who excels in an activity)
ACOMEDIDO -DA accommodating, obliging (see also COMEDIDO -DA)
ACOMEDIR vr. to serve or help without being asked; to be helpful, accomodating
ACCENTO (Eng.) accent
ACEITAR (var. of) aceptar
ACEITE m. kerosene; ACEITE DE CARRO motor oil; ACEITE DE COMER cooking oil, olive oil
ACELGA (fsg., also fpl.: ACELGAS) spinach
ACERO frying pan
ACETAR (var. of) aceptar
ÁCIDO msg. amphetamines, (slang) acid (="hard" drug used for narcotic purposes)
ACOMODADO -DA opportunistic
ACTOBÚS (var. of) autobús
ACTOMOBIL (var. of) automóbil
ACTOR -TORA mf. (vars. of) autor -tora
ACTUAL (Ang.) actual, real, factual
ACÚ (interj. said to babies) (nonsense syllables, probably onomatopoetic) coo, kitchy-kitchy coo
ACUADUCTO (var. of) acueducto
ACUAL (var. of) cual
ACULTRADO -DA (pej.) gringo-like, gringoized
ACUPAR (Ang?, or var. of?) ocupar
ACHANTAR (var. of) chantar
ACHAR (var. of) echar
ACHICHORRANAR (var. of) achicharrar
ACHINADO -DA curly (ref. to hair)
ACHINAR (var. of) chinar
ADELFINA (var. of) Delfina
ADIÓ (interj. of incredulity) Really?, You don't say?!
ADITORIO (var. of) auditorio
ADOLORADO -DA hypochondriac
ADOLORIDO -DA hypochondriac
ADOPTADO -DA adoptive; artificial, unreal
AFECTADO -DA tubercular, suffering from tuberculosis
AFECTAR vr. to become tubercular
AFILAR vr. to form a line; to stand in line; to march in a line; to take a walk
AFILERIAR (slang) va. to knife
AFILORIAR (slang) va. to knife
AFLOJAR va. to let out (clothing); (coll.) to cough up (money), pay; vr. to fart (vulg.), break wind
AFRAÑAR va. to understand
AGABACHADO -DA (pej.) gringo-like, gringoized
AGACHADO -DA humble, lowly
AGARRADERA (var. of) agarradero; fpl. love handles (slang), small rolls of fat on the human waist; breasts; TENER BUENAS AGARRADERAS to have a good shape (ref. to female body) (and therefore) to be sexually attractive
AGARRADO -DA: TENER AGARRADO -DA to have under arrest
AGARRAR va. to catch on, get (coll.), comprehend; to take in, reduce the dimensions of (e.g., clothes which are too large);

AGARRAR ABAJO to keep someone in his/her place, keep down (coll.); AGARRAR AIRE to get caught in cold air (folk medicine's belief is that such exposure will precipitate muscular pains or spasms); AGARRARLE A ALGUIEN DE SU CUENTA to have someone on a string (fig.), maintain in a position of dependency: "Ya déjalo, ya lo agarraste bastante de tu cuenta"; AGARRAR BIEN AGARRADITO -TA to grasp very tightly; to trap a criminal beyond the possibility of escape; AGARRAR CHANZA to take a chance, to risk; AGARRAR CLASES/CURSOS to take courses (in school); AGARRAR DE PURO PEDO to hound someone to death; AGARRAR DE UNA CUENTA to harp on the same theme; to hound someone to death (fig.), annoy in an extreme fashion; AGARRAR EL CHIVO (Ang.) to get someone's goat (fig.): "Juan le agarró el chivo a Pepe, por eso se peliaron" 'Juan got Pepe's goat, and that's why they got into a fight'; AGARRAR EL SUEÑO to fall asleep: "Me tomé una píldora pero no pude agarrar el sueño"; AGARRAR EN to fall into the habit of, to take a notion to: "En estos días ha agarrado en comer huevos y tortillas" 'Recently he's taken a notion to eating eggs and tortillas'; AGARRAR PA' TRAS (Ang.) to retract, take back (i.e., someone one has said); vn. AGARRAR CORRENTIA to gain momentum; AGARRAR GUSTO to develop a taste for: "Ya le agarró gusto a la cerveza" 'He's already developed a taste for beer'; AGARRAR LA BOTELLA to hit the bottle (coll.), drink to excess habitually; AGARRARLA SUAVE (coll.) to take it easy, be unconcerned; AGARRAR LA TETERA to hit the bottle (coll.), drink to excess habitually; AGARRAR PARA to go off to, head for: "¿Pa dónde agarró Pepe?" 'Where was Pepe going off to?'; AGARRAR PATADA DE (Ang.) to get a kick out of (coll.), receive gratification from; vr. to fight; AGARRAR TESÓN CON to harp on (a subject); to use or wear (repeatedly): "Agarró tesón con la corbata nueva" 'He kept on wearing the new tie'; AGARRAR VUELO to get a running start; AGARRARSE A CANCOS to come to blows (in a fight); AGARRARSE AL TIRÓN to fight, AGARRARSE A PORRAZOS to fight, get into a fight; AGARRARSE A REATAZOS/RIATAZOS to fight; AGARRARSE A LAS MECHAS or AGARRARSE DE LAS MECHAS to pull hair while fighting (usually said of women); AGARRARSE CON ALGUIEN to take up (relations) with (ref. to amorous relationships): "Dicen que Cuca se agarró con un cubano" 'They say that Cuca has taken up with a Cuban' (Note: it is usually the woman who "se agarra" with the man, not the reverse)

AGARRÓN (see DAR UN AGARRÓN)

AGOSOMAR vr. to become frightened or intimidated

AGRESIVO mf. agressor

AGRICOLTURA (var. of) agricultura

AGRINGADO -DA (pej.) gringo-like

AGRINGOLADO -DA (pej.) gringo-like

AGRINGOLAR va. to gringoize, cause to act like a gringo (Anglo-Saxon); vr. to become or act like a gringo

AGRITO prickly desert shrub

AGRURAS fpl. acidity, acid stomach condition; gaseous stomach condition, stomach gas

AGUA f. rain; (interj.) Watch out!; adj. DE AGUA soft, delicate (ref. to persons); effeminate; HACER (ALGO) COMO AGUA to perform a task with ease: "Para hacer eso se requiere bastante inteligencia.--Pues yo lo hago como agua"; HACER AGUA to urinate

AGUACERAL m. heavy rain shower, cloudburst

AGUADO -DA dilute, watered (said of liquids that lose the desired thickness when excessive amounts of water or, in the case of paint, thinners are added); soft, delicate; VENIR AGUADO to be no match for: "Sé que ese tipo me viene muy aguado" 'I know that guy is no match for me'

AGUADOR m. water-boy; (fig.) person always alert to shifts in the political wind

AGUANTADOR -DORA patient, forebearing

AGUANTAR: AGUANTAR BURI BARILLA to tolerate heavy kidding;

AGUANTAR LA VARA COMO VENGA (coll.) to withstand whatever comes, take whatever fortune brings; AGUANTAR MULETA to tolerate heavy kidding; vr. to resign oneself, be resigned to

AGUANTE m. strength to endure heavy emotional and physical stress

AGUANTÓN -TONA patient, forebearing, able to tolerate a great deal

AGUAZAL m. downpour, heavy rain shower

AGÜELO -LA (var. of) abuelo - la

AGUERRIDO -DA stubborn; relentless

ÁGUILA, EL (coll., Hispanization of) Eagle Pass, Texas

ÁGUILA (interj.) Watch out!, Be careful!; ÁGUILA AHI (interj.) Watch out!, Be careful!; ÁGUILA CON LOS V LISES (interj., coll.) Watch out!; ÁGUILAS (interj.) Watch out!, adj. alert, quick, careful, shrewd; ANDAR ÁGUILA to be on the alert, be watchful; PONERSE ÁGUILA to become alert, get smart (coll.)

AGUILÍA (var. of) aguililla

AGUILILLA buzzard (Buteo)

¡AGUILUCHAS TRUCHAS! (interj., slang) Watch out! Be careful!

AGÜITA drizzle, persistent light rain; annoyance, bother (frequently used as interj.: "¡Qué agüita!" 'What a bother!')

AGUITADO - DA downcast, sad; afflicted; frustrated; nervous; frightened; tired

AGÜITAR va. to make sad; to bore; to tire out; to frighten; to afflict; to make nervous;vr. to become frustrated, afflicted, frightened, bored, sad, tired, nervous, etc.

AGÜITE m. sadness; fear, fatigue; boredom; nervousness

AGUJERADO -DA (ref. to a baseball player who fails to snare grounders or other hits rolling on the ground); (vulg.)(f.) (ref. to any woman who is no longer a virgin);

AGUJERO -RA (vulg.) m. anus; vagina; f. hairpin

AGUZADILLO LA (coll.) smart-aleck kid, mischievous child

AGUZADÍO -IA (var. of) aguzadillo-lla

AGUZADO -DA (var. of) abusado -da

AHI (var. of) ahí

AHIJADO -DA mf. ward (person, usually a child, under the protection of an adult guardian)

AHINCADO -DA (var. of) hincado - da 'kneeling'

AHINCAR (var.) of hincar

AHOGADITO ring (child's game played with marbles)

AHOGADO -DA (slang) dead drunk

AHOGAR vr. (slang) to get soused (coll.), get very drunk

AHORA adv. today; AHORA PRONTO recently: "¿Cuándo pasó todo eso?-- Ahora pronto"

AHORCAR vr. (slang) to get married

AHOY (var. of) hoy

AHUA (var. of) agua

AHUEVADO -DA adamant, insistent, stubborn

AHUICHOTE m. pimp, whoremaster

AHUICHOTEAR or AHUICHOTIAR to encourage, stimulate

AHUITADO -DA (var. of) agüitado -da

AI (var. of ahí)

AIGRE (var. of) aire m.

AIGRIO -GRIA (var. of) agrio -gria

AIGRONAZO violent wind

AIRE m. (anal) gas; (interj., coll.) Scram!, Beat it!, AIRE AL QUEQUE (slang) Scram!, Beat it!, Bug off! (slang); DARLE AIRE A ALGUIEN to get rid of someone; to fire someone from a job; to give someone the brush off (slang), dismiss; EN TANTO QUE EL AIRE in a jiffy, in a split second, in no time at all

AIREPURETO (var. of) aeropuerto

AIROPLANO (var. of) aeroplano

AISCRIM (Eng.) (var. of) aiscrín

AISCRÍN (Eng.) m. ice cream

AISCRINERO -RA ice-cream vendor

AJEAR vr. to become wrinkled

AJERA (var. of) afuera

AJILAR (var. of) afilar

AJOLOTE m. salamander

AJUERA (var. of) afuera

AJUEVADO -DA (var. of) ahuevado -da

AJUEVAR (var. of) ahuevar

AJUITADO -DA (var. of) agüitado -da

AJUITAR (var. of) agüitar

ALA: ¡A VOLAR CON ALAS! Beat it! Scram! DAR ALAS to give free rein to; to side with someone

ALACRANADO -DA mad, angry; blond; (slang) feminine

ALACRANESCO -CA evil-tongued, malicious, viciously gossipy

ALAGARTO (var. of) lagarto

ALAMBRAZO telephone call; telephone message

ALAMBRE ELÉCTRICO (hum.) thin, skinny (ref. to persons)

ALAMBRISTA mf. illegal Mexican immigrant into the United States (so named for his/her skill in jumping or otherwise crossing

the wire fence that forms the border between California and Baja California)
ALAMBRITO inter-uterine device, coil, loop (form of contraception)
ALARMA: ALARMA DE LUMBRE fire alarm
ALARME m. (var. of) alarma
ALAVANTAR (var. of) levantar
ALBA: ¡AL ALBA! (interj., coll.) Cut it out!, Stop it!; Watch out!, Be careful; PONERSE AL ALBA to become alert, be careful;SER AL ALBA to be clever, astute, alert
ALBAJÓN m. (var. of) arvejón
ALBAYALDE m. face powder
ALBOCHARNAR (var. of) abochornar
ALBOROTADO -DA: ANDAR ALBOROTADO -DA CON to have a crush on, be smitten by
ALCAGÜETE mf. (var. of) alcahuete
ALCASO (var. of) acaso
ALCATRAZ m. paper bag
ALCOHOLISTA mf. alcoholic
ALCOL m. (var. of) alcohol
ALDABA f. small latch, catch (i.e., of a screen door, window screen, small box, etc.)
ALDILLA groin
ALDREDE (var. of) adrede
ALE (Eng.) m. alley
ALEBRASTAR or ALEBRESTAR vr. to brighten up, cheer up, regain one's good spirits (often said with ref. to sick persons on the road to recovery); (coll.) to smarten up, get smart
ALEGAR vn. to dispute, argue
ALEGRÓN -GRONA mf. flirt; good-time Charlie/Charlotte (coll.) f. woman of ill repute, prostitute
ALELADO -DA stupid, simple-minded
ALELUYA mf. (pej.) Protestant
ALERTO -TA intelligent
ALEVADOR (var. of) elevador
ALEVANTAR m. (var. of) levantar
ALFIDER m. (var. of) alfiler
ALFILEAR or ALFILIAR va. to cut (someone) with a knife, stab
ALFILERIAR (slang) va. to knife
ALFIREL (var. of) alfiler m. (cf. ALFIDER)
ALFOMBRÍA or ALFOMBRILLA (type of verbenaceous plant used as a ground cover in dry climates); German measles, rubella
ALFRENTE (var. of) enfrente
ALGODÓN m. cottonwood tree (Populus deltoides)
ALGODONERO -RA freeloader, sponge(r) (slang)
ALGOTRO -TRA (var. of) algún otro/ alguna otra (Std. otro -tra)
ALGUATE m. cactus sticker, cactus spine
ALGUEN (var. of) alguien pron.
ALIENTO -TA illegal Mexican immigrant to the United States
ALIMAL mf. (var. of) animal
ALIMAR mf. (var. of animal)
ALINEADO -DA or ALINIADO -DA dressed up, elegant; straight (slang) (i.e., not in trouble with the law)
ALINEAR or ALINIAR vr. to get dressed; to go straight (slang) cease to be in trouble with the law
ALIÑAR (var. of) alinear/aliniar
ALISTAR va. to dress up; vr. to get dressed up
ALIVIADO -DA adj. well, cured (of an illness)
ALIVIANADO -DA (slang) "high" on narcotics, "turned on" by a narcotic drug
ALIVIANAR va. to straighten (someone) out (e.g., to straighten out a criminal, assist a criminal in reforming); to lend a helping hand; vr. to go "straight" (case to engage in a criminal behavior)
ALIVIAR va. to cure; vr. to get well, cease to be sick; to end pregnancy by giving birth
ALÍZ (Hispanization of) Alice, Texas
ALMA: COMO CUANDO DIOS SE LLEVA UN ALMA in the twinkling of an eye (coll.), quite rapidly; TENER EL ALMA EN EL CUERPO to wear one's heart on one's sleeve
ALMETIR (var. of) admitir
ALMIRAR (var. of) admirar
ALMITIR (var. of) admitir
ALMUADA (var. of) almohada
ALMUERZAR (var.) of almorzar
ALÓ (Eng.) hello
ALOJA (interj., coll.) Hello!, Hi there!; Goodbye!
ALQUERIR (var. of) adquirir
ALREVESADO -DA (var. of) al revés
ALTA (see DAR DE ALTA)
ALTERO m. high pile of objects
ALTO: PARAR EL ALTO to put a stop to abusive behavior or to personal excesses: "Se está atacando mucho; hay que pararle el alto" 'He's becoming very abusive; we'll have to make him cut it out' (coll.); to put someone in his/her place, cut someone down to size (coll.); PONERSE ALTO (coll.) to get high, get drunk; DAR DE ALTA to discharge, fire (from a job);

PARAR LA ALTA (var. of) parar el alto
ALUMBRADO -DA (slang) drunk
ALUMINO (var. of) aluminio
ALUZAR va. to light up, cause light to shine or enter into (a room, etc.)
ALVERTIR (var. of) advertir
ALZADITO -TA (coll.) imprisoned
ALZADO -DA mf. loner, lone-wolf (coll.) (said of person who dislikes the company of others)
ALZAR va. to put away, return to an assigned place of storage (e.g., clothes, toys, etc., to their respective drawers); ALZAR LA CASA to clean house; vr.: ALZARSE UNA BOLA to rise up, form (said of wounds on the human body): "A Juanito se le alzó una bola en el brazo" 'Juanito got a lump on his arm'
ALLÁ: ALLÁ A LAS QUINIENTAS or ALLÁ A LAS CUANTAS after a long period of time (often ref. to a delayed reaction; also ref. to solutions or assistance coming too late to be of any good); ALLÁ EL that's up to him, that's his business (coll.)
AMÁ (var. of) mamá
AMACANAR vr. to grab something tightly; to refuse to budge from a place, refuse to move
AMACIZAR va. to tighten; to get a firm grip on; vr. to brace oneself; to make love, posses sexually: "Se amacizó con ella" 'He had his way with her' (coll.)
AMACHADO -DA stubborn, insistent
AMACHAR vr. to be stubborn: to resist
AMACHIMBRAR vr. to surrender, give up
AMACHINAR vr. to take what one wants: "Se amachinó con el libro" 'He made off with the book'; to strike a blow; to take sexual possession; to neck (coll.), pet (ant. slang), engage in noncopulative amatory activities
AMACHÓN -CHONA stubborn
AMAR: SABER LO QUE ES AMAR A DIOS EN TIERRA AJENA to know firsthand what trouble really is
AMARIHUANAR(SE) (var. of) enmarihuanar-(se)
AMARRADO -DA married, tied down (slang)
AMARRADOR -DORA employee who ties or bundles (e.g., vegetables into bunches, wool into packs, etc.)
AMARRAR va. to marry; vr. to get married, tie the knot (slang); AMARRARSE LA TRIPA to tighten one's belt (fig.), economize; to endure hunger; AMARRARSE LOS PANTALONES (fig.) to act resolutely
AMBALANCIA (var. of) ambulancia
AMBASADOR -DORA (Eng.) m. f. ambassador
AMBUSTERO -RA (var. of) embustero -ra
AMEJORAR (var. of) mejorar
AMENORAR (var. of) aminorar
AMERICANO -CA (non-pej.) Anglo-Saxon, gringo
AMIGUERO -RA person who makes friends easily
AMILCADO -DA (Eng.) milk, containing milk
AMOLADO -DA ruined, down and out (coll.)
AMOLAR va. to ruin, harm; vr. to ruin oneself, harm oneself; PARA ACABARLA DE AMOLAR on top of all that, to make things worse (fixed expressions): "Y para acabarla de amolar, robaron también la ropa y el carro"
AMOLINAR (var. of) arremolinar
ÁMONOS (var. of) vámonos
AMOS (var. of) vamos
AMOSOMADO -DA dull; ill-humored, sour (fig.)
AMOSOMAR (var. of) agosomar
ANCA prep. at the house of: "Estoy anca Juan" 'I'm at Juan's house' (Std. Estoy en casa de Juan)
ANCLAR vn. to arrive
ANCLEAR or ANCLIAR vn. to settle down permanently, establish permanent residence
ANCHETA (coll.) thingamagig, thingummy (said with ref. to an item whose name one has forgotten)
ANDA, VETE or ANDAVETE (command) Get out of here!
ANDADA distance covered by foot; very long walk
ANDADITO -TA m., f. manner of walking, gait, carriage
ANDANCIA light epidemic
ANDAR: ANDAR ALUMBRADO -DA (slang) to be drunk; ANDARLE A ALGUIEN to be in a very tight spot (fig.), be in serious trouble: "Ya me andaba" 'I was really up against the wall' (fig.,slang); ANDAR A LA LÍNEA to be well dressed; ANDAR AL ALBA to be on the alert, careful; ANDAR AL TROTE CON ALGO/ANDAR AL TROTE CON ALGUIEN to be wrapped up in

something/someone (fig.), be very involved with something/someone: "El niño anda al trote con el juguete que le compramos", ANDAR ÁGUILA to be on the alert, be careful; ANDAR AGÜITADO -DA to be downcast, sad, frustrated, tired, nervous (etc.); ANDAR ANDANDO to be up and about after an illness (said with ref. to persons who are sufficiently recuperated to be able to leave their sickbeds); ANDA QUE NO SE SIENTA/ANDA QUE NO SE AGUANTA (also pl.: ANDAN QUE NO SE SIENTAN, etc.) he's got ants in his pants (slang), he's extremely restless; ANDAR BAILANDO to be missing; ANDAR BOMBO to be drunk; to be dazed; ANDAR BRUJO/BRUJA to be penniless, stone broke (coll.) (note: only a man may ANDAR BRUJO while either sex may ANDAR BRUJA); ANDAR CABALLÓN -LLONA to be drunk; to be high on narcotic drugs; ANDAR CANICA(S) to be passionately in love; ANDAR CARGA to be carrying narcotic drugs; ANDAR CARGADO -DA to be carrying (to have possession of) narcotic drugs; ANDAR CATARRÍN to be drunk; ANDAR CLAVADO -DA to possess stolen money; to be in the money; (coll.), to possess a certain quantity of money in excess of the amount one is accustomed to have; ANDAR COMO BURRO SIN MECATE to run wild and free (said with ref. to persons); ANDAR CON ALGUIEN (coll.) to go steady, date one person exclusively; ANDAR CON EL RABO CAÍDO to feel depressed, low (coll.); ANDAR CON PELOTA (vulg.) to be passionately in love with (someone); to be carrying the torch for someone (coll.), suffer from unrequited love for; ANDAR CORTADO -DA DE DINERO to be low on funds; ANDAR CORTO -TA to be low on funds; ANDAR CRUDO -DA to have a hangover; ANDAR CHARCA to be well dressed; ANDAR CHIFLADO -DA to be love-lorn, obsessively in love; ANDAR CHUECO -CA to be involved in shady deals (coll.), be involved in dubious business practices; ANDAR DE A TIRO or ANDAR DIATIRO to be very drunk; ANDAR DE JACALERO -RA to go from house to house visiting or gossiping; ANDAR DE JILO to run rapidly, go like a bat out of hell (coll.); ANDAR DE MOJADO -DA to be an illegal immigrant from Mexico (see also MOJADO); ANDAR DE PASEO to be out on the town, to celebrate publicly (in various places of entertainment); ANDAR DE PUCHE to act as if one were the boss; ANDAR DE PUNTOS to walk on tiptoes; ANDAR (DE) SUELTO -TA to run around wild and free; ANDAR DE HOQUIS et al. (see DI HOQUIS et al.); ANDAR EL CUERPO to defecate (cf. HACER EL CUERPO); ANDAR ELÉCTRICO -CA to be drunk; ANDAR EMPALMADO -DA to be heavily bundled up (for protection against cold weather); ANDAR EMPELOTADO -DA to be passionately in love with (someone), to be carrying the torch for (someone), suffer from unrequited love for; ANDAR EN (+ __years of age) to be __years old: "Andrés anda en los 34"; ANDAR EN EL BABAY to be out on the town, to celebrate publicly (in various places of entertainment); ANDAR EN EL RESBALÓN to be having a love affair, having sexual relations; ANDAR EN LA LÍNEA to be drunk; ANDAR EN LA MOVIDA (slang) to sleep around (slang), have sexual relations frequently and promiscuously; to sow one's wild oats (fig.), behave wildly (esp. while one is young); to carouse; ANDAR EN LAS NUBES to be drunk; ANDAR EN PEDO CON (slang) to be in trouble with; ANDAR EN PELOTAS (vulg.) to go around mother-naked (vulg.), walk around completely nude; ANDAR ENTONADO -DA to be drunk; ANDAR ENTRADO -DA to be tipsy, slightly drunk; ANDAR FICHA to be broke, without money; ANDAR FICHA LISA (coll.) to be flat broke, completely without a cent; ANDAR HASTA EL COPETE (slang) to be very drunk; ANDAR HASTA LA RAYA COLORADA to be very drunk; ANDAR HASTA LAS CACHAS / ANDAR HASTA LAS CACHITAS to be very drunk; ANDAR HASTA LAS MANITAS to be very drunk; ANDAR JUNTOS to go steady (coll.), date one person exclusively; ANDAR LANA MORADA to be in love (note the process of disguise: enamorado > lana-morado); ANDAR LOCO -CA to be drunk; to be high on narcotic drugs, ANDAR LOCOTE drunk; high on narcotic drugs; ANDAR MAL to be involved in an illicit love affair; to be involved in a shady (questionable) business deal; ANDAR MEDIO SUATO -TA to be tipsy; ANDAR MOTEADO -DA / ANDAR MOTIADO -DA to be high on marihuana; ANDAR MOTOROL to be tipsy, slightly drunk; ANDAR MANITOS / ANDAR MUY MANITOS to be real buddy-buddy (slang), be on very friendly terms; ANDAR PANDO -DA to be staggering drunk, falling-down drunk; ANDAR PARA ARRIBA Y PARA ABAJO / ANDAR PARRIBA Y PABAJO to run around like a chicken with its head cut off (fig.), to rush about rapidly; ANDAR PEDO -DA to be drunk; ANDAR PIOCHA to be dressed neatly; ANDAR PISTO -TA to be drunk; ANDAR PLOCHA to be dressed neatly; ANDAR PUERCO -CA to be dirty, filthy; ANDAR QUE APENAS to be extremely drunk (so drunk one can scarcely walk); ANDAR QUEBRADO -DA (Ang?) to be broke, without money; ANDAR QUEDANDO BIEN to be trying to make a very favorable impression on someone (usually the object of one's amorous intentions--most often said of a male trying to ingratiate himself with a female): 'Héctor anda quedando bien con Yolanda'; ANDAR RAYADO -DA to have money on hand; to be in the money (coll.), be unaccustomedly wealthy; ANDAR RECORTADO -DA DE DINERO to be very low on funds; ANDAR ROSADO -DA (see ROSADO); ANDAR SOBRES (andar sobre alguien) to pursue a member of the opposite sex, run after someone (coll.); ANDAR SOCADO -DA to be cleaned out (said of someone who has lost his/her money in a game of chance); ANDAR SOCAS to be cleaned out (cf. ANDAR SOCADO); ANDAR SOLARES to be alone (cf. andar a solas); ANDAR SONÁMBULO -LA to be high on narcotic drugs or alcohol; ANDAR SOQUEADO -DA / ANDAR SOQUIADO -DA to be cleaned out (cf. ANDAR SOCADO); ANDAR SUBIDO -DA to be high on narcotic drugs or alcohol; ANDAR TINIADO -DA (Eng., thinner) to be high from sniffing paint thinner; ANDAR VOLADO -DA to go beserk; to be distracted ANDAR VOLANDO BAJO to be feeling low (coll.), sad, depressed

ANDARIEGO -GA m. adulteror, f. adultress

ANDARINO (var. of) andarín

ANDARON (var. of) anduvieron (3rd pers. pl. pret. of andar)

ANDASTE (var. of) anduviste (2nd pers. fam. sg. pret. of andar)

ÁNDATE PASEANDO / ÁNDATE PASIANDO (coll.) That's it! Now you've got it! (i.e., the correct answer to a question, the solution to a problem, etc.)

ANDURIEGO -GA (var. of) andariego -ga

ANGINAS fpl. tonsils

ANIMAS: ANIMAS (SANTAS) QUE interj. If only . . . ! (similar in intent and function to Std. Ojalá que . . .)

ANONERO -RA exaggerator

ANQUE (var. of) aunque; (var. of) anca (q.v. supra)

ANSÍ (var. of) así

ANSIA: COMER ANSIA to be impatient

ANTECRISTO (var. of) anticristo

ANTES: MÁS ANTES before, beforehand (Std. antes)

ÁNTICO -CA identical, similar

ANTICONCEPTIVO -VA contraceptive

ANTIFRÍS (Eng.) m. antifreeze

ANTIGÜIDAD (var. of) antigüedad f.

ANTINOCHE (var. of) anteanoche

ANTIOJOS (var. of) anteojos 'eyeglasses'

ANTONCES (var. of) entonces

ANUNCIO: DECIR UN ANUNCIO to announce; to advertise

AÑALES mpl. many years

AÑIDIR (var. of) añadir

AÑO DEL CALDO (coll.) very old; m. yesteryear, olden days, times gone by

AOLER (var. of) oler

APÁ (var. of) papá

APACHADO -DA (var. of) apapachado -da

APACHAR (var. of) apapachar

APACHURRADO -DA smashed, crushed; wrinkled (ref. to clothes)

APACHURRAR va. to smash, crush, squash; APACHURRAR (LA) OREJA (slang) to sleep; vr. to become smashed, crushed, squashed

APACHURRÓN m. act of smashing, crushing

APAGADORA fire engine

APAGAR: APAGAR LOS OJOS to give (someone) a black eye (in a fight): "Le apagaron los ojos

en el bochinche" 'They gave him a black eye in the brawl'
APALANCAR vr. to lift with a lever; to open with a level
APALIAR (var. of) apalear
APANTALLAR vn. to act important, show off
APAÑAR: APAÑAR AIRE to escape from (someone): "Tuvieron que apañar aire porque vieron venir a la polecía" 'They had to escape because they saw the police coming'; to steal
APAPACHADO -DA spoiled, pampered (ref. to children)
APAPACHAR va. to spoil, pamper (ref. to children); to encourage
APARADOR m. showcase, store counter; m. grass catcher (type of basket attached to rear or side of a lawn-mower)
APARAR va. to buy
APARATITO inter-uterine device, coil, loop (contraceptive)
APARATO msg. buttocks
APARENCIA (var. of) apariencia
APARTADO part (division in human hair)
APARTE reserved, somewhat standoffish (ref. to people); SER MUY APARTE to be a loner, be shy of human company
APELATIVO -VA surname (cf. Std. apellido)
APENADO -DA ashamed
APENAR va. to shame, make someone feel ashamed; vr. to be ashamed
APENAS: ANDAR QUE APENAS to be extremely drunk, be falling-down drunk
APENDIS m. (var. of) apéndice
APENTERAR va. to frighten; to surpass; to degrade, humiliate
APERLADO -DA pearl-colored (ref. to skin coloration mid-way between "white" and "brown")
APESTAR vn. to become out-of-date, passé: "Esa canción ya apesta" 'That song is already out-of-date'
APLADIR (var. of) aplaudir
APLANADORA steam roller
APLANAR va. to press, bear down upon
APLASTAR va. to leave speechless, cut down, put in one's place; vr. to overstay one's welcome; to sit down with the intention of staying a long while; to butt in, enter unwelcomed into (e.g., a conversation)
APLASTÓN m. unexpected scolding or punishment, reprimand; DARLE A ALGUIEN UN APLASTÓN to put someone in his/her place; ECHARLE A ALGUIEN UN APLASTÓN to put someone in his/her place
APLICACIÓN (Ang.) f. application (for funds, a job, admission to a school, etc.) (Std. solicitud etc.)
APLOGAR vr. to regain one's composure, become calm
APLOMAR vr. to be slow to react (because of inability, laziness, lack of preparation, etc.)
APORREADO -DA / APORRIADO -DA beaten up, thrashed (in a fight, etc.)
APORREAR or APORRIAR vr. to fight
APOYO last squirt of milk from a cow's udder
APREBAR (var. of) aprobar
APRECIO: HACER APRECIO to pay attention
APRENDER (Ang.) to find out, become aware of: "Aprendí que iba a venir el jueves" 'I learned (=found out) that he was coming Thursday'
APRENTERAR va. to outshine; to belittle; to scare
APRETADO -DA tight-fitting (ref. to clothes): "El vestido le queda muy apretado" 'The dress is too tight on her'
APRETADOR m. brassiere
APRETAR: APRETAR EL MONO to bewitch, hex: "A Pedro le están apretando el mono, por eso se está portando así"
APRETONES (see DAR APRETONES)
APRONTAR vr. to arrive unexpectedly
APROVECHADO -DA bully-like (said of persons), viciously aggresive
APROVECHAR vr. to bully someone
¡APUCHA! interj. (expression of surprise or astonishment)
APUCHAR (Eng.) (var. of) puchar
APUERCADO -DA poorly dressed
APURACIÓN f. haste, hurry
APURADO -DA in a hurry; in a tight spot (fig.), in trouble
APURAR vr. to hurry
APURÓN -RONA impatient (ref. to people)
APURREADO -DA / APURRIADO -DA (vars. of) aporriado -da
AQUELLA (see DE AQUELLA)
AQUELLO: POR AQUELLO DE LAS DUDAS just in case: "Lo voy a llamar por teléfono por aquello de las dudas"
AQUEO -A (var. of) aquello -lla
AQUÍ: AQUÍ ASÍ right here (Note: this fixed expression is accompanied by the speaker's pointing with his/her finger
ARACLÁN m. (var. of) alacrán

ARAÑADO -DA stolen
ARAÑAR va. to steal; (coll.) to try to get something for nothing
ARAÑON m. scratch
ARAS (var. of) arras fpl.
ARBOLERA (var. of) arboleda
ARCAS fpl. (seldom fsg.) armpits
ARCO: ARCO IRES (var. of arco iris m.
AREDOR (var. of) alrededor
ARENGUE m. trouble, difficulty
ARENTRO (rus.) (var. of) adentro
ARFILER (var. of) alfiler m.
ARGENTE adj. m. & f. accommodating
ARGOLLA wedding ring
ARGÜENDA m. piece of gossip
ARGÜENDERO -RA gossiper, gossipmonger
ARGULLO (var. of) orgullo
ARGUMENTO (Ang.) argument, dispute, verbal fight
ARISCAR va. to fight; ARISCAR MANGAS (coll.) to roll up one's sleeves (in preparation for a fight)
ARISCO -CA suspicious, distrustful; skittish; jealous
ARISMÉTICA (var. of) aritmética
ARMADO -DA flushed (slang), loaded (=possessed of considerable money or other assets)
ARMAR vr. to have it made (coll.), be assured of success or fortune; to have a stroke of good luck, come into good times
ARME (Eng.) m. army
AROPLANO (var. of) aeroplano
AROPUERTO (var. of aeropuerto
ARVEJÓN m. chick-pea (Cicer arietinum)
ARRACADA any type of earring
ARRACLE m. & f. show-off
ARRANADO -DA (hum.) married, hitched (hum.); peaceful; docile
ARRANAR va. to marry, marry off, hitch (hum.); vr. to get married, get hitched (hum.); to sit comfortably
ARRANCADO -DA penniless, broke (slang)
ARRANCAR vr. to move off rapidly from a standing position
ARRANE m. matrimony, married state
ARRANQUE: SER DE ARRANQUE(S) to be unpredictable; to be temperamental; ARRANQUES mpl. periods of strange and unusual behavior; TENER SUS ARRANQUES to anger quickly; to become angry unexpectedly
ARRASTRADERO: IRSE POR EL ARRASTRADERO to be guided by the tracks of an animal
ARRASTRADO-DA mean, despicable; mischievous, tricky; (slang) lousy, crumby, damned (coll.): ¡Sosiégate, huerco arrastrado!" 'Stop it, you damned little brat!"
ARRASTRAR va. to be good at doing things, excel: "A Juan le arrastra para jugar al tenis" 'Juan is very good at playing tennis'; ARRASTRAR EL APARATO to be good at doing things, excel
ARREADOR -DORA or ARRIADOR -DORA chauffeur, driver of a car
ARREAR or ARRIAR va. to drive (horses, mules, etc.); to drive any vehicle (including motorized vehicles)
ARREGLADA fsg. repairs; act of straightening out (the life of a person previously engaged in crime or otherwise "crooked" business); act of hexing or bewitching
ARREGLAR va. to hex, bewitch; ARREGLAR CUENTAS to settle a matter; vr. to reform, straighten oneself out (fig.)
ARREJUNTAR vr. (coll.) to cohabitate, live together out of wedlock, shack up (vulg. & slang)
ARREMPUJÓN m. (var. of) rempujón
ARRENDAR va. to return, give back: "¿Qué hiciste con la camisa? ¿Se la arrendaste?" 'What did you do with the shirt? Did you give it back to him?'; vr. to turn back after having started out, return: "Se arrendó antes de llegar a la casa"
ARREPENTIR vr. to change one's mind
ARREQUINTADO -DA tight-fitting; tightly pressed together (ref. to persons, e.g., in a crowd); mf. high-pressure artist (person who puts others under pressure, keeps them in a state of tension)
ARREQUINTAR var. to tighten (a wire); to get someone into trouble; to force someone into a corner; vr. to press tightly against someone (esp. while dancing)
ARRESTRAR (var. of) arrestar
ARRIADOR -DORA (var. of) ARREADOR -DORA
ARRIAR (var. of) ARREAR
ARRIESGAR vr.: ARRIEGARSE EL CUERO to risk one's neck

ARRIMADO: ESTAR DE ARRIMADOS to live with someone and be dependent upon them (often said with ref. to relatives who "move in with" a family)
ARRIMAR vr. to move in with a family (often relatives) and depend on them financially; ARRIMARLE A ALGUIEN LA CHANCLA to spank
ARRINCONAR va. to put in a corner
ARROLEAR or ARROLIAR (coll.) to go for a ride (in a car); to go for a walk
ARROÑA (var. of) roña
ARRUINAR: PARA ACABARLA DE ARRUINAR to make matters worse (set expressions)
ARRUMBADO -DA (var. of) rumbado -da
ASARRUCHAR (var. of) aserruchar
ASCO (see PONER DEL ASCO)
ASCRINERO -RA (var. of) aiscrinero -ra (Eng.)
ASEGÚN (var. of) según
ASEGURANZA (var. of) seguranza
ASEGURAR: NO ASEGURAR to not expect someone to live: "No la aseguran" 'They don't expect her to live'
ASEGURO (var. of) seguro
ASENTAR va. to tamp down, smooth, level, smooth out (press clothing lightly with a clothes-press or an iron)
ASÍ: ASÍ ES QUE so, therefore (conj.): "Nos quieren allí a las seis de la tarde en punto, así es que no vengas tarde"; ASÍ SÍ (SE VALE) That's more like it (general expression of approval); ASÍ NO (SE VALE) That's not it at all, That's just not right; That's not fair (Note: así no enjoys greater frequency than así sí); ASÍ Y ASADO so-and-so (used to ref. to person whose name one wishes to avoid mentioning): "¿Por qué te pones a hablar con ese así y asado?" 'Why do you talk with that old so-and-so?'
ASIENTO: mpl. ASIENTOS coffee grounds
ASIGUN (var. of) (a)según
ASILENCIAR (var. of) silenciar
ASINA (var. of) así
ASISTENTE -TA (Ang.) mf. assistant (Std. ayudante)
ASISTIR vr. to serve oneself (food); to eat
ASOLEADO -DA or ASOLIADO -DA scatter-brained, lame-brained, stupid; crazy, loony (slang); (said of a person dazed or stunned from over-exposure to the sun's rays); TONTO ASOLEADO crazy old fool
ASOLEAR vr. to overexpose oneself to the rays or heat of the sun; to show the effects of being out in the hot sun (by perspiring, being short of breath, etc.)
ASPERINA (var. of) aspirina
ASPIRINO -NA (coll.) person who becomes intoxicated by aspirins, person who "turns on" with aspirins
ASQUELA mosquito (Culicidae)
ASQUEROSO -SA squeamish
ASTRACTO -TA (var. of) abstracto -ta
ASTRONOTA mf. (var. of) astronauta
ASUAVIZAR (var. of) suavizar
ASUMIR (Ang.) to assume (i.e., that something has happened), suppose, conjecture (Std. suponer etc.)
ASUSTÓN -TONA (coll.) fraidy-cat (coll.), person easily frightened
ATACADO -DA (coll.) stuffed, full, filled (e.g., with food); opportunistic; abusive, vulgar, gross; tight fitting: "El vestido le queda muy atacado" 'The dress is too tight-fitting on her'
ATACAR vr. to overdo in a vulgar or greedy fashion; to behave abusively; to take more than one should (e.g., food); (coll.) to make a pig of oneself through overeating
ATACÓN -CONA bully(-like), abusive; stingy, cheap, parsimonious
ATAJO (pej.) bunch, group (of persons); ATAJO DE PENDEJOS bunch of idiots (fig.), group of fools
ATARANTADO -DA in trouble; absent-minded
ATARIADO -DA (var. of) atareado -da
ATASCADA (see DAR UNA ATASCADA)
ATASCADERO mess, jam (coll.), difficult situation
ATASCADO -DA ignorant; good-for-nothing; mean, base, vile; filthy, dirty
ATASCAR va. to jam (an object) into an opening; ATASCARLA (vulg.) to insert the male organ into the vagina; to force one's way in, crash (e.g., a party) (slang)
ATASCOSO -SA muddy
ATAÚR (var. of) ataúd m.
ATENDER (Ang.) va. to attend, be present at, go to (Std. asistir)
ATENDIENTE mf. clerk, attendant
ATENER vr. to depend upon someone to do one's work or dis-

charge one's responsibilities: "Si vienes a atenerte, es mejor que te vayas"
ATENIDO -DA dependent upon others to do one's work
ATEXANADO -DA Texanized, Texan-like
ATIBIARSE A HACER ALGO to get a move on (fig.), get busy doing something
ATIRANTADO -DA dead
ATIRANTAR vr. to go to bed, stretch out (fig.)
ATIRICIADO -DA sad, depressed
ATIRICIAR vr. to become sad
ATIZAR va. to stir, poke (a fire); to strike (someone); ¡ATIZALE! interj. Move it!, Get a move on!, Shake a leg! (coll.)
ATOCAR (var. of) tocar
ATOL m. (var. of) atole
ATOLE m. drink made of water, corn meal, sugar and sometimes chocolate and other ingredients; m. cream of wheat (cereal); ATOLE/ ATOLE DE AVENA oatmeal (cereal); DAR ATOLE CON EL DEDO to deceive one's husband with another woman; DESPUÉS DE ATOLE too late to do any good; HACER ATOLE to flatten, break every bone in one's body (ref. to person run over by a heavy vehicle); HACERSE ATOLE to become over-dilute, watery (usually said of food losing consistency while being prepared): "El arroz se hizo atole porque le echaste(s) mucha agua y lo dejaste(s) una hora sobre la lumbre"
ATOLERO -RA person who makes or sells atole; (also, pej. designation for any vulgar or ill-mannered person)
ATOLLADERO tight spot, jam (coll.), difficulty
ATOLLAR va. to anger; vn. to wander, roam; vr. to get confused, mixed up
ATOMOBIL (var. of) automóbil m.
ATOMÓBIL (var. of) automóbil m.
ATONTADO -DA dazed, stunned (as from a blow on the head)
ATOR -RA m., f. (var. of) autor -ra
ATORNILLADO -DA prudent, having common sense
ATOTACHADO adv. rapidly
ATRABANCADO -DA reckless
ATRABANCAR va. to act recklessly
ATRANCAR va. to latch (usually a screen door), lock (a door), bar
ATRASADO -DA (coll.) backward, slow to learn, dense; half-baked (coll.); relapsed, set back (said of medical patients); willfully ill-informed; ESTAR ATRASADO -DA to be incorregible; (as a reprimand for abusive behavior:) "¡Estás atrasado!" 'You're really something else again!' (iron.)
ATRASAR va. to cause a medical patient to suffer a relapse: "El doctor en vez de aliviarlo, lo atrasó"; vr. to have a relapse, suffer a setback: "Anoche estaba muy bien, pero esta mañana se atrasó"
ATREVIDO -DA insolent, abusive
ATROCIDADO -DA opportunistic, abusive
ATROJADO -DA behind, running slow (ref. to clocks and watches); behind schedule
ATROJAR vr. to fall behind, run slow (ref. to clocks and watches): "Voy a darle cuerda a mi reloj para que no se atroje otra vez"; to fall behind in one's work, on one's payments, etc.: "Me van a quitar la casa porque me atrojé en mis pagos"
ATUFAR vr. to become proud
ATULLAR (var. of) atollar
AUCUPADO -DA (vars. of) ocupado -da
AUDITOR (Ang?) m. bookkeeper
AÚJA (var. of) aguja
AURA (var. of) ahora
AUROPLANO (var. of) aeroplano
AUTOBUSERO -RA busdriver
AUTORIDAD fsg. the police, police force
AVENTAR va. to push; to throw (an object); vr. to fight; to excel, do well; AVENTAR A LOCO to ignore; AVENTAR A LEÓN to ignore
AVENTÓN m. lift, ride (in a car); push, shove
AVERIGUACIÓN f. dispute, argument
AVERIGUADERO dispute, argument
AVERIGUADOR -DORA argumentative person
AVERIGUAR va. to argue; vn. to argue; vr. AVERIGUÁRSELAS to resolve one's problems: "Carlos nunca se las va a averiguar"
AVERIGUATA noise and confusion created by an argument
AVIENTE mf. decoy; police informer
AVIROTE adj., mf. naked, nude
AVISPA bee
AVISPERO: PONERSE (EN EL) AVISPERO to become alert
AY: ¡AY TÚ!, ¡AY TÚ PEPE!, ¡AY TÚ PEPE, CUIDADO QUE TE VOY A

PEGAR!, ¡AY TÚ TÚ!, ¡AY TÚ PEPE, TÚ LA TRAIS!, ¡AY TÚ CHOCHÓN! interjs. (hum. or pej.) (used to mark or make fun of an effeminate person or else to mark or make fun of an effeminate-sounding statement); (var. of) ahí, (also of) allí; interj. Will you look at that!; ¡AY MIRA NOMÁS! Will you look at that!; AY NOS VEMOS / AY TE GUACHO / AY TE MIRO (coll.) See ya 'round, So long, Be seein' ya (coll.); AY TE MIRO, CASIMIRO / AY TE GUACHO, CUCARACHO (slang) (roughly equivalent to Eng. 'See ya later, alligator', etc.); POR AY/ POR AY NOMÁS (just) over there; more or less, approximately; AY VOY I'm coming (also AY VAMOS, AY VAN, etc.)

AZADONEAR or AZADONIAR (var. of) azadonar

AZODONEAR or AZADONIAR (var. of) azadonar

AZONZADO -DA stunned, dazed (from a blow, over-exposure to the sun, etc.)

AZONZAR va. to stun, stupify; vr. to become stunned, bewildered

AZORRILLAR va. to intimidate, frighten; vr. to become frightened; to become confused

AZOTAR va. to give (a present); to pay, fork over (coll.); vn. to yield, submit; to die; vn. to fall down hard, fall down with a bang; AZOTAR LA RES (var. of) caer la res; AZOTAR MUY FEO (slang) to die tragically

AZTLÁN m. ancient homeland of the Aztec people, roughly coincident with what is now the southwestern part of the United States (Texas, New Mexico, Arizona, California, etc.)

AZUCADERA (var. of) azucarera sugar bowl

AZUFRE (slang) m. heroin

AZUL (slang) m. policeman, "man in blue"

AZURCA f. (child language, var. of) azúcar

B

BABAY (Eng.) bye-bye (<good-bye); IR DE BABAY to take a walk; IR AL BABAY to "go out" (coll.) leave in search of amusement

BABICHE msg. beet(s); bitch; son-of-a-bitch (vulg.) (origin of BABICHE uncertain--possible blend of baba and biche bitch?)

BABITO (dim.) (Eng.) Bobby

BABOSADA foolish act; stupid idea, remark or act

BABOSO -SA ignorant, stupid

BABUCH (slang) foolish;stupid

BACALADO (var. of) bacalao

BACIERO chief shepherd

BACÍN m. bassinet; bed pan; slop jar

BACHA cigarette butt; (Eng.) (slang) badge, identification plate; barge, flat boat

BACHICHA (slang) cigarette butt (esp. marihuana cigarette butt)

BADÍA (var. of) bahía

BAI (Eng.) interj. good-bye; BAI BAI good-bye

BAICA (Eng.) bicycle

BAILADOR -DORA mf. fond of dancing; good dancer

BAILAR vr. BAILARSE A ALGUIEN to whip or spank someone; to defeat someone in a fight

BAILE: BAILE-CENA (Ang.) m. dinner-dance; BAILE ZAPATEADO/ ZAPOTIADO Mazurka (type of dance)

BAISA (coll. & underw. slang) hand (prob. < baes 'manos' in Spanish Romani [Gypsy] language)

BAISICLE (Eng.) m. bicycle

BAISICLETA (Eng.) bicycle

BAISÍQUEL (Eng.) m. bicycle

BAISO -SA (slang) young person

BAJAR: BAJAR PARA ABAJO (pleonasm) to go down, descend; to get off, climb down from; BAJAR DE ARRIBA to leave prison legally; BAJARLE LA REGLA A ALGUIEN to flow (said of menstrual fluid), have one's period

BAJO mpl. lower floors (of a building)
BALA m. or f. clever person, astute person; flirt, (f.) loose woman
BALACEADA or BALACIADA act or effect of firing a volley of shots (bullets); riddling (of a person with bullet shots)
BALACEAR or BALACIAR va. to riddle or spray with bullets, fire a volley of bullets
BALDE (dim. of) Baltasar
BALERINA (var. of) bailarina
BALONE or BALONI (Eng.) m. baloney sausage; (hum.) penis
BALÚN (Eng.) m. balloon
BAMBA Cuban dance; trick; accident
BANCO (Ang.) river bank; BANCO DE MADERA lumber yard; BANCO DE SANGRE blood bank
BANDA (Ang?) bandage, band-aid
BANDEJA washbasin; BANDEJAS fpl. pots and pans: "¿Por qué no has lavado las bandejas?"
BANDOLERO -RA lazybones (coll.), indolent (person)
BANQUEAR or BANQUIAR va. to bank, deposit money in a bank
BANQUETEAR or BANQUETIAR vn. to have a good time
BAÑO: BAÑO DE PIES foot bath; BAÑO DE REGADERA shower bath; BAÑO DE TOALLA sponge bath; DARSE BAÑOS DE PUREZA to glorify oneself, take a holier than thou attitude (coll.)
BAQUEAR or BAQUIAR (Eng.) va. & vr. to back up (a car), cause to move backwards; to support, back up; to back down, go back on one's word, chicken out (slang)
BARAJEAR or BARAJIAR (var. of barajar) va. to mix, jumble together; vn. to mix with a crowd (said of persons)
BARAJERO -RA card freak (slang), inordinately fond of playing cards
BARAÑA unkempt head of hair; (coll. & underw.) tomorrow; (coll. & underw.) morning; thickets, branches (fsg.)
BARATA bargain sale; BARATA DE QUEMAZÓN fire sale (sale at reduced prices of merchandise slightly damaged in a fire)
BARATEAR or BARATIAR vr. to mix with a crowd (said of persons)
BARATO deadbeat (coll.), person unwilling to pay and eager to borrow
BARATÓN -TONA ill-bred, coarse, vulgar
BARBA: HACER LA BARBA to apple-polish (coll.), flatter; BARBA DE ELOTE corn tassel (Zea mays) (herb prepared as a tea and used to treat kidney ailments); fpl. BARBAS TENGAS or BARBAS TENGAS Y CON ELLAS TE MANTENGAS (expression used mainly by children to taunt other children, roughly equivalent to Eng. "Phooey on you!")
BARBACOBA (var. of) barbacoa
BÁRBARO -RA excessive; tremendous, wonderful, marvellous; daring
BARBEAR or BARBIAR va. to apple-polish (coll.), flatter
BARER (var. of) barrer
BARRA bar (of metal); bar (barroom counter; the barroom itself)
BARRACA (Ang.) barrack (military)
BARRAL (coll. & underw.) m. muscular man
BARRANCO slope, hillside
BARRANQUEÑA: HACER BARRANQUEÑA to gather and take possession of a large number of articles for one's own use
BARREADA or BARRIADA fsg. citizenry of a barrio (collective reference to all persons in a given neighborhood)
BARRER va. to make the sign of the cross with wide, sweeping motions on a person's body to break the spell of a hex or an incantation (the act is performed by the healer as he/she recites several Our Fathers, Hail Marys and Credos)
BARRILITO -TA (coll.) chubby, tubby
BARRIO neighborhood (esp. with ref. to a Mexican-American neighborhood)
BARRO acne
BARRÓN -RRONA m.,f. materialist(ic)
BARROTE m. rafter
BAS (Eng.) m. bus
BASCA vomit
BÁSCULA (coll. & underw.) search; DAR BÁSCULA to frisk; PASAR BÁSCULA to frisk
BASE: BASE POR BOLAS (baseball slang) base on balls
BASQUEAR or BASQUIAR vr. to vomit
BASUDERO -RA (var. of) basurero -ra
BASURA scum of society (pej. ref. to persons); BASURA BLANCA (Ang.) (pej.) white trash (lower-class Anglo-Saxons); (see also PONER DE LA BASURA)
BASURITA foreign object that has gotten into one's eye
BATEAR or BATIAR (Eng.) va. to bat

a ball (in baseball)
BATEO (Eng.) act or effect of batting a ball (in baseball)
BATERÍA (electrical) battery; flashlight; a hard time: "No quiero que me den tanta batería" 'I don't want them to give me such a hard time'
BATERO -RA (Eng.) batter (of a ball, in baseball)
BATIADOR -RA mf. (var. of) bateador -dora (Eng.)
BATIAR (Eng.) (var. of) batear
BATIDERO disorderly and messy place
BATIDO -DA dirty, soiled (often ref. to persons)
BATIR vr. to get dirty: "Acabo de cambiarte; no te vayas a batir con ese chocolate"
BATO -TA (coll. & underw.) f. gal; m. guy, dude (slang); BATO CALOTE big guy; BATO DE COLEGIO educated person; guy who thinks he's smart; BATO RELAJE punk; ridiculous punk; BATO TIRILÍ Pachuco (q.v.); BATO TIRILONGO member of an adolescent or criminal gang; dude (slang); hood (slang)
BAUL (var. of) baúl
BAXEO (var. of boxeo
BAYONESA (var. of) mayonesa
BEBE va. to drink intoxicating beverages
BEBIDA act or effects of drinking intoxicating beverages
BECERRO -RRA ignorant person
BEDERO (var. of) babero
BEIBI (Eng.) mf. (var. of) bebé (cf. BEBE)
BEIBISIRA (Eng.) mf. baby-sitter
BEIBISIRIN (Eng.) m. baby-sitting
BEIQUINPAUDA or BEIQUINPAURA (Eng.) m. baking powder
BEIS (Eng.) m. base (in baseball)
BELDUQUE m. knife
BENDECIDO (var. of) bendicho (ppart. of bendecir)
BENDÉI (Eng.) m. band-aid
BENITO (dim. of) Benjamín
BENQUEAR or BENQUIAR (vars. of) banquear/banquiar
BEO -A (var. of) bello -lla
BEQUEAR or BEQUIAR (vars. of) baquear / baquiar (Eng.)
BEQUENPAURA or BEQUINPAUDA or BEQUINPAURA (Eng.) m. baking powder (cf. BEIQUINPAUDA et al.)
BERRONGO -GA bothersome (person)
BESBOL (Eng.) m. baseball
BESOTEAR or BESOTIAR va. to kiss repeatedly
BESUQUIAR (var. of) besuquear
BET (Eng.) m. baseball bat
BETABEL msg. sugar beet(s)
BETABELERO -RA harvester of sugar beets
BETEAR or BETIAR (vars. of) batear/batiar (q.v.)
BETEO (var. of) bateo (q.v.)
BETERO -RA (var. of) batero -ra (q.v.)
BETO -TA (dims. resp. of) Alberto -ta, Gilberto, Heriberto, Humberto, Roberto -ta
BI (Eng.) (dim. of) Beatriz
BIBEL or BIBÉL (Hispanizations of) Beeville, Texas
BICA (slang) money
BICARBONATO: BICARBONATO DE SODA bicarbonate of soda
BICECLETA tricycle
BICICLETERÍA bicycle shop
BICOCA (slang) money
BICORBONATE (var. of) bicarbonato
BIEN: BIEN DADO -DA wealthy, rich; (with ref. to a blow to the body) good solid blow, thorough blow or beating: "Te voy a dar una paliza bien dada"; ¡BIEN HAIGA! 'Good for you!' (expression of approbation); BIEN PARECIDO -DA handsome; BIEN SENTADO -DA rich, sitting pretty (coll.)
BIL (Eng.) m. bill of sale; tab, restaurant check
BINGO (Eng.) m. (game of) bingo
BINOCULAR (Ang.) mpl. binoculars
BIRONGA (coll. & underw.) beer
BIRONGUEAR or BIRONGUIAR (coll. & underw.) to drink beer; to drink any alcoholic beverage
BIRONGUERO -RA (slang) beer-drinker
BIROTE m. French bread
BÍRREA or BIRRIA barbecue; (Eng.) beer
BIRRIONGA (slang) beer
BÍSQUETE (Eng.) m. biscuit
BÍTARO beet; sugar
BITOQUE m. nozzle of a syringe used for enemas; nozzle of a hose
BIURE (Hispanization of) Buda, Texas
BIURE CHAP or BIURI CHAP (Eng.) m. or f. beauty shop, beauty parlor
BLAF (Eng.) m. bluff (deception, deliberate misleading)
BLANCANIEVE (var. of) Blancanieves
BLANQUILLO -LLA mf. (pej.) Anglo-Saxon; m. (euph.) testicle, ball (vulg.)
BLANQUÍO (var. of) blanquillo
BLICH or BLICHE or BLICHI (Eng.)

m. bleach
BLICHAR or BLICHEAR or BLICHIAR (Eng.) va. to bleach (hair)
BLÓAUT (Eng.) m. blowout (of a car's tire)
BLOC (Eng.) m. block
BLOFE (Eng.) m. bluff (deception, etc.--cf. BLAF)
BLOFEADOR -DORA or BLOFIADOR -DORA (Eng.) bluffer (deceiver)
BLOFEAR (Eng.) va. to bluff, deceive
BLOQUE (Ang.) m. city block; cement block
BOBITO (dim.) (Eng.) Bobby
BOBITO eye gnat (hippelates)
BOBO -BA (slang) drunk; crazy, nuts (coll.); m. balloon
BOCA: BOCA DE CHANCLA thick-lipped; BOCA DEL ESTÓMAGO esophagus, gullet; BOCA GRANDE (coll.) big mouth, excessive talker; HACERSE (DE) BOCA CHICA to pretend to be a small eater; TENER BOCA CHICA to talk very little
BOCÓN -CONA adj. (coll.) defamatory; mf. defamer; liar; gossiper; foul-mouthed person; loud-mouth (excessive and noisy talker)
BOCHINCHE m. gathering or crowd of lower-class or delinquent persons; party, celebration; melee
BOFO -FA soft, spongy; fat; VIEJA BOFA fat old bitch (vulg.); whore
BOGANVILIA (var. of) buganvilla
BOGUE (Eng.) m. buggy (esp. baby buggy)
BOICOTE (Eng.) m. boycott
BOICOTEAR or BOICOTIAR (Eng.) va. to boycott
BOI ESCAUT (Eng.) m. boy scout
BOILA (Eng.) boiler
BOÍTELAS interj. (coll.) Hot damn!, Gol-lee!
BOLA dollar; group of people; mob, disorderly gathering; baseball (Std. pelota); BOLAS fpl. knots (type of tissue swelling) "Dicen que las bolas en la nuca vienen de la nerviosidad" BOLA DE CARNE meatball; BOLA DE LA PUERTA door knob; HACER BOLA to confuse, puzzle, bewilder; HACERSE BOLA to mill around (said of groups of people); to become confused; VOLVERSE BOLA to become confused; (see also DAR CON BOLA); fpl. testicles, balls (vulg.)
BOLADO -DA m. adulteror; f. adultress
BOLEADA or BOLIADA shoe-shine
BOLEADOR or BOLIADOR m. shoeshine boy
BOLEAR or BOLIAR va. to shine shoes
BOLERO -RA m. shoeshine boy; f. mumps
BOLETO ticket; (pej.) gringo, Anglo-Saxon
BOLEVEAR or BELEVIAR vn. to dance
BOLILLO -LLA (pej.) gringo- Anglo-Saxon; BOLILLO CON COLA PRIETA gringoized Mexican-American, coconut (slang--ref. to Chicano who is "brown on the outside but white on the inside")
BOLÍO -LÍA (var. of) bolillo -lla
BOLITA yolk of egg; clay marble (used in game of marbles)
BOLO dollar, peso; gift; bunch of pennies traditionally thrown to children at baptisms by godfathers
BOLÓN m. multitude
BOLSA pocket (in trousers); BOLSA CHIQUITA watch pocket; BOLSA DE AGUAS amniotic sac: "El feto crece en la bolsa de aguas"; douche bag; enema bag
BOLSITA watch pocket, small pocket for storing watches
BOLSUDO -DA (coll.) monied, loaded (coll.); (said of clothes having an excessive number of large pockets)
BOLUDO -DA lumpy, full of lumps
BOMBO -BA (slang) rich, wealthy; tired; ANDAR BOMBO -BA to be drunk; to be dazed: VIEJO BOMBO / VIEJA BOMBA interjs. (pej.) You damned old bastard / bitch!
BOMBONES mpl. okra
BOMPA (Eng.) (automobile's) bumper
BOMPEAR or BOMPIAR (Eng.) va. to bump, bump into
BÓMPER (Eng.) m. (automobile's) bumper (cf. BOMPA)
BONCHE or BONCHI (Eng.) m. bunch, handful; (coll.) gang, bunch (of persons)
BÓNGALO bungalow
BONITO -TA handsome; QUÉ BONITO!, ¿NO? (iron.) Nice going! (iron.) (expression used to reprimand people for their improper behavior)
BONQUE (Eng.) (slang) m. bunk (type of bed); TIRAR BONQUE (coll.) to go to sleep
BONQUEAR or BONQUIAR (Eng.) vn. to sleep
BOÑUELO (var. of) buñuelo

BOQUINETA m. cleft palate
BORCELANA small chamber pot
BORCHINCHE (var. of) bochinche
BORDERA (Eng.) owner and operator of a boarding house
BORDO small dam or dike; (Eng.) food dispensed in a boarding house
BORLO dance; movie theater; agitated situation; any festivity
BORLOTE m. noise, agitation, tumult; scandal; trouble; HACER BORLOTE to make trouble; to liven things up, raise hell (coll.)
BORLOTEAR or BORLOTIAR vn. to raise hell (coll.), liven things up; to make trouble
BORLOTERO -RA mf. trouble-maker; agitator; adj. turbulent, noisy, rowdy
BOROL (Eng.) m. bottle
BORUCA: HACER BORUCA to confuse, disorient
BORUQUEAR or BORUQUIAR va. to confuse, disorient
BORRACHALES (usually mfsg.) habitual drunkard, lush (coll.)
BORRACHÍN -CHINA habitual drunkard
BORRACHINTO -TA alcoholic, drunkard
BORRADO -DA greenish-colored (esp. ref. to eyes)
BORRAR vr. to beat it (coll.), scram (coll.); BORRAR DEL MAPA (coll.) to kill (someone)
BORREGO -GA sheep; veal
BORREGUERO -RA country person, hick (coll. & pej.)
BOS (Eng.) m. bus; boss
BOSGO -GA glutton
BOSLAIN (Eng.) m. transportation network, busline; bus terminal
BOSTECEAR or BOSTECIAR (vars. of) bostezar
BOSTEZADA yawn
BOSTECEADA or BOSTECIADA (var. of) bostezada
BOTANA taco given free to tavern patrons
BOTE m. pail, bucket; bottle (in general); baby bottle; (slang) jail; ECHAR EN EL BOTE / ECHAR AL BOTE to hex, bewitch
BOTEA (var. of) botella
BOTELLA fsg. intoxicating beverages; AGARRAR LA BOTELLA to take to the bottle (fig.), become a habitual drunkard
BOTI (var. of) bote
BOTIJÓN -JONA large-bellied (usually ref. to women)
BOTO -TA alcoholic; PONERSE LAS BOTAS to take advantage of a situation
BOTÓN very young boy who constitutes the male half of the "miniture couple" at formal Catholic wedding ceremonies
BOX (Eng.) (var. of) boxeo m.
BÓXAR or BÓXER (Eng.) m. boxer (Std. pugilista)
BOXIAR (var. of) boxear
BOXIN (Eng.) m. boxing, fisticuffs
BRACA (Eng.) break, chance, opportunity
BRACERO day-laborer, esp. one of Mexican origin;(by extension) Mexican immigrant to the United States
BRANDI (Eng.) m. brandy
BRAVO -VA: A LA BRAVA by force
BRAZO: MÁS VALEN LAS PIERNAS QUE LOS BRAZOS (said by mothers when they see their sons paying more attention to their wives than to Mother)
BRECA (Eng.) break, rest period; brake (on a car or other vehicle)
BRENDI (Eng.) (var. of) brandi
BREÑA (var. of) greña
BREQUE (Eng.) m. brake (aut.)
BREQUEAR or BREQUIAR (Eng.) va. to brake, apply the brakes to stop a moving vehicle
BRETE m. eagerness to act
BRICH or BRICHE (Eng.) m. bridge (card game)
BRILLA (var. of) brillantina
BRILLANTINA (Eng?) hair tonic, hair oil
BRINCACHARCOS msg. high-water pants
BRINCAR: BRINCAR EL CHARCO to cross the river (understood to ref. to the Rio Grande/Río Bravo between Texas and Mexico); (by extension) to immigrate from Mexico to the United States
BRIZNA drizzle, light rain; crumb; chip, splinter, piece
BRÓCOLO (Eng.) m. broccoli
BRODA (Eng.) m. (coll.) brother
BROÍTA (Eng.) m. (var. of) brodita (dim. of broda, q.v.)
BRÓMFIL (Hispanization of) New Braunfels, Texas
BRÓNSVIL (Hispanization of) Brownsville, Texas
BRUJA broke (coll.), without money; ANDAR BRUJA to be penniless
BRUJO medicine man, curandero
BRUJEAR or BRUJIAR to go without sleep
BRUTAL (coll.) super, terrific, great, keen (etc.) (adj. of general approbation)
BRUTÁLICO -CA (coll.) super, terrific, great (etc.) (adj. of

general approbation)
BRUTO -TA (coll.) intelligent; tremendous, terrific; (said of problems or tasks that are very difficult to resolve or complete); stupid, dumb; f. sexually attractive
BUCA (slang) girl
BUCHACA billiard table pocket
BUCHE (vulg.) m. ass, buttocks; PESARLE A ALGUIEN EL BUCHE to be lazy; mpl.: HACER BUCHES (DE SAL) to fill one's mouth with warm salt water so as to kill germs and lessen the pain of a toothache
BUELITO -TA (var. of) abuelito -ta
BUEN adv. well (used instead of Std. bien)
BUENO -NA fine (e.g., BUEN TIEMPO fine weather); BUEN TIEMPO (Ang.) good time, enjoyable experience; BUENO PARA NADA (Ang.) good for nothing, lazy, useless; BUENO Y SANO healthy; ESTAR BUENO to be enough (said with ref. to actions the speaker finds excessive and wishes to terminate): "Ya está bueno con esa canción" 'That's enough of that song'; ESTAR DE BUENAS to be in a good mood
BUENOTE -TA (slang) sexually attractive, very good-looking
BUEVO (var. of) huevo
BUEY m. cuckold; adj. ignorant, dumb
BUEYADA (var. of) boyada
BUGANVILIA (var. of) buganvilla
BUIGA, BÚIGAS, BÚIGA, BÚIGAMOS/ BÚIGANOS, BÚIGAN (vars. of) bulla, bullas, etc. (pres. subjunctive of bullir)
BÚIGO (var. of) bullo (1st pers. pres. indic. of bullir)
BUJERO (var. of) agujero
BÚLAVA (Eng.) boulevard
BULCHITEAR or BULCHITIAR (Eng.) (vulg.) to bullshit (vulg.)
BULCHITERO -RA (Eng.) (vulg.) bullshitter (vulg.)
BULE (Eng.) mf. bully (person who intimidates others)
BULÍO -A (var. of) bolillo -lla
BULLIR va. to incite, provoke; BULLIR LA LENGUA to gossip, speak ill of (someone); to talk frequently
BULTO ghost, phantom
BUQUÉ m. bouquet (of flowers)
BUQUEAR or BUQUIAR (Eng.) va. to book (i.e., to enter a purchase as debit against future wages; this practice is typically carried out by owners of company stores
BUQUI -QUIA m., f. child, kid, youngster
BURE or BURI (slang) much, many, very
BURLISTA mf. joker; mocker
BURUCA (var. of) boruca
BURRO (fig.) dumbbell (coll.), stupid; ENTRE MENOS BURROS MÁS OLOTES the less you eat the more there'll be for someone else
BUS m. (var. of) autobús
BUSCAMOSCAS mfsg. agitator, trouble-maker
BUSCAPLEITOS mfsg. troublemaker; person who is always looking for a fight
BUSCAR va. to look for trouble; to incite, provoke; BUSCARLE LA CARA A ALGUIEN to seek someone out so as to effect a reconciliation; BUSCAR PEDO to look for trouble; BUSCARLE RUIDO AL CHICHARRÓN to make trouble for oneself needlessly; EL QUE LA BUSCA LA HALLA if you look for trouble you'll find it; (see also LADO-- BUSCARLE A ALGUIEN POR SU LADO-
BUSCATOQUES (slang & underw.) mfsg. addict in search of a narcotic fix
BUSCÓN -CONA troublemaker; sharpie (coll.), wheeler-dealer (slang); arriviste, person on the make (coll.)
BUSGO -GA dog; glutton; SER UN BUSGO to have a hollow leg (coll.), desire to eat incessantly
BUSO -SA clever, smart
BUSQUITA little extra advantage obtained in a business deal
BUTACA hope chest
BUTE or BUTI (vars. of) bure or buri (q.v.)
BUTLEGA or BUTLÉGUER (Eng.) mf. bootlegger

C

CABALLADA (coll.) group of disorderly or riotous persons
CABALLITOS (var. of) caballito 'merry-go-round'
CABALLO n. clumsy person; CABALLO CUATROALBO horse with four white hooves; CABALLO PINTO pinto horse; METER CABALLO (coll.) to put in a bad word about someone
CABALLÓN -LLONA high on drugs: "Pepe anda caballón" 'Pepe's high on drugs'; large; tall (both with ref. to persons)
CABANUELAS (var. of) cabañuelas
CABAR (var. of) acabar
CABARETEAR or CABARETIAR vn. to go nightclubbing
CABARETERO -RA frequenter (habitué) of nightclubs; worker in a nightclub
CABECILLA head (of a bed, table, etc.)
CABECITA (euph.) head of penis; CABECITA DE VENA red dots on the skin, angiomata
CABELLERA wig, toupee
CABEZA (underw.) U.S. black; CABEZA DE BÚFALO (pej.) U.S. black; ECHARLE POR LA CABEZA A ALGUIEN to tell on someone (coll.), betray a confidence; TENER BUENA CABEZA to have a good head (coll.) be intelligent; VOLTEARLE A ALGUIEN LA CABEZA to give someone a swell head (fig.), cause someone to assume an exaggerated sense of importance
CABEZUDO -DA hard-headed, recalcitrant
CABINETE (Eng.) m. cabinet
CABLAR (var. of) clavar
CABLE: CABLE DE BOCA word of mouth
CABO (var. of Std.) quepo (1st pers. sg. indic. of caber)
CABÓI (Eng.) m. cowboy
CABRA: CABRA QUE DA LECHE (said of a person with great promise)
CABRÓN m. husband deceived by an adulterous wife; (general term of insult, usually vulg.: son of a bitch, bastard, etc
CABRONAZO hard blow (with fist or blunt instrument)
CABRONZOTE -TA m.,f. large; tall (ref. to persons)
CÁBULA discord; mf. competitor
CABULEAR or CABULIAR va. to complete a chore
CABURRO (hum.) cowboy
CABÚS (Eng.) m. caboose; (hum.) buttocks; large buttocks, big butt (coll.) (ref. is usually to the posterior region of the female)
CACA (vulg.) excrement (Std. mierda)
CACAHUATE m. pill; barbituate pill; (slang) NO VALER UN CACAHUATE not to be worth a damn
CÁCARA (slang) girl; person with acne; acne
CACARAQUEAR or CACARAQUIAR (vars. of) cacarear or cacariar
CACARAQUEO (var. of) cacareo
CACAREAR or CACARIAR vn. to gossip
CACEROLA cooking pot
CACHAR (Eng.) va. to catch; to cash (a check, etc.)
CACHETADA slap
CACHETAR va. to slap (the face) (see also CACHETEAR et al.)
CACHETE m. cheek; EL OTRO CACHETE Mexico (= el otro cachete de la misma cara)
CACHETEAR or CACHETIAR va. to slap
CACHETÓN -TONA plump-cheeked; CACHETÓN DEL PURO m. fat man (esp. one who smokes cigars constantly)
CACHIRUL m. large comb, back comb
CACHO -CHA: CACHAS facial expressions of worry or displeasure; side of a gun's handle; ANDAR HASTA LAS CACHAS to be dead drunk; TRAER LAS CACHAS COLGANDO to be wearing a long face, have a hang-dog expression (coll.); CACHO bit, small amount, fraction: "Son las siete y cacho" 'It's a little after seven o'clock'
CACHUCHA drug supply; heroin capsule; (pej.) police, police force; hat
CACHUCHÓN m. mean or vengeful policeman
CACHUDO -DA stern-faced
CACHUMBEAR or CACHUMBIAR va. to nick, chip; (fig.) to neck (kiss and embrace)
CACHUQUEAR or CACHUQUIAR (slang) va. to blow a job (coll.), mess up (coll.); to doublecross

CADA: (DE) CADA EN CUANDO from time to time; once in a while
CADENA: CADENA DE TELEVISIÓN television channel; CADENA DE TIENDAS chain stores
CADE (var. of) cadilaque m.
CADILAQUE (Eng.) m. Cadillac (brand of automobile); any large, expensive car
CADILEC (Eng.) m. Cadillac (cf. CADILAQUE)
CAEDRÉ, CAEDRÁS, etc. (vars. of Std.) caeré, caerás, etc. (future forms of caer)
CAER va. to swoop down upon, catch off guard, fall upon; vr. to come across with (coll.), pay up, pay one's debts; vr. to scratch (in pool or billiards); CAER AGUA(S) to rain; CAER ATRAVESADO to rub someone the wrong way; CAERLE A ALGUIEN LA CHANCLA to receive a reprimand; CAER COMO LA BASURA / CAER COMO LA CHINGADA to be repellent; CAER CON ALGO to catch or come down with (coll.) a disease; CAER DE ESA / CAER COMO LA PATADA to be repellent, repulsive: "Ese bato me cayó como la patada" 'That guy really turned me off'; CAER DE AQUELLA to please, turn on (slang), be atractive to; CAER GACHO / CAER GORDO / CAER PESADO / CAER PESETA / CAER SURA to displease, turn off (slang), be unattractive to, be repellent, etc. (cf. CAER COMO LA BASURA et al., supra); CAER LA RES to fall into a trap; CAER TIERRA to get into trouble, get caught; CAERLE LA TIERRA A ALGUIEN to surprise, sweep down upon by surprise; to yield (said of someone who falls prey to the calculating advances or machinations of the opposite sex in a romantic involvement), fall into a trap, CAER TOSTÓN to turn off, displease, be repellent, etc.; NO TENER EN QUÉ CAERSE MUERTO to be destitute, dirt-poor (coll.); ¡CÁETE! / ¡CÁETE MUERTO! (coll.) Pay up!, Fork over!
CAFÉ: CAFÉ CON LECHE brownish or tan colored; CAFÉ CON LLANTAS (hum.) coffee with doughnuts; CAFÉ CON MOSCA (hum.) coffee with sweetroll; CAFÉ NEGRO (Ang?) coffee without cream
CAFECERO -RA coffee-fiend, person who drinks a great deal of coffee
CAFESES (var. of) cafés (Std. pl. of café)
CAFIRO (slang) coffee
CAFIRUCHO (slang) bad-tasting coffee
CAFRO (slang) coffee
CAGADERA (vulg.) diarrhea
CAGADERO (vulg.) bathroom, toilet; pile of excrement
CAGADO -DA (vulg.) angry, tired, infuriated; f. (vulg.) excrement underw.) heroin; (vulg.) brat, obstreperous child; CAGADA f. blunder, mess: "Hizo su cagada como siempre" 'He blew it as usual'
CAGÓN -GONA (said of persons who defecate with frequency); m.f. quick-tempered (person)
CAGUILLAS mfsg. quick-tempered person; scaredy-cat, person who is easily frightened
CAI (Hispanization of) Kyle, Texas
CAIBA, CAIBAS, CAIBA, CÁIBAMOS / CÁIBANOS, CAIBAN (vars. of) caía, caías, etc. (imperf. forms of caer)
CAIDO -DA (var. of) caído -da (ppart. of caer)
CAINDO (var. of) cayendo (ger. of caer)
CAIR (var. of) caer
CAIRÉ, CAIRÁS, etc. (vars. of) caeré, caerás, etc. (future forms of caer)
CAIS, CAI, CAIMOS/CAYEMOS/CAYIMOS, CAIN (vars. of) caes, etc. (pres. ind. forms of caer)
CAITE (Eng.) m. kite
CAJA: CAJA DE COLORES crayon box; CAJA DE CORREO (Ang.) mail box (Std. buzón)
CAJETA small round wooden box containing caramel candy
CAJETUDA adj. sexy (said of women); f. headache
CAJÓN DE CARTAS (Ang.) m. letter box, mail box
CAJONERÍA mortuary
CAJONERO -RA box-maker; funeral director
CALABACITA squash (vegetable); (coll. & hum.) woman's leg; fpl. little white lies (coll.), minor untruths
CALABAZA dummy, stupid person; air-filter of an automobile's carburator; (see also DAR CALABAZAS)
CALABOZ m. (var. of) calabozo
CALABURNIA stupid; eccentric
CALACA death; sign of death

CALAMBRE m. part of the human body fallen into a comatose state: "Tengo un calambre en la pierna derecha" 'My right leg has fallen asleep'
CALANGO -GA ambitious
CALAR va. to try out, test; to attack (e.g., hunger pangs): "Me está calando el hambre"; to hurt (fig.), offend: "Me caló lo que me dijo" 'What he said offended me'; vr. to have a try (at doing something), give it a try: "Se me hace que no lo puedo hacer porque ya me calé"
CALAVERA drunkard; stupid person, dullard; combination tractor and plow
CALCEAR or CALCIAR vn. to walk barefooted
CALCETA stocking, sock; DESENRROLLAR LA CALCETA (hum.) to dance
CALCETÍN: CALCETÍN DE SEDA (hum.) upper class, silk-stocking (fig.)
CALCO (slang) shoe
CALCOMANÍA decal; process and result of transfering a design to a wet surface
CALDEADO -DA or CALDIADO -DA angry, boiling mad
CALDEAR or CALDIAR va. to anger; to make love to; vr. to become angry
CALDO soup; AÑO DEL CALDO yesteryear, days gone by
CALENTADORA: ¡CALENTADORAS! interj. (slang) Shut up! (form of linguistic disguise--note the partial resemblance between the first syllables of this form and cállate)
CALENTAR va. to excite sexually; vr. to be in heat (said of animals), become sexually excited (said of persons)
CALENTÓN: DAR UN CALENTÓN to arouse sexually; to arouse anger; DARSE UN CALENTÓN to become aroused sexually; to become angry
CALIENTE adj. hot, sexually excited; ESTAR CALIENTE to be sexually excited; (Ang.) to be hot (ref. to the weather); (Ang.) to be hot, feel hot (ref. to one's body temperature)
CALIFA(S) California; m.& f. Californian
CÁLIZ: HACER EL CÁLIZ to try, make an effort: "No sabe si puede ganar, pero quiere hacer el cáliz"
CALMANTE m. snack before meals; ¡CALMANTES MONTES! (slang) interj. Quiet down!, Knock it off! (coll.), Take it easy!, etc.
CALMAR vr. to wait
CALMEROZ (slang) interj. Take it easy!, Knock it off!, etc.
CALO nickle, five cent piece; penny; attempt, effort
CALÓ slang (esp. Pachuco slang); dialect; jargon
CALOFRÍO hot flash (of the sort experience by women reaching the "change of life")
CALORCITO intense heat
CALOTA (slang) beautiful woman
CALOTE (slang) mf., adj. big; politically active; effective in politics
CALVITO (slang) God, the Deity
CALZONCILLOS mpl. man's long underwear
CALZONCÍOS (var. of) calzoncillos
CALZONES mpl. man's undershorts; woman's panties; trousers
CALZONUDO -DA (said of person wearing baggy trousers)
CALLEJA alley
CALLO: PAJUELEAR/PAJUELIAR EL CALLO to stink (said of feet); TENER CALLO to be experienced; to be callous
CAMADA: SER DE LA MISMA CAMADA (slang) to belong to the same generation; to be on the same social level
CAMALEÓN or CAMALIÓN: m. horned toad; FUMAR COMO UN CAMALEÓN to smoke like a chimney (fig.), smoke excessively
CAMARÁ (var. of) camarada
CAMBACHEAR or CAMBACHAR (vars. of) cambalachear or cambalachar
CAMBEADO -DA or CAMBIADO -DA m. homosexual; f. lesbian
CAMBEAR (var. of) cambiar
CAMBIAR: CAMBIAR CHAQUETA to change allegiance, be a turncoat; CAMBIAR EL DISCO to change the subject; to stop harping on the same theme
CAMEADOR -DORA or CAMIADOR -DORA hard worker
CAMEAR or CAMELLAR (vars. of) camiar
CAMELLO or CAMEO (slang) work, labor; job, employment
CAMIAR (slang) to work, labor
CAMINO: CAMINO DE FIERRO railroad
CAMITA baby's bed, crib; (slang) buddy, friend
CAMOTAZOS (slang) blows with the

fists or with a solid object
CAMPAMOCHA walking stick
CAMPANA electrical buzzer
CAMPEAR or CAMPIAR vn. to go camping
CAMPECHANO -NA countrified; mf. country person, peasant; f. type of Mexican sweetbread
CÁMPER (Eng.) m. camper (recreational vehicle)
CAMPIÓN -PIONA (var. of) campeón -peona
CAMPIONATO (var. of) campeonato
CAMPO: CAMPO TURISTA (Ang.) tourist camp; motel
CAMPOSANTERO -RA cemetery caretaker
CANA: CANAS VERDES: SACARLE A UNO CANAS VERDES (used by parents to reprimand children when they misbehave: "Espérate, tú también vas a ser padre, y tus hijos te van a sacar canas verdes"; the implication is that the next generation will be even harder to manage if the present generation misbehaves; CANAS VERDES is roughly equivalent to 'premature gray hairs')
CANALEAR or CANALIAR va. to cut
CANALERO -RA canal worker
CANCO (slang) blow with the hand or fist; mpl. fist fight; AGARRARSE A CANCOS / DARSE CANCOS / METERSE CANCOS to have a fist fight; to beat up (coll.) on one another
CANDE (dim. of) Candelario -ria
CANDELÍA or CANDELILLA icicle
CANDELIAR or CANDELILLAR vn. to fall lightly (said of freezing rain or hail)
CANDI m. candy
CANDILAR va. to lure into a trap
CANICA: ANDAR CANICA(S) / CARGAR CANICA (slang) to be passionately in love with, carry the torch for (coll.)
CANIJO -JA mischievous person, little devil (coll. & hum.)
CANILLA wrist
CANQUEAR or CANQUIAR va. to beat someone up in a fight; vn. to fight with the fists; vr. to have a fist fight; to beat up on (coll.) one another
CANQUIZA beating, thrashing (in a fight)
CANTAR (slang) va. to ask for; to degrade, humiliate; to tell off (coll.), reprimand severely
CANTEAR or CANTIAR vr. to incline, lay on edge
CANTINERA dance-hall girl
CANTO (slang) house; home
CANTÓN (slang) m. house EL CANTÓN DE LA PERRA GALGA (hum.) the Greyhound bus terminal
CANUTILLO herbal tea ("Mormon tea," ephedra trifurca) used to treat anemia
CANUTO (see SALIR CANUTO)
CAÑONETA (var. of) camioneta
CAPA raincoat; (slang) heroin capsule; CAPA DE AGUA raincoat
CAPABLE (Ang.) capable
CAPACETA m. convertible top (of an automobile)
CAPEAR or CAPIAR va. to catch; to put heroin in capsules; vn. to tattle on someone
CAPIROTADA m. dessert made out of bread, cheese, raisins, honey and shortening; the same type of dish made with meat and without any form of sweetening
CAPIRUCHE or CAPIRUCHO m. captain
CAPITAL f. capitol (building) (Std. capitolio)
CAPÓN -PONA sterile (ref. to persons unable to bear or procreate children)
CAPOTE (see DAR CAPOTE)
CAPOTEADA (see DAR CAPOTEADA)
CAPOTEAR or CAPOTIAR va. to snatch an object (usually a ball) on way to its intended receiver; to leave scoreless in an athletic competition, to blank (coll.)
CAPOTIZA: DAR UNA CAPOTIZA to leave scoreless, blank (in an athletic competition); to shellack (coll.), achieve a high number of points while leaving the opponent scoreless
CAPOTUDO: OJOS CAPOTUDOS bulging eyes, pop eyes (slang); drooping eyelids
CAPTIVO -VA (var. of) cautivo -va
CAQUIS msg. fecal matter (euph. often applied to babies' feces); CAQUIS MAQUIS: ESTAR CAQUIS MAQUIS--"El bebito está caquis maquis" 'The baby is "dirty"' (i.e., the baby had defecated in his/her pants)
CARA: ECHAR EN CARA to hold something over someone: "Después del favor que me hiciste ahora quieres echármelo en cara"; TENER CUERPO DE TENTACIÓN Y CARA DE ARREPENTIMIENTO to have a beautiful body and a homely face (said of a woman); TORCER LA CARA to snub; (see also DAR EN CARA)

CARÁCTER (Ang.) personage in a play, character; odd-ball (slang), eccentric person
CARÁCTERES (var. of Std. pl.) caracteres
CARAJADA booboo, stupid thing, dumb act
CARAJAZO blow (with fist or object)
CARAJO interj. (mild or violent according to intonation); CARAJOS (var. of) carajo: "¿Qué carajos quieres?" 'What in the Sam Hill/tarnation (etc.) do you want?'; CARAJO -JA mischievous, tricky; difficult, hard to resolve
CARAMELO peppermint stick
CARANCHADA trick, mischief; stroke of bad luck
CARANCHO -CHA mischievous, tricky
CARANTIZAR (var. of) garantizar
CARÁTULA (slang) face
CARBULADOR (var. of) carburador m.
CARCACHA old car, jalopy (coll.)
CARCAJEAR or CARCAJIAR vn. to laugh heartily, guffaw
CARCAMONÍA (var. of) calcomanía
CARCELEJA type of children's game played with marbles
CAREADO -DA adj. at par, beginning a sports competition on an equal footing; f. sports competition not involving a handicap
CARGA (slang & underw.) load of narcotics
CARGADO -DA bothersome; overbearing; boring; strong (e.g., strong coffee): "El café está muy cargado" 'The coffee is too strong'; thick (e.g., beard or hair); ANDAR CARGADO -DA (underw.) to be carrying drugs
CARGADOR m. pall bearer
CARGAR va. to charge (merchandise to an account); CARGAR CANICA to be passionately in love with, carry the forch for (coll.); CARGAR LA CALENTURA to increase or persist (ref. to fever): "Anoche le cargó la calentura al niño" 'The child's fever went up last night'; CARGAR LA CARRETA (for one person to do most of the work in a supposedly cooperative venture, to take the lion's share of the burden); CARGAR LA EDUCACIÓN EN LA PUNTA DE LOS PIES/CARGAR LA EDUCACIÓN EN LOS TALONES (ref. to an educated person who behaves in an ill-bred manner); CARGAR PELOTA (slang) to be passionately in love with, carry the torch for (coll.); CARGÁRSELE A ALGUIEN MUCHO to take someone's death very hard: "A Julio se le cargó mucho la muerte de su bisabuela"
CARGO: HACERLE CARGOS A ALGUIEN (Ang.) to bring charges against someone (in a law suit)
CARGUERO freight train
CARIÑOSO -SA likeable
CARITA flirt, tease
CARLANGO -GA raggedy; m. coat (in general)
CARLANGUIENTO -TA raggedy; sickly-looking
CARMESA (var. of) quermés or quermese (also spelled kermés, kermese)
CARMÍN m. lipstick
CARNAL (slang) m. brother
CARNALA (slang) f. sister
CARNALISMO comradeship
CARNALONGO -GA (slang) m. big brother; f. big sister
CARNE: BOLAS DE CARNE meat balls; CARNE DEL DIABLO devilled ham; CARNE MOLIDA hamburger meat, ground meat; CARNE PICADA hamburger meat, ground meat
CARNOSIDAD: CARNOSIDAD DEL OJO fleshy eye growth (pterigium)
CARPANTA multitude
CARPETA (Ang.) rug
CARTELÓN m. placard
CARTITA small card (e.g., a filing card)
CARTUCHERA holster
CARTÚN (Eng.) m. cartoon
CARRANCLÁN m. type of cloth used for women's dresses
CARRAZO luxurious automobile
CARREREAR or CARRERIAR va. to hurry someone along; vn. to hurry, rush
CARRERÍA mass or bunch of automobiles
CARRETÍA or CARRETILLA spool (e.g., spool of thread)
CARRETÓN m. child's toy wagon
CARRÍA or CARRILLA: ¡CARRILLA! interj. Hurry up!; AGARRAR A CARRILLA to give chase to; DAR CARRILLA to bother, pester; ECHAR EN CARRILLA to give chase to; HACER ALGO A CARRILLA to do something hurriedly
CARRITO streetcar, tram; TENER CARRITO to harp on the same subject
CARRIZO fishing rod
CARRUCHA (coll.) jalopy, clunker (slang), old worthless car
CARRUCHAR va. to cart off, carry

off; vn. to ride in a car
CARRUCHO automobile (usually pej.)
CARRUMFLA (slang) jalopy, old car; (hum.) face
CASA: CASA DE ALTO two-story house; CASA DE APARTAMENTOS (Ang.) apartment house, apartment building; CASA DE BORDE or CASA DE BORDEROS or CASA DE BORDOS (Eng.) boarding house; CASA DE CAMBIO currency exchange; CASA DE CORTE (S) (Ang.) courthouse; CASA DE RENTA (Ang.) house for rent; rented house; CASA GRANDE (Ang?) (slang) big house (i.e., penitentiary); CASA MORTUORIA funeral home; CASA REDONDA (Ang.) round house (for the switching and repairing of trains)
CASANOVA m. adulteror
CASCAR va. to ask for and receive something
CASCAREAR or CASCARIAR vn. to use one's last ounce of strength in order to accomplish something
CASCARÓN (used mainly in mpl.: CASCARONES) egg shells filled with confetti, then painted, and subsequently broken over people's heads, festively, at Eastertime
CAS: CAS DE (see A CAS DE)
CASE prep. at the home of: "Está case Felipe" 'He's at Felipe's house'
CASERA babysitter; person who enjoys doing household chores
CASIMIRO GUERRA (slang & hum.) m. young man about to be drafted
CASITA out-house, privvy
CASPIENTO -TA full of dandruff
CASQUETA masturbation; HACERSE LA CASQUETA to masturbate
CASQUETEAR or CASQUETIAR va. & vr. to masturbate
CASQUILLA cartridge case; empty cartridge
CASTAÑO chest, trunk
CATÁGALO or CATÁGOLO (vars. of) catálogo
CATAPLÚN (var. of) cataplum (interj.)
CATARINO -NA (var. of) Catalino -na
CATARRIENTO -TA (var. of) catarroso -sa
CATARRO: CATARRO CONSTIPADO chronic cold in the head; hay fever
CATE (dim. of) Catalino -na, Catarino -na
CATEADO -DA or CATIADO -DA mf. victim of a beating
CATEAR or CATIAR (slang) va.to beat up (in a fight); vr. to beat up on one another in a fight
CATIZA (slang) beating, thrashing (in a fight)
CATO (slang) blow with a fist; CATOS fist fight; boxing match; AGARRARSE A CATOS to have a fist fight; METERSE CATOS to beat up on one another in a fight
CATOLECISMO (var. of) catolicismo
¡CATORCE! interj. (of varying intensity according to intonation)
CATORRAZO heavy blow with the fist; heavy slap
CATRÍN m. dandy, fop, dude, (slang)
CAUBÓI (Eng.) m. cowboy
CAUCH or CAUCHO (Eng.) m. couch, sofa
CAUSULA (var. of) cápsula
CAVARRUBIAS (var. of) Covarrubias (surname)
CAYER (var. of) caer
CAYÍ, CAYISTE, CAYIMOS (vars. of) caí, caíste, caímos (various pret. forms of caer)
CAYO (dim. of) Arcadio
CAZO large kettle used for boiling clothes; bowl
CAZUELEJA children's game played with tops
CEBOLLA (hum.) watch, wristwatch
CEBOLLITA children's game similar to tug-of-war
CEDRÓN m. bucket
CELAFÁN or CELAFÉIN (Eng.) m. cellophane
CELEBRAR: ¿QUÉ CELEBRAS? (set expression) What are you up to?, What are you doing?; What is wrong with you?
CÉLEBRE adj. thankful; cute
CELEBRE (var. of) célebre
CELEBRO (var. of) cerebro
CELGA (var. of) acelga
CEMETERIO (var. of) cementerio
CEMITA (var. of) acemita 'bran bread'
CENCIA (var. of) ciencia
CENICERA (var. of) cenicero ashtray
CENTRO: CENTRO ABARROTERO shopping center
CENTURA (var. of) cintura
CENZONCLE or CENZONTE or CENZONTLE mf. mocking bird (Mimus polyglottos)
CEQUIA (var. of) acequia
CER (var. of) hacer
CERCA adj. m. & f. stingy
CERCAS (var. of) cerca
CEREBRO nape of neck
CERILLO any type of match (Std.

fósforo)
CERO kindergarten
CEROTE large-statured, tall
CERVECERO -RA very fond of beer
CERRADO: CERRADO DE BARBA thick-bearded
CERRAR: CERRAR EL PICO (coll.) to shut up, be quiet
CESTÓN m. kitchen cupboard
CICLETA (var. of) bicicleta 'bicycle'; tricycle
CIELO (vocative) darling
CIEN (var. of) ciento (when Std. requires the full form, e.g.:) "cien treinta" "ciento treinta", etc. (also in adjectival constructions:) "¿Cuántos libros tienes? -- Cien."
CIENTÍFICO -CA well-educated, knowledgeable
CIERTO -TA: CIERTOS ELOTES (VERDES) /CIERTOS ELOTES Y CAÑAS HELADAS certain so-and-sos (said to avoid naming someone specifically)
CIGARRERA ash-tray
CIMENTERO -RA (var. of) cementero -ra
CIMENTO (var. of) cemento
CINC (Eng.) m. sink (for washing dishes)
CINCO nickel, five cents; DAR CINCO: "Dame cinco" (slang) 'Shake hands', 'Slap me five' (slang)
CINCHO (Eng.) (slang) cinch, sure thing; DE CINCHO certainly, for sure
CINIA (Eng.) zinnia
CINQUE (coll.) five; fifteen
CINTA shoelace
CINTO woman's belt (never ref. to male belt)
CINTURA small of back, area surrounding the small of the back
CINZONCLE or CINZONTE or CINZONTLE (vars. of) CENZONCLE et al.
CIODI (Eng.) m. C.O.D. (abbrev. of Collect On Delivery; the abbrev. has been reconstituted in Spanish as Cobrar o devolver)
CIRGÜELA f. or CIRGÜELO m. (vars. of) ciruela
CIRQUERO -RA fond of circuses; mf. circus performer; person working for a circus
CISCA shame
CISCAR va. to frighten away
CISCO (dim. of) Francisco
CISNERO -RA liar
CIZOTE m. sore; wound
CLAB (Eng.) m. (var. of) club
CLACO (slang) nickel, five cents
CLAPIAR (Eng.) va. to applaud; to cut in on someone at a dance; vn. to clap, applaud
CLARIDOSO -SA frank, blunt
CLAS or CLASIA (vars. of) clase f.
CLAVADO -DA (underw.) stolen; ECHARSE UN CLAVADO / TIRARSE UN CLAVADO to dive into water
CLAVAR (slang) vr. to steal; to fail to return a borrowed item; CLAVAR LA UÑA to sell (often through high-pressure tactics); to borrow money; to stab
CLAVEL (slang) adj. thieving; m. thief (ref. to male thieves only)
CLAVELITO -TA (slang) adj. thieving; mf. thief
CLAVETE (slang) adj. thieving; m. thief (ref. to male thieves only)
CLAVETEAR or CLAVETIAR (slang) (vars. of) clavar
CLAVETÍN (slang) m. robbery
CLEIMIAR (Eng.) va. & vn. to claim
CLEMO (slang) penny, one-cent piece
CLEPEAR or CLEPIAR (Eng.) (vars. of) clapiar
CLEPTO -TA (var. of) cleptomaníaco -ca
CLETA (dim. of) Henriqueta
CLETA (var. of) bicicleta, tricicleta
CLÍNERS (Eng.) mpl. cleaners, dry cleaners; LLEVAR A LOS CLÍNERS (slang) to clean someone out (fig.), impoverish someone
CLIPA (Eng.) f. (usually fpl.: CLIPAS) clippers, shears
CLOB (var. of Eng.) club m.
CLOCHE (Eng.) m. clutch (automotive)
CLORAX or CLOROX (Eng.) m. bleach, chlorine
CLOROFORME (var. of) cloroformo
COBIJA(S): PEGÁRSELE A ALGUIEN LA(S) COBIJA(S) to oversleep
COBRADOR -DORA persistent in collecting money that is due
COBRE m. penny, one-cent piece
COBRÓN -BRONA persistent in collecting money that is due
CÓCCIZ m. tailbone, coccyx
COCEDOR m. oven
COCINIAR (var. of) cocinar
COCO (hum.) head, skull; (child language) hurt, injury
COCOLES mpl. beans
COCOMALETAS msg. bogyman
COCOLMECA herbal tea (sarsaparilla, Smilax mexicana) used to treat kidney ailments
CÓCONO turkey; gigolo; (slang)

male homosexual; mf. person high on drugs
COCTEL or CÓCTEL or COCTEIL (Eng.) m. cocktail party; cocktail (alcoholic drink)
COCHE (Eng.) m. coach, athletic trainer
COCHINO -NA nasty; indecent
COCHITO -TA conformist, square (coll.)
COCHOTAS: COCHOTAS DE PAPÁ (term of endearment with a slight tinge of vulgarity to it; possible Eng. equivalent: 'Daddy's sweet mama')
COCHOTE -TA m. sugar daddy; f. sweet mamma (terms of endearment, often used in the vocative; cf. COCHOTAS supra); mf. fat person
CODO stingy; EMPINAR EL CODO to drink (usually intoxicating beverages)
COGEDERA (vulg.) fornication
COGEDOR -DORA m. sex fiend, satyr; f. nymphomaniac
COGER (vulg.) va. to fornicate, COGER EN LAS MORAS (coll.) to catch red-handed; COGER FRÍO (Ang.) to catch cold, get a cold; COGER PARA to head toward, go in the direction of; COGERSE ALGO to steal
COGIDO -DA (vulg.) adj. screwed (vulg. slang); f. screwing (vulg.), fornication: "Le dieron su buena cogida" 'They really ____ her over'
COIL (Eng.) m. inter-uterine device, coil, loop (contraceptive)
COJÍN m. adultress; unmarried woman who enjoys sex frequently
COLA fsg. buttocks; (Eng.) long-distance telephone call; (fig. and slang) tail, shadow, probation officer (i.e., anyone who "follows" a criminal, a suspect or an ex-criminal); COLA AFUERA (Eng.) long-distance telephone call; COLA LARGA sly, astute, tricky; PONER COLA to put a tail on (someone) (e.g., to have someone follow a suspect); SALIR CON COLA to travel with one's family; to leave prison on parole; TENER COLA to be on probation; NO TENER COLA QUE LE PISEN to have nothing to be ashamed of, have no skeletons in the closet; TRAER COLA (for underclothing to be showing)
COLAR vr. to slip in and out, sneak in and out
COLCRIM or COLCRÍN (Eng.) m. cold-cream
COLCHA: ¡¿CUÁLES COLCHAS?! (interj.) What do you mean?, What the hell are you talking about?! (esp. with the implication: I didn't promise you anything); PEGARSE LAS COLCHAS to oversleep: "A Luis se le pegaron las colchas, por eso llegó tarde"
COLEAR or COLIAR va. to follow, tail (slang); to grab by the seat of the pants or by the skirt; to borrow; to color (var. of colorear)
COLECTADOR -DORA collector (e.g., of taxes)
COLECTAR va. to collect
COLEGIANTE mf. student; college student
COLEREAR or COLERIAR va. to borrow
COLERO -RA sponger, freeloader (coll.)
COLGAR: COLGAR LOS GUANTES (fig.) to retire from boxing; COLGAR LOS TENIS (fig. & hum.) to die (<tennis shoes)
COLICHE mf. tag-along, person (usually youngster) who follows others wherever they go
COLMAR: COLMARLE A ALGUIEN EL PLATO to cause someone to come to the end of his/her rope (coll.): "Ya me colmaste el plato con tu abuso. ¡Vete!"
COLMENA bee
COLOPEAR or COLOPIAR to go out on the town (coll.), have a good time in nightclubs, etc. (<columpiar 'to swing'?)
COLOR: COLORES mpl. type of children's game; DAR COLORES to show off
COLORADA (slang) secconal capsule; blood; SACAR LA COLORADA to give someone a bloody nose
COLOTE (var. of) culote m.
COLTURA (var. of) cultura
COLUDO -DA showing, hanging out (said of underclothing, shirt-tails, etc.)
COLUMPIO -PIA tight-wad (coll.), person who never pays; person who walks with an exaggerated swinging gait; CADA CHANGO A SU COLUMPIO Y A COLUMPIARSE LUEGO let each one attend to his/her own affairs
COMA (var. of) goma
COMBIAR (Eng.) va. to comb
COMELÓN -LONA glutton
COMENZÓN (var. of) comezón
COMER: COMER ANSIA to be impatient;

COMER CON LA VISTA to devour with glances; COMER GALLO to become agressive; to hit foul balls (note bilingual pun: foul--baseball term--equated with fowl 'gallo'); COMERSE UNA CARTA to fail to answer a letter; COMERSE A UNA PERSONA to browbeat someone; COMERSE A ALGUIEN CON LOS OJOS to stare at someone with hatred or anxiety; COMERSE A ALGUIEN VIVO to tell someone where to get off (slang) in no uncertain terms, reprimand someone severely; COMERSE ALGUIEN SUS PALABRAS (Ang.) to eat one's words (fig.), retract something one has said

COMIDO -DA full, awash with, blighted by: "Tiene la cara comida de espinillas" 'His face is full of pimples'; COMIDA DE BUFÉ (Eng.) buffet supper; f. COMIDA EMPACADA canned food

COMIDOR (var. of) comedor m.

COMILÓN -LONA (var. of) comelón -lona

COMO: CÓMO ALMA QUE (SE) LLEVA EL DIABLO/COMO CUANDO DIOS SE LLEVA UN ALMA in the twinkling of an eye (fig.), very rapidly; COMO ÉL SOLO as only he can be: "Es loco como él solo" 'He's crazy as only he can be' (also: COMO ELLA SOLA, COMO ELLOS SOLOS, etc.); ¿CÓMO LES QUEDÓ EL OJO? (slang) How does that grab you?, How do you like them apples? (slang)

COMPA (<compadre) (slang) m. Mac, Bub, Jack, mister, etc. (frequent vocative used to address person whose name one does not know): "Ese, compa, páseme un frajo" 'Hey Mac, gimme a cigarette'

COMPANÍA (var. of) compañía

COMPAÑERO: EL ______ ÉSE MI COMPAÑERO (ironic or festive reference to a quality shared by both the speaker and the person referred to; the remark is sometimes made to take revenge on an initial criticism from the person referred to, e.g., "el chaparro ése mi compañero" 'that guy was just as short as I am')

COMPITA (var. of) compadre, compa m.

COMPLEAÑOS or COMPLIAÑOS msg. (vars. of) cumpleaños

COMPLETAR: COMPLETAR CON to take care of as well, finish up the job with (you) too: "Y si tú te entremetes, completo contigo" 'And if you stick your nose into this, I'll take care of you afterwards' (i.e., after having defeated the original antagonist, as in a fight)

COMPONEDOR -DORA handy-man, Mr. Fix-It (coll.); distorter of the truth

COMPONER va. to cast a spell, bewitch; vr. to reform, go straight (after a life of crime); to clear up (said of cloudy skies)

COMPRAR: COMPRAR A TIEMPO (Ang.) to buy on time (coll.), buy on the installment plan

COMPROMISO debt

COMPUESTITO -TA (coll.) straightened out (i.e., after having led a life of crime); bewitched, hexed (often used in the context of I-told-you-so, or He-had-it-coming-to-him, e.g., "Pues ya está compuestito" 'I told you they would put a spell on him sooner or later')

CON (Eng.): CON DE NIEVE (var. of) cono de nieve

CON prep. CON SAFOS or CON ZAFOS (insulting) The same to you!, The same goes for you!, Now I've said the last word!; CON EL GORDO hitch-hiking; (Eng.) m. cone (Std. cono); (see also CON DON--v.s. DON)

CONCENCIA (var. of) consciencia

CONCUÑO (var. of) concuñado

CONCHA (dim. of) Concepción

CONCHABAR vr. to live in free union, form a common-law marriage

CONDENADO -DA (pej.) bastard, son-of-a-bitch (terms of insult)

CONDO (rus.) (var. of) cuando

CONDUCÍ, CONDUCISTE, CONDUCIÓ, CONDUCIMOS, CONDUCIERON (vars. of) conduje, condujiste, etc. (pret. forms of conducir)

CONDUCTOR -TORA or CONDUTOR -TORA railroad conductor, ticket collector

CONE (Eng., dim. of) Connie

CONECTACIÓN (var. of) conexión

CONEJO msg. biceps

CONFERENCIAL m. meeting; small conference meeting

CONFIDENCIA (Ang.) trust, confidence

CONFIDENTE -TA faithful; CONFIDENTE

m. sofa (in general)
CONFORMAR va. to adjust, harmonize, reconcile; vr. to reconcile
CONFORME reconciled (adj.)
CONGA type of Cuban dance
CONGAL (slang) m. brothel, whore house; beer joint
CONO: CONO DE NIEVE ice cream cone
CONOCENCIA acquaintanceship, group of friends
CONQUIÁN m. type of card game similar to whist
CONSCIENCIA: TENER LA CONSCIENCIA LIMPIA to have a clear conscience; TENER LA CONSCIENCIA SUCIA to have a guilty conscience
CONSECUENTAR va. to tolerate, bear with
CONSERVATIVO -VA stingy, tightfisted
CONSIGUIR (var. of) conseguir
CONSTIPADO -DA (Ang.) constipated, unable to move one's bowels
CONTAR: CONTAR LAS MUELAS to pull the wool over someone's eyes (coll.), to deceive
CONTENTAR va. to reconcile; vr. to become reconciled
CONTENTO -TA reconciled
CONTESTABLE (var. of) condestable
CONTIMÁS (var. of) cuantimás 'at least'
CONTOY TODO (var. of) con todo y todo 'lock, stock and barrel' (coll.=absolutely everything)
CONTRA (see DAR LA CONTRA)
CONTRABANDISTA mf. illegal immigrant (esp. one from Mexico to the United States)
CONTRABANDO illegal (male) immigrant
CONTRECHO -CHA contradictory
CONTROL -LA (slang) m. gang leader; f. (hum.) wife
CONVENENCIA (var. of) conveniencia
CONVENCIERO -RA or CONVENENCIERO -RA opportunistic
CONVERTIBLE m. (Ang.) convertible (car with folding roof); pick up truck
CONVIENCIA (var. of) conveniencia
CONVITE m. group of persons announcing a forthcoming event from a truck
CÓNYUGUE (var. of) cónyuge
COPALA perch (perca flavescens)
COPEAR (var. of) copiar
COPEÓN -PEONA or COPIÓN -PIONA m., f. copycat
COPEQUIEC (Eng.) m. cupcake
COPETÓN -TONA (ref. to person whose hair is piled up high in front)
COPERAR (var. of) cooperar
COPETE m. top rim of a measuring glass; ANDAR HASTA EL COPETE to be very drunk; ESTAR HASTA EL COPETE to come to the end of the road (fig.), be completely fed up with (fig.), want nothing more with: "Ya estoy hasta el copete con Enrique" 'I've just come to the end of the road with Henry'; TENERLE A ALGUIEN HASTA EL COPETE: "Ya me tienes hasta el copete" 'I've just had it up to here with you'
COPETEAR or COPETIAR va. to fill a glass to the brim
COPQUEIC (Eng.) (var. of) copequiec
CORA (var. of) corazón m.; (see also DE CORA)
CORAJE: m. pathologically angry condition believed to cause miscarriage, spoil breast milk, etc.; DA-CORAJE (hum. or ironic) m. Cadillac (or any other expensive brand of automobile)
CORBATA: CORBATA DE GATO (hum.) bowtie
CORBATERO tie rack (perch for hanging neckties); man fond of wearing neckties
CORBEADOR -DORA or CORBIADOR -DORA freeloader, sponge (coll.)
CORBERO -RA freeloader, sponge (coll.)
CORCHOLATA bottle cap
CORDÓN m. string; street curb
CORONA V.I.P., big-shot (coll.), important or influential person
CORONA DE SAN DIEGO climbing red rose (Antigonon leptopus)
CORPOS (Hispanization or var. of) Corpus Christi, Texas
CORSAJE m. corsage
CORTADO -DA m. (var. of) cortadura; ANDAR CORTADO DE DINERO to be low on funds; ANDAR RECORTADO DE DINERO to be very low on funds
CORTAR va. to put down (slang), put someone in his/her place, deprecate; vr. (slang) to leave; CORTAR EL MITO to stop talking (used esp. as a command: "¡Corta el mito"); CORTAR LAS NUBES to "cut" storm clouds (acc. to folk belief, if an innocent child makes the sign of the cross with a knife out of doors, storm clouds will disappear); CORTARSE LA CALENTURA (for a fever to break, cease to be intense): "Anoche se le cortó la calentura" 'His fever broke last night'
CORTE (Ang.) f. court, courthouse;

slight trim (haircut)
CASA DE CORTE(S) (Ang.) courthouse
CORTINA: ¡CORTINAS! (slang) Cut it out!, Stop it!
CORTO -TA f. short film preceding the main feature; m. (coll.) brushoff; (elec.) short circuit; ANDAR CORTO DE DINERO to be low on funds
CORTÓN m. brushoff, snub
CORVAS fpl. TEMBLARLE A ALGUIEN LAS CORVAS to be afraid
CORRE (casa de corrección) (underw.) f. prison, jail
CORREA immigration or customs officer (esp. U.S. immigration officer on the U.S.-Mexican border)
CORRECTAR (Ang.) va. to correct
CORREDERA diarrhea
CORRELÓN -LONA scaredy-cat (slang) (said of person who consistently runs away from a situation which he/she finds threatening)
CORRELLÓN or CORREÓN m. thick belt (article of clothing)
CORRENTÍA impetus, momentum; AGARRAR CORRENTÍA to get a running start
CORRENTÓN -TONA common, ordinary, cheap
CORRER va. to chase; (Ang.) to run off, reproduce, duplicate: "¿Cuántas copias corriste?"; (Ang.) to operate, run (e.g., a business); va. (Ang.) to run, supervise; CORRER EL CUERPO to defecate; CORRER LA CABEZA to talk excessively; CORRER PARA UNA OFICINA (Ang.) to run for political office
CORRETEAR or CORRETIAR va. to run ragged
CORRIDA: EN CORRIDA written by hand
CORRIENTE ordinary, common, cheap, lowclass
COSA: CREERSE LA GRAN COSA / HACERSE LA GRAN COSA to act superior; COSA QUE conj. therefore, and so, hence; LA OTRA COSA (any narcotic drug substitute); ¡QUÉ COSAS! (fixed expression of endearment and approbation frequently used with ref. to a child's actions) How nice!, How adorable!, etc.
COSITA: fpl. HACER COSITAS (euph.) to copulate
COSOTA: fpl. COSOTAS (DE MAMÁ) (term of endearment usually used when addressing one's female sweetheart; poss. Eng. equivalent: 'Sweet mamma'); COSOTAS (DE PAPÁ) (term of endearment with a slight tinge of vulgarity; poss. Eng. equivalent: 'Daddy's sweet mamma'); (cf. COCHOTAS et al.)
COSTAL: SER HARINA DEL MISMO COSTAL to share the same charcteristics, be cut from the same cloth (fig.); SER HARINA DE OTRO COSTAL to belong to a different tribe (fig.), belong to someone else (often said sarcastically be parents to married offspring who seldom return to the parental home to visit)
COSTALAZO precipitous tumble, heavy fall; DAR EL COSTALAZO to keel over, go down like a sack of meal (fig.)
COSTEAR or COSTIAR to be worth the trouble, worthwile
COSTILLA f. girl friend; f. boy friend; girl who keeps a gigolo
COSTILLITA: SER MUY COSTILLITA to be a stinker (slang), be disagreeable to others
COSTIPADO -DA (vars. of) constipado -da
COSTURERÍA seamstress's shop
COTACO (Eng.) m. "Kotex" (female sanitary napkin)
COTACHÍS (Eng.) m. cottage cheese
COTIN m. cloth used to cover chairs or sofas; slip cover
COTINCHÓN -CHONA meddler (usually ref. to man who meddles in women's affairs)
COTORRAZO blow, heavy hit
COTORREAR or COTORRIAR vn. to converse amiable, gossip, chat
COTORRO -RRA talkative person, chatterbox, gossip
COUC (Eng.) f. coca-cola (soft drink)
COUCH (Eng.) mf. coach, trainer
COYOTE mf. youngest member of a family; person easily frightened; exploiter; unscrupulous politician; halfbreed; person who works for a commission (fixed rate of pay)
COYOTEAR or COYOTIAR va. to rob; vn. to goof off (slang), fool around, enjoy oneself aimlessly
COZCO devil
CRACA (Eng.) wise crack, would-be clever remark
CRANQUE (Eng.) m. crank (tool); crank (grumpy person)
CRAQUEADO -DA or CRAQUIADO -DA (Eng.) cracked (slang), crazy
CRAQUEAR or CRAQUIAR (Eng.) va. to

crack, break open
CREADA (var. of) criada
CREATURA (var. of) criatura
CRECER vn. to mature, gain experience
CRECIDOTE -TA ponderous and overgrown young person
CREER: CREERSE LA DIVINA GARZA ENVUELTA EN TORTILLA / CREERSE LA DIVINA GRACIA / CREERSE LA GRAN COSA / CREERSE LA GRAN CACA (vulg.) / CREERSE MUY MALDITO -TA / CREERSE MUY CHICOTUDO -DA / CREERSE MUY CHICHO -CHA to consider oneself superior / CREERSE MUY MACHÍN to consider oneself to be a real stud (slang): "Él se cree muy machín" 'He thinks he's a real stud'; / CREERSE SABROSO -SA to feel superior, consider oneself superior; ¡NO CREAS! (interj., iron.) Don't doubt it for a moment!
CREIBA, CREIBAS, etc. (vars. of) creía, etc. (imperf. conjugation of creer)
CREÍDO -DA credulous, gullible, vain, presumptuous
CREIDO -DA (var. of) creído -da (ppart. of creer)
CRENQUEAR or CRENQUIAR (Eng.) va. to crank a car
CREP or CREPÉ: CREPÉ ROMANO type of coarse cloth
CREPA (Eng.) (vulg.) crapper (i.e., toilet)
CREQUEAR or CREQUIAR (Eng.)(vars. of) craquear or craquiar
CRER (var. of) creer
CRESTA: IR LA CRESTA to rise (said of bodies of water during floods)
CREYER (var. of) creer
CREYON (Eng.) m. crayon
CRIAR: CRIAR CON PECHO to breast feed
CRIS (dim. of) Cristóbal
CRISMAS or CRISMES (Eng.) msg. Christmas (season); Christmas present
CRISTAL m. multicolored marble; mf. (mildly pej.) Anglo-Saxon; (dim. of) Crystal City, Texas
CRO (var. of) creo (1st pers. sg. pres. ind. of creer)
CRUCIFICO (var. of) crucifijo
CRUDO -DA adj. hungover; mf. person suffering from a hangover
CRÚNER (Eng.) m. crooner, singer of popular love songs
CRUZ: HACER LA CRUZ to make one's first sale of the day (said of merchants)
CRUZACALLES mfsg. gadabout, loafer
CRUZADO -DA halfbreed
CUACO horn of an animal; mpl. animal horns; handle bars of a bicycle
CUACHA chicken dung; HACER CUACHA (vulg., slang) to make mincemeat of (fig.), beat up soundly (in a fight)
CUACHALOTE ugly; bad; clumsy
CUACHÓN -CHONA fat and flabby; slovenly dresser, infrequent bather
CUACHONÓN -NONA very fat and flabby
CUADRO field for cultivation; field under cultivation
CUAI (cuate) m. buddy, pal (slang)
CUAJAR vn. to lie, tell falsehoods
CUALQUIERA prostitute, whore
CUANDO: (DE) CADA EN CUANDO from time to time
CUANTIMÁS (coll.) at least; let alone
CUANTO -TA: ¡A LAS CUÁNTAS! It's about time!, ¿A QUIÉN Y A CUÁNTOS? What business is that of anyone's?
CUARENTAIDÓS or CUARENTAIUNO (slang) male homosexual (so named after the disputed number of men caught in flagrante delicto at a private party by the police in Mexico City in the late 1930's)
CUARENTENA forty days following parturition (birth of a child): "Antes, las mujeres tenían que evitar baños y varios alimentos durante la cuarentena"
CUARTA belt (article of clothing)
CUARTADA spanking or whipping with a belt
CUARTAZO msg. single blow with a belt; mpl. spanking, whipping (with a belt)
CUARTERÓN -RONA person of mixed Hispanic and African ancestry
CUARTILLA quarter, twenty-five cent piece
CUARTITO outhouse, outdoor toilet
CUARTIZA spanking or whipping with a belt
CUARTO: CUARTO REDONDO (Ang.) quarter round (piece of corner furniture similar to a night stand)
CUATE -TA twin; pal, buddy (coll.); peer, equal; m. double-barreled shotgun; CUATES mpl. (slang) testicles
CUATEZÓN -ZONA intimate friend
CUATROJOS (slang) mfsg. four-eyes (i.e., person who wears eyeglasses)

CUATRO: CUATRO REALES / RIALES fifty cent piece
CUAY m. guy, fellow
CUBRIDO (var. of) cubierto (ppart. of cubrir)
CUCARACHA (coll.) jalopy, old car
CUCARACHERO place infested with cockroaches
CUCARACHO (var. of) cucaracha
CUCO or CUCA (dims. of) Refugio (m. & f.)
CUCOMALETAS (var. of) cocomaletas
¡CÚCHALE! or ¡CÚCHELE! interj. Sic'-em! (said to animals as encouragement to attack someone or retrieve something)
CUCHARA: CUCHARA DE VIERNES busybody, interfering person
CUCHÍA or CUCHILLA: PANTALONES DE CUCHILLA bellbottomed trousers
CUCHILLERO -RA troublemaker
CUCHO -CHA twisted, misshapen; harelipped
CUELA or CUÉLALE or CUÉLATE or CUELE or CUÉLELE or CUÉLESE interjs. (slang) Scram!, Beat it!, Bug off!, etc.
CUELLO: CUELLO DE LA MATRIZ cervix, entrance to the uterus
CUENTA: GARRAR ALGO DE UNA CUENTA to keep harping on something; HACER DE CUENTA QUE to suppose, assume
CUENTAZO several related pieces of gossip (all of which make for a long story)
CUENTO: pretext: "Ahora con el cuento de que está enfermo se porta como niño" 'Acting now under the pretext that he is sick, he's behaving like a child' CUENTO CHINO (often mpl.) lie, falsehood; CON EL CUENTO DE QUE under the pretext that: "Con el cuento de que estaba enfermo, no quiso hacer el trabajo"; ESTAR MALO EL CUENTO (said of situations which have become precarious): "Si mandaron traer (a) la ley, es que está malo el cuento" 'If they sent for the cops then things have really gotten bad'
CUERA (slang) girl friend, sweetheart; (pej.) mistress, kept woman; woman of considerable beauty
CUERAZO (slang) sexually attractive or very beautiful woman
CUERDO -DA (slang) adj. reckless, bold; (slang) f. boss, leader; ¡CUERDA! interj. What!, Bam!, Pow!; CUERDA DE LEÑA cord of wood
CUERERÍA leather goods shop
CUERÍN m. scab (over a wound on the skin); trap for small animals (e.g., mouse trap)
CUERITO scab (over a wound on the skin)
CUERIZA spanking
CUERNO -NA mean; wicked; PONER CUERNOS to deceive one's spouse through adultery
CUERNADO -DA buck-toothed; lean-faced
CUERO -RA (slang) handsome (m.), pretty (f.); m. fiancé, sweetheart; man living in free union with a woman, common-law husband; m. gang, circle of friends; ARRIESGAR EL CUERO to risk one's life, rise one's hide (slang); CUERO DE RANA dollar bill, greenback (slang)
CUERPAZO sexy female body
CUERPO (slang) woman with a sexy body; ANDAR EL CUERPO / CORRER EL CUERPO to defecate; CUERPO DE COCA-COLA shapely (ref. to a woman's body) CUERPO DE ESTUDIANTES (Ang.) student body, totality of students (Std. estudiantado); HACER EL CUERPO to defecate; HACÉRSELE EL CUERPO CHINITO A ALGUIEN to get goose-pimples; TENER EL ALMA EN EL CUERPO to be sensitive about things, wear one's heart on one's sleeve (coll.)
CUERVO (pej.) U.S. black person
CUESTIÓN (Ang.) f. question (i.e., one that asks for information; Std. pregunta)
CUETAZO pistol shot; shot from any weapon
CUETE drunk, high as a kite (coll.); m. drunken binge; gun, pistol; CUETES mpl. curls, ringlets
CUETEAR or CUETIAR va. to shoot
CUEVA (vulg. slang) vagina
CUEVENO -NA light-colored (usually said of eyes)
CUIDADO: PONER CUIDADO to pay attention
CUIDADORA babysitter
CUIDANDERA babysitter
CUIDANIÑOS fsg. babysitter
CUIDAR: CUIDAR A LA ESPOSA for a man to "take care of" his wife by ejaculating outside of the uterus
CUIJA personal defect attracting sympathy
CUILCA cover, blanket, quilt
CUILMAS: SAN CUILMAS (hum.) San

Antonio, Texas; (hum.) (name applied to any town one wishes to burlesque)
CUILTA (Eng.) quilt, blanket
CUININICHE mf. uncooperative person
CUIRA (slang) quarter, twenty-five cent piece
CUIZA (slang) prostitute (cf. huiza)
CUITEAR or CUITIAR (Eng.) va. to quit
CULA (slang, vulg.) (var. of) culo
CULEBRA: CULEBRA DE AGUA sudden storm, cloudburst
CULEBRÍA or CULEBRILLA undulating line
CULECO -CA brooding (said of hens); adj. m. recently become a father (said of a man whose first child has just been born)
CULEQUILLAS: EN CULEQUILLAS (var. of) en cuclillas
CÚLER (Eng.) m. water cooler, drinking fountain
CULERO -RA cowardly, fearful; eccentric; m. (slang & vulg.) homosexual; mf. (slang & vulg.) son-of-a-bitch
CULO fear, fright; CULO AGUADO large, flabby ass (vulg.; ref. is usually to the feminine posterior); FRUNCÍRSELE A ALGUIEN EL CULO to be afraid, become frightened
CULÓN -LONA (slang & vulg.) son-of-a-bitch
CULOTE m. female buttocks (ref. may be pej. or flattering, depending on the context)
CUMPRIAÑOS (var. of) cumpleaños
CUÑADO (term used to address a stranger)
CUOTIZAR va. & vr. to set the price on an article
CUQUEAR or CUQUIAR (Eng.) va. to cook
CUQUI (Eng.) f. cookie
CURA (slang) f. fix (of a narcotic drug); medicinal preparation for someone with a hangover
CURANDERO -RA witch doctor cum herbalist
CURAR va. to remove a hex or spell; to provide an addict with a fix (slang); CURAR DE SUSTO to cure, by sorcery, the after-affects of a traumatic experience; CURARLE A ALGUIEN LOS CALLOS to stop annoying someone; CURARSE (DE) LA CRUDA to "cure" a hangover by drinking more alcohol; to cure a hangover by drinking menudo (q.v.)
CURIOSITO -TA m. & f. cartoon film or humorous short feature shown before the main feature in movie theaters; comic relief, in a play or movie
CURIOSO -SA funny, humorous; fpl. comic strips in a newspaper; comic relief in a play or movie
CURITA (Eng., through metonymy Curity) band-aid, bandage
CURSI embittered, sour
CURSIENTO -TA diarrhetic, suffering from diarrhea
CURSIO (var. of) curso
CURSO (normally msg.) loose bowels, diarrhea
CURVAR (Ang.) va. to curve, grade on a curve (manner of assigning grades on examinations)
CURVIA insinuation, innuendo
CUSQUEAR or CUSQUIAR va. to pick up with a utensil; to eat
CUTE (Eng.) m. coat

CH

CHABACÁN (var. of) chabacano 'apricot'
CHABELA (dim. of) Isabel(a)
CHACOTEAR or CHACOTIAR vn. to engage in lewd behavior
CHACUACO (slang) cigarette; cigar butt
CHACHALACA talkative
CHACHALAQUERO -RA talkative
CHACHO -CHA (vars. of) muchacho -cha
CHAFO -FA worthless, substandard; tired, fatigued
CHAGO (dim. of) Santiago
CHÁGÜER or CHAHUER (Eng.) m. shower (bath and apparatus); party (at which gifts are given in honor of a new-born baby or a woman engaged to be married
CHAHUA or CHÁHUER (Eng.) m. shower, party to bestow gifts
CHAIN (Eng.) m. shine, polish; shoeshine; DAR CHAIN to shine or polish (esp. shoes)
CHAINADA (Eng.) shine, polish, (esp. of shoes)
CHAINAR or CHAINEAR or CHAINIAR (Eng.) va. to shine or polish

(esp. shoes)
CHAINERO (Eng.) shoe-shine boy
CHAIRA (slang) watch chain; sweetheart; fiancée
CHALÁN m. shoe
CHALAR (used only as interj.:) ¡CHÁLESE! or ¡CHALE! Shut up!, Cool it!, Knock it off!, etc.
CHALE (dim. of) Carlos
CHALE (vulg.) m. penis
CHALECO: DE CHALECO as a freeloader, without paying; free, gratis
CHALICE (Eng.) m. & f. chalice
CHALITO (dim. of) Carlos
CHALITO (vulg.) penis
CHALUPA shoe
CHALLO -LLA (dim. of) Rosario (m. & f.)
CHAMACO -CA m. boy; f. girl
CHAMARRA sweater
CHAMBA (coll.) job
CHAMBEAR or CHAMBIAR vn. to work at a job
CHAMBELÁN or CHAMBERLÁN or CHAMBELÁIN m. escort
CHAMBONEAR or CHAMBONIAR vn. to do a job awkwardly
CHAMORRO calf (of the leg)
CHAMPIÓN -PIONA (Eng.) champion
CHAMPIONATO (Eng.) championship
CHAMPÚ (see DARSE CHAMPÚ)
CHAMPUCERO -RA (vars. of) chapucero -ra
CHAMPURRADO gruel made of sugar, chocolate and corn meal
CHAMUCO devil
CHAMUSCADO -DA scorched, burnt
CHANATE adj. black; m. coffee; (pej.) U.S. black person
CHANCAQUÍA or CHANCAQUILLA thistle, burr
CHANCLA slipper (bedroom slipper); ARRIMAR LA CHANCLA to dance; to spank; CAERLE A ALGUIEN LA CHANCLA to receive a reprimand (esp. said of husbands whose wives put a stop to their flirtations or other misbehavings); TIRAR CHANCLA to dance
CHANCLAR or CHANCLEAR or CHANCLIAR va. to spank; vn. to dance; to walk
CHANCLAZO spanking; dance, party
CHANCLE m. dance; TIRAR CHANCLE to dance
CHANCLEO dance, party
CHANCLETEAR or CHANCLETIAR (vars. of) chanclar et al.
CHANCLÓN -CLONA good dancer
¡CHANE (SU PICO)! or ¡CHÁNESE! interjs. Shut up!, Cool it! (slang), etc.
CHANGARRETE m. business establishment
CHANGLE mf. & adj. useless, good-for-nothing (usually ref. to persons)
CHANGO -GA monkey; (slang) young person; (pej.) U.S. black person; (slang) fiancé(e); f. tomboy; f. amusing little show-offish girl; CADA CHANGO A SU COLUMPIO Y A COLUMPIARSE LUEGO / CADA CHANGO A SU MECATE Y A DARSE VUELO everyone (should) mind his/her own business; every man for himself; PONERSE CHANGO to become alert, get smart; to get all dressed up
CHANGUEAR or CHANGUIAR va. to imitate, mock, ape (coll.)
CHANO (dim. of) Feliciano, Graciano, Luciano
CHANQUILEAR or CHANQUILIAR vn. to walk, take a walk
CHANSA (common orthog. var. of) chanza
CHANSIAR (slang) va. to two-time (slang), commit adultery
CHANTAR vn. to live, dwell; vr. to get married; (coll. & vulg.) to shack up (Std. vivir amancebados)
CHANTE m. house, home
CHANZA (Eng.) f. chance, opportunity; risk; mumps; adv. perhaps; AGARRAR CHANZA to take a chance, risk; (HAY) CHANZA QUE there's a chance that, it's possible that
CHAPA door knob; door latch; (Eng.) porkchop; any chop of meat; fpl. (Ang.) false teeth, choppers (slang)
CHAPANECAS fpl. popular Mexican dance
CHAPANECO -CA short-statured
CHAPARRAL m. road runner (Geococcyx californianius)
CHAPARRO -RRA short person; ¡QUÉ SUERTE TAN CHAPARRA! What lousy luck!
CHAPEADO -DA or CHAPIADO -DA flushed (said of cheeks)
CHAPEAR or CHAPIAR vr. to blush; to apply rouge to cheeks
CHAPETA earring; diaper
CHAPETE f. (var. of) chapeta; ¡QUÉ CHAPETE! What a bod! (slang--said of an attractive woman); CHAPETE'S PLEIS (Eng.) (said of a sexually attractive woman's body): "¿Tú conoces a Mariana?--Uj, ¡Chapete's Pleis!"
CHAPETEADO -DA or CHAPETIADO -DA rosy-cheeked

CHAPETEAR or CHAPETIAR va. to rouge one's cheeks; to fornicate
CHAPETONA: ¡QUÉ CHAPETONA! What a bod! (slang--said of sexually attractive woman's body)
CHAPETUDA sexy woman
CHAPETURA (var. of) chapetuda
CHAPÍN -PINA misshapen (said of legs)
CHAPO -PA short-statured (person); (coll. & hum.) Japanese
CHAPOPOTE (var. of) chapapote
CHAPOTE m. live-oak tree (Quercus virginiana)
CHAPUCEAR or CHAPUCIAR va. to deceive, cheat
CHAPUCERO -RA cheat, deceiver
CHAPUL m. child
CHAPULÍN -LINA grasshopper
CHAPULINADA group of children (fig.); swarm of grasshoppers
CHAPUZA fraud, deception; HACER CHAPUZA A ALGUIEN to cheat someone
CHAPUZAR va. to cheat, deceive
CHAQUETEAR or CHAQUETIAR va. to betray
CHAQUETERO -RA turn-coat, betrayer
CHÁQUIRA (Eng.) (slang) jacket
CHARA (Eng.) charter
CHARAMUSCA taffy in twisted or spiral form
CHARCA: ANDAR CHARCA to be well dressed
CHARCO: AHOGARSE EN CUALQUIER CHARCO to be incapable of doing anything right, not able to fight one's way out of a paper bag (fig.); BRINCAR EL CHARCO to cross the Rio Grande/Río Bravo (Texas-Mexican border) (said with ref. to persons immigrating from Mexico to Texas)
CHARCHAR or CHARCHIAR (Eng.) va. to charge purchases on a charge account
CHARCHINA jalopy, old car; (slang) girl
CHARIFE (var. of) cherife (Eng.)
CHARLADOR -DORA liar
CHAROLA tray (of whatever sort); fpl. pots and pans
CHARPIAR (Eng.) va. to sharpen
CHARRASQUEAR or CHARRASQUIAR va. to scar with a knife
CHARREADA or CHARRIADA party or get-together of charros
CHASÍS m. SER EL PURO CHASÍS to be nothing but skin and bones (coll.), be extremely thin
CHAT (Eng.) m. shot, injection
CHATO -TA (term of endearment used between husband and wife); f. marihuana; CHATOS mpl. crab lice (usually found in the genital region); HACERSE CHATO -TA to turn a deaf ear (coll.)
CHAVAL -VALA sweetheart; m. fiancé; f. fiancée
CHAVALÓN -LONA child
CHAVETA (slang) head (Std. cabeza); fiancée; sweetheart (f.)
CHAVO -VA (slang) young person; sweetheart
CHAYO (dim. of) Eduardo; CHAYO -YA (dim. of) Rosario (m. & f.)
CHAYOTE m. tom-boy; (slang) dollar
CHECADITA (Eng.) check-up, examination
CHECAR (Eng.) va. to review; to verify; to check; to correct; to examine
CHECHE (m.), -CHA (f.) young child, little shaver (coll.)
CHEIQUEAR or CHEIQUIAR (Eng.) va. to shake, agitate
CHELA (dim. of) Graciela, Celia
CHELO (dim. of) Consuelo
CHEMA m. (dim. of) José María
CHEMBI (slang) adv. perhaps, maybe
CHENCHO -CHA (dim. of) Cresencia, Cresencio (m. & f.), Inocencio (m. & f.)
CHENDO -DA (dims. of, resp.: Rosendo, Rosenda)
CHENTE -TA (dims. of, resp.: Vicente, Vicenta)
CHEPE mf. hypocrite
CHEQUE (Eng.) m. investigation, examination (see also DAR SU CHEQUE)
CHEQUEADITA or CHEQUIADITA (Eng.) (vars. of) checadita
CHEQUEADOR -DORA or CHEQUIADOR -RA m., f. (Eng.) checker, inspector
CHEQUEAR or CHEQUIAR (Eng.) (vars. of) checar
CHEQUEO (Eng.) check, check-up; examination
CHÉRBET (Eng.) m. sherbert
CHERIFE (Eng.) m. sherrif
CHERMÉS m. silk cloth
CHI f. (vulg.) urine; HACER (LA) CHI (var. of) hacer chis
CHIAPANECO -CA (var. of) chapaneco -ca
CHICABACHO -CHA chicano (Mexican-American) who acts and thinks like an Anglo-Saxon (gabacho, q.v.)
CHICAGO (slang, vulg. & hum.) toilet, restroom, bathroom (etc.) (< chi 'urine' + cago 'I defecate')
CHICALES mpl. corn-meal stew
CHICANADA (slang) action or behavior typifying a Chicano; group of

Chicanos
CHICANEADA or CHICANIADA (slang) (vars. of) chicanada
CHICANEAR or CHICANIAR (slang) vn. to behave in a Chicano-like fashion; (coll., said of Chicanos) to do one's thing (slang), act as one feels like acting
CHICANEO action or behavior typifying a Chicano
CHICANERÍA (slang) (id. to CHICANEO)
CHICANGLO Chicano who acts like an Anglo-Saxon; Anglo-Saxon who identifies with the Chicano and the Chicano cause(s)
CHICANISMO ideology and ethnic spirit typifying the Chicano Movement(s)
CHICANO -NA Mexican-American, person of Mexican heritage born and raised in the United States or person born in Mexico of Mexican ethnic background who has become a United States citizen or permanent resident; any person of Mexican ethnic background
CHICLE m. tar; asphalt; pest, uninvited person, tag-along (colloquial)
CHICLOSO -SA pest, tag-along (coll.); m. (vulg.) anus
CHICO -CA mocking-bird (Mimun polyglottos); adj. mf. (iron.) big, large; CHICAS PATAS mfsg. Mexican: "Él es un chicas patas"; A LAS CHICAS PATAS in the Mexican fashion
CHICOLITO -TA small, tiny
CHICOTAZO whiplash, blow with a whip
CHICOTE (slang) m. penis
CHICOTEADA or CHICOTIADA whipping, lashing
CHICOTEAR or CHICOTIAR (slang): CHICOTEARLE A ALGUIEN EL APARATO / EL MANGO / CHICOTEARLE A ALGUIEN PARA HACER ALGO: to excell at doing something: "A él le chicotea para jugar a la pelota" 'He is really good at playing ball'
CHICOTUDO -DA very large; difficult; m. extremely handsome male, an Adonis (coll.); (slang) V.I.P., man of considerable importance
CHICURA ragweed herb (Ambrosia ambrocoides) (whose roots are made into a douching solution)
CHÍCHARO pea, green or sweet pea (Lathyrus odoratus); (slang) mpl. household goods (e.g., furniture, etc.)
CHICHARRO (hum.) cigar
CHICHARRONEAR or CHICHARRONIAR va. to burn to a crisp
CHICHARRÓN: BUSCARLE RUIDO AL CHICHARRÓN to look for trouble; HACER CHICHARRÓN to burn to a crisp
CHICHE or CHICHI f. breast (female) sinecure, soft job (coll.) often obtained as a political favor; DAR CHICHE to breastfeed a child; MAMAR CHICHE to sponge (coll.), live off other people, live at someone's expense
CHICHECANO -NA or CHICHICANO -NA (slang) Chicano who enjoys a sinecure (cf. CHICHE/CHICHI) (the word appears to have been born in 1968 at the Kelly Air Force Base in San Antonio, Texas)
CHICHERO (coll. & mildly vulg.) brassiere, bra
CHICHITA welt
CHICHO (dim. of) Narciso; CHICHOCHA adj., mf. crazy, daffy, screwy (slang); wonderful, great
CHICHÓN -CHONA large-breasted (usually f., ref. to women)
CHIFLADO -DA daffy, scatter-brained (coll.); stuck up (coll.), presumptuous; smitten, head over heels in love (coll.); ANDAR CHIFLADO -DA to be smitten in love
CHIFLAR va. to elate; to cause to swell with a (false) sense of pride or self-importance; to spoil, pamper; vr. to swell with a (false) sense of pride
CHIFLETA (var. of) chiflete; (var. of) chufleta; f. sarcastic remark, innuendo
CHIFLÓN -FLONA person very susceptible to the flattery of others
CHIFÓN m. chiffon
CHIFONÍA chiffonier, chest of drawers
CHIHUA or CHIHUAHUA interj. (of varying intensity of meaning, according to intonation, e.g., everything from 'Goodness gracious' through 'Hell!')
CHILE m. penis; CHILE PARADO erect penis, hard-on (slang); CHILE PELÓN (in the sexual act, penis not encased in a condom); IR HECHO CHILE to go like a bat out of hell (slang), move very quickly; chilli pepper (and the following variant types) CHILE ANCHO bell pepper; CHILE BOLITA

small round red pepper; CHILE CASCABEL dry red pepper whose seeds rattle inside the cask; CHILE DEL MONTE round red pepper measuring one centimeter in diameter; CHILE DULCE sweet pepper; CHILE EN ESCABECHE chile preserved in vinagre; CHILE JALAPEÑO large and piquant green pepper; CHILE JAPONÉS elongated piquant red pepper about four centimeters in length; CHILE PIQUÍN very piquant caper-sized green or red pepper; CHILE PISADO large red dry pepper measuring about ten centimeters in length and six in width; CHILE PITÍN (var. of) chile piquín; CHILE RELLENO large green pepper filled with meat and sauces and then baked

CHILERO -RA fond of eating chilli peppers; m. small yellow bird with gray wings (Pitangus sulfuratus)

CHILETE m. (id. to chilipiquín or CHILE PIQUÍN) (Capsicum baccatum)

CHILPASÍA dry and ripe chile artificially dried in the sun

CHILPAYATE mf. small child

CHILPITIN (var. of) chile piquín/ chile pitín

CHILUCA (slang, underw.) head (human)

CHILUDO m. (vulg.) man with a big penis

CHILLA: ESTAR EN LA CHILLA to be hardpressed financially (usually for just a short time)

CHILLADOR -DORA: TROMPO CHILLADOR wind-up top which makes a whining noise when spinning; (VÍBORA) CHILLADORA rattlesnake

CHILLANTE loud (said of colors)

CHILLAR vn. to cry; vr. to become very angry

CHILLÓN -LLONA cry-baby

CHIMENEA: TENER LA CHIMENEA MUY CERCA to be very hot-tempered

CHIMINEA (var. of) chimenea

CHIMOLEAR or CHIMOLIAR (vars. of) chismorrear or chismorriar

CHIMOLERO -RA (var. of) chismolero -ra

CHIMPA hair

CHIMUELO -LA lacking teeth, with some teeth missing

CHINANERO any stick used to remove a hot lid from a kettle

CHINAR va. to comb; vr. CHINÁRSELE EL CUERPO A ALGUIEN to get goosebumps (goosepimples)

CHINCORRAZO blow on the head

CHINCUALES mpl. type of small skin eruption; (fig.) nervousness: "Parece que traes chincuales" !You'd think you had ants in your pants' (coll.) (said of persons, usually children, who are restless and who continually squirm around)

CHINCUÍS m. ocular sty

CHINCHE adj. miserly; m. & f. CHINCHE PEDORRA / CHINCHE PERRODA stink-bug (Pentatomida); HACERSE CHINCHE to act stingy, miserly; to overstay one's welcome; TENER LA SANGRE DE CHINCHE to be repugnant to, repellent to (said of persons)

CHINCHERÍA squalor, filth; place infested with chinch bugs (bed bugs)

CHINCHERO messy room; messy house; any room, mattress, etc., infested with bed-bugs; (hum.) small business establishment; jail

¡CHÍNELAS! interj. (slightly euph.) 'Son of a . . . !'

CHINGADA (lit., woman on whom the act of coition has been performed) (vulg.); ESTAR COMO LA CHINGADA to be as ugly/mean/ timid/insensitive (etc.) as one can possibly be; ¡HIJO DE LA CHINGADA MADRE! interj. (strongest and most vulg. interj. possible) 'XXXXXXX XXXX!'; ¡HIJO DE TU CHINGADA MADRE! (very vulg.); MANDAR A LA CHINGADA to tell someone to go to hell; ¡¿QUÉ CHINGADOS QUIERES?! (very strong and vulg.) What the hell ya want?; ¡ME LLEVA LA CHINGADA! (strong and vulg.) I'll be God-damned! ¡VÁMONOS A LA CHINGADA! Let's get the hell out of here!

CHINGADAZO (var. of) chingazo

CHINGADERA nuisance, annoyance; damn(ed) thing

CHINGAL: UN CHINGAL a great deal, to a high degree (cf. UN CHINGATAL)

CHINGAR (vulg.) va. to copulate (etc.); to cheat; to avenge; to defeat (in a contest); to get what one is after: "Ya chingó" 'He got what he wanted'; vr. (slang & vulg.) to get married; interjs.: ¡CHINGA CAGADA! (very strong and vulg.) 'XXXXXX XXXX!'; CHINGAR LA

PACIENCIA to bother; PARA ACABARLA DE CHINGAR to make matters worse
CHINGATAL: UN CHINGATAL a great deal, to a high degree (cf. UN CHINGAL)
CHINGAZO blow with the hand or with a heavy object; CHINGAZOS mpl. a fist fight; AGARRARSE A CHINGAZOS to get into a fist fight
CHINGÓN -GONA: large; tall (ref. to persons); EL MERO CHINGÓN (hum.) the big boss, the big cheese (slang)
CHINGONÓN -NONA (var. of) chingonote
CHINGOS mpl. (used adjectivally) several, many; (used adverbially) a great deal, to a considerable extent
CHINGUIZA (see DAR UNA CHINGUIZA)
CHINITA: ¡CHINITA POR TU AMOR! interj. (slightly euph.) Son of a ... !; ¡CHÍNITAS! interj. (slightly euph.)
CHINITO: HACÉRSELE A ALGUIEN EL CUERPO CHINITO to get goosebumps (goose-pimples); TRAER LOS OJOS CHINITOS to have sleepy(-looking) eyes
CHINO -NA m. curl (of hair); comb (in general); comb for removing body lice or hair lice; mf. darling (term of endearment); CHINA POBLANA Mexican regional costume (worn by women); PAPEL DE CHINA tissue paper
CHIPIAR vn. to drizzle, rain very lightly
CHIPIL or CHÍPILI mf. spoiled or overindulged child (cf. CHIPLE)
CHIPÓN -PONA spoiled child
CHIQUEADOR -DORA or CHIQUIADOR -DORA mf. pamperer (person who pampers); adj. fond of pampering
CHIQUEAR or CHIQUIAR va. & vr. to spoil, pamper; vr. to play hard to get, be evasive (esp. in amorous games)
CHIQUEO act or effect of pampering
CHEQUEÓN -QUEONA or CHIQUIÓN -QUIONA spoiled child; person who enjoys being pampered
CHIQUERO dirty and messy place, pigpen (fig.)
CHÍQUETE m. chewing gum; asphalt; tar
CHIQUININGO -GA or CHIQUIRRINGO -GA or CHIQUITINGO -GA small child
CHIQUITO -TA son/daughter who bears the first name of the parent of the same sex (esp. used after parent's first name with ref. to the child, e.g., "Eva chiquita"; also used when ref. to a child who imitates the parent, even though the two are not identically named); m. (slang) buttocks; (vulg.) anus
CHIRA (Eng.) mf. cheater, deceiver
CHIRIAR (Eng.) va. & vn. to cheat, defraud
CHIRINOLA gossiper; group of gossips; fuss, bother
CHIRIÓN -RIONA cheater, deceiver
CHIRIPADA (var. of) chiripá
CHIRRIONA (var. of) chirona
CHISCA or CHISCURA bicycle
CHISMARAJO gossiping, gossip
CHISMOLEAR or CHISMOLIAR (vars. of) chismorrear
CHISMOLERO -RA gossiper
CHISPA f. (ref. to both men and women) astute, sly, sharp; ¡CHISPAS! (mild interj.) Holy cow!, Golly!
CHISPUDO -DA curly (said of hair); daffy, crazy, screwy (coll.)
CHISQUEADO -DA or CHISQUIADO -DA (slang) adv. very rapidly, like crazy (coll.)
CHISQUEAR or CHISQUIAR va. to drive crazy, madden; vr. to become crazy
CHISTAR or CHISTEAR or CHISTIAR vn. to complain (esp. with interj. ¡chst! as to request silence in a theater), to shush
CHISTE m. NO TENER CHISTE to be worthless, of no importance; to be dull (said of persons); to to be easy to accomplish: "Eso no tiene chiste" 'There's nothing to doing that'
CHITO -TA (muchachito -ta) m. (dim.) little boy; f. (dim.) little girl
CHITO -TA (dims. of) Jesús, Jesusa; Felícito, Felícita
CHIVAS fpl. trinkets, objects of little value; (slang) interj. Give me whatever you have! (used for example by a thief to a victim: 'Hand it over!)
CHIVATO -TA mischievous youngster, "kid" (coll.)
¡CHIVE! (slang) interj. Don't be frightened!
CHIVEAR or CHIVIAR vr. to back down, back out, retract (a statement), be afraid or bashful
CHIVERO -RA skittish person, scaredy-cat (coll.); (pej.) Anglo-Saxon; m. goatherd; f. young girl
CHIVETAL m. fold for goats (young goats)

CHIVETE m. fear
CHIVETERO -RA frightened; m. fold for kids (young goats)
CHIVINOLERA gossipy person
CHIVO -VA (slang) adj. afraid, shy; handsome, beautiful; mf. (slang) coward; f. ten dollar bill; heroin; thingamagig (used as a substitute for a forgotten designation); coin; nanny goat; AGARRAR EL CHIVO (Ang.) to get someone's goat (fig.): "Juan le agarró el chivo a Pepe, por eso se peliaron" 'Juan got Pepe's goat, and that's why they got into a fight'; HACERLE A ALGUIEN LOS TAMALES DE CHIVO (fig.) to deceive a spouse, commit adultery
CHIVOTE (slang) m. handsome man
CHO (Eng.) show, spectacle, exhibition; movie theater
CHOC (Eng.) m. shock; choke (automotive); chalk (writing instrument)
CHOCADO -DA at odds with one another (said of two or more persons); ESTAR CHOCADOS not to be on speaking terms
CHOCANTE repugnant; presumptuous
CHOCANTERIA repugnant act
CHOCANTÓN -TONA repulsive, repugnant (usually ref. to persons)
CHOCAR va. to shock, repel, be repulsive to: "Ese tipo me choca mucho"; vr. to become enemies; to cease to be on speaking terms: "¿Por qué no invitastes a María y a Juana?--Porque ayer se chocaron"; CHOCAR LAS MANOS to shake hands
CHOCLE (Eng.) m. chalk (writing instrument)
CHOCHE m. small boy; (Eng.) George; (Hispanization of) George West, Texas (city in south Texas) (cf. YOCHE)
CHOCHO -CHA chubby; slow-moving; f. small girl
CHOCHÓN -CHONA (term of endearment)
CHOFERO -RA chauffeur, driver of a car
CHOFLEAR or CHOFLIAR (Eng.) vn. to shuffle
CHOLA or CHOLE (dim. of) Soledad f.
¡CHOLE! or ¡CHÓLESE! (slang) Shut up!, Knock it off!, Cool it!, etc.
CHOLENCO -CA weak, worn, weary; (said of persons who appear to be coming down with an illness); sickly, prone to infirmities
CHOLENQUE m.,f. (var. of) cholenco -ca
CHOMPA or CHOMPE or CHOMPETA (slang) f. head (human)
CHON or CHONA (dims. of) Asunción, Encarnación (m. & f.) (dims. of) Concepción (f. only)
CHONES mpl. (calzones) long underwear
CHONGO knot of hair tied up in the back of the head; AGARRARSE DE LOS CHONGOS to fight by pulling one another's hair
CHONGUEADA or CHONGUIADA fight wherein one woman pulls another's hair
CHONTE m. mocking bird (Mimus polyglottos)
CHOPA (f.) or CHOPE (m.) (Eng.) shop, store
CHOPETEAR or CHOPETIAR (slang) vn. to have sexual intercourse
CHOQUEAR or CHOQUIAR (Eng.) va. to choke, manipulate the choke (on a car); vr. (var. of chocar 'to shake hands')
CHOPO (hum.) nose
CHOPUCERO -RA (var. of) chapucero -ra
CHORA sweetheart, fiancée; cigarette butt
CHORALO -LA small child
CHORCHA (Eng.) (little used) church; (more frequently) group of people; HACERSE LA CHORCHA for a group to form, congregate
CHORE (Eng.) m. short-statured
CHORICERO -RA sausage vendor; member of the family of a sausage vendor
CHORIZO type of Mexican sausage; (vulg.) penis, etc.
CHORREADO -DA or CHORRIADO -DA dirty, soiled
CHORREAR or CHORRIAR va. to soil with a liquid, make dirty; vr. to spill a liquid on oneself; to drip: "La pompa está chorriando"
CHORRERA or CHORRERÍA diarrhea; (id. to chorrero)
CHORRERO long string of (things or person): "Traiba un chorrero de huercos" 'He had with him a long string of brats' (see also CHORRERÍA)
CHORRO diarrhea; multitude (of people);(euph.) gonorrhea; LLOVER A CHORROS to rain cats and dogs (fig.), rain heavily
CHORROS (Eng. sure) (slang) (affirmative response to a question) "¿Vas al pueblo?-- Chorros"
CHOT (Eng.) (var. of chat, also Eng.)
CHOTA (slang) policeman; police

force
CHOTEADO -DA or CHOTIADO -DA (slang, vulg.) promiscuous, loose-living (usually ref. to women), with a lot of mileage on (slang)
CHOTEAR or CHOTIAR va. to use to excess; to abuse; to ridicule; to defame, ruin; to make a fool of someone; to caress heavily, pet (slang)
CHOTEO act and effect of using to excess, abusing, ridiculing, defaming, etc. (see CHOTEAR, supra)
CHOU (Eng.) (var. of cho, also Eng.)
CHUCO , EL (slang) El Paso, Texas
CHUCO -CA (slang) (var. of) pachuco-ca
CHUCHALUCAR va. to take advantage of a woman sexually
CHUCHO -CHA (dims. of) Jesús, María de Jesús
CHUCHO -CHA sly, astute, foxy (coll.) m. dog
CHUCHULUCO little toy
CHUECO -CA twisted, not straight, tilted; bowlegged; crooked, dishonest
CHUGA (pej.) U.S. black person
CHÚINGOM (Eng.) m. chewing gum
CHULADA cute remark or gesture (can be used ironically, e.g., "¡Qué chulada!" 'Well isn't that just something!')
CHULEAR or CHULIAR va. to caress; to speak affectionately to; to flatter (usually 'to flatter a woman'); to primp; vr. to pimp
CHULO -LA pretty (often said to children)
CHUPACHARCOS (slang) mpl. tennis shoes; homosexual
CHUPADA pull, inhalation (on a cigar or cigarette)
CHUPADERA act of smoking; chain smoking, continual smoking of cigarettes
CHUPADOR -DORA smoker; heavy smoker
CHUPAMIEL m. unscrupulous politician
CHUPÓN -PONA (slang., vulg.) homosexual
CHUPONCITO puff on a cigar or cigarette
CHUPARROSA humming bird (Trochilidae)
CHUSAR or CHUSEAR or CHUSIAR (Eng.) va. to choose, select
CHUSEADOR -DORA or CHUSIADOR -DORA (Eng.) person who does the choosing
CHUTAR or CHUTEAR or CHUTIAR (Eng.) va. to shoot
CHUTEADO -DA or CHUTIADO -DA embarrassed
CHUTEO (Eng.) act of shooting; shoot-out (with guns, between two or more people); (var. of) choteo
CHUY (dim. of) Jesús

D

DA-CORAJE (see CORAJE)
DAGAZO stab with a dagger
DAILEAR or DAILIAR or DALEAR or DALIAR (Eng.) va. to dial (a telephone)
DAIME (Eng.) m. dime, ten cent piece
DALLAS (see IR A DALLAS)
DAMA: DAMA DE HONOR bridesmaid
DAMIANA damiana (Turnera diffusa) (herb prepared as a solution and either drunk or else used as a douch for treatment of FRÍO DE LA MATRIZ, q.v. infra)
DAR va. to show, project (a film); A MÍ NO ME LA DAS You can't fool me!; DAR A BAJAR to ill-treat, mistreat; DAR AIRE to fire, discharge; to dismiss one's boy-(girl) friend; give him/her the air (slang); to give cause to suspect: "No le des aire de lo que ha pasado aquí; DAR ALAS to give someone free rein; to side with someone (in a dispute, etc.) DAR A OLER to give cause to suspect: "No le den a oler que su amigo se murío ayer" 'Don't give him cause to suspect that his friend died yesterday'; A COMO DÉ LUGAR one way or another, any way it can be done: "¿Cómo piensan hacerlo?-- A como dé lugar."; DAR APRETONES (folk medicine:) sharp squeezes administered, from behind, to a sick person, typically one with a cold and aching bones and muscles; the sick person grabs himself by the hands behind the neck so that the elbows jut out from the body at a 90° angle; the treatment is said to cure the cold and relieve the muscular ache; DAR ATOLE CON EL DEDO to deceive one's spouse with another person, have

adulterous sexual relations; DAR BÁSCULA to frisk for concealed weapons, stolen goods, etc.; DAR BEBITO (coll.) to impregnate, make pregnant; DAR BOLA to cause unnecessary problems; DAR CALABAZAS to give someone the air (slang), reject (as a suitor); to make a fool out of someone; DAR CAPOTE to blank (sports slang), hold an opponent to zero points in a game; DAR CAPOTEADA/DAR CAPOTIADA to blank (sports slang), achieve a very high score while holding the opponent to zero points; DAR CAPOTIZA (id. to DAR CAPOTEADA); DAR CARRILLA to bother, molest; DAR CATOS (coll.) to beat someone up, usually with one's fists; DAR COLOR to show something off (usually a new possession); DAR CHAMPÚ to shampoo someone's hair; DAR DE ALTA to discharge (i.e., from a hospital); to discharge from the armed forces (usually ref. to an honorable dischange); DAR DE PECHO to breast feed; DAR DE SÍ to yield, be reasonable, be willing to compromise (the expression is used more frequently in the negative: NO DAR DE SÍ to be adamant, uncompromising, hard to convince, etc.); to stretch (said of clothing); DAR EL GOLPE AL CIGARRO to inhale deeply on a cigarette; DAR EN CARA to be fed up with (coll.), satiated with: "Ya me dio en cara esa sopa"; DAR EN EL (MERO) MATE to hit where it hurts; to hit right on the button; DAR EN EL MOCO to punch on the nose; to adminster a beating (usually in a fist fight); DAR EN LA MADRE (id. to DAR EN EL MOCO); DAR EN LA MERA MADRE to administer a severe beating; DAR EN LA TORRE to administer a beating (usually in a fist fight); DAR EN TODA LA MADRE to give someone a severe beating (usually in a fist fight) DAR FAMA to praise, eulogize; DAR GUERRA to annoy, irritate, bother; DAR LA CONTRA to contradict, oppose, disagree with; DAR (LA) LATA to bother, pester: "Llévate ese niño pa' fuera, está dando mucha lata"; DAR LA PATADA to dismiss, fire (from a job); to sever ties, break with, terminate (e.g. an amorous relationship); to stink, emit a foul odor; DARLAS to have sexual intercourse promiscuously, be up for (grabs) (slang) (usually said of women), put out (slang) (cf. IR A DALLAS); DAR LAS DOCE to be in a tight spot: "Ya me daban las doce" 'I was sure in a tight spot'; to be worried stiff: "Ya me daban las doce con el niño porque tenía una calentura de 105°"; DAR LAS NALGAS (hum.) to lose in a game or sports contest; to have sexual intercourse promiscuously, be up for grabs (slang) (usually said of women); DAR LÁSTIMA CON to feel sorry for: "Me dio lástima con Juan" 'I felt sorry for Juan'; DAR LA SUAVE to humor; DAR LA VUELTA to look in on (someone): "Dame la vuelta mientras me baño, no vaya a ser que me desmaye" 'Look in on me while I'm taking a bath, just to make sure I haven't fainted'; DARLE AL GAS (Ang.?) to step on the gas (fig.), hurry (also vn.: to hurry, speed up, get a move on [slang]; DARLE DE REVERSA to back up, reverse (a vehicle); DARLE GAS to speed up (esp. a motor vehicle); DAR LIJA to put the finishing touches on a job; DAR LUZ to give the go-ahead, approve a request; to give a light (to someone lighting a cigarette, etc.); (var. of dar a luz 'to give birth to'); DAR MADERA to flatter, apple-polish (coll.), give a snow job (slang); DAR PA' DENTRO (vulg.) to copulate (vulg.): "Le dio pa' dentro"; DAR PATADAS DE AHOGADO/DIOGADO to be in a tight spot, a precarious situation; to fight a losing battle: "Ese pobre señor está dando patadas de ahogado"; DAR PA' FUERA to fire, dismiss (from a job); DAR PA' TRAS (Ang.) to return, give back; to back up, reverse: "Le dio pa' tras al coche" 'He backed up his car'; DAR PENA to embarrass: "Me da mucha pena" 'It embarrasses me'; DAR POR to take a notion to: "Le dio por irse temprano" 'He got it into his head to go early'; DAR POR SU LADO to humor: "Dale por su lado para que te dé lo que quieres"; DAR PUERTA to show the body's "private parts" (genitalia, etc.) or to show one's undergarments unintentionally; DAR QUEBRADA (Ang.) to give a break, allow to have a chance; DAR REATAZOS/RIATAZOS to administer a beating (usually with fists); DAR SU CHEQUE to fire (coll.), dismiss, discharge from a job; DAR SU LONCHE to put someone in his/her place, tell someone where to get off (slang): "Mamá te está esperando para darte tu lonche" 'Ma is waiting to give you what you've got coming to you', DAR UN AGARRÓN to scold; to browbeat; (vulg.) to copulate (with); DAR UN APLASTÓN to humiliate, cut down (coll.); DAR UN REATAZO/RIATAZO to strike a blow with one's fist; DAR UNA CHINGUIZA to administer a beating (usually with fists); DAR UNA ATASCADA (vulg.) to copulate; DAR UNA FREGUIZA to beat up (coll.), administer a beating (usually with fists); DAR UNA MANITA to lend a helping hand; DAR UNA MANO (id. to DAR UNA MANITA); DAR UNA METIDA (vulg.) to copulate, (coll.) slip it in (vulg. slang); DAR UNA PALIZA to beat (coll.), soundly triumph over (in a sport's competition); DAR UNA REATIZA/RIATIZA to give a severe beating (usually with fists) (cf. DAR REATAZOS, DAR UN REATAZO); DAR UNA TAMBORIZA to administer a severe beating, beat to a pulp (coll.); DAR UNA TIRADA (vulg.) to copulate (vulg.); vn. to go off in a specific direction (usually used as a command): "Dale pa' la casa" 'Get on home': DAR ABASTO to suffice, be enough (usually employed in the negative): "Estas tortillas no dan abasto" 'These tortillas aren't going to be enough to feed the number of people expected'; to be coped with: "Estos niños no dan abasto; se ensucian la ropa cuatro veces por día"; DAR CON BOLA to realize one's goals; DAR LA VUELTA to pass by, drop by (a place), drop over (for a visit): "Mañana no dejes de dar la vuelta" 'Don't forget to come by tomorrow'; DAR UNA VUELTA to make a complete turn; to go for a stroll or a ride; DAR UN RAUND (Eng.) to last out a round (said of boxers in a boxing match); vr. to give up, yield, produce: "Este año se van a dar muchas nueces"; to submit to sexual advances; DARSE A BAJAR to act in such a manner as to bring on ill treatment or abuse: "Te tratan así porque das a bajar" 'They treat you like that because you bring it on yourself'; DARSE BAÑOS DE PUREZA to boast of one's decorum and behavior; to justify one's words and deeds; DARSE CABRONAZOS to beat up on one another (usually in a fist fight); DARSE CANCOS to have a fist fight; DARSE CATOS to have a fist fight; DARSE CHAMPÚ to shampoo one's own hair; DARSE CHINGAZOS to beat up one another (usually in a fist fight); DARSE DE SANTOS to thank one's lucky stars (coll.), be thankful for favors received; DARSE EN to bump: "El niño se dio en la cabeza con la mesa" 'The child bumped his head on the table'; DARSE FREGADAZOS/DARSE FREGAZOS to beat up on one another (usually in a fist fight); DARSE GUSTO to have fun, have a good time; DÁRSELA A ALGUIEN to fool, deceive (used only in the negative): "Tú no me la das" 'You can't fool me'; DARSE LIJA to exalt oneself, praise oneself; DARSE MADERA (id. to DARSE LIJA); DARSE PAQUETE to give oneself importance, boast of one's abilities; DARSE TOPES to bump heads; to try to outdo each other (said of two or more persons); DARSE TROMPA to become aware of something; DARSE TROMPAZOS to beat up one another; DARSE UNA AGARRADA/DARSE UN AGARRÓN to get into an argument; to get into a fist fight; DARSE UNA CHINGUIZA to beat up one another severely (usually in a fist fight); DARSE UNA REATIZA/RIATIZA to give one another a severe beating; DARSE UN AGARRÓN (vulg.) to engage in copulation; DARSE UN CALENTÓN to become sexually excited; to anger one another; DARSE UN FREGADAZO/DARSE UN

FREGAZO to hit oneself on an object
DANDO Y DANDO (said as a request for simultaneous exchange of objects, roughly equivalent to Eng. 'Share and share alike')

DE: DE ABURI many; DE AGUA incomplete; weak, soft (said of persons); effeminate, faggy (slang); DE A MADRE totally, completely; a great deal, a considerable amount; super, magnificent, swell; DE AQUELLA very nice, super, neat, swell (etc.) (all coll.); DE AQUELLA MELAZA terrific, super, swell (etc.); DE A TIRO totally, completely; DE A VOLADA fast, rapidly, quickly; DE CINCHO assuredly, certainly (cf. CINCHO); DE CORA enthusiastically; ¿DE CUÁNDO ACÁ? Since when? (used to indicate disbelief and incredulity): "Ahora ya no le tengo rencor a nadie porque he cambiado.--¿De cuańdo acá?"; DE CHALECO free, gratis; DE DEVERAS in truth, in earnest, seriously; DE DIARIO daily, every day; DE HILO in a straight line, directly; very fast; DE HOQUIS in vain; with no strings attached (coll.), with no hidden complications; DE JILO (var. of) de hilo; DE MALAS: at least: "De malas ya mero pagamos por la casa" 'At least we've almost paid for the house'; DE OQUIS (orthog. var. of) de hoquis; DE PASADA on the way to; DE PASO on the way to; DE PATITAS feet first (i.e., to go out feet first, be thrown out of a place feet first in a prone position); DE POR SÍ QUE as things now stand; as it is: "No hables de él; de por sí que no quiere venir a la fiesta"; DE PRIMERO at first, in the beginning; DE PUERTA nice, swell, good, excellent (etc.); DE RANCHO from the sticks, countrified, hickish, farm-fresh (fig.): "Mi primo es bien de rancho" 'My cousin is straight from the farm' (fig.); DE SEGUNDO second-hand; DE SEGURO for sure, a certainty, a sure thing; DE TODO VUELO beautiful, enticing, shapely, sexy, (etc.) (said of women); DE UN SOPETÓN in one gulp; DE VOLADA (see DE A VOLADA); DE VUELTA again; after returning; DEL (contraction): DEL OTRO LADO (coll.) from Mexico; DEL TIRO totally, completely

DEÁN (Ang.) m. dean (of a college)
DEBELIDAD (var. of) debilidad
DEBELITAR (var. of) debilitar
DECEDIR (var. of) decidir
DECIDO (rus.) (var. of) dicho (ppart. of decir)
DECINUEVE (var. of) diecinueve
DECIOCHO (var. of) dieciocho
DECIR: A (inf) SE HA DICHO Let's (inf.) : "A comer se ha dicho" 'Let's eat'; DECIR BIEN to predict accurately: "Te dije que iba a venir.--Dijiste bien"; DECIR MAL to err in what one has said, misspeak oneself: "Ya se fue ... No no, digo mal, todavía está aquí" 'He went off already ... No, I'm wrong, he's still here'; DECIR PA' TRAS (Ang.) to talk back to, respond aggresively: "No te dejes; dile pa' tras" 'Don't just stand there and take it, talk back to him'; DECIR UN ANUNCIO to announce; NO DECIR NI MI ALMA to say nary a word, keep absolute silence (esp. after a scolding); ¿NO TE DIGO? (also ¿NO LE(S) DIGO?) interj. Well I'll be!, Son of a pup! (etc.); QUE SE DIGA so to speak, to speak of: "Él no tiene muy buena voz, que se diga"; USTED DIRÁ It's up to you; you tell me
DECISÉIS (var. of) dieciséis
DECISIETE (var. of) diecisiete
DECORA (Hispanization of) (North and South) Dakota
DEDAL (coll.) m. finger
DEDO: APUNTAR EL DEDO to tell on someone, tattle on someone; DEDO CHIQUITO little finger (fifth finger on the hand); DEDO DE LOS ANILLOS ring finger (fourth finger); METER DEDO (slang, vulg.) to simulate copulation, insert the finger into a woman's vagina to simulate coition; PONER EL DEDO (id. to APUNTAR EL DEDO)
DEFENSA: DEFENSA DEL CARRO bumper (automobile)
DEFENSIA (var. of) defensa
DEFÍCIL (var. of) difícil
DEFOULT (Eng.) m. default (in a sports competition)
DEFUNTO (var. of) difunto
DEGUAL (var. of) desigual
DEIT (Eng.) m. date, social appointment
DEJADO -DA negligent in dress and

personal hygiene, slovenly; lazy; meek

DEJAR: DEJAR A LA DESIDIA to procrastinate; DEJAR LA PUERTA ABIERTA to leave good feelings behind; DEJAR PLANTADO -DA to fail to keep a date or an appointment; DEJARSE (CAER) to yield to the seductive advances of the opposite sex; DEJAR SABER to inform, advise; NO DEJARSE to take nothing from nobody (slang), refuse to accept insult, abuse, etc.; to fight back, return insult for insult; (NOMÁS) POR NO DEJAR (just) to while the time away (to do something just to be doing something); DEJAR POR LA PAZ to quit, let something rest, leave something be, leave well enough alone; vr. (slang, vulg.) to put out, give freely of one's sexual favors: "¿Te dejas?" 'Do you 'do' it?' 'Do you put out?'

DEJÓN -NA person who lets others bully or manipulate him/her

DELANTAR (var. of) delantal m.

DELGADO -DA thin (ref. to persons only; flaco -ca is applied by many to both animals and persons, though some insist that flaco designates animal thinness only)

DELINCUENTE: DELINCUENTE JUVENIL mf. (Ang.) juvenile delinquent

DEMO(N)STRACIÓN (Ang.) f. demonstration (ref. to political demonstration) (Std. manifestación)

DEMO(N)STRAR (Ang.) vn. to demonstrate (for a political cause, etc.)

DEN (Eng.) m. secluded room for studying or relaxing, den

DENDE (var. of) desde

DENGUE m. gesture (body or facial)

DENTRAR (var. of) entrar

DENUNCIANTE m. cruel and ruthless policeman

DEO (var. of) dedo

DEODORANTE (Eng.) m. (var. of) desodorante

DEPACHAR (var. of) despachar

DEPENDER: DEPENDER EN (Ang.) (var. of) depender de

DEPONER, va. to vomit

DEPRESIÓN (Ang.) f. economic depression

DEPUÉS (var. of) después

DEPUTADO -DA (var. of) diputado -da

DERECHAZO hard blow with the right fist (usually in a boxing match)

DERECHERO -RA straight shooter, person whose aim is consistently accurate

DERECHITO adv. straight ahead (said in giving route directions)

DERECHO: DECIR POR DERECHO to speak frankly, get to the point (coll.)

DERRAME: DERRAME DEL CEREBRO stroke, cerebral hemorrhage

DERRITIR (var. of) derretir

DESABROCHADOR m. clasp, fastener, clip

DESACOMEDIDO -DA non-accommodating, disobliging

DESAFANAR vn. to get out of jail

DESAFISFECHO -CHA (Eng.) (var. of) desatisfecho -cha (Eng.)

DESAHIJAR va. to prune (plants)

DESAHIJE m. act or affect of pruning (plants)

DESAIGRAR (var. of) desairar

DESANIVELADO -DA (var. of) desnivelado -da

DESANIVELAR (var. of) desnivelar

DESAPARECIDO -DA (euph.) deceased, dead

DESAPARTAR (var. of) apartar

DESARMADOR m. screwdriver

DESATINAR: HACER DESATINAR A ALGUIEN to make someone lose his cool (slang), cause someone to become very angry and quite disoriented

DESATISFECHO -CHA mean, base, dispicable (ref. to persons)

DESAYUNO light breakfast taken during the early part of the morning

DESBALAGADO -DA dispersed, spread out; lost

DESBARATAR va. to change a larger monetary unit unto smaller ones

DESBORRADOR m. eraser

DESBORRAR va. to erase; to expunge

DESCADECIMIENTO (var. of) descaecimiento 'weakness, lack of energy'

DESCARAPELAR (var. of) escarapelar

DESCARGADOR -RA freeloader (coll.), sponger, parasite

DESCARRILADO -DA crazy, screwy (coll.), off one's rocker (fig.)

DESCÍPULO (var. of) discípulo

DESCOGER (var. of) escoger

DESCOLGAR vn. to leave unannounced, take French leave (coll.)

DESCOLORIDO -DA (pej.) Anglo-Saxon

DESCOMPASAR vr. to overstep the bounds of reasonable behavior or decorum

DESCONCHI(N)FLADO -DA in a state of disrepair, in poor working order

DESCONCHINFLAR va. to put out of order, render unusable; vr. to break down, become inoperative
DESCONTAR (slang) vr. to beat it (slang), go away, leave; vr. to avenge oneself; to settle a financial debt
DESCONTROLADO -DA out of control, uncontrolled
DESCONTROLAR vr. to lose control of oneself
DESCOSER vr. (fig.) to shout it from the rooftops (coll.), open up and tell everything
DESCUACHARRANGADO -DA (slang) broken, shattered; in a bad state of disrepair
DESCUACHARRANGAR (slang) va. to put out of order, render inoperable; vr. to break down, become inoperative
DESCUALIFICAR (Eng.) va. to disqualify
DESCHARCHAR (Eng.) va. to discharge (from the armed forces); (hum.) to break off an amorous relationship, give the gate to one's sweetheart (slang)
DESCHARCHE or DESCHARCHI (Eng.) m. discharge from the armed forces (ref. to the act of discharge or the document certifying same); (hum.) dismissal given to the partner in an amorous relationship, walking papers (slang), the old heave-ho (slang)
DESDE: adv. DESDE CUANDO for a long time now: "Eso ya lo sé desde cuando" 'I've known that for a long time now'
DESEMBARAÑADOR m. comb
DESEMBARAÑAR va. to comb hair
DESENRAICE m. act and effect of uprooting (i.e., plants, shrubs, etc.)
DESENRAIZADO -DA bad off (coll.), hopeless, incorrigible; LOCO DESENRAIZADO crazy old fool
DESENRAIZAR va. to uproot (plants)
DESENROLLAR: DESENROLLAR LA CALCETA (slang) to dance
DESEPAQUETAR (var. of) desempaquetar
DESFENDER (var. of) defender
DESFLECHADO -DA disoriented
DESFROZAR (Eng.) va. to defrost
DESGANCHAR (var. of) desenganchar
DESGARRADO -DA ragged, in rags
DESGARRANCHADO -DA raggedy, torn, worn out (ref. to clothes and also to person wearing such clothes)
DESGARRANCHAR vr. to tear one's clothes to shreds
DESGARRAR (var. of) esgarrar 'to cough up phlegm'
DESGARREATE or DESGARRIATE m. heavy destruction of property; upheaval
DESGASNATAR vr. to yell, shout; to talk too freely
DESGOTADO -DA (var. of) escotado -da 'low (of neckline, i.e., dress which barely reaches above wearer's breast)'
DESGRACIADO -DA (pej.) base, vile, mean, son-of-a-bitch
DESGRACIAR va. to ruin, injure badly
DESGRANAR va. to tear apart; vr. (hum.) DESGRANARSE LA MAZORCA to fall down (said of persons)
DESGUSTAR (var. of) disgustar
DESHERMANABLE unbrotherly, unsisterly (said of person who mistreats his/her siblings)
DESIAR (var. of) desear
DESIDIOSO -SA procrastinating; negligent
DESIMULAR (var. of) disimular
DESINFESTANTE (var. of) desinfectante
DESINFESTAR (Ang.) va. to disinfect
DESMADRAR va. to beat up (in a fight); to destroy or deface maliciously; vr. to hurt oneself
DESMANCHAR va. to remove spots
DESMECHAR va. & vr. to pull at one another's hair in a fight
DESNARIZADO -DA (var. of) desnarigado -da
DESOBLIGADO -DA irresponsible
DESOCUPAR va. to dismiss from a job, fire
DESPACHADOR -RA mf. store clerk
DESPAGAR va. to cut weeds
DESPARRAMAR va. to broadcast news or gossip far and wide
DESPENSA medicine cabinet
DESPERCUDIDO -DA light-complexioned, light-skinned; pale
DESPERJUICIO (var. of) perjuicio
DESPIDIR (var. of) despedir
DESPILFARRERO (var. of) despilfarro
DESPLUMAR va. to defeat (in a contest)
DESPUÉS: DESPUÉS DE: (Ang.) in honor of, after: "Lo nombraron después de Benito Juárez" 'They named him after Benito Juárez'; DESPUÉS DE ATOLE (said of solutions or assistance appearing too late to do any good)
DESPUESITO adv. right after, immediately after: "Se fue despuesito de ti" 'He left just

after you did'
DESPUESTO -TA (var. of) dispuesto
DESPULMONAR vr. to work hard (often to excess)
DESTAPADO -DA hatless, without a head covering
DESTAPADOR m. plunger (used to clean out clogged drains, etc.)
DESTAPAR vr. to obtain relief from constipation; vr. to remove one's headgear, uncover one's head
DESTENDER (var. of) extender; DESTENDER LA CAMA to make the bed
DESTETE m. weaning
DESTORNUDAR (var. of) estornudar
DESTORNUDO (var. of) estornudo
DESTRAÍDO -DA or DESTRAIDO -DA (vars. of) distraído -da
DESTRIBUIDOR (var. of) distribuidor m.
DESTRUIGO, DESTRUIGUES, etc. (vars. of) destruyo, destruyes, etc. (pres. ind. forms of destruir)
DETECTA (Eng?) m. detective
DETECTIVA mf. (var. of) detective
DETENIDO -DA freeloader (coll.), stingy person
DETIRAR (var. of) retirar
DETRATO (var. of) retrato
DETUR m. (Eng.) detour
DEVALGAR (var. of) divulgar
DEVERAS (see DE DEVERAS)
DEVERTIR (var. of) divertir
DEVINO (var. of) divino
DEVISAR (var. of) divisar
DEVOLVER: DEVOLVER PA' TRAS (Ang.) va. to return, take back; vr. (var. of volverse 'to turn back, return')
DEVORCIO (var. of) divorcio
DÍA m. (EL) DÍA DE FINADOS All Souls' Day (Nov. 2nd); (EL) DÍA DE LA CONEJA Easter, Easter Sunday; (EL)DÍA DE VALENTÍN (St.) Valentine's Day
DI AY (var. of) de ahí: "Di ay se jueron a casa" 'From there they went on home' or 'And then they went on home'
DIÁLAGO (var. of) diálogo
DIAME (Eng.) m. dime, ten-cent piece (cf. DAIME, DIME et al.)
DIANTRE mf. devil; DIANTRE DE: "¡Diantre de huerquito éste!" 'You damnable mischievous little brat, you!
¡DIANTRES! interj. (var. of)¡diantre!
DIAVOLADA (see DE A VOLADA)
DIBILIDAD (var. of) debilidad f.
DIBILITAR (var. of) debilitar
DICEMOS or DICIMOS (var. of) decimos (1st pers pl. pres. ind. of decir)
DICER or DICIR (vars. of) decir (cf. DIJIR)
DICINUEVE (var. of) diecinueve
DICIOCHO (var. of) dieciocho
DICIPELA (var. of) ericipela erysipelas (type of contagious skin disease)
DICISIETE (var. of) diecisiete
DICHE (Eng.) m. irrigation canal; any type of ditch
DIEGO (DE RIVERA) (slang) m. dime, ten-cent piece
DIENTE: DIENTE PICADO tooth with a cavity or tooth decay; PELAR EL DIENTE to smile; to show one's teeth (often in anger)
DIENTISTA (var. of) dentista
DIENTÓN -TONA (var. of) dentudo -da
DIFORME (var. of) deforme
DIGNATARIO -A (var. of) dignitario -a
DIJIA, DIJÍAS, etc. (vars. of) decía, decías, etc. (imperfect forms of decir)
DIJIERA, DIJIERAS, etc. (vars. of) dijera, dijeras, etc. (past subj. of decir)
DIJIERON (var. of) dijeron (3rd pers. pl. pret of decir)
DIJIR (var. of) decir
DIJUNTO -TA (vars. of) difunto -ta
DILE (Hispanization of) Dilley, Texas
DILEAR or DILIAR (Eng.) vn. to deal or traffic in narcotic drugs
DILICADO -DA (vars. of) delicado -da
DIMA or DIMO (Eng.) (slang) dime, ten-cent piece (cf. DAIME, DIAME et al.)
DINERO-ORO United States currency (cf. DINERO-PLATA)
DINERO-PLATA Mexican currency
DINO -NA (var. of) digno -na
DINTISTA (var. of) dentista mf.
DIONDE (var. of) donde
DIOQUIS (see OQUIS, also DE HOQUIS)
DIOS: ¡DIOS NOS (ME) FAVOREZCA! DIOS NO LO QUIERA Heaven forbid!; EN EL NOMBRE SEA DE DIOS Amen, So be it; ¡NI LO MANDE DIOS! Heaven forbid!, Saints preserve us!; SEA POR DIOS Amen, So be it; (slang) That's the way the cookie crumbles (slang); SI DIOS ES SERVIDO God willing: "Buenas noches, hasta mañana.--Si Dios es servido"; SI DIOS ES SERVIDO God willing; SABER LO QUE ES AMAR A DIOS EN TIERRA AJENA to know firsthand what trouble really is
DIPA (Eng.) dipper, ladle
DIPARTAMENTO (var. of) departamento

DIPO (Eng.) depot, train station
DIPTONGUIZAR (var. of) diptongar
DIPUTADO deputy policeman
DIRECCIÓN f. steering wheel (automobile)
DIRRETIR or DIRRITIR (vars. of) derretir
DISCHARCHAR (var. of) descharchar (Eng.)
DISCO: CAMBIAR EL DISCO to stop harping on the same theme, change the topic of conversation; DISCO RAYADO (fig.) (said of a person who keeps harping on the same theme; the "harped-upon" conversational theme itself)
DISCONFIADO -DA (vars. of) desconfiado - da
DISCUTO (var. of) discurso m. 'discourse'
DISGUSTADO -DA hard to please
DISINTERESADO -DA (vars. of) desinteresado -da
DISISÉIS (var. of) dieciséis
DISMINUIGO (var. of) disminuyo (1st pers. pres. ind. sg. of disminuir)
DISPACIO (var. of) despacio
DISPEDIR (var. of) despedir
DISPERTAR (var. of) despertar
DISPIERTO, DISPIERTAS, etc. (vars. of) despierto, despiertas, etc. (pres. ind. --conjugation of despertar)
DISPUÉS (var. of) después
DISTRAIDO -DA (var. of) distraído - da
DISTRICTO (var. of) distrito
DISTRITAL adj. mf. of or pertaining to a district
DISTRUIGO, DISTRUIGUES, etc. (vars. of) destruyo, destruyes, etc. (pres. ind. conjugation of destruir) (cf. destruigo et al.)
DISVARIAR (var. of) desvariar
DITADO (var. of) dictado
DITECTO (Eng?) detective
DITUR (Eng.) m. detour
DIVIRSIÓN (var. of) diversión f.
DIVURCEAR or DIVURCIAR (vars. of) divorciar
DIVURCIO (var. of) divorcio
DIZQUE (var. of) dice que
DOBLEPLEY (Eng.) m. double play (in baseball)
DOCE (see DAR LAS DOCE)
DOCTOR: VISITA DE DOCTOR very brief visit (expression usually in the form of a complaint voiced by a host when visitors depart after a stay the host feels was too brief; the complaint is common among members of the same family who feel they should "see"each other more frequently)
DOCHE (Eng.) m. Dodge (brand of automobile)
DOLER: DOLER LA CINTURA to have a backache
DÓLOR (var. of) dólar m. 'dollar'
DOLOR: DOLOR DE BAZO spleen pain, "stitch in the side"; DOLOR DE CINTURA backache (esp. in the lower back); HACÉRSELE DOLOR A ALGUIEN HACER ALGO for it to hurt (fig.) someone to do something (ref. to ungenerous attitude): "Se te hizo dolor darme un pedacito de manzana" 'It hurt you to give me a little piece of the apple'
DOMÁS (var. of) nomás adv.
DOMECILIO (var. of) domicilio
DOMINGUERO suit of clothes reserved for formal occasions, "Sunday best" (coll.); DOMINGUERO -RA mf. & adj. (said of person who enjoys going out to have a good time or to visit on Sundays)
DOMPE (Eng.) m. garbage dump; dump truck; (fig.) house or room in a filthy condition
DOMPEAR or DOMPIAR (Eng.) va. to dump, dispose of; to vomit; to dump, give someone the slip (fig.), get rid of someone
DON: AY VA CON DON (hum. and also vulg.) (said of a passing woman; double entendre: 'There she goes with Don' and also 'There she goes with a condom')
DONA (Eng.) doughnut
DOÑAJUANITA (slang) marihuana
DORMELÓN -LONA (var. of) dormilón - lona
DORMIERA, DORMIERAS, etc. (past subj. forms of dormir) (vars. of) durmiera, durmieras, etc.
DORMIÓ, DORMIERON, DORMIENDO (vars. of) durmió, durmieron, durmiendo (resp. 3rd pers. sg. pret. 3rd pers. pl pret., and ger. of dormir)
DORMIR: DORMIR COMO UN TRONCO to sleep like a log (fig.), sleep very soundly; DORMIR LA BORRACHERA to sleep off an alcoholic binge; DORMIR LA CRUDA to sleep off a hangover; DORMÍRSELE A ALGUIEN EL GALLO to be caught napping, caught off guard (e.g. in a business deal or other competitive effort); to fail to take advantage of a favorable situation; to fail in the sex act (said of men who lose their

erection); PONER A DORMIR to knock out in a fist fight or boxing match
DORMITORIO (Ang.) dormitory (student residence)
DORREALES or DORRIALES (vars. of) dos reales
DOS: EN UN DOS POR TRES in the twinkling of an eye (coll.), with extreme rapidity; DOS REALES or DOS RIALES quarter, twenty-five cent piece
DOSTEAR or DOSTIAR (Eng.) va. to dust, remove dust (as in cleaning a room)
DOTA (Eng?) m. doctor, physician
DOTOR (var. of) doctor m.
DRAIVEAR or DRAIVIAR (Eng.) va. to drive (an automobile)
DRENAJE m. drain, catheter
DRIBLEAR or DRIBLIAR (Eng.) va. to dribble (a ball, in basketball)
DRINC or DRINQUE (Eng.) m. drink (esp. an alcoholic drink)
DROGA (slang) debt
DROMA (Eng.) m. traveling salesman (< drummer [dated slang expression for traveling salesman])
DROPEAR or DROPIAR (Eng.) va. to drop, let fall
DUÉRMAMOS (var. of) durmamos (1st pers. pl. subjunc. of dormir)
DULCE: SER DE DULCE (slang, pej.) to be a pansy (slang, pej.), be a homosexual; DULCE CON SAL m. hog skin crackling; DULCE DE PALITO m. (any sweet object embedded on a stick, e.g., an all-day sucker)
DUQUE m. tobacco (loan metonymy, < Duke brand tobacco?)
DURMIR (var. of) dormir
DURO -RA (slang) stiff (slang), dead

E

EA (var. of) ella
ECHADA f. boast; bluff, fib; brooding hen; SER MÁS LAS ECHADAS QUE LAS CULECAS (lit., for there to be more hens on the nest than the number that are actually laying eggs; said of persons who claim to have accomplished much but who actually have not)
ECHADOR -DORA mf. braggart; bluffer
ECHAR va. ECHAR A CUESTAS to throw someone on his/her back; ECHAR CARNES to curse; ECHAR DE PATITAS A LA CALLE to fire, dismiss (from a job) in short order; to run off, tell to leave (e.g., a home--usually ref. to the manner in which one common law partner tells the other to depart); ECHAR UN APLASTÓN / ECHAR UN TAPÓN to put someone in his/her place, put someone down (slang), tell someone where to get off (slang), reprimand; ECHAR A LA BOLSA / ECHAR EN LA BOLSA to defeat; ECHAR AL BOTE to bewitch; ECHAR A PERDER to spoil, pamper (esp. ref. to children); ECHAR DE LA MADRE to curse at someone (the taboo word madre is usually included in the cursing); ECHAR EL GATO A RETOZAR to let out a secret, let the cat out of the bag (coll.); ECHAR EN CARRILLA to give chase to, chase away: "Juan le echaron en carrilla porque estaba molestando mucho"; ECHAR HABLADAS to insinuate; ECHAR LA SAL to jinx, bring bad luck; ECHAR LA TRANCA to latch (usually ref. to a screen door); ECHAR (SU) LONCHE to put someone in his/her place, tell someone where to get off (slang): "Pásale, papá va a echarte tu lonche" 'Come on, daddy's going to give you what you've got coming' (said to a child who has misbehaved); ECHAR MADRES to curse, cuss out (cf. ECHAR DE LA MADRE); ECHARLE LA LEY A ALGUIEN to get the law after someone; to bring a lawsuit against someone; ECHAR MENOS (var. of) echar de menos; ECHAR MOSCA to tease; ECHAR PAPAS to tell lies, lie; ECHAR UN PEDO (vulg.) to expel wind; ECHAR PIQUETE to provoke, needle (coll.); ECHAR POR LA CABEZA to betray, tell the secrets of someone else: "Primitivo se enojó con Inocencio porque le echó por la cabeza"; ECHAR TRANCA (A LA PUERTA) to lock (a door with a key), latch (a screen door); vn. ECHAR(SELAS) DE LADO to brag, boast; ECHAR MAROMAS to do somersaults; ECHAR PULGAS to cause trouble; ECHAR(SE) UNA POLCA to dance a polka (or another other dance); ECHAR UN PALITO (slang) (for a male to have sexual intercourse);

vr. to lie down (said only of animals or, in anger or sarcastically, of humans); ECHARLO AL JUEGO (var. of) echarlo a juego to tell as a joke, tell in fun; ECHARSE AL PLATO / ECHÁRSELO to get the best of someone, beat someone out; to seduce; to kill; ECHARSE DE VER to be evident, show: "Es muy mezquino. --Se echa de ver." 'He's very stingy. --It shows.' ECHARSE EL TROMPO EN LA UÑA (usually said as a command:) "¡Échate el trompo en la uña!" 'Put that in your pipe and smoke it!' (said as an admonishment or by way of revenge); ECHARSE ENCIMA to jump on someone; ECHARSE TRÁCALA(S) to fall into debt; ECHARSE UN PEDO to expel wind; ECHARSE UN PEDO DE AQUELLOS (slang, vulg.) to let out a real stinker (ref. to a very bad-smelling expulsion of bodily wind)

EDEFICIO (var. of) edificio

EDITOR (Ang.) m. newspaper editor (Std. redactor)

EDUCACIÓN (Ang.) f. education (in all senses of the word in Eng., not solely 'upbringing' as per Std.)

EDUCACIONAL (Ang.) adj. educational, that which serves to enhance the learning process

¡EIT! or ¡ÉITALE! (slang, used to call a person's attention:) Hey you!

¡ÉJELE! interj. (used to poke fun at someone:) "¡Éjele, perdieron el juego!"

EJIR (rus.) (var. of) decir

EJOTE msg. string beans, green beans

ELANTE (var. of) delante

ELÁSTICO rubber band

ELBA (slang) m. barber (< el ba [rbero])

ELECTAR (Eng.) va. to elect, elect to office

ELECTRECIDAD (var. of) electricidad f.

ELÉCTRICO -CA (slang) drunk

ELIGIR (var. of) elegir

ELOISA (var. of) Eloísa

ELOTE: CIERTOS ELOTES certain (well-known) persons, certain so-and-sos (would-be oblique ref. to persons whom one coyly does not wish to name)

EMBACHICHAR va. to con, dupe, swindle

EMBARADO -DA bloated (ref. to stomach bloated from indigestion)

EMBARAZADO -DA (Ang.) embarrassed

EMBARRADA (var. of) embarradura

EMBARAÑADO -DA (var. of) enmarañado -da

EMBARRAR va. to run over (e.g. a person with a vehicle); to spread (e.g. butter on a slice of bread)

EMBIJAR va. to paint; to smear, grease

EMBOLAR va. to confuse, mix up; vr. to get confused or mixed up

EMBOLIO (var. of) embolia 'stroke'

EMBONO (var. of) abono

EMBORUCAR va. to confuse, mix up; vr. to get confused or mixed up

EMBORRACHAR va. to make dizzy; vr. to become dizzy

EMBUSTEROSO -SA liar

EMITERIO (var. of) Emeterio

EMPACADOR -DORA mf. packer (person who works in a packing house)

EMPACAR (slang) va. to eat; vr. to stuff oneself (coll.), eat to satiation

EMPACHADO -DA fed up (fig.), extremely annoyed (with)

EMPACHAR va. to irritate, annoy

EMPALMADO -DA bundled up, wearing lots of clothes

EMPALMAR va. to pile up items one top of the other; vr. to bundle up, wear plenty of clothing (as for protection against the cold)

EMPALME: TRAER EMPALME to be heavily bundled up, be wearing many clothes

EMPANADA semi-circular-shaped jelly roll or doughnut

EMPANAL m. type of small bread roll

EMPANTURRAR va. to stuff (a person) with food; vr. to stuff oneself with food, eat to excess

EMPANZADO -DA stuffed, full (said of stomachs replete with food)

EMPANZAR va. to stuff (a person) with food; vr. to stuff oneself with food, eat gluttonously

EMPAQUE (slang) m. chow (slang), food, meal, dinner; tooth packing (temporary filling for cavity)

EMPAREJAR vr. to tie the score in a game; to avenge

EMPEDAR vr. to get drunk (cf. PEDO)

EMPELOTADO -DA passionately in love

EMPELOTAR vr. to be passionately in love

EMPINADO -DA bent over

EMPINAR va. to bend (usually ref. to persons); vr. to bend over

EMPISTOLADO -DA armed with a gun

EMPLEADO -DA or EMPLIADO -DA police officer; (esp.) immigration officer
EMPLUMAR vn. to become of age
EN: EN CAS DE (var. of) en casa de; EN EL COLORADO (Ang.) in the red (slang), in debt; (DE) EN SEGUIDA DE alongside, next door: "Vive en la casa de en seguida de nosotros"; EN TANTO QUE NADA in a jiffy, very quickly; EN UN DOS POR CUATRO/EN UN TRES POR CUATRO (vars. of) en un dos por tres in a jiffy, in a wink; EN VECES (var. of Std. a veces 'at times'); EN VISITAS (var. of Std. de visita 'on a visit')
ENAMORAR: ENAMORARSE CON (Ang., var. of Std. enamorarse de)
ENCÁ or ENCA prep. (var. of) en casa de
ENCAJAR va. to blame; vr. to climb on someone's back; to get on top of one's partner to have sexual intercourse
ENCALMADO -DA dying of thirst, extremely thirsty
ENCAMORRADO -DA ill-tempered
ENCANDILADO -DA tired
ENCANDILAR va. to tire; to lure, tempt; vr. to get tired, tire out
ENCANICADO -DA (slang) passionately in love
ENCANICAR vr. to fall passionately in love
ENCANTONEADO -DA or ENCANTONIADO -DA (slang) married, hitched (slang)
ENCANTONEAR or ENCANTONIAR (slang) vr. to get married, get hitched (slang)
ENCAPUCHADO -DA (slang) well-dressed
ENCARAMADO -DA on top of
ENCARAMAR vr. to mount a horse; to "mount" someone to have sexual intercourse
ENCARTADO -DA halfbreed, of mixed racial background
ENCEBAR vr. to get grease on one's hands
ENCENDIDO m. match (used for igniting
ENCIMAR vr. to be where one is not wanted; to be or become a pest
ENCIMÓN -MONA (vars. of) encimoso -sa: ANDAR ENCIMÓN or SER ENCIMÓN to be a pest (fig.), be bothersome
ENCIMOSO -SA pest, annoying person
ENCONTONEAR or ENCONTONIAR (vars. of) encantonear, encantoniar
ENCORRALAR va. to corner
ENCUERADO -DA naked
ENCUERAR va. to strip, take the clothes off of; vr. to undress
ENCUETAR va. to inebriate; vr. to get drunk
ENCHALECAR (slang) va. to shoplift
ENCHAQUETAR va. to help (someone) put on a jacket; vr. to put on one's jacket
ENCHARCADO -DA adj. stuck in the mud; m. mistake
ENCHARCAR vr. to make a mistake; to get stuck in the mud
ENCHILADA m. burned mouth or tongue (resulting from the ingestion of any type of food that contains hot chile)
ENCHILADO -DA infuriated, outraged
ENCHILAR va. to burn someone's tongue with hot food; vr. to burn oneself (in the mouth) with hot food (esp. food containing hot chile)
ENCHINADO -DA in curls
ENCHINADOR m. hair curler
ENCHINAR va. & vr. to curl hair; vr. ENCHINÁRSELE EL CUERPO A ALGUIEN to get goosepimples (goosebumps)
ENCHINCHADO -DA infested with chinch bugs
ENCHINCHAR va. to fill with bedbugs; vr. to become infested with bedbugs (usually said of mattresses)
ENCHUECAR va. to twist; vr. to become twisted
ENDENANTES adv. a little while ago
ENDEREZAR va. to straighten out (fig.), reform, rehabilitate; vr. to straighten oneself out, reform oneself
ENDEVERAS (var. of) de veras
ENDOMINGAR vr. to dress up in style, dress up in one's "Sunday best"
ENDROGAR va. to get someone into debt; vr. to get into debt
ENFAJAR va. to put a belt or sash on someone; vr. to put on one's belt or sash
ENFATIZAR va. to emphasize
ENFERMA adj. f. (euph.) menstruating, having one's period
ENFERMAR va. to hex, make sick through witchcraft; vr. to begin labor pains; to be in labor
ENFERMEDAD: ENFERMEDAD DE ANDANCIA disease that is "going around," mild epidemic (cf. ENFERMEDAD QUE ANDA); ENFERMEDAD DEL CARÁCTER character disorder, disease of social pathology (often considered innate); ENFERMEDAD ENDAÑADA disease resulting from an act of witch-

craft; ENFERMEDAD QUE ANDA disease that is "going around," mild epidemic; ENFERMEDAD SECRETA venereal disease

ENFLACAR va. to cause someone to become thin: "Lo enflacó de tantas penas"; vr. to become thin, lose weight; to diet (so as to lose weight)

ENFRIFOLAR or ENFRIJOLAR vr. to eat an excessive amount of beans, stuff oneself with beans (usually pinto beans)

ENGANCHAR va. to hook or trick into marriage; vr. (hum.) to become engaged to be married; to get married, get "hooked" (slang)

ENGANCHE m. engagement, promise to marry; downpayment; contract to obtain bracero laborers

ENGANCHISTA m. (sometimes pej.) contractor of bracero labor

ENGARRUñAR vr. to get into a fight; to double up, shrink (esp. when extremely angry)

ENGARTUSAR (var. of) engatusar

ENGRASADA shoe-shine; DAR UNA ENGRASADA to apply shoe paste to shoes (as to shine them)

ENGRASAR va. to apply shoe paste to shoes (so as to shine them)

ENGRASE m. applications of shoe paste to shoes for purposes of shining

ENGREÍR vr. to become attached to, fond of

ENGRIDO -DA (var. of) engreído -da

ENGRIFAR va. to administer marihuana; to someone; vr. to take marihuana; to feel the effects of marihuana

ENGRINGOLAR va. to cause someone to become gringo-like, to gringoize; vr. to become like a gringo

ENGUAYNAR (Eng.) va. to get someone drunk on wine; vr. to get drunk on wine

ENGÜERAR vr. to become addled (ref. to people); to become rotten (ref. to eggs)

ENGUSANAR vr. to become wormy (ref. to animals and persons who fall prey to worms in their intestines)

ENHUEVAR vr. to become stubborn

ENJAULADO -DA jailed, in jail

ENJAULE (slang) m. jail

ENJETADO -DA (said of person who is pouting; also said of person making a facial expression denoting anger

ENLISTAR (Eng.) vr. to enlist in the armed forces

ENMAIZADO -DA: LOCO -CA ENMAIZADO -DA screwball (coll.), crazy old fool

ENMANTECAR va. to dirty with grease or lard; vr. to become dirty with grease or lard

ENMAñADO -DA deceptive, fraudulent, tricky (ref. to persons)

ENMARIHUANAR va. to administer marihuana to, cause to take marihuana; vr. to take marihuana

ENMUGRAR (var. of) enmugrecer

ENMUGRENTAR to soil, dirty

ENMULAR vr. to become obstinate, stubborn

ENRAIZADO -DA: LOCO -CA ENRAIZADO -DA screwball (coll.), crazy old fool (cf. ENMAIZADO)

ENREDADO -DA (hum.) engaged to be married

ENRODAR vr. to become tangled, rolled up

ENROLLAR vr. to become tangled

ENSARTAR (vulg.) va. & vr. to insert one's penis into a vagina

ENSEÑAR: ENSEñAR LA OREJA to show one's bad side, reveal one's defects; to reveal one's true colors; ENSEñAR UNA PELICULA (Ang?) to show a movie

ENTABICAR (slang) va. to jail, lock up in jail

ENTABLAZÔN f. obstruction, severe constipation

ENTACUACHADO -DA (var. of) entacuchado -da

ENTACUCHADO -DA (slang) well-dressed, dressed up (coll.)

ENTELIGIR (var. of) inteligir

ENTENDER (see HACER ENTENDER)

ENTERRAR va. to stick with a pointed instrument; vr. to stick a pointed object into oneself (usually through accident): "Me enterré una astilla en el pie"

ENTONADO -DA: ANDAR ENTONADO -DA to be drunk

ENTONCE (var. of) entonces

ENTOSEQUIDO -DA (Eng.) intoxicated, drunk

ENTRACALADO -DA in debt

ENTRACALAR va. to put into debt; vr. to become indebted, accumulate debts

ENTRADA inning (in baseball); permission officially given by the father of a girl to a boy desirous of visiting her at home; VENIR DE ENTRADA Y SALIDA to visit or call upon someone briefly

ENTRADERA: ENTRADERA Y SALIDERA (ref. to person) gadabout

ENTRADITO -TA slightly drunk

ENTRADO -DA slighty drunk

ENTRADOR -DORA mf. dare-devil, taker of risks
¡ÉNTRALE! interj. (used to encourage or stimulate) Go at it!, Do it!: "Entrale, no le tengas miedo!"
ENTRAR va. to tackle, take on (e.g. a job, a challenge, etc.)
ENTRE: ENTRE MÁS ... MÁS the more ... the more; ENTRE MENOS ... MENOS the less/fewer ... the less/fewer
ENTRESACAR va. to thin hair (as done by barbers to customers so requesting)
ENTRESEMANA fsg. weekdays
ENTRETENER va. to delay; vr. to be delayed
ENTRIEGO, ENTRIEGAS, etc. (vars. of) entrego, entregas, etc. (pres. ind. of entregar)
ENTRINCAR: ENTRINCAR LOS DIENTES to clench one's teeth
ENTRO (var. of) adentro adv.
ENTRÓN -TRONA mf. dare-devil, taker of risks, dreadnought
ENTUMIDO -DA (var. of) entumecido -da
ENTUMIR vr. to get cold feet (fig.), shy away from something
ENVITADO -DA (var. of) invitado -da
ENVITAR (var. of) invitar
ENVOLTIJO (var. of) envoltorio 'bundle'
ENVOLVER (Eng.) va. to involve (someone in something:) "Querían envolverlo en ese problema"; vr. to become involved in: "Siempre se envuelve en mucho mugrero"
ENYERBADO -DA bewitched, hexed
ENYERBAR va. to bewitch, hex
ENVUELTOS mpl. enchiladas
ENZOQUETAR va. to muddy up, splatter with mud; vr. to get muddied up
¡EPA! or ¡ÉPALE! interj. Watch that!, Hey!, Careful!, etc.
EPAZOTE m. wormseed (Chenopodium embrosioides)(herbal tea used to treat stomach ache or as a vermicide)
EPISODIO motion picture presented in serial form (e.g. in 15 parts, one each week)
ERJOSTES (Eng.)fsg. stewardess, airline hostess (ant.)
ERO (rus.) (var. of) soy (1st pers. sg. pres. indic. of ser)
ERUTAR (var. of) eructar
ÉSA ES DE AY or ÉSE ES DE AY (general expression of approval) (slang) Right on! (slang), That's right!
¡ÉSA(LE)! or ¡ÉSE(LE)! (slang)(interj. used to call someone's attention) Hey you!
ESCALERA (hum.) tall person, daddy long legs (coll.)
ESCAME m. fear, terror
ESCAMOSO -SA fearful, frightened
ESCANDALOSO -SA squeamish
ESCANSAR (var. of) descansar
ESCANTE m. short while, moment: "Espérame un escante"
ESCARAPELAR va. to chip off; vr. to get chipped off
ESCARBAR to dig, excavate deeply (not merely 'to scratch' as in Std.)
ESCARCHA cold weather, cold season
ESCOBÓN (slang, hum.) m. guitar
ESCOCH (Eng.) m. Scotch whiskey; ESCOCH TEIP (Eng.) m. scotch tape
ESCONDIDAS: JUGAR A LAS ESCONDIDAS to play hide and seek (child's game)
ESCOR (Eng.) m. score
ESCORCÉS (var. of) escocés
ESCRACHAR (Eng.) va. to scratch (slang= to cancel, eliminate)
ESCREBIDO -DA (rus.) (var. of) escrito -ta (ppart. of escribir)
ESCREBIR (var. of) escribir
ESCREPÓN (Eng.) m. shoe with thick soles (scrape)
ESCRECHAR (Eng.) va. to scratch (cf. ESCRACHAR)
ESCRIBIDO -DA (rus.) (var. of) escrito -ta (ppart. of escribir)
ÉSCRIN or ESCRÍN (Eng.) m. ice cream
ESCRÍN (Eng.) m. movie screen
ESCUADRA pistol (usually automatic); gun (in general); (fig.) square shooter, honest person; square deal, honest treatment
ESCUELA (Ang.) classes, school day: "No hay escuela hoy" (Std. no hay clases hoy); ESCUELA ALTA (Ang.) high school
ESCUETO -TA quiet, tranquil
ESCUINCLE mf. child
ESCULCÓN -CONA (pej.) snoop, person who enjoys searching through others' possessions without permission
ESCUPE (slang) m. gun
ESCUPIDA (slang) (fig.) gun blast
ESCUPIDERA (slang) pistol, gun
ESCURA (Eng.) motor scooter; child's (motorless) scooter
ESCURECER (var. of) o(b)scurecer
ESCÚRER (Eng.) m. scooter, motorcycle; child's (motorless) scooter
ESCURO -RA adj. (var. of) oscuro-ra

ESGADO -DA sideways, crossways: "El carro quedó esgado en medio de la calle" 'The car was left in a diagonal position in the middle of the street'
ESLECS (Eng.) mpl. slacks, pants
ESO: EN ESO at that moment, just then: "En eso llegó María" 'Just then María arrived'
ESPALDA: ESPALDA MOJADA wet-back (illegal immigrant from Mexico)
ESPALDAR m. headboard; back of a chair
ESPATEAR or ESPATIAR (Eng.) va. to spot, recognize
ESPAUDA or ESPAURA (Eng.) (<yeast powder) baking powder
ESPELEAR or ESPELIAR (Eng.) va. to spell (words)
ESPELETEAR or ESPELETIAR (Eng.) (vars. of) espelear, espeliar
ESPERANZA: ¡QUE ESPERANZA(S)! interj. (used to express strong doubt as to whether something will take place) That'll be the day!
ESPICHADITO -TA (Eng?<speech?) quiet, repressed, not talkative
ESPICHE (Eng.) m. speech, discourse
ESPINECHE (Eng.) m. spinach
ESPINIENTO -TA or ESPINILLENTO -TA pimpled, beset with facial pimples
ESPIRINA (var. of) aspirina
ESPÍRITO (var. of) espíritu
ESPORTE (Eng.) m. sport
ESPRÍN (Eng.) m. spring (Std. resorte); spring (Std. primavera)
ESPUÉS (var. of) después
ESQUECHAR (Eng.) va. to sketch, draw, design
ESQUECHE (Eng.) m. sketch, design
ESQUINADO -DA or ESQUINIADO -DA adj. placed at an angle (usually ref. to a piece of furniture)
ESQUINAR or ESQUINIAR va. to place at an angle or in a corner of a room
ESQUINEAR or ESQUINIAR (slang) vn. to go along with (fig.), assent to
ESQUIPEAR or ESQUIPIAR (Eng.) va. to skip (i.e., to miss, e.g. a class, a lesson, an appointment); va. & vn. to skip, jump, hop
ESQUITE m. popcorn
ESTACA: POLLITO DE ESTACA person approaching old age; adult or person approaching adulthood
ESTACAR (Eng.) va. to stack, pile up
ESTACIÓN: ESTACIÓN DE GASOLINA (Ang?) f. gas(oline) station
ESTADO: ESTADO DE LA ESTRELLA SOLITARIA Lone Star State (i.e., Texas); ESTADO INTERESANTE (euph.) pregnancy
ESTAFEATE or ESTAFIATE m. medicinal herb used for stomach disorders
ESTAMPA (Ang.) stamp, postage stamp
ESTAQUITA mumbletypeg (children's game played with a jack-knife)
ESTAR: ESTAR A MANOS to owe nothing to anyone, be even; to have avenged oneself; ESTAR A TODA MADRE (for something to be) terrific, tremendous; ESTAR A UNA Y UN PEDAZO to be penniless, stone broke (coll.); ESTAR BUENO to suffice, be enough: "¡Ya está bueno!" 'That's enough!'; ESTAR CALIENTE (Ang.) to be hot (said of the weather; Std. hacer calor); ESTAR COMO LA FREGADA to be as _____ as can be (e.g., 'to be as ugly as sin', 'as mean as a junkyard dog', etc.--ref. usually to any negative quality known both to speaker and listener) ESTAR COMO LA JODIDA to be as ____as can be (usual ref. to a negative characteristic of which both speaker and listener are cognizant, e.g.:) "Ella está como la jodida" 'She's as ugly as sin'; ESTAR CON EL ESPOSO/ESTAR CON LA ESPOSA (euph.) to be having sexual intercourse; ESTAR CON FAMILIA to be pregnant; ESTAR CURADO -DA DE SUSTO fearless (ref. to person who does not frighten easily); ESTAR DE AQUE(LL)A (slang) to be tremendous, terrific, great, etc.; ESTAR DE LADO (coll.) to be in a good mood; ESTAR DE LA PATADA (slang) to stink, smell highly; to be incorrigible; to be very ugly, homely (usually ref. to women); ESTAR DIOQUIS (see DE HOQUIS); ESTAR EN CALLE to be destitute, in extreme poverty; ESTAR EN LA CHILLA to be destitute, down and out, desperate; ESTAR EN LA LÍNEA / LINIA to be drunk; ESTAR EN TODO (MENOS EN MISA) to mind everyone's business but one's own, attend to everyone's affairs but one's own; ESTAR FEBRERO / ESTAR MARZO to be crazy (also: ESTAR FEBRERO LOCO Y MARZO OTRO POCO, id.) ESTAR FRÍO (Ang.) to be cold (said of the weather; Std. hacer frío) ESTAR HASTA EL COPETE to be

fed up, to have stood as much as possible; to be extremely drunk; ESTAR HASTA LAS MANITAS to be extremely drunk; ESTAR LA PATRIA MUY POBRE/ESTAR LA PATRIA MUY FREGADA to be in a poor financial situation, be at the end of one's rope (fig.): "¿Vas a comprar el carro?--No puedo, está muy fregada la patria"; ESTAR MADRE (slang) (for something to be) terrific, tremendous, super, great, etc.; ESTAR MALO EL CUENTO (for things to be in a bad state:) "¡Está malo el cuento!" 'Things have come to a pretty pass!' (coll.); ESTAR PADRE (,BATO -TA) (slang) (iron. expression used to indicate that one's feelings have been hurt; the implication is that revenge will be taken or poetic justice will prevail); ESTAR PAREJOS to be tied, end up in a tie; ESTAR PONIÉNDOSELA A ALGUIEN to be having sexual relations with someone; ESTAR QUE HASTA/ESTAR QUE NOMÁS to be very tense, fit to be tied, on pins and needles (fig.), at one's wits' end (etc.); to be very ugly/beautiful/drunk (etc.-- ref. to an extreme manifestation of an obvious quality known to both speaker and listener); ESTAR QUE SE LO LLEVA EL DIABLO / ESTAR QUE SE LO LLEVA JUDÁS / ESTAR QUE SE LO LLEVA EL TREN / ESTAR QUE SE LO LLEVA LA CHINGADA to be very tense, fit to be tied, on pins and needles, at one's wits end; ESTAR SALADO -DA to be having a stroke of bad luck; to be jinxed, unlucky; ESTAR TAMAÑITO -TA to be edgy, be on pins and needles (as in anticipation of something to happen momentarily); ESTAR TIRADO -DA to be abed, lying in bed (usual ref. to sick or lazy person); ESTAR TORCIDOS not to be on friendly terms (see also TORCERLE LA CARA A ALGUIEN); ESTAR TRES PIEDRAS to be terrific, tremendous, very beautiful, etc.

ESTARA or ESTÁRER (Eng.) m. starter (on an automobile)

ESTAREAR or ESTARIAR (Eng.) va. to start (an automobile)

ESTE (used as a stalling device, i.e., inserted when the speaker cannot think of what to say next)

ESTECHE HUEGUEN (Eng.) m. station wagon (type of car)

ESTILACHO (slang) style, fashion

ESTILLA (var. of) astilla

ESTIRADA act or result of growing taller (usually said with ref. to teenagers): "No reconocí a tu hijo; se dio una estirada tremenda" 'I didn't recognize your son, he had grown so much'

ESTIRAR va. ESTIRAR IGUAL to cooperate, pull together (coll.); ESTIRAR LA PATA (slang) to die; ESTIRARLE AL EXCUSADO to flush the toilet; vr. to grow taller (usually said with ref. to teenagers)

ESTIRÓN (slang) m. DARSE UN ESTIRÓN to grow like a weed (fig.), grow considerably and suddenly (usually said with ref. to teenagers)

ESTEPLES (slang) (Hispanization of) Staples, Texas

ESTÉRICO -CA (var. of) histérico -ca

ESTO (see A TODO ESTO)

ESTÓGAMO: (var. of) estómago; ESTÓMAGO SUCIO indigestion, dyspepsia; "infected stomach"

ESTOR (Eng.) m. store, shop

ESTRAIQUE (Eng.) m. strike, work stoppage; strike (in baseball)

ESTRAIQUEADO or ESTRAIQUIADO (Eng.) strike-out

ESTRAIQUEAR or ESTRAIQUIAR (Eng.) va. to strike at and miss a pitched ball (in baseball); to strike someone out (baseball); vn. to strike, go on strike (Std. estar de huelga, ponerse de huelga)

ESTRAMBÓLICO -CA (var. of) estrambótico -ca 'strange, unusual, eccentric, queer'

ESTRELLAR vr. to faint, see stars (coll.); vr. to excel, shine (in a game, etc.)

ESTROC (Eng.) m. stroke, cerebral hemorrhage

ESTROPOJO (var. of) estropajo

ESTRUJAR va. to shake violently

ESTRUJÓN m. violent shaking (usually admininstered to a person)

ESTUATA or ESTUATUA (vars. of) estatua

ESTUFA: ¡ESTUFAS CALIFORNIA! (slang) Knock it off!, Quiet down!, Shut up!; ¡YA ESTUFAS! (id.)

ESTUFEAR or ESTUFIAR (slang) va. to sniff the residue of powdered

narcotic drugs
ESTULE (Eng.) (slang) m. stoolie (slang), stool pigeon (slang), person who betrays one's companions by serving as a police informer
ESTULEAR or ESTULIAR (Eng.) va. to "stool" on someone, serve as a police informer (cf. ESTULE)
ESTUTO -TA (vars. of) astuto -ta
ESTUVO (3rd pers. sg. pret. of estar): ¡YA ESTUVO! That's it!, We've got it made!, The job's done! (etc.)
EXAMINACIÓN f. exam (in a school subject)
EXCLUIGO (var. of) excluyo (1st per. pres. sg. ind. of excluir)
EXCUSADO: EXCUSADO DE AFUERA outhouse, outdoor toilet
EXCUSAR (Ang.) va. to pardon, forgive
ÉXITO (Ang.) exit, way out
EXPERENCIA (var. of) experiencia
EXPLOTAR (Ang.) va. to explode, detonate; vn. (fig.) to explode with anger
EXPRÉS (Ang.) m. express (i.e., express train, express bus); carriage pulled by one or two horses
EXTRA f. spare tire
EXTRAORDENARIO -RIA (var. of) extraordinario -ria
EXTRAVIADO -DA half-crazy, slightly tetched (coll.)
EXTRORDINARIO -RIA (var. of) extraordinario -ria

F

FACHAS fpl. unkempt and messy appearance: "Andaba de unas fachas que daba lástima" 'He looked so messy that one felt sorry for him'
FACHAZO (slang) alcoholic drink; shot of liquor
FACULTOSO -SA usurper of privileges, taker of rights one has not been authorized to enjoy
FAIN (Eng.) adj. fine, okay, all right
FAJA belt used for medicinal or therapeutic purposes; corset
FAJAR va. to spank; to beat (with a belt); to put a collar on someone (fig., i.e. to control)
FAJAZO blow administered with a belt
FAJERO wrapping or swaddling cloth for newborn babies; belt for medicinal or therapeutic purposes (esp. to hold in the navel of the newborn child)
FALDA shirt tail; part of a woman's slip accidentally showing: "Te sale la falda, métetela"
FALDÓN m. fender (automobile)
FALTAR (slang) FALTARLE A ALGUIEN UN TORNILLO to be daffy, have a screw loose (slang), be someone crazy
FALSEAR or FALSIAR: FALSEÁRSELE A ALGUIEN LA RODILLA to sprain one's knee
FALSEO sprain
FALLAR: FALLARLE A ALGUIEN EL COCO to go off one's rocker (slang), become slightly crazy
¡FALLÁU! (Eng.) (interj.) (slang) Far out! (indicating approval of something)
FAMA: DAR FAMA to praise, eulogize
FAMILIA: ESTAR CON FAMILIA to be pregnant
FANEAR or FANIAR (Eng.) va. to fan (baseball slang), strike out; FANEAR EL AIRE to attempt and fail to hit the ball (baseball)
FANTOCHE mf. presumptuous or pretentious
FARMACÉTICO (var. of) farmacéutico
FAROLAZO: ECHARSE UN FAROLAZO (slang) to drink down a shot of hard liquor
FARUCAS (slang) Falfurrias, Texas
FAUBOL or FÁUBOL (Eng.) m. foul ball (in ball sports, e.g., in baseball, said of a ball hit to the left or the right of the field of play)
FAUL (Eng.) m. foul (in sports competitions)
FEDERAL (<feo) (slang) adj. ugly
FEDERICO -CA (slang) ugly (cf. FEDERAL); crazy, insane, lunatic; fsg. federal police, federal troops
FEILAR or FEILEAR or FEILIAR (Eng.) va. to fail, flunk (someone in a school subject); va. & vn. to fail (in a school subject)
FENDA (Eng.) fender (automobile); (slang ant.) hair heavily greased and combed straight back on the sides, "DA" haircut, "fenders" (slang ant.)
FÉNDER (Eng.) f. (var. of) fenda

(Eng.)
FENÓMENO -NA big-headed, large-headed; m. monstrosity
FEO: OLER FEO to stink (said of persons or things); PONERSE FEO to become dangerous, threatening, to turn bad (said of weather): "¿Trajiste tu capa?--¿Por qué preguntas?--Porque se está poniendo feo el cielo"
FEÓN -ONA (var. of) feúcho -cha
FEREAR or FERIAR va. & vn. to barter; make change for: "Por favor, feréame este dólar"
FERIA change, money due from a larger monetary unit; loose change, assortment of coins; TENER FERIA to be flushed, have a great deal of money; to have more money than one customarily has on one's person
FERNI (nickname for) Fernando
FEYO -YA (var. of) feo -a
FIANCE m.(var. of) fianza
FICHA bottle cap; slug; adj. broke, without money; ANDAR FICHA (LISA) to be stone broke, completely without money; CIERTAS FICHAS certain so-and-so's
FICHAR va. to look for money
FICHAZO change, money returned from a larger monetary unit
FICHERA (slang) whore, prostitute

FIEBRE: FIEBRE DEL VALLE f. valley fever, coccidiodomycosis
FIERRITO hat pin
FIERRO (var. of) hierro; FIERROS mpl. tools of a barber's trade; CAMINO DE FIERRO railroad
FIERROCARRIL (var. of) ferrocarril
FIESTERO -RA fond of going to parties
FIFÍ or FIFIRICHE or FIFIRUCHO (slang) effeminate (male), faggot, pansy, swish, Miss Nancy, Miss Molly, nelly (etc.) (slang)
FÍJESE or FÍJESE NOMÁS Fancy that!, Can you imagine that! (expressions of surprise or incredulity)
FIL (Eng.) m. field (ref. to both athletic and agricultural fields); field = specialty (i.e., academic "field", academic major)
FILA (slang) wife; knife; CARGAR or TRAER FILA to carry a knife, a switchblade, etc.; SACARLE LA FILA A ALGUIEN to pull a knife on someone
FILDEAR or FILDIAR vn. to play the position of fielder (in baseball)
FILDEO act or technique of fielding (in baseball)
FÍLDER (Eng.) m. fielder (in baseball)
FILERA knife
FILEREAR or FILERIAR va. to knife, cut with a knife
FILERO knife
FILETEAR or FILETIAR (slang) va. to knife, cut with a knife
FILORAZO knife wound (usually one inflicted in a knife fight)
FILOREAR or FILORIAR (vars. of) filerear, fileriar
FILOSA (slang) knife
FINA (dim. of) Josefina (see also PEPA)
FINCA building, edifice
FINCAR va. to construct a building
FISGADERA act of snooping or peeping
FISGÓN -GONA mf. peeping tom, person who snoops or peeps on others (observes them surreptitiously)
FITO (nickname for) Adolfo
FLACO -CA thin (usually ref. to animals)
FLACÓN -CONA somewhat thin (usually prefaced by medio: MEDIO FLACÓN / MEDIO FLACONA)
FLANQUEAR or FLANQUIAR (Eng.) (vars. of) flonquear, flonquiar
FLETEAR or FLETIAR (Eng.) va. to flatten (a tire, by letting the air out) (a person, by knocking him/her down with a blow of the fists); vr. to go flat: "La llanta se flatió"
FLET (Eng.) m. flat, flat tire; ANDAR FLET to be flat broke (coll.), completely without money; adj. flat, out of tune (ref. to musical instruments)
FLIPEAR or FLIPIAR (Eng.) va. to flip, flip over; vr. (slang) to go crazy, flip one's lid (slang)
FLIRTIAR (var. of) flirtear
FLOCHAR (Eng.) va. to flush
FLOJÓN -JONA somewhat lazy (often prefaced by medio: MEDIO FLOJÓN/MEDIO FLOJONA)
FLONQUEAR or FLONQUIAR (Eng.) va. to fail, flunk (someone in a school subject); v. & vn. to fail (in a school subject)
FLOR (slang) f. homosexual, pansy (pej.)

FLORE (dim. of) Florinda
FLORIAR (var. of) florear
FLORINDO (slang) homosexual
FLOTAR: FLOTARSE UNA (slang) to drink a beer: "Se flotó una"
FLOUT (Eng.) m. float (Std. carro alegórico)
FLU (Eng.) f. influenza
FLUNQUEAR or FLUNQUIAR (Eng.) (var. of) flonquear, flonquiar
FOCO: FOCOS mpl. eyeglasses
FODONGO (Eng. <Ford) old battered-up car
FÓLDER (Eng.) m. folder (envelope or filing apparatus)
FONAZO (slang) (Eng.) fun, enjoyment
FONCHAR vn. to cheat in a marble game by placing or pushing the marble shooter closer to the target (see also HACER FONCHE)
FONCHE: HACER FONCHE: to cheat in a marble game by placing or pushing the marble shooter closer to the target
FONDONGO (slang) buttocks, ass (vulg.)
FONE (Eng.) adj. mf. funny, amusing
FONES or FONIS (Eng.) mpl. comic strips, funnies (coll.)
FONO (var. of) teléfono
FORCITO (Eng.) old battered-up car (cf. FODONGO)
FOREHUÉS(T) or FOROHUÉS(T) (Hispanization of) Fort Worth, Texas
FOREHUOR (Hispanization of) Fort Worth, Texas
FORIHUÁN or FORITÚ (slang) (Eng.) m. male homosexual (cf. CUARENTAIDÓS/CUARENTAIUNO)
FORJE (slang) m. female figure, woman's body
FORMAL m. (Ang?) formal (dance, gathering, etc.); TRAJE FORMAL m. formal evening wear
FORNITURA (Eng.) (infreq.) furniture
FORTIGO or FORTINGO (Eng.) old battered-up car (cf. FODONGO)
FORRO (slang) good-looking person; mpl. (said of two people who resemble each other): "Son forros" 'They're look-alikes'
FRAGO (slang) cigar
FRAILECILLO or FRAILECÍO blister bug, blister beetle (meloidae)
FRAJEAR or FRAJIAR (slang) va. to smoke
FRAJO (slang) cigarette; FRAJO DE SEDA (slang) marihuana cigarette
FRANQUE (Eng.) (dim. of) Frank or Francisco
FRANQUE (Eng.) adj. frank, honest
FREGADA -DO penniless, down and out, destitute; (almost always adj.) (said of a woman who looks prematurely old as the result of excessive sexual activity); tricky, roguish, damned (fig.): ESTAR COMO LA FREGADA to be as ____ as can be (e.g., 'to be as ugly as sin', 'as mean as a junkyard dog', etc.--ref. usually to any negative quality known both to speaker and listener); HUERCO FREGADO damned little brat; m. shady dealer, sneaky person; f. hard time, difficult time; IRSE A LA FREGADA (usually a command:) ¡Vete a la fregada!" 'Go to hell!', 'Get the hell out of here!'; LLEVÁRSELO A ALGUIEN A LA FREGADA to die; to fall onto hard times, be ruined (often financially): "Se lo llevó a la fregada porque no hizo lo que debía"; NO IMPORTARLE A ALGUIEN UNA FREGADA not to give a damn (about something): "A mí no me importa una fregada" 'I don't give a damn about it'
FREGADAL m. much, many, large quantity (of something): "Tiene un fregadal de huercos" 'He has a huge bunch of kids' (fig., i.e., a large family)
FREGADAZO blow with the fist or any other object
FREGADERA action of washing dishes; harassment, annoyances; nagging; "thingamagig" (coll., said when one fails to remember the name of a particular object); junk, trash
FREGADITO -TA adj. m. deceitful (usually prefaced by medio: MEDIO FREGADITO); adj., mf. ruthless opportunist
FREGADIZA severe beating; hard time, difficult time
FREGADOR -DORA mf. deceiver, cheater; freeloader; opportunist
FREGAR va. to cheat; to take advantage of; vn. to bear the brunt of, be forced to take the lion's share (of a job), have a real work out with; DE A TIRO LA FRIEGAS (FRIEGA/FRIEGAN etc.) (used to reprimand for abusive behavior) 'You're really something else' 'You're a real lulu' 'You're really just too much' (all used ironically and with critical intent); FREGAR LA BORREGA to bother, pester, annoy;

PARA ACABARLA DE FREGAR to make matters worse, on top of all that (fig.); YA NI LA FRIEGAS (FRIEGA, FRIEGAN, etc.) (set expression used to censure abusive behavior)
FREGAZO blow with the fist or any other object
FREGÓN -GONA complainer, chronic bitcher (slang); bothersome, annoying; fraud, cheat, ruthless opportunist; (coll.) the boss, the big cheese
FREGUIZA (see DAR UNA FREGUIZA, LLEVAR UNA FREGUIZA)
FREIMIAR (Eng.) va. to frame (coll.) conspire to have convicted
FREJOLES (var. of) frijoles
FRENTAZO bumping together of two foreheads
FRENTE: EN FRENTE DE LA GENTE (Eng?) in public: "Lo regañaron en frente de la gente"
FRENTUDO -DA big-browed; broad-faced
FRESCO male homosexual
FRIADOR -DORA m.,f. refrigerator
FRIAR (var. of) freír 'to fry' (va. & vn.) (friar is conjugated like criar)
FRIFOL (var. of) frijol
FRIFOLERO -RA (var. of) frijolero -ra
FRIJOLERO -RA fond of eating beans
FRÍO: FRÍO -A (slang) dead; FRIO DE LA MATRIZ "cold womb", frigidity, lack of (feminine) sexual desire; female sterility; (TIEMPO DE) FRÍO winter, winter time (the cold season)
FRISA (Eng.) freezer (type of refrigerator)
FRISCAR (Eng.) va. to frisk, search a person for hidden objects
FRÍSER (Eng.) m. & f. freezer (type of refrigerator) (cf. FRISA)
FRIYAR (var. of) friar
FRUNCIR: FRUNCÍRSELE A ALGUIEN (EL CULO) (slang, vulg.) to be afraid
FRUTA (slang) m. male homosexual
FUCHE or FUCHEFUCHE or FUCHI or FUCHIFUCHI interjs. Phew! (used to express disgust, repulsion, etc.); TENER FUCHIFUCHI to be afraid
FUEGO (var. of) juego 'game'
FUEREÑO -ÑA stranger, someone not from the particular locality, outsider
FUERTE m. influential person, someone with "pull"; male to whom all women are attracted; lucky person, someone who "has it made"; boss, strong man (fig.); HACERSE FUERTE to show great strength (often under emotional strain); to rise to the occasion
FUERTÍSIMO -MA (var. of) fortísimo -ma
FUERZA: A FUERZA QUE SÍ most likely, in all likelihood, more likely than not: "¿Tendrán frío los gatos?--A fuerza que sí" 'Are the cats cold?--More likely than not.'; A TODA FUERZA in full swing: "El baile esta a a toda fuerza" 'The dance was in full swing'; HACER FUERZA to faze, affect: "Se murío su mamá y ni fuerza le hace" 'His mother died and it doesn't affect him in the least'
FULEAR or FULIAR (Eng.) va. to fool, deceive
FULTAIM (Eng.) adv. full-time (Std. horario completo, tiempo completo)
FUMADA act of smoking a cigar or cigarette
FUNDILLO or FUNDÍO (slang, vulg.) piece of ass (vulg.): "Tiene allí su fundillo cuando lo quiere" 'He's got a piece of ass [opportunity for sexual relations] right there whenever he wants it'
FUNDILLON (m.) -LLONA (f.) or FUNDILLOTE (m.)-TA (f.) big- bottomed (coll.) (said of person with a large buttocks)
FUNDILLUDO -DA adj. and mf. (ref. to person with a sexually-appetizing rear end)
FUNTA (var. of) junta
FURRIAS mfpl. (pej.) (said of persons) base, mean, despicable; clumsy; lusterless, dull, uninteresting; sloppy, careless; (said of things) shoddily-made
FUTBOLERO (Eng.) football player

G

GABA (abbrev., var. of) gabacho -cha
GABACHERO -RA (pej.) gringoized, gringo-like; (pej.) gringo-lover, (person) obsequious to gringos
GABACHO -CHA (pej.) Anglo-Saxon, gringo
GABARDINO -NA (pej.) (var. of) gabacho -cha

GABINETE: GABINETE (DE COCINA) kitchen cabinet
GABO -BA (pej.) (var. of) gabacho -cha
GACHO (usually pej.) crude; mean, base; bad; ugly; ridiculous; ¡QUÉ GACHO! How humiliating!, How disgusting!, TORCER MUY GACHO to die a horrible death
GAI (Eng.) (slang) m. guy, fellow
GAITA trick
GALLAZO (slang), shot, puff or "fix" of a narcotic drug
GALLETA cookie; GALLETA DE SODA saltine cracker
GALLINA: GALLINA PORPUJADA (type of child's game)
GALLO (slang) guy, fellow; hero; he-man, stud (coll.); street serenade; (slang) blood issuing from a wound received in a fight; mpl. articles of hand-me-down or second-hand clothing; DORMÍRSELE EL GALLO A ALGUIEN to fail in the sex act, lose one's erection (said of a man); SACAR GALLO to show off a new possession (esp. an article of clothing)
GALLÓN -LLONA brave; terrific, tremendous; m. he-man, stud (coll.)
GAJO cotton
GALGO -GA thin; sickly-looking
GANAR vn. to go toward, head toward: "Ganó para el río" 'He headed off toward the river'
GANAS: GANAS TIENES You'd like that, wouldn't you: "La maistra te va a flonquiar. --Ganas tienes."
GANCHAR va. to hook onto (an object); to force commitment; to hook, trap (as into marriage); vr. to become engaged to be married; to get married
GANCHO (clothes) hanger
GANDAYA uneaten food that is thrown away after a meal
GANGA (Eng.) gang, group of delinquent youths; circle of friends
GANGOSO -SA hair-lipped
GÁNGSTER (Eng.) m. gangster, hoodlum
GARABATOS mpl. poor or unintelligible handwriting, scribblings
GARACHE (Eng.) m. garage
GARAJE m. filling station, gasoline station
GARCÍA: ACÁ GARCÍA (hum.) toilet: "Voy acá García" 'I'm going to the toilet' (play on words: a cagar + [Gar] -cía)
GARGANTA: DOÑA GARGANTA agressive, influential, powerful woman; shrew
GARITA customs house (on a border between two countries)
GARNUCHO fillip (flip) with one's fingers against someone's head
GARRA fsg. old cheap clothes; ESTIRAR GARRA or SACAR LA GARRA (slang) to gossip; to run someone down (slang), speak ill of someone; ESTAR MALA DE LA GARRA / TENER or TRAER LA GARRA to be having one's menstrual period (ref. to women); TIRAR GARRA to dress up, dress elegantly
GARRANCHAR va. to slash, gash
GAR(R)AR (vars. of) agarrar
GARRASPERA (var. of) carraspera
GARRERO vendor of second-hand clothing; dealer in second-hand clothing; piles of rags
GARRIENTO -TA ragged
GARROTE (slang) m. large male organ, big penis; (see also LIMOSNERO Y CON GARROTE)
GARROTEAR or GARROTIAR va. to rout, defeat decisively in a sports match (usually in baseball); to batter, beat up; to collect many hits off a pitcher (in baseball)
GARROTERO batter (baseball); slugger, batter successful in hitting
GARROTIZA severe beating (usually administered with a club); shellacking, decisive defeat in a game (usually baseball)
GARRUÑO scratch
GAS: ACABÁRSELE A ALGUIEN EL GAS (Ang?, fig.?) to run out of gas, lose one's stamina; (see also DARLE AL GAS); PEDAL DE GAS accelerator
GASELÍN m. (var. of) gasolina
GASELINA (var. of) gasolina
GASOFA (slang) gasoline; GASOFA DE LA BUENA (slang) premium gasoline
GASOLÍN (Eng.) m. gasoline
GATA maid, female servant
GATO (slang) fraidy-cat, fearful person; CORBATA DE GATO (slang) bow tie
GENTE: HASTA DÓNDE LLEGA LA GENTE (set expression) My, what some people are capable of!
GENTECITA rabble, bunch of lower-class persons
GENTIAZO or GENTILLAZO multitude of people
GIOMETRÍA (var. of) geometría
GLADIOLA (Eng.) (Std. gladíolo)
GLOBO (slang) (type of barbituate pill swallowed for narcotic effect)
GLU or GLUFA (Eng.) f.: HACER(SE)

A LA GLU(FA) to sniff glue (for the mildly narcotic effect it produces)
GLUFO -FA high from sniffing glue (cf. GLU); mf. glue-sniffer
GODORNIZ (var. of) codorniz f.
GOGOTE (var. of) cogote m.
GOLAR (var. of) volar
GOLEAR or GOLIAR (Eng.) vn. to make a goal (in an athletic contest, e.g. in soccer)
GOLFO (Eng.) golf (game of golf)
GOLPANAZO severe, heavy blow
GOLPE: DARLE EL GOLPE AL CIGARRO / DARLE EL GOLPE AL CIGARRILLO to inhale a cigarette or cigar
GOLPIAR (var. of) golpear
GOLPIZA series of blows; severe beating
GOMA paste (sticking paste)
GOMITADERA (var. of) vomitadera
GOMITAR (var. of) vomitar
GÓMITO (var. of) vómito
GORDO -DA f. & adj. (coll.) pregnant; SALIR GORDA to get pregnant; f. thick corn tortilla; CAER GORDO to be repugnant, repellent: "Ese tipo me cae gordo"
GORILA or GORRILA f. (cf. Std. mf.)
GORILÓN -LONA or GORRILÓN -LONA large and ponderous person
GORUPERO place infested with gorupos (chicken fleas)
GORUPIENTO -TA infested with gorupos (chicken fleas)
GORUPO chicken flea
GORRA (slang) heroin capsule
GOTA (slang) gasoline; (see also SUDAR)
GOTEADOR or GOTIADOR m. eye-dropper, medicine dropper
GOYO -YA (dims. for, resp.) Gregorio -ria
GRÁBOL (Eng.) m. gravel
GRACIAS: PARA ESAS GRACIAS if that's the way it's going to be, if that's how it is: "Mañana vamos a tu casa a celebrar la fiesta. --Muy bien, traigan su guajolote. --Újule, para esas gracias mejor nos lo comemos en casa."
GRACIA(S): ¡QUÉ GRACIA(S)! Thanks a lot! (iron.) Thanks for nothing
GRADACIÓN (var. of) graduación f.
GRADAR (var. of) graduar
GRADO (Ang.) grade, mark in a school subject; HACER GRADOS to receive grades, make a certain grade: (Ang.) "Hice puras 'A's el semestre pasado" 'I made straight A's last semester'; year or level in school: "Pedro está en el segundo grado"
GRAJEA sleet
GRAJEAR vn. to sleet
GRAMO (slang) packet of heroin
GRAMPA (var. of) grapa
GRANDE advanced in years, old; MÁS GRANDE older (Std. mayor); (slang) m. a thousand dollars (Ang? 'one grand'); CASA GRANDE (slang) the big house (slang), penitentiary
GRANDOTOTE or GRANDOTOTOTE adj. mf. extremely large, immense, gargantuan
GRANIENTO -TA full of sores
GRANIZAZO major hail storm
GRANJEAR or GRANJIAR to fawn, flatter, do favors so as to ingratiate oneself or receive favors in return
GRANO sore, open skin lesion; ulcer; wound
GRASA shoe paste; DAR GRASA to apply shoe paste (in order to shine shoes)
GREÑERO -RA disheveled and unkempt hair: "Trae un greñero de la mierda" (vulg.) 'He's got a messy head of hair'
GREVE or GREIVE or GREIVI (Eng.) m. gravy
GRIFA (slang) marihuana
GRIFO -FA marihuana user; adj. mf. kinky (ref. to hair)
GRIPA (var. of) gripe
GRITADERA or GRITADERO (vars. of) gritería
GROCERÍA (Eng.) grocery store
GROCERÍAS (Eng.) fpl. groceries, food, provisions
GRULLA cold air; police, police force; adj. ugly: "¡Tu madre! --¡La tuya, que está más grulla!" (exchange of insults among children)
GUACHA (Eng.) wrist watch; washer (used in plumbing)
GUACHAR (Eng.) va. to watch
GUACHATERIA (Eng.) washateria, laundromat
GUACHE (var. of) guacha (Eng.) f.
GUACHIMÁN (Eng.) m. watchman, guard
GUAFLERA (Eng.) waffle maker, machine for making waffles
GUÁFOL (Eng.) m. waffle
GUAIFA (Eng.) (slang, hum.) wife
GUAIN (Eng.) (slang) m. wine
GUAINERO -RA (Eng., cf. GUAIN) habitual drinker of wine; heavy drinker (of any alcoholic beverage)
GUÁIPER (Eng.) m. windshield wiper
GUAJOLOTE mf. (fig.) fool, idiot
GUAMAZO hard blow (with the fist or

other object) (see also GÜEMAZO, HUAMAZO, HUEMAZO)
GUANGO -GA loose-fitting; flabby; VENIRLE A ALGUIEN GUANGO -GA to compare unfavorably (often in the physical sense): "Ese tipo me viene guango" 'That guy is a pushover for me' (i.e., it will be easy for me to defeat him in physical combat)
GUANTADA blow or slap
GUAPO -PA industrious; intelligent; talented
GUAREAR or GUARIAR (slang) va. to say hello to; to plan to meet
GUATO festivity; commotion
GUATOSO -SA noisy
GUAYÍN (Eng.) m. wagon drawn by horses
GÜELAR (var. of) volar
GÜELDEAR or GÜELDIAR (vars. of) hueldear or hueldiar
GÜELITO -TA (var. of) abuelito -ta
GÜELO, GÜELES, etc. (vars. of) huelo, hueles, etc. (pres. ind. conjugation of oler)
GÜELTA (var. of) vuelta
GÜELVA, GÜELVAS, etc. (var. of) huela, huelas, etc. (pres. subj. of oler)
GÜELVO, GÜELVES, etc. (vars. of) vuelvo, vuelves, etc. (pres. ind. of volver)
GÜEMAZO hard blow, slap (cf. GUAMAZO)
GÜENO -NA (var. of) bueno -na
GUENGSTA (Eng.) m. (cf. GÁNGSTER)
GÜERCO -CA (var. of) huerco -ca
GÜERGÜENZA (var. of) vergüenza
GÜERINCHE or GÜERINCHI (pej.) blond, fair-complexioned (cf. GÜERO)
GÜERO -RA blond, fair-complexioned; mf. Anglo-Saxon
GÜERTA (var. of) huerta
GUERRA (see DAR GUERRA)
GÜESO (var. of) hueso
GÜETE (var. of) cuete m. 'gun'
GÜETEAR or GÜETIAR va. to shoot
GÜEY (var. of) buey mf.
GUÍA steering wheel (automobile)
GÜICHOL (var. of) huichol m.
GÜILA (var. of) huila
GÜILE (Eng.) (dim. of) William
GÜÍNCHIL (Eng.) m. windshield (automobile)
GUINDO dark red color
GÜINE (Eng.) m. wienie, wiener sausage; COMER GÜINES (slang, tag question equivalent to Eng. "...or something?") "¿Estás loco o comiste güines?" 'Are you crazy or something?'; (vulg.) m. penis, male member (euph.)
GUISAR va. to fry
GÜIZA (var. of) huiza
GUSGO -GA (slang) glutton, chow hound (coll.) (cf. BUSGO -GA)
GUSJEAR or GUSJIAR (slang) va. to eat, "chow down" (slang)

H

HA, HAMOS (vars. resp. of) he, hemos (1st pers. sg. and pl. of pres. ind. haber)
HABER: HAY: "Y ¿qué hay con eso?" 'So?', 'So what?', 'What about it?'
HABLADA f. offensive word; innuendo, insinuation; fpl. ECHAR HABLADAS to make sarcastic remarks; to offend
HABLADERÍA (var. of) habladuría
HABLADERO -RA m. chatter, excessive talk; mf., adj. boastful, bragging
HABLADOR -DORA m., f. liar; gossiper
HABLANTINO mf. (var. of) hablantín
HABLAR va. to call, telephone: "Te hablan por teléfono" 'Someone's calling you on the phone'; vn. to gossip; to speak ill of someone; HABLARLE A UNA MUJER to ask a woman to go steady; to tell a woman how one feels about her (romantically); HABLAR NOMÁS POR NO DEJAR to talk just to be talking (for no particular reason); HABLAR PA' TRAS (Ang.) to talk back to, answer in a sassy manner: "No le hables pa' tras a tu papá" 'Don't talk back to your dad'; HABLAR RECIO to speak loudly
HACER va. to figure, imagine, assume: "Yo te hacía en el centro" 'I figured you were downtown'; HACER AGUA (Std. hacer aguas menores) to urinate; HACER A ALGUIEN VER SU FORTUNA to give someone a hard time; HACER A LA LEY to win over (to a particular way of thinking): "Tú no le puedes decir nada. Él ya la hizo a su ley." 'You can't tell her anything. He already won her over.'; HACER A(L) TROCHEMOCHE to do a half-assed job (slang), do

poorly, do with a lick and a promise (coll.); HACER APRECIO to pay attention; HACER ATOLE (see ATOLE); HACER BARRANQUEÑA to assemble and carry along a large quantity of items HACER BOLA to fluster, confuse; HACER BORUCA to fluster, confuse; HACER BUENO (Ang.) to replace, "make good" (ref. to replacement of belongings lost or destroyed); HACER CARGOS to place charges against; HACER CAQUIS/HACER CAQUIS MAQUIS (euph.) to go potty (euph.), do number two (euph.), defecate (said of infants or small children); HACER COMO AGUA to do effortlessly; HACER CHICHARRÓN to burn to a crisp; HACER CHILLAR to cause to cry; to anger; HACER ENTENDER to get through after repeated efforts (coll.), succeed in getting (someone) to listen to reason; HACER GARRAS to tear to shreds; HACER JALE (slang) to steal; to cheat; to work; to make advances to a member of the opposite sex; HACER JALÓN (slang) to make advances to a member of the opposite sex; HACER JAMBERGA/JAMBORGA/JAMBÓRGUER DE (slang) to make mince-meat of (coll.), beat up soundly (in a fight); HACER LA BARBA to flatter; HACER LA LUCHA to try to convince, try to get someone to change his/her mind; HACER LA PALA to accompany; HACER LA PARADA to humor, go along with, tolerate, put up with; HACER LOS TAMALES DE CHIVO to cheat on one's spouse, commit adultery; HACER MAJE to fool, deceive; HACER OJO to cast a spell upon, cast the evil eye upon; HACER PEDO (slang) to make trouble; to harass; to make advances to a member of the opposite sex; to make a scene, an uproar: "Jorge estaba haciendo pedo en la cantina"; HACER PICADILLO to grind; to squash; HACER PLACER to be courteous and attentive; to humor, go along with: "Mejor es que le hagas placer al jefe para que no te desocupe"; HACER POR (var. of) hacer el esfuerzo por; HACER TOPILLO (slang) to make a fool of; HACER UNA (MALA) PARADA to do someone a bad turn, play a dirty trick on; vn. HACER A LA GLU(FA) to sniff glue (for mildly narcotic effect); HACER BIEN (Ang.) to do will, earn money in copious amounts; to be wise, act prudently: "Haces bien en no decírselo"; HACER BORLOTE (slang) to make trouble; to make noise; make a scene (slang), cause an uproar; to make advances to a member of the opposite sex; HACER BUCHES(DE SAL) to fill one's mouth with warm salt water so as to kill germs and lessen the pain of a toothache; HACER (LA) CACA (vulg.) to defecate (Std. cagar); HACER CARRITO to harp on the same subject, talk incessantly about the same topic; HACER CHAPUZA A ALGUIEN to cheat someone; HACER COMO QUE to pretend, act as if, feign: "Haz como que te pegué muy recio" 'Act as if I struck you real hard'; HACER CORAJE(S) to throw fits of anger, throw a tantrum; HACER COSITAS (euph.) to have sexual relations; HACER CUACHA (vulg., slang) to make mincemeat of (fig.), beat up soundly (in a fight); HACER DE LAS SUYAS to blunder as usual; to misbehave as always; HACER DESATINAR A ALGUIEN to make someone lose his cool (slang), cause someone to become very angry and quite disoriented; HACER DINERO (Ang.) to make money, get rich; HACER DINERO A MANOS LLENAS to make money hand over fist (fig.), make large quantities of money, get very rich quick; HACER EL CÁLIZ to try, make an effort: "No sabe si puede ganar, pero quiere hacer el cáliz"; HACER EL CUERPO to defecate; HACER FUERZA to faze, affect: "Se murió su mamá y ni fuerza le hace." 'His mother died and it doesn't affect him in the least'; HACER GASTOS to spend money (usually unexpectedly and at times unnecessarily); HACER GENTE A ALGUIEN to treat an undeserving person decently; HACER GRADOS (Ang.) to receive grades, make a certain grade (Std. sacar notas): "Esteban está haciendo muy malos grados"; HACER HAMBRE to work up an appetite; HACER LA CRUZ to make one's first sale of the day (ref. to storekeepers); HACER LA CHI(S) (euph.) to urinate, make "wee-wee" (euph., also baby talk); HACER LA PERRA (slang) to loaf, while away the time; HACER MAL MODO to slight, be rude to; HACER PANTOMINAS to create a scene, make trouble, make a spectacle of oneself: "No te contentaste hasta que hiciste tus pantominas" 'You just weren't happy until you could make an idiot of yourself in public'; HACER PAPELES id. to HACER PANTOMINAS supra; HACER PEDO (vulg.) to make a fuss, raise a stink, create trouble; HACER PENDEJO -JA A ALGUIEN to cheat on someone, deceive (e.g., one's spouse, fiancé(e) etc.); HACER PININOS (for a baby to make amusing and endearing little gestures); (for a baby to begin to take his/her first steps); HACER (LA) PIPI / HACER (LA) PIPI (slightly euph.) to urinate, "make water" (euph.) (esp. said of and to children) HACER POR to try to; HACER RONCHA to run up one's winnings in a game of chance after starting out with a very small amount of money; HACER SUERTES to do magical tricks; HACER TIEMPO (Ang.) to do time in jail, comply with one's jail term; (Ang.) to "make time" with the object of one's affections, engage in a display of affection toward; HACER TRACALADA to make much noise, raise a ruckus; HACER TRAMPA to resort to crooked tactics (e.g., in a business deal); HACER TROMPAS to put on a sad or annoyed facial expression; HACER VACA to run up one's winnings in a game of chance after starting out with a very small amount of money; vr. HACERLA DE to play the role of: "Luis Aguilar la hace de trampe" 'Luis Aguilar plays the role of the villain'; HACERLE PEDO A ALGUIEN (vulg.) to make a play for someone (with amorous intentions); HACERLE PLÁTICA A ALGUIEN to strike up a conversation with someone; HACERSE BOCA CERRADA to pretend to be quiet and reserved; HACERSE BOCA CHIQUITA to pretend to be a small eater; HACERSE CACHETÓN -TONA to ignore an assignment; to conveniently forget a debt or a commitment (see also HACERSE CHATO); HACERSE CIRCO to make a fool of oneself; HACERSE CHATO-TA to ignore an assignment; to conveniently forget a debt or commitment; HACERSE CHINCHE to act stingy, miserly; to overstay one's welcome; HACERSE DE: ¿QUÉ SE HIZO DE ___? (fixed expression) 'Whatever became of _____?' HACERSE DEL ROGAR (var. of hacerse de rogar 'to want to be coaxed'); HACERSE FUERTE to arm oneself with fortitude and patience to face difficult times, be strong enough to ward off difficult situations; HACERSE GACHO to be unpleasant; HACERSE GRANDE to act big, act superior, give oneself airs; HACERSE LA CASQUETA to masturbate; HACERSE LA GRAN CACA (vulg. and offensive) to act like a big shit (vulg.), put on airs; HACERSE LA GRAN COSA to put on airs, act presumptuously; HACERSE LA PUÑETA (vulg., slang) to do a hand job (coll.), masturbate; HACERSE MOSQUITA MUERTA to give the (false) impression that one is reticent, quiet and reserved; HACERSE PATO to retract (a statement), renege, back down; HACERSE PA'TRAS (Ang.) to back out, renege; to take back, apologize for; HACERSE PESADO EL BULTO (fig., coll.) (for one's responsibilities to become burdensome); HACÉRSELA (vulg., slang) to pull on it (coll.), masturbate; HACÉRSELE DOLOR A ALGUIEN HACER ALGO for it to hurt (fig.) someone to do something (ref. to ungenerous attitude): "Se te hizo dolor darme un pedacito de manzana" 'It hurt you to give me a little piece of the apple'; HACÉRSELE EL CUERPO CHINITO to get goosepimples (goosebumps); misc. (fixed expressions); HACERLA (Ang?) to make it, arrive (fig.), be successful: "El bato ese ya la hizo" 'That guy has got it made'; NO LE HACE 'It doesn't matter'; NO LE HAGAS leave well enough alone; ¿QUÉ LE HACE? 'What does it matter?' 'So what?'; QUE MANDADO HACER (set expression used to indicate any quality in excess): "Está más loco que mandado hacer" 'He's crazier than a hoot owl'; ¡QUÉ SUAVE (LE HACES/HACE/ HACEN)! Nice going! (iron.), That's a fine howdy do!; TENERLA HECHA (Ang?) to have it made (to have achieved a level of accomplishment sufficient to insure future success)

HACHA: ¡HIJO DEL HACHA! interj. (mildly euph. though considered lower-class)

HAIGA (var. of) haya (3rd pers. subj. of haber); ¡BIEN HAIGA! 'Good for you!' (expression of approbation); YA TE LO HAIGA/ YA SE LO HAIGA/ YA SE LOS HAIGA (set expression of admonition, warning, etc.): "¿Estudiaron?--No.-- Ya se los haiga."

HALLAR: HALLARSE EN LA CALLE to be broke, penniless; NO HALLARSE to be ill at ease, uncomfortable, not to feel at home (fig.): "Estoy impuesto a la ciudad; no me hallo en los pueblos chiquitos"

HAMBORGUESA (var. of) hamburguesa (Eng.)

HAMBRE: MUERTO -TA DE HAMBRE (fig. and ironic: said with ref. to a greedy, selfish person)

HAMBRIADO -DA famished, very hungry

HARINA: SER HARINA DEL MISMO COSTAL to share the same characteristics, be cut from the same cloth (fig.)

HOMBRE: EL HOMBRE DE LA HORA (Ang.) the man of the hour (coll.), the person currently held in highest regard

HAMBREADO -DA or HAMBRIADO -DA hungry; starving

HAMBRIENTO -TA stingy, mean

HARTADA act and effect of over-eating: "Se murió de la gran hartada que se dio"

HARTO -TA glutton

HARTÓN -TONA glutton

HASTA: HASTA PA' VENTAR PA' RIBA (=hasta para aventar para arriba) with much to spare, with many to spare, in excess; HASTA QUE NO until (the no is superfluous): "No nos vamos a ir hasta que no lo hagas" 'We won't go until you do it'; HASTA QUE SE LE/TE/NOS/LES HIZO or HASTA QUE SE LE (etc.) CUMPLIÓ He/she (etc.) finally got what he/she had wanted (=finally realized his/her goals)

HECHO -CHA: HECHO -CHA BOLA very flustered, very confused; HECHO -CHA MADRE / HECHO -CHA MÁQUINA adv. quite rapidly; TENERLA HECHA (Ang.) to have it made (coll.), be very successful: "Ya la tienes hecha"

HELADA beer (in cans or bottles)

HELADO popsicle

HERVIENDO (var. of) hirviendo (ger. of hervir)

HESPITAL m. (var. of) hospital

HESTÉRICO -CA (var. of) histérico -ca

HESTORIA (var. of) historia

HIELERA refrigerator; ice-box (ant.)

HIELERÍA ice plant (place where ice is made and sold), ice house (id.)

HIELERO ice man (vendor and deliverer of ice) (ant.)

HIERBA (slang) marihuana; (slang) mf. & adj. mean, base, low; HIERBA ANÍS (var. of) anís; HIERBA COLORADA dock herb (Rumex crispus) (prepared as a solution and gargled to treat tonsilitis); HIERBA DEL BURRO burro bush herb (Hymenoclea sp.) (prepared as a solution and applied to arthritic areas and infected cuts); HIERBA DEL INDIO desert milkweed (Asclepias sp.) (prepared as a tea and used to treat kidney ailments); HIERBA DEL MANZO swamp root (Anemopsis californica) (prepared as a tea and used to treat stomach ache); HIERBA DEL PASMO spasm herb (Haplopappus larincofolius) (prepared as a tea and either drunk or inhaled in the treatment of pasmo); HIERBA MALA (var. of) mala hierba; Y DEMÁS HIERBAS (fixed expression) and so on and so forth (=Std. y así sucesivamente)

HIERBAJAL or HIERBAJAR or HIERBAZAL (vars. of) herbazal m.

HIERBERO grassland (=herbazal); herbalist

HIJO: ¡HIJO! interj. (varies in meaning according to intensity and type of articulation: from mild--Damn!--through strong--Son of a bitch!--esp. when followed by a prep. phrase e.g.:) ¡HIJO DE CABRÓN!, ¡HIJO DE LA CHINGADA! (This last is esp. strong: 'Mother-XXXXXX' bastard!', etc.); HIJO DEL HACHA (see HACHA); HIJO DE POLICÍA person to whom no attention has been paid or who has not re-

ceived any share of something: "¿Acaso soy hijo de policía?" (ref. to traditional popular antipathy towards the police); HIJO DE LA GUAYABA (see GUAYABA); ¡HÍJOLE! (see also ¡JÍJOLE!) interjs. (vary in meaning according to intensity and situation, from a mild 'Damn!' through something much stronger)
HINCHAR: HINCHÁRSELE A ALGUIEN (slang) to do what one damn well pleases: "¿Cuándo te vas a ir? -- Cuando se me hinche"
HINDIDURA (var. of) hendedura
HIPROCRESÍA (var. of) hipocresía
HITO -TA (var. of) hijito -ta
HOCICÓN -CONA loud-mouthed; foul-mouthed
HOGADO -DA (var. of) ahogado -da
HOGAR (var. of) ahogar va.
HOJARASCA type of sweetroll
HOJELATA (var. of) hojalata
HOMBRAZO he-man, stud (slang)
HOMBRE (can also be used as vocative when addressing a woman:) "No hombre, ni siquiera sabía que estabas enferma"
HOMBRERA woman strongly attracted to men
HOMBRO: METER HOMBRO (slang) to lend a helping hand, put one's shoulder to the wheel (fig., coll.)
HOQUIS (orthog. var. of) oquis
HORA (var. of) ahora
HORA: A LA HORA DE LA HORA / A L'ORA DE L'ORA at the moment of truth, at the time of crisis, when all is said and done (coll.)
HORALE interj. Knock it off!; Move it!, Hurry up!, (etc.); That's it! (=You're right!); (with interrogative intonation:) How about it?, What do you say to that?, And ... ?
HORCADO -DA (var. of) ahorcado -da
HORCAR (var. of) ahorcar
HORITA or HORITITA or HORITITITA (etc.) (vars. of) ahorita (etc.)
HORONGO (vars. of) jorongo
HORQUETA slingshot
HORQUÍA or HORQUILLA clothes pin
HOTEL: HOTEL MUNICIPAL (hum.) county or city jail
HOY: HOY EN LA NOCHE tonight
HOYITO: HOYITO DEL CHI urinary opening (female)
HUACHA (var. of) guacha
HUACHAR (Eng.) va. to watch, observe, watch out; ¡HUÁCHALO! (slang) Watch out!, Be careful!
HUACHETERÍA (Eng.) washeteria, self-service automatic laundry
HUACHIMÁN (var. of) guachimán
HUAFLERA (var. of) guaflera
HUAINO -NA (var. of) guaino -na
HUAMAZO (Eng?) (var. of) guamazo et al.
HUANGO (var. of) guango
HUARACHAZO (slang) dance
HUARACHE (slang) mf. Mexican citizen
HUAREAR or HUARIAR (vars. of) guarear, guariar
HUATO (var. of) guato
HUATOSO -SA (var. of) guatoso -sa
HUAYÍN (Eng.) (var. of) guayín m.
HUAYO (dim. of) Eduardo (see also Yayo)
HUELDEAR or HUELDIAR (Eng.) va. to weld, solder
HUELVA, HUELVAS, etc. (vars. of) güelva, güelvas, etc. (in turn vars. of) vuelva, vuelvas, etc. (pres. subj. of volver)
HUEMAZO (var. of) güemazo (see also GUAMAZO et al.)
HUENO -NA (var. of) bueno -na
HUERCO -CA kid, brat, young child
HUERFANATO or HUERFANATORIO (vars. of) orfanato orphanage
HUERTE (var. of) fuerte
HUESO: HUESOS mpl. (slang) dice; HUESO SABROSO funny bone (coll.) (point near the elbow where the nerve may be pressed against the bone to produce a tingling sensation)
HUEVO: A HUEVO forcibly, by force; HUEVO HUERO (coll.) rotten egg; ¡HUEVOS! (interj.) Hell no! (strong negative); HUEVOS RANCHEROS Mexican-style scrambled eggs with peppers, onions, tomatoes, etc.; TENER HUEVOS (vulg.) to have balls (semi-vulg. & slang), possess considerable strength of character, intestinal fortitude
HUEVÓN -VONA (pej.) lazy, no account (coll.), good-for-nothing
HUEVONADA laziness
HUEVONEAR or HUEVONIAR (coll.) vn. to loaf, be idle
HUEY (var. of) buey m.
HUICHACA billiard pocket
HUICHOL m. wide-brimmed straw hat
HUIFA (Eng.) (slang) wife (see also GUAIFA)
HÚIGA, HÚIGAS, etc. (vars. of) huya, huyas, etc. (pres. subj. of huir)
¡HUIJE! interj. (expression used to make fun of someone or to

provoke to anger) (see also IJE, IJI)
HUILA or HUILACHA (slang, pej.) prostitute, whore; two-dimensional quadrangular kite
HUIMBLE (Hispanization of) Wimberly, Texas
HUINE (Eng.) (var. of) güine m.
HUIQUÉN (Eng.) m. week-end
HUIRIHUIRI (slang) gossip, idle talk
HUIRLOCHA (slang) jalopy, old car
HUISCLE m. (var. of) whiski (Eng.)
HUÍVORA (child language var. of) víbora
HUIZA (slang, pej.) whore, prostitute; (non-pej.) girlfriend; fiancée
HULE m. inner tube; floor linoleum; shoe sole; (slang) condom, rubber (slang); (slang) QUEMAR HULE to burn rubber (slang), accelerate a car rapidly from a standing position
HUMADERA (var. of) humareda
HUMADO -DA (var. of) ahumado -da
HÚNGARO -RA gypsy
HURGONEAR or HURGONIAR va. to shake violently
HUYAR (var. of) aullar vn.
HUYIR (var. of) huir vn.

I

ICIR (var. of) decir
IDEAR or IDIAR vn. to idle the time away by daydreaming about things beyond one's means to acquire or achieve
IDEOMA (var. of) idioma m. (f.)
IDEOSO -SA or IDIOSO -SA daydreamer (cf. IDEAR, IDIAR)
IDIOMA (often f.: LA IDIOMA)
IDIOSO -SA fancier, aficionado (of something)
IDO -DA or MEDIO -DA nuts (slang), crazy, cuckoo (slang)
IGLE (PAS) (coll., Hispanization of) Eagle Pass, Texas
IGNORAR (Ang.) va. to ignore, not to pay attention to (Std. no hacer caso)
IGUALADO -DA social-climber (ref. to person, often overbearing, who tries to achieve a superior social level)
IGUALAR vr. to social climb (coll.), try to achieve a superior social level
ILUMINIO (var. of) aluminio
INACIO -CIA (vars. of) Ignacio -cia
INCONVINIENTE (var. of) inconveniente
INFLUENCIA (var. of) influenza
INFRIAR (var. of) enfriar
INGLESADO -DA (non-pej.) Anglo-ized, Anglo-like
INSPECTAR (Ang.) to inspect (Std. inspeccionar)
INSTRUCTAR (Eng.) va. to instruct, teach
INSTRUCTEAR or INSTRUCTIAR (vars. of) instructar (Eng.)
IMPERIAL f. type of bleached cotton cloth
IMPIDIR (var. of) impedir
IMPLEMENTO (Ang.) tool, implement
IMPLIADO -DA (var. of) empleado -da
IMPONER va. to accustom, train, get (someone) used to: "No lo impusiste a trabajar, por eso es tan huevón"; vr. to get used to, accustomed to; to be dependent on (someone)
IMPRUVEAR or IMPRUVIAR (Eng.) va. & vn. to improve
IMPUESTO -TA accustomed, used to
INCENSO (Eng?) incense (Std. incienso)
INCOMTAX (Eng.) m. income tax
INCONTRAR (var. of) encontrar
INCORDIO (slang) chicken's egg
INDECCIÓN (var. of) inyección f.
INDIADA (pej.) disorderly mob; ill-bred persons belonging to the same clan, etc.
INDIGESTO -TA: SENTIRSE INDIGESTO -TA to feel bloated; to feel one has a stomach disorder
INDIVIDO -DA (var. of) individuo -dua
INFANTE mf. (poss. Ang.) infant, baby
INFECCIÓN: INFECCIÓN DE LA SANGRE (euph.) syphilis
INFILDA or INFILDER (Eng.) m. infielder (baseball)
INFLENCIA (var. of) influencia
INOCENTE adj. (euph.) (ref. to various degrees of mental retardation:) "Los niños inocentes no pueden asistir a la escuela con los demás niños"
INORANTE (var. of) ignorante
INORAR (var. of) ignorar
INSULTATIVO -VA (vars. of) insultador -dora
INSULTO digestive indisposition (upset stomach, etc.)
INTELIGIR vn. (for someone to be good at something:) "Le intelige a las matemáticas" 'He's very good at math'; INTELIGIR-

SE CON to be in charge of: "¿Quién se intelige con este negocito?" 'Who's in charge of this business?'
INTERO -RA (var. of) entero -ra
INTILIGENTE (var. of) inteligente
INTONADO -DA up on (coll.), tuned in (slang), abreast of the latest news and happenings
INTRODUCIR (Ang.) va. to introduce, present (two people previously unacquainted to each other) (Std. presentar)
IR: IR ACÁ GARCÍA (slang) to go to the toilet (see discussion s. GARCÍA); IR A DALLAS (slang) to have sexual intercourse, come across (slang), put out (slang) (play on words: DALLAS = DARLAS 'to give out with one's sexual favors, come across with'; commentary: the expression is pr. ir a dal las, the last two words representing a rough Hispanicization of the name of the Texas city, Dallas); IR A PATÍN / IR A PATINA (slang) to go on foot; IR CAYENDO POCO A POQUITO to come around bit by bit, yield (cease to resist) little by little; IR CHISQUEADO -DA or CHISQUIADO -DA to run at top speed, go like a bat out of hell (coll.); IR DE JILO (slang) to run rapidly, go like a bat out of hell (coll.); to go directly (without stopping) to one's destination; IR DE PERLA to have a good time; to have good luck: "Le dieron el primer premio. --¡Caray, le fue de perla!"; IR DIOQUIS (see DIOQUIS, DE HOQUIS); IR HECHO CHILE (slang) to run rapidly, go like a bat out of hell (coll.); IR HECHO MÁQUINA to be going very rapidly; IRLE A (coll.) to bet on: "¿Quién va a ganar?--Pues yo le voy al campeón" ' ...--Well I bet on the champ'; IR PA' TRAS (Ang.) to go back, fail to keep (i.e., one's word, a promise, etc.); vn. to return: "Se fue pa' tras pa' México"; IRSE A LAS GREÑAS to go at one another in a fight which involves pulling hair (usually said of two women); ÍRSELE A ALGUIEN EL SUEÑO to lose one's sleepiness, get over one's tiredness; ÍRSELE A ALGUIEN LA MANO to slip up, lose control; to miscalculate; ÍRSELE A ALGUIEN LA VOZ to hit a sour note while singing; IRSELE LA ONDA A ALGUIEN to go off on a tangent; ÍRSELE A ALGUIEN LAS PATAS (slang) to slip up, lose control of oneself, lose one's head; to throw caution to the wind (often used in a sexual context, e.g., "Mírala, está gorda, se le fueron las patas"); SI A ÉSAS VAMOS If that's the case, If that's how things stack up: "Si a ésas vamos, yo también puedo usar dos camisas por día" VÁMONOS A LA FREGADA Beat it!, Scram!; ¿VAMOS LLEGANDO ...? How's about stopping off ...?: "¿Vamos llegando a ca Pedro?" 'How's about stopping off at Pedro's house?'; Y VAMOS QUE even though: "Y no terminó su tesis el pendejo ese, y vamos que le dimos dos años" 'And that S.O.B. didn't finish his thesis, even though we gave him two years';
IRRIGAR (Eng.) va. to irrigate
ISTAFIATE (var. of) estafeate, estafiate
IXTLE m. fiber of the century plant (used to make lariats, etc.)
IZQUIERDISTA mf., adj. left-handed person (Std. izquierdo -da)

J

JABALÍN m. (ref. to person whose hair stands straight on end, as in a crewcut)
JABLA (var. of) jaula
JACALEAR or JACALIAR vn. to habitually go around visiting one home after another in order to bear tales and gossip
JACALERA woman who goes from house to house bearing tales and gossip; busy-body (coll.)
JAIBOL (m.; pl. JAIBOLES) or JAIBOLA (f.) (Eng.) highball (cocktail)
JAIBOLEADA or JAIBOLIADA (Eng.) cocktail party
JAIC (Eng.) m. hike, long walk in the countryside
JAIGUEY or JAIHUEY or JAÍHUEY (Eng.) m. highway
JAINIAR (slang) vn. to make love, engage in the sexual act; to

engage in sexual foreplay, make out (slang)
JAINO -NA (slang) m. boy friend; fiancé; f. girl friend; fiancée
JAIPO (Eng.) (slang) needle used to inject narcotic drugs into the veins of the human body; mf. or JAIPO (m.) -PA (f.) person who "mainlines" narcotic drugs into his/her veins
JAITÓN - TONA (Eng.) high-toned (coll.), snobbish; stylish; elegant
JALADO -DA (slang) drunk; f. pull, jerk (cf. JALAR)
JALADOR -DORA hard-working, diligent, industrious
JALAR va. (slang) to steal; vn. (coll.) to work; vr. JALARSELA (vulg., slang) to masturbate: "Lo pescaron jalándosela" 'They caught him pulling away at it!; ¡JÁLALE! interj. (slang) Hurry up!, Move it!
JALE (coll.) m. work, job; HACER JALE; (coll.) to work; (slang) to steal
JALEA (slang) adj. very elegant, dressed to kill (usually with ANDAR: "Anda muy jalea") (poss. Ang? < jelly bean, ant. slant=elegant, well dressed)
JALETINA (var. of) gelatina
JALÓ (Eng.) hello
JALÓN: ANDAR DE JALÓN (slang) to be on the make (slang), be out looking for a date or a sexual partner; DE UN JALÓN once and for all; all at once: "Se tomó todo el vino de un jalón" 'He drank the wine down in a single gulp'; HACER JALONES to flirt, make passes at a member of the opposite sex; HACERLE JALÓN A ALGUIEN to make passes at someone (with amorous intentions)
JALONEAR or JALONIAR va. to jerk; to pull
JALLAR (var. of) hallar
JAMBADO -DA (slang) stolen, ripped off (slang)
JAMBAR (slang) to steal
JAMBERGA (hum., m. & f.) or JAMBORGA (m. & f.) or JAMBÓRGUER (m.) (Eng.) hamburger; HACER JAMBERGA (et al.) DE (slang) to make mince-meat of (someone), beat up soundly (in a fight)
JAMBO -BA (slang) m.,f. thief; adj. thieving
JAMBÓN - BONA (slang) m., f. thief; adj. thieving
JAMÓN m. bacon; (slang) JAMON TORTILLA straight-forward and honest person
JANDO (slang) money
JAQUETA (Eng?, Ang?) jacket, coat
JARDÍN INFANTIL m. kindergarten
JARIA (slang) hunger
JARIPEO (type of rodeo)
JAROCHA or JARUCHA lively and alert (said of women)
JASPE (slang) m. meal (dinner, supper, etc.)
JASPEAR or JASPIAR (slang) va. to eat
JASPIA (slang) hunger
JATANA (slang) guitar
JAULA (slang) jail, cage (coll.)
JAULE (slang) m. burglary
JEDER (var. of) heder
JEDIONDEZ (var. of) hediondez f.
JEDIONDO -DA (var. of) hediondo -da
JEFA (slang) wife; mother
JEFE (slang) m. father
JETEAR or JETIAR vn. to pout
JEY FÍVER (Eng.) m. or f. hay fever
JI interj. (slightly euph.) (< jijo = hijo, q.v.)
JIEDO, JIEDES, JIEDE, JEDEMOS/JIÉDEMOS, JIEDEN (vars. of) hiedo, hiedes, etc. (pres. ind. of heder)
JIJO (var. of) hijo; interjs.: ¡JIJO! (varies in intensity according to degree of emphasis, type of intonation, etc.); ¡JIJO DEL HACHA! or ¡JIJO DE LA MAÑANA! or ¡JIJO DE LA GUAYABA! (all vary in intensity, though all tend to be fairly euphemistic--'Golly Moses!' is an average gloss for most); ¡JÍJOLE! interj. (varies in meaning according to intensity and situation, from a mild 'Damn!' through something much stronger)
JILO: ANDAR DE JILO to be in a hurry; IR DE JILO to pass by in a hurry; interj. ¡JILO! (rather euph.) Gosh!, Gee!; ¡JILO DE LA CHINGADA! (not quite as strong as the correspondent ¡Hijo de la chingada!); ¡JILO E LA MAÑANA! (var. of) ¡Jijo de la mañana!
JINCAR (var. of) hincar
JIORGE (var. of) Jorge
JIPO -PA (Eng.) hippopotamus; (n. & adj.) obese; m. "Hippo Size" (soft drink manufactured in San Antonio, Texas)
JIRA (Eng.) m. & f. heater, heating

device
JIRICUA pie baldness, vitiglio
JIRIMIQUEAR or JIRIMIQUIAR vn. to whimper
JIRIOLA: IR(SE) DE JIRIOLA (slang) vn. to cut classes, not to attend school
JIT (Eng.) m. hit, musical success, successful musical composition; base hit (baseball)
JITAZO (Eng.) (slang) tremendous hit, exremely popular musical composition
¡JITO! interj. (euph.) Golly!, Gosh!
JOCOQUE m. curdled milk; yogurt
JODARRIA (slang) harassment
JODEDERA (slang) harassment; nagging
JODER va. to deceive, cheat; to take sexual possession through deception; PARA ACABARLA DE JODER (set expression) To make matters worse, As if that were not enough
JODIDO -DA down and out, desitute; in poor health; (coll.) out of one's gourd (slang), crazy: "Pues ese tipo está jodido si cree que vamos a hacer todo esto en quince minutos"; ESTAR COMO LA JODIDA to be as _____ as can be (usual ref. to a negative characteristic of which both speaker and listener are cognizant, e.g.:) "Ella está como la jodida" 'She's as ugly as sin'
JODÓN -DONA ruthless, opportunistic; deceptive; EL MERO JODÓN (slang) the big boss, the head honcho (slang)
JOGAR (rus.) (var. of) jugar
JOL (Eng.) m. hall, corridor
JOLA (slang) money
JOLINO -NA short, not tall, not long
JOM (Eng.) m. home base (baseball)
JOMRÓN (Eng.) m. home run (baseball)
JONCHAR (Eng? < to hunch?) va. & vn. to cheat in a game of marbles by moving the marble shooter closer to the target
JONCHE: HACER JONCHE (id. to JONCHAR)
JONDO (local rendition of) Hondo, Texas
JONDO -DA (var. of) hondo -da
JONE or JONI (Eng.) (vocative, term of endearment) honey
JONQUI (Eng.) (pej.) mf. honky, hunky (both pej.), Anglo-Saxon
JONRÓN (Eng.) (var. of) jomrón m.
JOROBAS msg., fsg. (also adj.) (var. of) jorobado -da
JORONCHE (slang) mf. hunch-back
JOSCO -CA (var. of) hosco -ca; m. (fig.) bad boy
JOSLA (Eng? < hustler?) adj. keen; neat, terrific, swell, etc.
JOSLEAR or JOSLIAR (Eng? cf. JOSLA) va. & vr. to steal: "Se joslió dos dulces" 'He stole two bars of candy'
JOTINGO -GA (slang) m. faggot, male homosexual; f. lesbian
JOTITO (slang) young male homosexual
JOTO -TA (slang) m. fag, male homosexual; f., dike, lesbian
JOTQUEY (Eng.) m. hot cake (type of pancake)
JOVENTUD (var. of) juventud f.
JUAN (slang) m. cockroach (see also TALTASCUÁN et. al.)
JUANI (dim. of) Juan
JUANITA (slang) marihuana
JUAQUÍN (var. of) Joaquín
JUARILES (also orthog. var. JUARÍLEZ) (slang) Ciudad Juárez, México
JUDÁS: ESTAR UNO QUE SE LO LLEVA JUDÁS to be very angry, very hot under the collar (coll.); ME LLEVA JUDÁS (set expression) Well I'll be, Well I'll be darned
JUEGAR (rus.) (var. of) jugar
JUEGO (var. of) fuego
JUERTE (var. of) fuerte
JUEZ DE PAZ (Ang.) m. justice of the peace
JUGADA (ref. to a woman who has frequently indulged her carnal appetites, who has "played around" a lot
JUGARSE PLANCHA to be slow to react (because of lack of preparation, laziness, etc.)
JUGUETÓN -TONA (hum.) m. adulteror; f. adultress
JUI, JUI(S)TE(S), JUE, JUIMOS, JUERON (vars. of) fui, fuiste, etc. (pret. of ser/ir)
JUILA (Eng? <wheeler?) bicycle
JUISQUE (Eng.) m. whiskey
JUIZA (var. of) huiza
JULIA (slang, underw.) police wagon, paddy wagon (coll.); ambulance
JUM (Eng.) (var. of) jomrón m.
JUMADERA (var. of) humadera, humareda
JUMAR (var. of) fumar
JUMARADA (var. of) humarada
JUMEDAD (var. of) humedad f.
JUMO (var. of) humo
JUMRÓN (Eng.) (var. of) jomrón m.
JUNIOR (Eng.) m. and adj. junior (see also YÚNIER et al.)
JUNRÓN (Eng.) (var. of) jomrón m.
JUNTAR vr. to become reconciled

(usually ref. to lovers, husbands and wives, etc., who have separated)
JUNTO: ANDAR JUNTOS to go steady (coll.) (ref. to boy and girl who date each other exclusively); JUNTO DE (var. of) junto a: "Vive junto de su hermano"
JUQUEAR or JUQUIAR (Eng.) vn. to play hookey, absent oneself from school (see also JUQUI)
JUQUI (Eng.) m. hookey, unexcused absence from school; JUGAR JUQUI to play hookey, absent oneself from school without permission
JURA (slang) fsg. policeman; fpl. police force
JURGONEAR or JURGONIAR (vars. of) hurgonear, hurgoniar
JUSTICIA (slang) fsg. police force
JUT m. (Eng.) hood (aut.)

K

KANSES (Eng., var. of) Kansas
KARMESA (orthog, var. of) carmesa

L

LABERINTO scandal; noise; intrigue
LABERINTOSO -SA squeamish; exaggerating; mf. rabble rouser
LABIO: LABIO CUCHO harelip
LABIOSO -SA mf. flatterer; smooth talker (coll.)
LABOR f. cultivated field; field used for farming
LA: LA DE MALAS (coll.) bad luck: "Le tocó la de malas" 'He had some bad luck'
LADO: BUSCARLE A ALGUIEN POR SU LADO to approach someone from his good side (fig.), get someone in a good moment; EL MEJOR LADO (Eng.) someone's best side, most appealing personality traits; EL OTRO LADO (coll.) Mexico; (see also DARLE A ALGUIEN POR SU LADO; ESTAR DE LADO)
LADRERÍA barking of dogs
LAGARTIZO (var. of) lagartijo
LAGARTO -TA alligator
LAIRA (Eng.) f. lighter, cigarette lighter
LALO -LA (dims. of) Eulalio -lia
LAMBEACHE or LAMBIACHE (vulg.) ass-kisser (vulg.), flatter, obsequious person (mf.)
LAMBECULOS (var. of) lameculos mfsg.
LAMBEHUEVOS (vulg.) mfsg. apple-polisher, ass-kisser (vulg.)
LAMBER (var. of) lamer
LAMBICHE (var. of) lambeache, lambiache (mf.)
LAMBIDA (var. of) lamida
LAMBION -BIONA mf. flatterer, apple-polisher, ass-kisser (vulg.)
LAMBIZQUE mf. (coll.) freeloader, person who avoids paying
LAMBIZQUIAR (var. of) lambuzquiar
LAMBUZCO -CA hollow leg (coll.), person perpetually looking for something to eat; person perpetually eating
LAMBUZQUEAR or LAMBUZQUIAR va. to nibble at food in between mealtimes; to go around looking for food to eat in between mealtimes; vn. to be obsequiously and hypocritically courteous
LAMEACHE or LAMIACHE (vars. of) lambeache, lambiache (mf.)
LAMECULOS (vulg.) mfsg. flatterer, apple-polisher, ass-kisser (vulg.)
LAMER (vulg.) va. to kiss ass (vulg.), ingratiate oneself (with someone)
LAMPAREAR or LAMPARIAR (slang) va. to look at: "Está lampariando a las batas que pasan"
LAMPREADO -DA or LAMPRIADO -DA roasted; roasted with a beaten egg covering
LAMPREAR or LAMPRIAR va. to roast meat; to cover a roast with beaten eggs
LANA (slang) money; LANA MORADO: ANDAR LANA MORADO (slang) to be in love with (play on words: lana morado = ena-morado)
LANERO -RA wool worker; person who gathers the sheep's wool from the ground and places it on a platform where it is bundled
LÁNGARA sly, astute, cunning: "Pedro es una lángara"
LANUDO -DA flushed with money (ref. to person carrying around an unaccustomed amount of money or to a person suddenly much richer than before)

LAO (var. of) lado
LÁPIZ msg. & mpl. (word wrongly interpreted as already bearing the plural marker, thus") "Traigo un lápiz...no, parece que traigo dos lápiz"
LAQUIAR (Eng.) va. to lock shut
LARGADO -DA estranged, abandoned (by a spouse): "Pobre María está largada ¡y con tanta familia!"
LARGAR va. to abandon (leave) one's spouse, run away from one's mate: "Juan largó a su esposa"
LÁSTICO (var. of) elástico
LASTIMADA action and effect of injuring or hurting (physically or emotionally)
LASTIMÓN m. (var. of) lastimada
LATA (see DAR LA LATA)
LATIDO stomach spasms or palpitations
LAVADERO act of washing clothes
LAVADO douche
LAZAZO blow with a rope
LAZO clothesline
LEACHO (var. of) liacho
LECIÓN (var. of) lección f.
LECTRICIDAD (var. of) electricidad f.
LECHE f.(vulg.) (male) semen, sperm; LECHE AGRIA sour milk, curdled milk; MOSCA EN LECHE dark-complected person married to (or associating with) a fair-skinned person)
LECHUDO -DA (slang) lucky
LECHUZA bat
LEIDO -DA (var. of) leído -da (ppart. of leer)
LEJECITOS (iron.) adv. quite far away, quite a distance
LENCHO -CHA lame; ANDAR LENCHO to be lame; to be foolish
LENCHO -CHA (dim. of) Lorenzo -za
LENGÓN - GONA (var. of) lenguón -guona
LENGONEAR or LENGONIAR (slang) vn. to gossip; to chat, converse
LENGUA (slang) necktie; BULLIR LA LENGUA to gossip; to talk excessively; ECHAR LENGUA to work excessively; to walk a long distance on a wild goose chase (coll.), walk a long distance in vain; LENGUA DE ZAPATO shoe's tongue (Std. lengüeta de zapato); LENGUA GRANDE big-mouthed (coll.), talkative, garrulous; LENGUA, LENGUA PA' LORENZO (set expression used to poke fun at someone who has walked a long distance on a wild goose chase, i.e., without accomplishing his objective); TENER LENGUA MOCHA to talk very little; TENER LENGUA SUELTA to talk frequently; to be garrulous; TIRAR LENGUA (slang) to talk too much, be very garrulous
LENGUÓN -GUONA m., f. liar; malicious gossiper; foul-mouthed, filthy-mouthed
LENTODOS (slang) mpl. eyeglasses
LEÑA (slang) marihuana
LEÑITO (slang) marihuana cigarette
LEÓN, LEONA greedy; ambitious; unrelenting in the pursuit of something: "Ella es una leona para las estampillas; nunca deja de pedírnoslas cuando viene de compras"; TIRAR A LEÓN to ignore, not pay attention to
LEPE (coll.) mf. brat, squirt, annoying young child; short-legged, heavy-set person
LER (var. of) leer
LES: JUGAR A LA LES to play tag; TRAER LA LES (also TRAERLA) to be "it" in a game of tag (LES <Eng. last, i.e., 'Last one in is the loser'?, or perhaps <lass 'young girl'?)
LEVANTADA pick-up, woman who allows herself to be solicited for sexual activity: "Tú eres pura levantada" 'You're nothing but a pick-up'
LEVANTAR: LEVANTAR ACEITE (slang) to blow off steam (coll.), get angry; LEVANTAR CHANCLA / LEVANTAR CHANCLE (slang) to move rapidly, really "pick up one's feet" (coll.); LEVANTAR EL ALARME / LEVANTAR LA ALARMA to raise an alarm, give warning; LEVANTAR LA BANDERA (Ang.) to raise the flag (i.e., run the flag up the flagpole) (Std. izar la bandera); LEVANTARSE CON LAS GALLINAS (Ang?) to get up with the chickens (fig.), arise very early in the morning
LEVANTE (slang) mf. pick-up, person "picked up" (usually in an anonymous fashion) by another for subsequent sexual activity; act of picking up for subsequent sexual activity
LEVANTÓN m. boost in one's morale: "Hay que darle un levantón, está muy triste"
LEY (slang) fsg. police force; METER A LA LEY / METER EN LA LEY to bring suit against (someone)
LEYER (var. of) leer

LIACHO badly-tied bundle (e.g., of clothes)
LIAL (var. of) leal
LICAR (slang) va. to look at, observe: "Está licando la tienda que piensa robar;" to see
LICO (dim. of) Federico
LICOREAR or LICORIAR (slang) va. to look at, observe; to see (cf. LICAR)
LICUADOR m. blender, machine used to blend food
LICHA (dim. of) Alicia
LIEBRE (slang) f. odd job
LIMA (slang) shirt
LIMAR (slang) va. to degrade, humiliate
LIMBURGO (slang) Edinburg, Texas
LIMOSNERO -RA: LIMOSNERO Y CON GARROTE (ref. to person who wants to have his/her cake and eat it too, one who wants a mile when offered an inch, etc.)
LIMPIO -PIA (slang) cleaned-out, stone broke, penniless
LINAR (var. of) alinear
LINDA (slang) vagina; QUITAR LA LINDA to cause to lose one's virginity, to deflower (said of women): "Si no te cuidas te van a quitar la linda"
LÍNEA penny pitching (mild type of gambling game); (Ang.) line, falsehood used to convince: "Le estaba dando una línea" 'He was handing (feeding) her a line'; ANDAR EN LA LÍNEA / ESTAR EN LA LÍNEA (coll.) to be drunk; TIRAR LÍNEA (slang) to flatter, "hand someone a line" (slang)
LINIA (var. of) línea
LINOLIO (var. of) linóleo
LINTERNA small store or business; (slang) eye; (coll.) fire-fly
LÍO (Eng.) Leo (proper name)
LIÓN (var. of) león m.
LIONA (slang) jail
LIPESTIC or LIPESTIQUE or LIPISTIC or LIPISTIQUE (Eng.) m. lipstick
LIQUEAR or LIQUIAR (Eng.) va. to lick; vn. to leak
LIQUELLAR (slang) va. to see; to look
LIRA (slang) guitar
LÍRICO -CA self-taught (ref. to persons who play instruments "by ear" or to persons who recite poems etc. from memory without having learned them from a script); a born ____ (ref. to someone who is said to have inherent talent for something, e.g.:) "un músico lírico" ' a born musician'
LIS m. (Eng.) lease, rental contract
LISA (slang) shirt
LISTERINA (Eng.) mouth-wash (in general) (loan metonymy Listerine)
LISTONES mpl. children's game played thus: the children divide into two bands; band one decides upon a particular color, which band two then tries to guess by knocking on an imaginary "door" and participating in the following dialogue: "Tantan.--¿Quién es? (response from band two) -- La vieja Inés.-- ¿Qué quería? -- Un listón. -- ¿De qué color?" At this point the second band names a color. If named correctly, band two receives a point; if not then it is the turn of band one to guess the color
LITO -TA (dims. of) Carmen (mf.), Carmelito (m.), Carmelita (f.)
LIVIANO -NA adj. (ref. to persons with a bad reputation); f. woman of ill repute
LOBATISMO (Ang.) cub scouting
LOBI (Eng.) m. lobby, hall, vestibule
LOBICA (slang, Hispanization of) Lubbock, Texas
LOBO (hum. slang, Hispanization of) Lubbock, Texas
LOBO (fig.) astute and clever person
LOCARIO -RIA (slang) crazy
LÓCAT (slang, Hispanization of) Lockhart, Texas
LOCO -CA (slang) drunk; m. (slang) dollar bill; ANDAR LOCO -CA (slang) to be high on narcotic drugs; LOCO DE ATIRO crazy through and through; LOCO -CA ENMAIZADO -DA (coll.) crazy old fool, doddering old idiot; TIRAL AL LOCO (slang) to ignore: "Se enojaron porque los tiraron al loco"; ¡QUÉ LOCO! or ¡QUÉ LOCOTE! (slang) (set expression used to praise an accomplishment:) "Gané el primer premio. --¡Qué loco!"
LOCOTE: ANDAR LOCOTE (slang) to be high on narcotic drugs
LOGO (var. of) luego (adv.)
LONAS fpl. overalls, coveralls (type of men's workclothes)
LONCHAR (Eng.) vn. to eat lunch (see also LONCHEAR, LONCHIAR)
LONCHE (Eng.) m. lunch (light midday meal); sandwich (Std. emparedado): "¿Cuántos lonches quieres hoy?"; ECHARLE A ALGUIEN SU LONCHE (slang) to tell some-

one off, bawl someone out (slang); "¡Qué bueno que le echó su lonche; lo merecía!"; ECHARSE A ALGUIEN DE LONCHE to defeat someone in a sports competition; to beat someone up in a fight
LONCHEAR or LONCHIAR (Eng.) vn. to eat lunch (see also LONCHAR)
LONCHERA (Eng., cf. LONCHE) lunch pail, lunch bucket (container used to carry one's lunch to work)
LONCHERÍA (Eng., cf. LONCHE) lunchroom; small café
LONDRE or LONDRI (Eng.) m. laundry, place where clothes are cleaned; laundry, dirty clothes to be cleaned
LONJONUDO -DA very fat and flabby
LORE: ¡JI LORE! (Eng. Lordy, dim. of Lord) interj. (euph.) Lordy me! (cf. other interjs. with JIJO)
LOS (slang) Los Angeles, California: "Ese bato es de Los" 'That guy is from Los Angeles'
LOS (var. of) <u>nos</u> (1st pers. pl. object pron.): "Él siempre que los ve los pide que véngamos a casa" 'Every time he sees us he asks us to come over to his house'
LOSOTROS -TRAS (var. of) <u>nosotros -tras</u>
LUCARIO -RIA (var. of) <u>locario -ria</u>
LUCAS (slang) adj. mfsg. crazy, foolish; TIRAR A LUCAS (slang) to ignore
LUCE or LUCI (dim. of) <u>Lucía</u>
LUCIR vr. to show off, act ostentatiously
LUCHA (dim. of) <u>Lucía</u>, <u>Luz</u>
LUCHA: HACERLE LA LUCHA A ALGUIEN to try to convince someone (usually against his/her will), try to get someone to change his/her mind
LUCHISTA mf. go-getter (coll.), agressive person
LUCHÓN -CHONA (id. to LUCHISTA supra)
LUEGO: LUEGO LUEGO or LUEGO LUEGUITO adv. right away, immediately
LUENGA (var. of) <u>lengua</u>
LULI (Hispanization of) Luling, Texas
LUIS MORALES (hum.) m. man with low moral standards (bilingual play on words: <u>loose morals</u>)
LUISA MORALES (hum.) f. woman with low moral standards (bilingual wordplay, cf. LUIS MORALES supra)
LUMBRE: SER MUY LUMBRE (said of a person who wears things out, i.e., clothes, or who puts them in a state of disrepair in a short time); SACAR LUMBRE to harp on the same subject, talk incessantly about the same topic
LUMBRE f. light, match (for lighting cigarettes, etc.): "Dame lumbre" 'Give me a light'
LUMBRERO -RA firefighter, fireman
LUMBRIZ (fig.) mf. thin (person) (var. of <u>lombriz</u>, a form which is seldom heard in Texas)
LUNA menstruation period; ESTAR MALA DE LA LUNA to be having one's (menstruation) period
LUNADA moonlight party
LUP (Eng.) m. loop
LUPE (dim. of) <u>Guadalupe</u> (m., f.)
LUQUIS (slang) mf. crazy person
LURIO -RIA or LURIAS (mfsg.) (slang) crazy: "Ese bato está lurias" 'That guy is crazy'
LUTO: TRAER LUTO (fig.) to have dirty fingernails

LL

LLAMAR vr. to go back on one's word, retract a promise: "Carlos se llamó, por eso estoy enojado"
LLAMÓN -MONA person who goes back on his/her word, fails to carry out a promise
LLANTA (fig., hum.) doughnut; (fig., slang) "spare tire" (slang), role of fat around a person's waist; fpl. gifts given at a wedding
LLANTÓN -TONA (slang, pej.) U.S. black person
LLEGAR: LLEGARLE A ALGUIEN to get to someone, get the best of someone; ¿VAMOS LLEGANDO ... ? How's about stopping off ...?: "¿Vamos llegando a ca Pedro?" 'How's about stopping off at Pedro's house?'
LLENAR va. & vr. to soil, dirty, stain (esp. clothes): "Le llenaste la camisa de jugo" 'You stained his shirt with juice'; vn. LLENAR DE _______ to have enough _______, e.g., LLENAR DE SUEÑO to have enough sleep
LLEVAR va. LLEVAR PA' TRAS (Ang.)

to return, take back; to retract (e.g., a promise), go back on (one's word); vn. LLEVAR UNA FREGUIZA to have a hard time of (something); vr. to kid around (slang), direct humor towards (someone) with apparent offensive intent though never with genuine malice; LLEVARLA to pay for, be given the responsibility for, have to shoulder the blame for: "Cuando el hogar se desbarata la mujer es la que la lleva" 'When a home breaks up it's the woman who pays for it'; to take out on: "Todo el día el profesor mira a las muchachas bonitas y después cuando llega a casa es la mujer la que la lleva" 'All day the professor is looking at pretty girls and then when he gets home he takes it out on his wife'; LLEVARSE A ALGUIEN EL TREN / LLEVARSE A ALGUIEN LA CHINGADA / LLEVARSE A ALGUIEN LA JODIDA (vulg.) (fixed expressions): "¡Me lleva la chingada!" 'Well I'll be doubled damned!'; (also used in the sense of 'to find oneself in a tight spot': "¡Ya me llevaba el tren!" 'I was really in trouble then!'); LLEVARSE A ALGUIEN to get the best of one in a business deal, "take" someone (slang): "Ese chico sí que te llevó" 'That boy really got the best of you'; (slang) to knife (someone); LLEVARSE DE ENCUENTRO to run over (someone)

LLORADA act of crying: "Tuvo su buena llorada" 'He had a real good cry'

LLORAR: YA NI LLORAR ES BUENO No use crying over spilled milk

LLORETAS mfsg. crybaby, whimperer

LLORIDO cries, act of crying: "Nos despertaron sus lloridos" 'His crying woke us up'

LLORONA (slang) patrol car (police); fire engine; siren (of a fire engine or a police car); LA LLORONA: ghost-woman who, according to folk legend, killed her baby and afterwards threw it into the water; when she died she was forced to atone for her crime by wandering along the banks of the river, mourning the child; many towns and villages are said to have their own "local Lloronas" who haunt the banks of the local stream

LLOVEDERO -RA mf. heavy rainfall, cloudburst; continuous rainfall

M

MACALEN (Hispanization of) McAllen, Texas

MACALILILILIÁ children's game in which the participants form two human chains facing each other; a type of sung dialogue transpires, during which one child and then another asks something of a child from the other group

MACANAZO blow with a blackjack

MACANEAR or MACANIAR va. to strike over the head with a blackjack or other heavy instrument

MACÁNICO -CA (var. of) <u>mecánico -ca</u>

MACANO -CA adj. cheap, common, ordinary; f. cheapskate, parsimonious person; blackjack (weapon)

MACETA (slang) head; (slang) hand; slow poke, person who acts or learns slowly

MACITA beautiful and desirable woman; (slang, often vocative) sweet mamma

MACIZAR va. to secure something for oneself, appropriate

MACIZO (slang) boy friend; gang leader; favorite son (ref. to local or regional politicians who enjoy considerable popularity)

MACUACHE mf. useless person

MACUCO -CA old

MACUECO -CA left-handed

MACHACAR: MACHACAR LA MUELA (slang) to eat

MACHETE adj. (var. of) <u>machetón -tona</u>; m. (slang) tomboy; mfpl. KID MACHETES (Eng. 'kid' + <u>machetes</u>) (ref. to person who does everything wrong)

MACHETEAR or MACHETIAR va. to do a job clumsily, leave a job half done

MACHETÓN -TONA lazy; clumsy, awkward

MACHÍN -CHINA strong; outstanding, excellent

MACHITO type of Mexican food prepared in the same way as the chittling and consisting of the same ingredients (pig entrails)

MACHO adj. very masculine, studly (slang); m. type of roast dish of liver, sweetbreads and other meat; adv. A LO MACHO in a manly manner: "Pórtate a lo macho" 'Act like a man' ; NO APEARSE DE SU MACHO / NO BAJARSE DE SU MAHCO to be unyielding, stubborn (in an opinion or on a stand one has taken)

MACHÓN -CHONA adj. (var. of amachón -chona 'stubborn'); f. woman who acts mannishly; tomboy

MADAMA (Eng.) madame (title of address which maids give to the women they work for)

MADERA flattery; MADERA GACHA flattery, adulation; falsehood, lie; interj. ¡MADERA (GACHA)! Hog wash!, Bull roar!; (see also DAR MADERA)

MADEREAR or MADERIAR va. to flatter; to lie, deceive; vr. to pass the time; to boast, brag

MADERERA or MADERÍA lumber yard

MADERISTA mf. braggart; liar; flatterer

MADRE f. (slang) shapely and sexy woman; ACÁ LA MADRE DE LOS BURROS / ACÁ LA MADRE DE LOS CABALLOS adv. very far away; DAR EN LA MERA MADRE / DAR EN TODA LA MADRE (slang) to beat up severely (usually in a fist fight); ECHARLE A ALGUIEN LA MADRE / MENTARLE A ALGUIEN DE LA MADRE to insult someone by referring to his/her mother (in however veiled or cryptic a fashion); ECHAR MADRES to curse, speak obscenities; EN LA MADRE where it hurts (coll.), in a vulnerable spot (physical or emotional): "Le van a dar en la madre"; ¡MADRE SANTA! interj. (fairly euph.) Good Lord! Heavens!; NO IMPORTARLE A ALGUIEN MADRE not to give a damn about anything; NO TENER MADRE (expression used as mild or hum. criticism of someone's boldness or bad behavior); NO VALER MADRE not to be worth a damn; ¡PURA MADRE! interj. Hell no!, The hell (you say)!; ¡QUÉ PADRE MADRE! (slang) What a gorgeous hunk of woman!; (see also: A TODA MADRE s. TODO, DAR EN LA MADRE, DE A MADRE)

MADRECITA (slang) beautiful and sexy woman

MADRUGUERO -RA early riser

MAGACÍN or (orthog. var.) MAGAZÍN (Eng.) magazine, periodical

MAGUE (dim. of) Margarita (Eng. Maggie?)

MAIESTRO -TRA or MAISTRO -RA (var. of) maestro -tra

MAIQUE (Eng.) (dim.) Mike (< Michael)

MAIQUE pron. I; me; mine (probable hum. substitution of MAIQUE Mike, Eng., + my/mine)

MAIZ (var. of) maíz m.

MAJE adj. (slang) dumb, ignorant; HACERLE MAJE A ALGUIEN to make a fool of someone

MAJADERO -RA loud mouth (coll.) (ref. to boisterous and aggressive talker)

MAL adv./adj. MAL AVERIGUADO -DA hot-tempered, easily provoked; MAL DADO -DA damaging (ref. to a hard blow to the body's more vulnerable parts); MAL DE HIEL gall bladder disease; MAL DE LA SANGRE (euph.) syphilis

MALAJOS interj. (used to express impatience) Dammit to hell!; ¡MALAJOS SEAS! Damn you!

MALAMÉ m. corn, maize; chicken feed

MALANCO -CA somewhat rotten (fruit); sick; slightly under the weather (coll., ref. to persons who are mildly sick); mean, base, vile; SALIR MALANCO -CA to turn out to be bad (ref. to persons, e.g., a bad spouse, a bad son, etc.)

MALANCON -CONA sick, ill; disreputable (ref. to persons); SALIR MALANCÓN -CONA (id. to SALIR MALANCO -CA)

MALAVERIGUADO -DA pugnacious, quarrelsome

MALCREADAR or MALCRIADAR to talk back to, be insolent with: "No le malcriadees a tus mayores" 'Don't talk back to your elders'

MALCRIADO -DA sassy, impudent

MALDICIENTO -TA (var. of) maldiciente

MALDITO -TA superior: "Ella se cree muy maldita" 'She thinks she's really some big deal' (coll.)

MALE (Eng.) Molly (personal name)

MALECITO slight but bothersome cold in the head; cold on the verge of becoming flu

MALES (mpl.) (var. of) malas 'enfermedades'; ¿CÓMO SIGUE DE MALES? (set expression) How are things with you?; PARA COLMO DE MIS MALES (set expression) To make things worse, As if that weren't enough

MALETA baby's excrement found on a diaper
MALETUDO -DA baggy (ref. to person wearing baggy pants)
MALHAYA or MALHAYA SEA interjs. Cursed be ... ! "¡Malhaya sea el día en que naciste!"
MALI (Eng.) (var. of) Male 'Molly'
MALIA or MALILLA m. male actor who plays the "heavy" (villain) in movies; adj. cruel
MALICIÓN (rus.) (var. of) maldición f.
MALINCHE mf. & adj. bad, evil; turncoat, betrayer
MALO -LA adj. MALA DIGESTIÓN (pleonasm for) indigestion; MAL GENIO bad tempered; MAL HABLADO -DA foul-mouthed, given to insults; MALA REATA / MALA RIATA m. tough guy (coll.), mean bastard: "No hay que negarlo, es mala riata"; MALA YERBA (fig.) bad seed, person marked for tragedy or bad deeds from birth onward; untrustworthy person; DE MALAS at least: "De malas no perdí todo el dinero"; LA DE MALAS bad luck: "Le tocó la de malas" 'He had some bad luck'
MALORA mf. & adj. perverse, malevolent: "Pedro es un malora"; f. evil deed
MALPASADO -DA ill-nourished; irregularly fed
MALPASAR vr. not to eat regularly
MALTRATADO -DA beat, beaten down (ref. to someone who shows all the signs of having lived a hard life); f. reprimand, scolding
MALVA adj. astute, clever
MALLATE (orthog. var. of) mayate
MALLUGADO -DA (var. of) magullado-da
MALLUGAR (var. of) magullar
MALLUGÓN m. (var. of) magullón / magulladura / magullamiento
MAMA (Eng.) mamma (Std. mamá)
MAMACITA (slang) pretty girl
MAMADA act of sponging off of someone (coll.), living at someone else's expense
MAMADERA sinecure
MAMADOR -DORA sponger (coll.), parasite, person who lives off a sinecure
MAMÁ GRANDE grandmother (Std. abuela)
MAMALECHE f. hopscotch (children's game) (see also BEBELECHE)
MAMALÓN -LONA (slang) m. male homosexual; f. lesbian
MAMAR va. & vn. to sponge (coll.), live off of someone else's work or income; MAMAR CHICHE to be fed from the breast (said of babies): "El bebé mama chiche, no necesita botella"; to sponge (coll.) (id. to MAMAR); MAMAR Y DAR TOPE to have one's cake and eat it too (coll., ref. to the desire to receive the maximum possible)
MAMASES (var. of) mamás (pl. of mamá) fpl.
MAMASOTA (slang) beautiful woman
MAMI (Eng.) f. mommy, mamma
MAMIS fsg. (var. of) mami
MAMÓN m. baby's pacifier
MANA (var. of) hermana; (often used in the vocative and then not necessarily to one's own sister): "Oye, mana" 'Listen woman'
MANCILLA (var. of) manecilla
MANCORNÍA / MANCORNILLA or MANCUERNÍA (usually fpl.) cufflinks
MANCHA NEGRA black sheep (fig.), member of a family who brings disgrace upon the rest
MANDA religious vow; PAGAR UNA MANDA to fulfill a religious vow
MANDADERO -RA errand boy/girl; messenger
MANDADO errand; order (i.e., of groceries, at or from a store); groceries, foodstuffs
MANDAR: MANDAR A LA CHINGADA / MANDAR AL DIABLO / MANDAR A LA FREGADA / MANDAR A LA PORRA to tell (someone) to go to hell (coll.), dismiss someone in extreme anger; MANDAR A LA CHINITA POR TU AMOR (euph. var. of MANDAR A LA CHINGADA et al.) to tell someone to go to "heck"; MANDAR MUY LEJOS to tell someone to go fly a kite (fig.), tell someone off, get angry at someone; ¿QUIÉN TE MANDA? (¿QUIÉN ME MANDA? etc.) Who told you to get involved in this business?
MANEA brake (on a vehicle); ECHAR LA(S) MANEA(S) to apply the brakes, put the brakes on (lit. and fig.; fig.= to restrain)
MANEADO -DA or MANIADO -DA limited in talent, with limited competency
MANEAR or MANIAR va. to brake
MANEJADOR -DORA m., f. (Ang.) manager; MANEJADOR -DORA DE LA CIUDAD (Ang.) city manager
MANEJERA handlebars (on a bicycle); steering wheel (on a car); any

type of handle; ÍRSELE A ALGUIEN LA MANEJERA to lose control of the steering wheel
MANFLOR -FLORA m. male homosexual; f. lesbian
MANGA (slang) attractive (adj. ref. to persons); sharp dresser (coll.), person who dresses stylishly; fpl. ARISCAR MANGAS to roll up one's sleeves (for any reason, but esp. in preparation for a fist fight)
MANGAZA (slang) girl with an attractive figure
MANGO -GA mf. handle (of a kitchen utensil; of any apparatus); m. (slang) penis; PAJUELEARLE EL MANGO A ALGUIEN to be good at something, excel: "A Godofredo le pajuela el mango pa' jugar beisbol"
MANIJAR (var. of) manejar
MANIJERA (var. of) manejera
MANIL (slang) m. money
MANITA: DAR (UNA) MANITA to lend a helping hand; ANDAR HASTA LAS MANITAS to be very drunk
MANITO (var. of) hermanito; ANDAR MANITOS to be real buddy-buddy (slang), be on very friendly terms
MANO (var. of) hermano; (coll.) friend, buddy, pal; (also used as a verbal stalling device, i. e., inserted when the speaker cannot think of what to say next); fpl. CHOCAR (LAS) MANOS to shake hands; ESTAR A MANOS / PONERSE A MANOS / QUEDARSE A MANOS to owe nothing to anyone, be even (coll.); to have avenged oneself; IRLE A ALGUIEN A LA MANO to discipline a child by spanking him/her; ÍRSELE A ALGUIEN LA MANO to slip up, lose control; to miscalculate; MANO A MANO on equal terms, even, tied; METER MANO (vulg.) to engage in manual coitus, insert one's finger into a vagina to simulate copulation; to engage in enthusiastic and vigorous sexual foreplay; PASÁRSELE A ALGUIEN LA MANO (var. of ÍRSELE A ALGUIEN LA MANO, supra); SALIR A MANOS to break even in a game of chance
MANOPLA (slang) hand
MANOSEADA or MANOSIADA (ref. to a woman who has indulged her carnal appetities frequently, a a woman who has been "handled" frequently
MANOSEADERA or MANOSIADERA act of "handling" a woman; sexual foreplay
MANOSEADOR or MANOSIADOR m. (ref. to man who "handles" or engages in sexual foreplay with a woman)
MANOSEAR or MANOSIAR va. to handle, pet, paw (etc., i.e., engage in vigorous sexual foreplay)
MANOSEO (id. to MANOSEADERA, supra)
MANQUE conj. (var. of) aunque
MANTELITO table napkin
MANTENIDO -DA m. gigolo; f. kept woman, mistress
MANTEQUÍA (var. of) mantequilla
MANTIA (var. of) mantilla
MANZANEAR or MANZANIAR va. to seek to gain favor through gifts
MAÑANEAR or MAÑANIAR (slang) va. to steal
MAÑANITAS fpl. early morning serenade on the occasion of someone's birthday, typically sung outside the house of the celebrant
MAPA or (more frequently) MAPE (both m.) (Eng.) mop (cf. MOPE et al.)
MAPEADA or MAPIADA action and effect of mopping (Eng., cf. MAPA, MAPE et al.)
MAPEADOR or MAPIADOR (Eng.) m. mop; person who mops floors, mopper (see also MAPERO -RA)
MAPEAR or MAPIAR (Eng.) va. to mop (see also MOPEAR et al.)
MAPERO -RA (Eng.) person who mops floors, mopper (see also MAPEADOR et al.)
MÁQUINA car, automobile; (coll.) fire engine; locomotive; HECHO -CHA MÁQUINA (coll.) adv. very rapidly (see also A TODA MÁQUINA); MÁQUINA DE (CORTAR) ZACATE lawn mower
MAQUIS or MAQUISHUEL (slang, Hispanization of) Maxwell, Texas
MARACA (slang) dollar, dollar bill
MARAVIOSO -SA (var. of) maravilloso -sa
MARCA person ostracized by his/her own peers or compatriots
MARCADO (var. of) mercado
MARCADO -DA scar-faced
MARCAR va. to brand, scar
MARCHANTA woman customer
MARCHO (slang) convict, prisoner
MARGAYATES mpl. confusion, disorder
MARÍA JUANITA (slang) marihuana
MARICOCAIMORFI (slang) mf. person who habitually uses marihuana, cocain and morphine
MARIGUANA (var. of) marihuana
MARIGUANO -NA or MARIHUANO -NA habitual marihuana user
MARIJUANA (var. of) marihuana

MARIOLA (slang) marihuana
MARIPOSA (slang) prostitute
MARITATA mf. street vendor, peddler
MARMAJA (slang) money
MAROMA sommersault (see also MAROMETA)
MAROMEAR or MAROMIAR va. to set a trap for, seek to entrap; vn. to turn sommersaults; (fig.) to betray
MAROMEO act of betrayal
MAROMETA sommersault (see also MAROMA)
MAROTA tomboy, slightly masculine girl
MARQUETA (Eng.) market; meat market
MARQUETERO -RA (Eng., cf. MARQUETA) clerk in a store or market; butcher
MARTIAR or MARTILLAR (slang) to eat
MARTILLO or MARTÍO (slang) food
MARZO (slang) daffy, screwy, slightly crazy; FEBRERO LOCO Y MARZO OTRO POCO a little bit crazier with each passing day
MARRANA (pej.) bitch (term of insult); MARRANA CUINA (pej.) fat and ugly old bitch (insult directed at a woman)
MARRAR (var. of) amarrar
MARROQUIANO -NA (var. of) parroquiano -na
MARRULLERO -RA lazy, sluggish
MÁS: MÁS AL RATO (pleonasm) (var. of) al rato; MÁS ANTES (pleonastic var. of) antes 'before, beforehand'; MÁS DESPUÉS (pleonasm) (var. of) después; MÁS MEJOR (pleonastic var. of) mejor 'better'; MÁS QUE QUIÉN SABE QUÉ a lot, a great amount: "Ahora la ama más que quién sabe qué"; MÁS NADA (var. of) nada más: "No tengo más nada acá conmigo" 'I don't have anything else with me here'; MÁS _______ QUE QUIÉN SABE QUÉ (coll.) more _______ than you could possibly imagine; ENTRE MÁS ____ MÁS the more _______ the more
MASA (slang) mf. slowpoke, lethargic person; flabby, blubber-bellied (coll.)
MASACOTA or MASACOTE f. disorganized mixture, jumble of various items
MASCADA scarf
MÁSCARA (coll.) woman with an ugly face
MASERO -RA vendor of ready-made dough for tortillas
MASES (Hispanization of) Mathis, Texas
MASOTA beautiful and sexy woman, red hot mamma (slang)
MASUDO -DA doughy, not well-baked (ref. to pastry or other dough product)
MATA: plant (any plant in general); LA MERA MATA the real McCoy (coll.), the genuine article
MATABURROS msg. (coll.) dictionary, lexicon; cheap grade of whiskey
MATAGUSANOS msg. worm-killer, medicine used for purposes of deworming people or animals; any de-worming agent
MATALOTE m. type of spine-backed fish
MATAMOSCA m. (var. of) matamoscas 'flyswatter'
MATANZA slaughter-house
MATATENA children's game in which stones are thrown in the air
MATE: DARLE A ALGUIEN EN EL MERO MATE to hit someone right where it hurts
MATÓN -TONA m. (slang) gangster; self-styled lady killer, Don Juan type; f. wicked and evil woman; m., f. killer, assassin, murderer
MATRACA mf. chatterbox (coll.), person who talks incessantly
MATRALLADORA (var. of) amatralladora (in turn var. of) ametralladora
MATRIMONIAR vr. to get married
MATRIZ (slang) f. prostitute
MATUTENA (var. of) matatena
MAULA adj. clever, astute; TRAER MAULA (coll.) to be up to something, have something up one's sleeve (coll.)
MAYATE (pej.) mf. U.S. black person
MAYESTRO -TRA (var. of) maestro -tra
MAYOR (Ang.) m. mayor (of a city) (Std. alcalde)
MAYOTE m. nag, old horse
MAYUGAR (var. of) magullar
MAZORCA (slang) fsg. teeth, set of teeth
MAZUMA (slang) money (<mazuma, ant. English <Yiddish, slang of the 1930's)
MEADERA frequent urinating
MEADERO (var. of) meadera
MECANEAR or MECANIAR vn. to do mechanical work, work as a mechanic
MECATAZO whiplash, lash of a whip
MECATE: ANDAR COMO BURRO SIN MECATE to run wild and free, do as one pleases; CADA CHANGO A SU MECATE Y A DARSE VUELO (lit. 'each monkey to his rope and start swinging') every man for himself, let each person do his own thing (slang)

MECETA (var. of) maceta
MECO -CA lower-class person; person in a bad mood; MECOS mpl. (vulg.) semen, seminal fluid
MECHA (Ang.) match (for lighting fire) (Std. cerilla, fósforo)
MECHACHITO -TA (vars. of) muchachito -ta
MECHAR (Eng.) va. to match, compare (one thing with another); to match, harmonize (attempt to make two items harmonize with each other)
MECHAS fpl. disheveled hair, "mop" of hair (coll.); AGARRARSE A LAS MECHAS / AGARRARSE DE LAS MECHAS to pull one another's hair in a fight; IRSE A LAS MECHAS / IRSE DE LAS MECHAS to pass from a verbal to a physical battle (esp. one in which hair is pulled)
MECHUDO -DA person with long and unkempt hair; hippie
MEDECINA (var. of) medicina
MEDIAGUA: ESTAR MEDIAGUA to be drunk
MEDICINA: MEDICINA DE LA BOTICA/ MEDICINA DE LA FARMACIA patent medicine
MEDIERO -RA sharecropper (unequal "partner" on a ranch or farm")
MEDIO nickel, five-cent piece
MEJICLE (slang) Mexico
MEJOR: A LA MEJOR (Std. a lo mejor); MÁS MEJOR (pleonasm) better (Std. mejor); MEJOR MITAD (Ang.) f. wife
MELA (nickname for) Carmela
MELA (slang) human head
MELE (nickname for) Guillermo
MELENA (slang) head (body: neck upward)
MELITAR (var. of) militar m. 'soldier'
MELÓN m. hornless or dehorned bull; or MELONA f. (slang) human head
MEMBRECÍA membership
MEME (Eng.) Mamie (woman's name)
MEMO (nickname for) Guillermo
MENARDE or MENARVE (Hispanization of) Menard, Texas
MÉNDIGO (var. of) mendigo. (latter is infrequently used in Texas); m. rogue, trickster; adj. mf. MÉNDIGO -GA cheap, stingy; mean, base, wicked
MENEADA or MENIADA or MENEADERO -RA or MENIADERO -RA mf. the act of stirring (esp. a liquid in a container): "Dale una meniada al caldo" 'Stir up the soup'
MENEAR: MENEARLAS or MENEAR LAS NALGAS to wiggle one's hind quarters
MENIJAR (var. of) manejar
MENIU (Eng.) m. menu
MENJURGE (var. of) mejunge m.'disorderly pile of objects jumbled together'
MENORAR (var. of) minorar
MENOS: DE MENOS at least (Std. a lo menos, por lo menos); ENTRE MENOS BURROS, MÁS OLOTES / MIENTRAS MENOS BURROS, MÁS OLOTES the fewer people, the more there is to go around (often said with ref. to food); ESTAR EN TODO MENOS EN MISA be minding everybody's business except one's own; ENTRE MENOS ______, MENOS ______ the fewer ______, the fewer ______
MENSO -SA ignorant; foolish
MENSUAL (slang) (hum. var. of menso -sa)
MENTIDERA (coll.) several lies at once, string of lies
MENTIR vn. to be wrong, be in error: "Pues, vino a las ocho... No, miento, vino a las ocho y media"
MENTIRITAS: DE MENTIRITAS in make-believe fashion
MENTOLATO (Eng?) mentholatum
MENUDO soup or stew made with various types of tripe and well seasoned, esp. with salt; menudo is popularly known as an efficacious hangover cure
MEÓN, MEONA m., f. person who urinates frequently, weak-bladdered (coll.)
MERO: EL MERO BEBÉ the one and only (coll.); EL MERO MERO / EL MERO PETATERO (slang) the big boss, the big cheese, the head honcho (slang); the real McCoy, the genuine article (slang); EL MERO JODÓN (slang) the big boss, the head honcho (slang); YA MERO / YA MERITO almost, nearly
MES m. menstrual period; TENER EL MES to have one's (menstrual) period
MESA: SALIR POR DEBAJO DE LA MESA to always come out on the short end of the stick (fig.), always fail in whatever one attempts
MESMO (var. of) mismo
MESTRO -TRA (var. of) maestro -tra
¡MÉTELE! interj. Hit 'em!; Hurry up!; Get to work! (etc.)
METER va. to stick, sting (slang), charge excessively for: "Le metieron quinientos dólares por esa carrucha" 'They stung him $500 for that old heap'; A LA

QUE ME METÍ A fine mess I got myself into; A TODO METER full speed ahead, very rapidly; (adj.) stupendous, exceptional, marvelous (etc.); METER A ALGUIEN EN BOLA to get someone into trouble, involve someone in a conflict; METER A ALGUIEN EN LA LEY to bring a lawsuit against someone; METER A ALGUIEN EN UN TRABAJO to use one's influence to obtain a job for someone; METERLE A ALGUIEN UNA PALIZA / REATIZA / PORRIZA (etc.) to give someone a severe beating; vn. METER CABALLO (slang) to put in a bad word (about someone), speak ill of; METER EL CODO (slang) to put in a good word for someone, speak well of; METER HOMBRO to help out, lend a helping hand; to put in a good word for someone, speak well of; METER MANO (vulg.) to engage in manual coitus, insert one's finger into a vagina to simulate copulation; to engage in enthusiastic and vigorous sexual foreplay; METERLE DURO / METERLE MUCHO to do something to excess (esp. the drinking of alcohol): "Le mete duro a la tomada" 'He really drinks heavily'; vr. to consume, eat up: "Me metí dos platos de frijoles"; to cover territory, travel: "Me metí 20 millas en una hora"; METERSE EN EL EJÉRCITO/CUERPO AÉREO/MARINA (etc.) to enlist in the army (etc.); METÉRSELA DOBLADA A ALGUIEN to get the best of someone in a business deal, a sports competition, etc.: "A Pedro se la metieron doblada en es juego"; METÉRSELE A ALGUIEN EN LA CABEZA (coll.) to get (something) into one's head, for an idea to occur to someone; to be bullheaded about something

METICHE or METICHI mf. busybody, meddler

METIDO -DA: ESTAR MUY METIDO -DA CON ALGUIEN to be very involved with someone (esp. in a love affair); ESTAR MUY METIDO -DA EN ALGO to be very absorbed in something; f. (vulg.) act of fornication (see also DAR UNA METIDA)

METRALLADORA (var. of) ametralladora

MEXICANO-AMERICANO (Ang.) Mexican-American (Std. mexicoamericano)

MÉXICO: MÉXICO VEN POR TU GENTE (expression of disapproval directed at Mexican-Americans who are making a spectacle of themselves); MÉXICO VIEJO (Old) Mexico (as distinct from New Mexico, U.S. state)

MEZQUINO wart

MEZQUITE (slang) m. month

MÍ (pers. pron.): A MÍ ¿QUÉ?/¿A MÍ QUÉ ME DA? What's that to me?, What concern's that of mine? (expresses indifference)

MIADERA (var. of) meadera

MIAR (var. of) mear

MICAILA (var. of) Micaela (woman's name)

MIEMBRECÍA (var. of) membrecía

MIENTRAS: MIENTRAS MENOS at the very least (Std. cuanto menos); POR MIENTRAS for the time being, meanwhile

MIÉRCOLES (euph.) msg. feces, "number two" (euph.--the word that miércoles avoids is mierda); ¡MIÉRCOLES! interj. (mildly euph.) Damn!, Hell!

MIERDA (vulg.) excrement, feces (also with ref. to persons:) (vulg.) Son-of-a-bitch, No-good bastard (etc.)

MIGRA (slang) immigration service (U.S.); U.S. border patrol

MIGUEL (slang) (pers. pron.) I; me (hum. identification between mí and Miguel)

MILAGRO: ¡QUÉ MILAGRO! 'What a pleasant surprise!'

MILITARIO (var. of) militar (n. & adj.)

MILO -LA (dims. of) Emilio -lia

MILQUE (Eng.) f. milk

MIMELA (slang) (pers. pron.) I (Std. yo) (cf. MIGUEL, supra)

MINE (dim. of) Minerva, Herminia

MINGO (dim. of) Domingo

MIÓN, MIONA (var. of) meón, meona

MIRA (Eng.) f. meter (e.g., parking meter)

MIRAMONTE (slang) (3rd pers. sg. pres. ind. of mirar)

MIRAR: MIRAR ADELANTE PARA (Ang.) to look forward to, anticipate; ESTAR DE MÍRAME Y DÉJAME (pej., said with ref. to a homely woman): "Esa mujer está de mírame y déjame"; ¡MIRA NOMÁS! (interj. of surprise:) Well I'll be damned!, Will you look at that!

MIRELES (slang) (pers. pron.) I (Std. yo) (1st pers. sg. subject pron.) (cf. MIGUEL, MIMELA et al.)

MIROJEAR or MIROJIAR va. to peep, sneak a look at, glance at covertly and often with lust

aforethought
MISA: LA MISA (hum. or else mock Eng. for) La Mesa, Texas
MISA: MISA DE GALLO (var. of) misa del gallo; ESTAR EN TODO MENOS EN MISA to mind everyone else's business but one's own
MISIÓN (re-Hispanization of) Mission, Texas
MISIRICORDIA (var. of) misericordia
MÍSPERO (var. of) níspero (Japanese plum tree)
MISTEAR or MISTIAR (Eng.) va. to miss; to fail to attend (e.g. a class); to feel the absence of: "Te misteo mucho, vuelve pronto"; to fail to hit (e.g. a target): "Le mistié al pajarito con mi rifle"
MÍSTER (Eng.) m. mister, Mr.
MITA Y MITA (var. of) mitá y mitá (mitad y mitad) half and half (as when one person shares something with another)
MITO: CORTAR EL MITO (slang) to silence, shut up: "Le cortaron el mito" 'They shut him up'
MITOTE m. uproar, din; disturbance; trouble; noisy party, loud festivity
MITOTEAR or MITOTIAR va. to stir up, incite; vn. to make trouble, raise hell (coll.), to go on a wild spree
MITOTERO -RA adj. rowdy, noisy; troublesome, hard to handle; mf. instigator, rabble rouser, troublemaker
MIXEAR or MIXIAR (Eng.) va. to mix (see also MIXTEAR et. al.) (note: of the four variants, mixiar is the most prevalent)
MIXTEAR or MIXTIAR (Eng.) va. to mix
MOCA (Eng?) mug (e.g. for drinking coffee)
MOCO: TIRAR MOCO (slang) to cry; (see also DAR EN EL MOCO)
MOCHA switch-engine (locomotive used to shuffle cars in a trainyard)
MOCHACHO -CHA (var. of) muchacho -cha
MOCHAR (Eng?) va. & vn. to mooch off of (slang), sponge (coll.), live off the earnings of others; ¡MÓCHATE! (slang) Bug off!, Get out of here!, Cut out! (slang)
MOCHERA camp-follower (woman who resides near a military base so as to be proximate to the amorous attentions of military personnel, who often pay her for services rendered)
MOCHO -CHA (said of someone missing an extremity, i.e., one-handed, one-armed, one-legged); m. soldier (usually of low rank); adj. impudent, sassy
MOFLA or MOFLE (Eng.) m. muffler (aut.) (Std. silenciador m.)
MOGOTE m. brush land, brush country
MOJADO -DA illegal immigrant to the U.S. from Mexico, wetback (pej.)
MOJARRA mf. illegal immigrant to the U.S. from Mexico, wetback (pej.)
MOJO (var. of) moho 'rust'
MOJÓN m. solid drenching, thorough soaking
MOJOSO -SA (var. of) mohoso -sa 'rusty'
MOLCAJETE: CARA DE MOLCAJETE (slang) (pej.) (insult used to indicate a very ugly face)
MOLCAS (var. of) molcajete; CIERTAS MOLCAS (used to ref. to person whose name one wishes to avoid mentioning; cf. CIERTOS ELOTES)
MOLER: MOLER GENTE to bother (someone), make a nuisance of oneself: "¡Cómo te gusta moler gente!"
MOLÓN -LONA m., f. pest, bothersome person; complainer
MOLOTE m. bun of hair, topknot
MOLLEJA pocket watch
MOLLERA: MOLLERA CAÍDA fallen fontanelle (the soft part of a baby's skull which sometimes "falls" or retracts before becoming fully hardened); MOLLERA CERRADA (fig.) (ref. to person who is slow to learn)
MOLLETE m. cake baked in the shape of a loaf
MOMIO -MIA dunderhead, blockhead, dolt
MOMIO (var. of) momia
MOMPES (Eng.) mpl. mumps
MONA (dim. of) Ramona
MONARCO movie theater, cinema (<?, perhaps mono, q.v., or, through metonymy Monarco, name of a particular theater)
MONEADA or MONEADERA or MONIADA or MONIADERA act of being or attempting to be cute or amusing
MONESTERIO (var. of) monasterio
MONI (msg.) or MONIS (mpl.) (Eng.) money
MONITO -TA (rus.) (var. of) bonito -ta
MONITA paper doll, cartoon cut-out doll
MONO (slang) movie theater, cinema; movie, film; APRETARLE A ALGUIEN EL MONO to bewitch someone;

MONO DE AGUA fireplug; SER MUY MONO -NA to dress very elegantly
MONONTEROS (var. of) montoneros mpl. 'gang of attackers'
MONQUIAR (Eng.) (slang) vn. to monkey around with, engage in often meaningless activities for the sake of killing time
MONSTRO -TRA (vars. of) monstruo -trua
MOPE (Eng.) m. (infrequently used var. of mape)
MOPEADA or MOPIADA (vars. of) mapeada, mapiada (Eng.)
MOPEADOR -DORA or MOPIADOR -DORA (vars. of) mapeador -dora, mapiador -dora (Eng.)
MOPEAR or MOPIAR (vars. of) mapear, mapiar (Eng.)
MOQUEADERA or MOQUIADERA act of crying; nasal drip
MOQUEAR or MOQUIAR (slang) vn. to cry; to drip (said of noses)
MOQUERA or MOQUERIA act of crying; nasal drip
MOQUETAZO punch in the nose
MOQUIENTO -TA (var. of) mocoso -sa
MORA (slang) juvenile detention home, house of correction for boys or girls; fpl. PESCAR EN LAS MORAS to catch (someone) red-handed, catch in the act
MORAS: LAS MORAS (Spanish name for) Brackettville, Texas
MORDELÓN -LONA (pej.) policeman (m.), policewoman (f.) (usually ref. to corrupt policemen, i.e., those who accept mordidas)
MORDIDA bribe; pay-off, kick-back
MORE (Hispanization of) Moran, Texas
MORETEADO -DA or MORETIADO -DA bruised, covered with bruises
MORETEAR or MORETIAR va. to bruise; vr. to bruise oneself
MORFINIENTO -TA user of narcotic drugs (esp. morphine)
MORIDO -DA (var. of) muerto -ta (ppart. of morir)
MORIENDO (var. of) muriendo (ger. of morir)
MORIERA, MORIERAS, etc. (vars. of) muriera, murieras, etc. (past subj. conjugation of morir)
MORIERON (var. of) murieron (3rd pers. pl. pret. of morir)
MORIÓ (var. of) murió (3rd pers. sg. pret. of morir)
MORMACIÓN f. nasal obstruction
MORMADO -DA nasal (ref. to sound of the voice of a person with a temporary articulatory defect resulting from a stopped-up nose, a throat inflamation, etc.)
MORMAR vr. to contact an inflamation of the nasal passages, the throat, etc. (and which serves to nasalize or otherwise distort the vocal quality)
MORMULLO (var. of) murmullo
MORMURAR (var. of) murmurar
MORO or MORONDEL (slang, Hispanization of) Martindale, Texas
MOROSAICO (Eng.) motorcycle
MORRAGIA (var. of) hemorragia
MORRALUDO (ref. to man wearing baggy pants)
MORRO -RRA short and chubby
MORROCOYO (slang) any type of insect
MORTIFICACIÓN f. worry, preoccupation
MORTIFICAR va. & vr. to worry
MOSCA (fig.) pest, bothersome person; MOSCA EN LECHE dark-complected person married to (or associating with) a fair-skinned person; POR SI LAS MOSCAS just in case
MOSQUERÍO swarm of flies
MOSQUIENTO -TA fly-ridden, abounding in flies
MOSQUITA MUERTA person who pretends to be timid and reserved but is not; wolf in sheep's clothing (fig.), person pretending to be harmless
MOTA f. moss balls on trees (type of tree fungus); LA MOTA (slang) (Spanish name for) Hunter, Texas
MOTA (slang) marihuana
MOTEA or MOTELLA (rus.) (var. of) botella
MOTEADO -DA or MOTIADO -DA (var. of) goteado -da or gotiado -da; (slang) ANDAR MOTIADO -DA to be high from using marihuana
MOTEAR or MOTIAR (slang) vn. to smoke pot (slang), smoke marihuana
MOTEL (Eng.) m. motel
MOTO (slang) mf. marihuana freak, habitual user of marihuana
MOTORCICLETA (var. of) motocicleta
MOTOSAICA m. (Eng.) motorcycle
MOVER: MOVER LA JICOTERA to stir things up, get things moving (coll.); vr. MOVERSE DE CASA (Ang.) to move, change residences (Std. mudarse de casa); NO LE MUEVAS Leave well enough alone
MOVIDA: MOVIDA CHUECA (slang) crooked move, unsavory deal; illicit love affair; TENER MOVIDA (slang) to have plans for

a sexual assignation
MOYOTE m. mosquito
MU (var. of) muy
MUCHACHON -CHONA m. boyish; f. girlish: "Se ve muy muchachón" 'He looks very boyish'
MUCHAR (var. of) mochar 'to cut (off)'
MUCHAR (var. of) mochar
MUCHITO -TA (var. of) muchachito -ta
MUEBLE (rus.) m. automobile, car
MUELA fpl. CONTAR LAS MUELAS to pull the wool over one's eyes (fig.), deceive: "A mí no me cuentes las muelas; tú me robaste ese dinero"
MUELÓN -LONA m., f. bothersome person, pest
MUERTO -TA: m. adj. CAER(SE) MUERTO to drop dead; (slang) to pay up, pay, cough up (slang); ESTAR MUERTO -TA to be unaware of a fraud or a deception; to be adamant, stubborn, hard to convince; MUERTO -TA DE HAMBRE (fig.) (said of a greedy and selfish person); NO TENER EN QUÉ CAERSE MUERTO to be totally broke, penniless
MUGRAR (rus.) va. to dirty, make dirty; vr. to get dirty, dirty oneself
MUGRE f. (word used to name something whose name the speaker has forgotten, 'whatchamacallit', 'thingamagig','gizmo', etc.); prostitute
MUGRERO junkyard (fig.), place filled up with useless and dirty objects; botch-job, work badly done
MUJER: MUJER DE LA CALLE (pej.) street-walker, prostitute; MUJER JUGADA / MUJER PASEADA or PASIADA / MUJER PATEADA or PATIADA woman with a lot of mileage on her (coll.), woman with considerable sexual experience
MUJERERO (var. of) mujeriego
MUJERINGO (pej.) effeminate, sissy, fruity (slang)
MULO -LA: SER MULO -LA (fig.) to be stubborn; f. (Eng.) (ant. slang) money
MULETA: AGUANTAR MULETA (v.s. AGUANTAR)
MUNCHO -CHA (var. of) mucho -cha
MUNINCIPAL (var. of) municipal
MURIR (var. of) morir
MÚSICA: TENER or LLEVAR LA MÚSICA POR DENTRO (said of an introverted person) to have one's real self hidden; MÚSICA DE BOCA harmonica, mouth organ
MUSIQUERO -RA musician
MUSTIO -TIA ill-humored; dull, lusterless

N

NA (var. of) nada 'nothing'
NACIONAL mf. Mexican, Mexican national, someone from Mexico; mpl. (coll.) beans, frijoles
NACHO -CHA (dim. of) Anastasio -sia
NACHO (Eng., <natch, naturally) (slang) naturally, sure thing (coll.), you bet (coll.)
NADA: NADA VALE There's nothing to, The ____ is insignificant .... (expression used to indicate that one thing is of little importance compared to something else, which is worse:) "Nada vale la borrachera, lo peor es la cruda" "Being drunk is nothing, the worst part is the hangover'
NADIEN (var. of) nadie (pron.)
NAGUA or NAHUA fsg. (vars. of) naguas fpl. 'petticoat'; 'skirt'
NAGUAS fpl. (var. of) enaguas fpl.
NAIDE(N) (vars. of) nadie (pron.)
NAIFA (Eng.) knife
NAILÓN (Eng.) m. nylon
NALGAS: NALGAS PELONAS (vulg.) (hum.) bare-assed: "Él anda con las nalgas pelonas" 'He's going around bare-assed'; (see DAR LAS NALGAS)
NALGATORIO (hum.) big buttocks
NALGÓN -GONA (var. of) nalgudo -da
NALGUEADA or NALQUIADA spanking
NALGUEAR or NALGUIAR va. to spank; to pat someone on the buttocks
NANA baby-sitter
NANDO -DA (dims. of) Fernando -da
NAPQUETÍN (Eng.) m. napkin (Std. servilleta)
NAQUEADO -DA or NAQUIADO -DA (Eng.) knocked out, unconscious (see also NOQUEADO et al.)
NAQUEAR or NAQUIAR (Eng.) va. to knock out, render unconscious; vn. to knock on a door
NAQUIN (Eng.) m. napkin
NARANJADO -DA (var. of) anaranjado -

-da
NARANJAS (slang) adv. no (negative response to a question): "¿Vienes conmigo? ---¡Naranjas!"
NARANJILES (slang) adv. no (negative response to a question) (cf. NARANJAS)
NARANJO (Hispanization of) Orange Grove, Texas
NARCO (slang) member of the narcotics squad of the police force; detective (in general) (Eng?, nark)
NARIZ f. SER NARIZ to be a busybody (coll.), be overly interested in the affairs of others (see also NARIZÓN -ZONA); fpl. NARICES DE TÍSICO good sense of smell: "Tienes unas narices de tísico" (often said in exasperation, as by a mother to a child who has succeeded in smelling out a cake that was to be kept whole until dinner time)
NARANJA DULCE f. children's game in which the following verse is sung by a moving circle of participants: "Naranja dulce, limón partido / Dame un abrazo que yo te pido"; one child is stationed inside the circle, and when he/she succeeds in embracing one of those forming part of the circle, that child enters the center and is replaced by its former occupant
NATO (dim. of) Natividad or Natalio -lia
NATURAL m. "regular" haircut, however defined (traditionally a cut in which the hair does not cover the ears or descend below the collar line)
NAYOTAS (slang) fpl. nose
NAVAJEAR or NAVAJIAR va. to cut with a knife
NAVAJERO -RA flatterer; knife wielder (person whose favorite weapon is a knife)
NECEDERA (var. of) necedad 'foolishness'
NECESIDAD fpl. HACER LAS NECESIDADES (euph.) to go to the bathroom (for purposes of fecal or urinary evacuation)
NECIO -CIA annoying, bothersome; fussy, fidgety, irritable: "Yo creo que el niño tiene calentura porque está muy necio" 'I think the child has a temperature because he's very fussy'
NECITAR (var. of) necesitar
NEGRADA large group of U.S. black persons
NEGRITA elderberry (Sambucus mexicana) (prepared as a tea and used to treat colic)
NEGRO (pej.) mpl. CENA DE NEGROS any disorderly gathering
NEI mf. Inez
NEJO -JA dirty; yellowed (ref. to old tortillas)
NEL or NELA or NELA CANELA (slang) no (negative response to a question)
NELO -LA (dim. of) Manuel -la
NEQUIN (Eng.) f. napkin
NETA (Eng.) net (tennis or volleyball net)
NETO (dim. of) Ernesto
NI: NI MADRE (coll.) not a thing, not a single mother-lovin' thing (slang): "¿Qué hay en la hielera? -- Ni madre"; NI PELIGRO not a chance, fat chance (slang); NI POR AHI TE PUDRES (said to a friend or close relative who has not visited you in a while) 'What's become of you?'; NI SOCA not a bit, not at all
NICLE (Ang.) m. five-cent piece
NIERVO (var. of) nervio
NIEVE f. ice-cream (Std. helado); NIEVE DE PALITO eskimo pie, ice-cream on a stick; f. cocaine
NIEVERÍA (var. of) nevería
NIEVERO (var. of) nevero 'ice-cream vendor'
NIGACHURA or NIGASURA or NIGUESURA (Eng.) sling shot, nigger's shooter (ant. slang)
NIGUAS (slang) no (negative response to a question)
NINGUNEAR or NINGUNIAR (slang) va. to kill, wipe out (slang), off (slang)
NINO -NA (dims. of) Bernardino -dina
NIÑO: EL NIÑO MÁS (ref. to person whose name one wishes to avoid mentioning; cf. CIERTOS ELOTES (VERDES), MOLCAS); NIÑO DEL OJO pupil (of eye)
NIUNCA (var. of) nunca
NIUQUIS (slang) New Braunfels, Texas (see also NUIQUIS)
NO: ¡NO DIGO! interj. I told you so!, Didn't I tell you?!; How about that? (indicates admiration for a thing, a feat, etc.); ¿NO QUE NO? Didn't you say that ...?: "¿No que no te casabas?" 'I thought you said you were never going to get married!; ¿NO QUE NO, CHIQUITO -TA? I thought you told me

you weren't (going to do whatever you said you weren't)
NOBLADO -DA (var. of) nublado -da
NOCAUT (Eng.) m. knockout (in boxing) (see also NACAUT)
NOCHE late at night, late hours of the night: "Vino muy noche" 'He came very late last night'
NOCHEBUENA Poinsetta plant (Euphorbia pulcherrima)
NOCHECITA adv. fairly late at night
NODRIZA nurse (in general) (Std. enfermera)
NOJADO -DA (rus.) (var. of) enojado -da
NOJAR (var. of) enojar
NOJOTROS -TRAS (rus.) (var. of) nosotros -tras
NOMÁS adv. just; only; no sooner; AQUÍ NOMÁS / AY NOMÁS just so-so: "¿Cómo le va?-- Ay nomás"; How about that?, What do you think of that (often a slightly self-congratulatory response to a compliment); NO NOMÁS not just; not only; NOMÁS EN CUANTO (var. of) en cuanto 'as soon as'; NOMÁS NO (resolute negative reply to a request or a suggestion): "¿Nos puedes hacer ese favor? -- ¡Nomás no!"; (iron.) Yes indeed, Yes sirree: "¿Se lo llevaron a la cárcel?-- Nomás no"
NOPALERO -RA person employed to cut nopales or to clear land covered with nopales
NOQUEAR or NOQUIAR (Eng.) va. to knock out (in boxing); vn. to knock on a door (see also NAQUEAR et al.)
NORIA well (in general, e.g., NORIA DE AGUA 'water well', NORIA DE ACEITE 'oil well'); drain
NORTEADO -DA or NORTIADO -DA crazy, nutty, cracked (coll.)
NORTEAR or NORTIAR va. to drive crazy; vr. to go crazy
NORTECITO cold front accompanied by strong winds from the north
NOVIERO -RA easily enamored, quick to fall in love (ref. to person who flits from novio -via to novio -via)
NUBLAZÓN f. (var. of) nublado 'storm cloud'; cloudiness
NUBLINA (var. of) neblina
NUECERA person (invariably a woman) who works in a pecan factory as a processor, packager, etc.
NUECERÍA pecan factory, pecan processing plant
NUEVAS fpl. news (i.e., information forming part of a newspaper account or media broadcast)
NUEVECÍSIMO -MA very new, brand new
NUEVECITO -TA very new, brand new
NUIQUIS (slang) New Braunfels, Texas (see also NIUQUIS)

Ñ

ÑANGO -GA thin, scrawny
ÑUDO (var. of) nudo

O

OBEDENCIA (var. of) obediencia
OCEANO or OCIANO (vars. of) océano
ODIOSO -SA incorrigible; overbearing
OFECINA (var. of) oficina
OFENDOR -DORA m.,f. (Eng.) offender; juvenile delinquent
OFICINA (Ang.) political office, elective office (e.g., mayor, congressman, etc.): "¿Pa' qué oficina estás corriendo?" 'What office are you running for?'
OFRECIDO -DA apple-polisher, flatterer; f. woman who is prone to throwing herself at a man's feet, putting herself thereby at his mercy
OIDO -DA (var. of) oído -da
ÓJALA (var. of) ojalá
OJALÁ Y (var. of) ojalá (que): "Ojalá y vengas pronto" 'I hope you come soon'
OJETE (vulg.) anus; adj. stingy, cheap, parsimonious
OJO: OJOS CAPOTUDOS bulging eyes, pop eyes (slang); drooping eyelids; OJO DE BOTÓN buttonhole; OJO DE CHÍCHARO (slang) alert, sharp; OJO DE VENADO deer's eye (Muzuna sloani) (used as an amulet for protection against El Ojo--the Evil Eye)

HACER OJO to cast a spell on someone, give someone the mal de ojo; QUEDARLE A ALGUIEN EL OJO: "¿Cómo le quedó el ojo?" 'How does that grab you?' (slang), 'How do you like that as a result?'; TRAER A ALGUIEN ENTRE OJOS to have one's eye on someone, be watching someone for any little slip (misbehavior)

OLO, OLES, OLE, etc. (vars. chiefly rus.,of) huelo, hueles, huele, etc. (pres. indic. conj.of oler)

OLOTE m. corn-cob (ear of corn with husk and grains removed); ENTRE MENOS BURROS MÁS OLOTES the less you eat the more there'll be for someone else (often said as a reprimand to a child who refuses to eat)

OLLA (slang) buttocks,ass; PATALEARLE or PATALIARLE A ALGUIEN LA OLLA to kick someone in the ass; to beat someone up in a fight

OMBLIGÓN -GONA ponderous, heavy-set (ref. to persons); (said of a person with a large navel)

ONDA trend of the moment (in style, thought, speech, etc.), latest fad; ESTAR EN LA ONDA to be up-to-date, "with it" (slang); EN ONDA turned on, "with it", up-to-date

ONDE (var. of) donde

ONQUE (rus.) (var. of) aunque

¿ONTÁ? (rus.) (var. of) ¿Dónde está?

¡OPA! or ¡ÓPALE! Hey!, Hey you! Watch out!; uff! (grunt issued when lifting a heavy object)

OQUIS (var. of) de oquis, dioquis (advs.) (see also ANDAR DIOQUIS, ESTAR DIOQUIS)

ORA (var. of) ahora

¡ÓRALE! interj. Hurry up!; That's it, That's right!; fine by me, okay, sure; Throw it!, Let's have it!, Over here!; Stop it!, Knock it off! (coll.); ÓRALE ÓRALE Do it right now!

ORALIA (slang) (var. of) órale

ORDEN m. (Ang.) any request for merchandise (Std. pedido)

ORDENAR (Ang.) va. to order, request merchandise (Std. pedir)

OREJA handle (on a pitcher, a mug, etc.); telephone receiver and mouthpiece; hearing aid; fpl. (slang) yes (affirmative response to a question); APACHURRAR OREJA / PLANCHAR OREJA / TRAMPAR OREJA (slang) to sleep; PARAR (LA[S]) OREJA(S) to perk up one's ear(s), listen attentively (usually so as to hear what one should not); TIRAR OREJA (slang) to listen

ORGULLECER (var. of) enorgullecer

ORILLA: ESTAR DE ORILLA to be in a good mood; SER DE ORILLA to be temperamental, mercurial

ORILLAR vr. to pull over to the curb of the street (when driving a car)

ORINADA act of urinating

ORITA (var. of) ahorita 'right now'

ORMI (Eng.) m. army

ORQUESTRA (var. of) orquesta

ORUTAR (var. of) eru(c)tar

ORUTO (var. of) eru(c)to

OTATE m. bamboo pole or stick (Bambu arundinacea)

OTRO: EL OTRO CACHETE (DE LA CARA) or EL OTRO LADO (DEL CHARCO) Mexico; mpl. SER DE LOS OTROS (slang) to be a (male) homosexual; fpl. SER DE LAS OTRAS to be a lesbian

OVAROLES (Eng.) mpl. overalls (type of work pants) (see also OVEROLES)

OVEN (Eng.) m. oven (Std. horno)

OVEROLES (Eng.) mpl. overalls (type of work pants)

ÓVULOS mpl. vaginal suppositories (which may be used as contraceptives)

OYÍ, OYISTE, OYIMOS (vars. of) oí, oíste, oímos (1st pers. sg., 2nd pers. sg. and 1st pers. pl. pret. forms of oír)

OYIDO -DA (var. of) oído -da

P

PA' (var. of) para (prep.)

PACA bale; pack

PACA (var. of) para acá: "Ven pacá" 'Come here'

PACENCIA (var. of) paciencia

PACIENTA (var. of) paciente f.: "El paciente y la pacienta tenían mucha pacencia"

PACITO (dim. of) papacito 'daddy' (term of endearment in child language)

PACO -CA (dim. of) Francisco -ca

PACOIMA (slang) square (slang), person not up-to-date, not "with" whichever current trends

PACÓN (Eng.) m. popcorn
PACHANGA (coll.) party, festivity
PACHOCHA (slang) money
PACHORRAS mf. slowpoke
PACHORRUDO -DA slowpoke
PACHUCO -CA Chicano "zoot-suiter" of the 1940's; m. boy or f. girl from El Paso, Texas; EL PACHUCO (slang) El Paso, Texas. (There are several possible explanations of the word's origin: that it is a deliberate deformation of Paso with probable support from the Mexican city of Pachuca, or that the deformation of Paso may form part of the well-known process whereby nicknames beginning with c derive from syllables whose initial consonant is s, thus: Chente <Vicente.)
PACHUQUISMO linguistic oddity said to be typical of pachucos
PADED f. (child language var. of) pared
PADER (var. of) pared f.
PADRASTO (var. of) padrastro
PADRE (slang) adj. keen, terrific, neat, etc.: ESTÁ PADRE (,BATO -TA) (slang) (iron. expression used to indicate that one's feelings have been hurt; the implication is that revenge will be taken or poetic justice will prevail); ¡QUÉ PADRE MADRE! (slang) What a broad!, What a doll! (ref. to a very attractive woman); PADRE DE MÁS DE CUATRO (slang) he-man, stud, macho
PADROTE (slang) m. pimp; gigolo
PAENTRO or PA'ENTRO (vars. of) para adentro
PAFUELA (var. of) pajuela
PAFUELAZO (var. of) pajuelazo
PAFUELEADA or PAFUELIADA (vars. of) pajueleada or pajueliada
PAFUELEAR or PAFUELIAR (vars. of) pajuelear or pajueliar
PA' FUERA (see DAR PA' FUERA)
PAGADOR -DORA m., f. person who settles debts promptly
PAGO pay, wages
PAGRE (rus.) (var. of) padre
PAGRECITO (rus.) (var. of) padrecito
PAGULEAR or PAGULIAR (slang) to pay (see also paulear or pauliar)
PAI (Eng.) m. pie
PAINE (rus.) (var. of) peine m.
PAIPA (Eng.) pipe, smoking pipe; waterpipe
PAIS (var. of) país m.
PAISA mf. (var. of) paisano -na
PAJAREAR or PAJARIAR (slang) va. to look; to see; to watch, keep an eye on (coll.)
PÁJARO (slang) jail bird, prison inmate; PÁJARO -RA NALGÓN -GONA (slang) person with a large posterior, fat ass (vulg.)
PAJUELA woman of easy virtue, whore
PAJUELAZO whipping, (physical) blow; shot or gulp of liquor
PAJUELEADA or PAJUELIADA whipping
PAJUELEAR or PAJUELIAR va. to whip; PAJUELEARLE A ALGUIEN (EL MANGO) PARA HACER ALGO: to excel at doing something: "A Roberto le pajuelea el mango pa enseñar idiomas"; PAJUELEARLE EL CALLO A ALGUIEN (said of feet which smell badly): "A Primitivo le pajuelea el callo"
PAL (var., i.e., contraction, of) para el: "¡Vámonos pal centro!"
PALABRA: PALABRA MALA swearword, dirty word
PALABROTA very erudite and learned word
PALE (Eng.) m. pal, friend
PALEDAR (var. of) paladar m.
PALERO -RA (coll.) cover, cover-up agent, person who covers up the unintentional or deliberate mistakes of others
PALETA popsicle; ice-cream on a stick
PALÍO (var. of) palillo 'toothpick'
PALITO game resembling cricket; (euph.) penis; ECHAR UN PALITO to have sexual intercourse; DULCE DE PALITO lollipop; mpl. (usually pl.) clothes pins
PALIZA (see DAR UNA PALIZA)
PALO tree; (slang) penis; interj. Wham!, Crash!; PALO BLANCO aspen tree; SER DE PALO to be insensitive, hard as a rock (coll.)
PALOMA butterfly
PALOMÍA (var. of) palomilla
PALOMILLA gang, street corner gang; circle of friends
PALOMITA moth
PALOTAZO blow with a rolling pin
PALOTE m. rolling pin; (vulg.) large penis
PALLÁ or PA' ALLÁ (vars. of) para allá: "¿Onta Jorge?-- Se jue pallá" 'Where's Jorge?-- He went over there'
PALLAMAS (orthog. var. of) payama(s) (see also pijama)
PAMITA tansy mustard herb (Descurainia pinnata) (prepared as a tea for the treatment of empacho)

PAN (vulg., slang) vagina (see also PANOCHA, PANOCHO; PAN (DE) DULCE sweetbread; PAN DE HUEVO type of sweetbread in semi-spherical form; PAN DE MAÍZ or PAN DE MAIZ cornbread; type of old-fashioned dance
PANA lint, fluff
PANASCO -CA fat
PANCÁ (var. of) para la casa de: "¿Onta Chente? --Se jue pancá su buelita"
PANCHO -CHA (dims. of) Francisco -ca
PANCHO -CHA: PANCHO RIATA tough guy, mean bastard: "Ése es un pancho riata de verdad"; SER MUY PANCHO -CHA to be lacking in good taste, esp. with ref. to clothes: "Ése es muy pancho pa vestirse" 'That guy's got lousy taste in clothing'; (in general) to be lusterless, plain, dull, colorless; to be unsophisticated
PANDEADO -DA or PANDIADO -DA (vars. of) pando -da
PANDEAR or PANDIAR vr. to retract, take back: "Cuando se lo reclamaron, se pandió" 'When they confronted him with what he had said, he took it back'
PANDO -DA tilted, lopsided; (slang) drunk, looped
PANECÍO (var. of) panecillo
PÁNEL (Eng.) m. panel van (type of small truck similar to a delivery van)
PANITA lint, fluff
PANOCHA or PANOCHO (slang) vulva
PANOCHUDA (vulg.) adj. ref. to woman with a large vagina
PANQUEQUE (Eng.) m. pancake
PANTALETAS fpl. woman's panties
PANTALÓN m. (usually mpl.) PANTALONES CORTOS shorts, short pants; PANTALONES DE CUCHILLA bell-bottom(ed) trousers; PANTALONES DE PECHERA bib overalls; PANTALONES DE PLITS (Eng.) pleated trousers (Std. pantalones de pliegue); PANTALONES PEGADOS overalls (work trousers)
PANTALONUDO -DA (ref. to person with baggy pants)
PANTAS (Eng.) fpl. pants, trousers
PANTASMA (var. of) fantasma
PANTERA adj. elegant, groovy, (slang) (said. esp. of attractive and noticeable woman): "¡Qué pantera!"
PANTIÓN (var. of) panteón 'cemetery'
PANTOMINA (var. of) pantomima
PANTOMINA: HACER PANTOMINAS to make a scene (coll.), make a public spectacle of oneself, make a fool of oneself: "No te asilenciaste hasta que hiciste tus pantominas" 'You didn't shut up until you could make a scene in public'
PANZAZO (var. of) panzada 'push or shove with one's belly'
PANZONA (vulg.) knocked up (vulg.), pregnant
PANZONCITA (hum.) (ref. to a chubby woman who is pregnant)
PANZONZOTA (ref. to woman who is enormously pregnant)
PAÑO handkerchief
PAPA: ¡LA PAPA! interj. Great!, Terrific!, Swell!; PAPA MACEADA or PAPA MACIADA or PAPA MOLIDA mashed potatoes; fpl. ECHAR PAPAS to lie, tell lies
PAPACHADO -DA (var. of) apapachado -da
PAPACHADOR -DORA (var. of) apapachador -dora
PAPACHAR (var. of) apapachar
PAPACHOS m. (usually pl.) fondling, pampering, indulging; HACER PAPACHOS to pamper, fondle, spoil (said of children), indulge
PAPA GRANDE or PAPÁ GRANDE m. grandfather
PAPALOTE m. paper kite; windmill; propeller
PAPALOTEAR/PAPALOTIARLE A ALGUIEN PARA HACER ALGO to excel at doing something: "A Nino le papalotea pa pichar"
PAPASES (var. of Std. pl.) papás mpl.
PAPASOTE (slang) m. handsome man; sexy male; sugar daddy; daddy-o (slang)
PAPEL (Ang.) m. newspaper; PAPEL DE CHINA tissue paper (used for packing gifts); mpl. HACER PAPELES to make a spectacle of oneself or play the fool in public, create a scene in public; PAPEL PICADO confetti
PAPELERÍA establishment that buys used papers and magazines for recycling
PAPELERO -RA m. newsboy, newspaper seller; adj. mf. showoff; braggart; fraud; person prone to making scenes in public or to making a fool of him/herself; exhibitionist; mess of papers, scattered papers
PAPERO -RA liar; pretender

PAPI (Eng.) m. pappy, daddy
PAPIRO paper (in general); newspaper, periodical; PAPIRO DE CÍTICEN (Ang.) citizenship paper, document attesting to citizenship
PAPIS (Eng.) msg. (var. of) papi
PAPITA little white lie, falsehood of generally minor proportions
PAPULAR (Eng.) (var. of) popular adj.
PAQUETE m. the best part of anything; first prize; mf. opportunist
PAQUETUDO -DA (slang) excellent, topnotch
PARA: PARA ACABARLA DE FREGAR to make matters worse, on top of all that (fig.);PA(RA) ESAS GRACIAS in that case: "Vete por el perro. -- ¿Dónde está y qué hago con él cuando lo encuentre? --Bueno, pa' esas gracias yo voy mejor"
PARADA dirty deal, unfair bargain; HACERLE A ALGUIEN UNA (MALA) PARADA to play a dirty trick on someone; give someone a dirty deal; HACERLE LA PARADA A ALGUIEN to go along with someone's stand (position on an issue) or joke
PARADO -DA adj. m. on foot; standing; adj. mf. DEJAR A ALGUIEN PARADO -DA (in baseball) to strike someone out without a chance (i.e., with pitches so aimed that the batter has no chance to even swing at the ball); to stand someone up, fail to keep an appointment or show up for a date; f. TRAERLA PARADA to have a hard-on (slang, vulg.), have an erection
PARALIS (var. of) parálisis msg.
PARAR: ¡PÁRE(N)LE AHÍ! interj., coll.: Knock it off!, That's enough of that!; va. to stand something up perpendicularly; PARARLE EL ALTO A ALGUIEN / PARARLE LOS PEDOS A ALGUIEN to put a stop to someone's abusive behavior, put someone down (slang); PARARSE EN UNA BODA to stand up for (the bride/the groom) at a wedding, participate as one of the nuptual couple's sponsors; vr. to leave a sick bed upon getting well; NO PARARLE LA COLA A ALGUIEN: "Llámale por teléfono a ver si está en casa, porque a ése nunca le para la cola" 'Call him up to see if he's at home, because he's constantly on the go'
PARCHE mf. disagreeable person; leech, sponge, person who lives off of others
PARDE (rus.) (var. of) padre m.
PARDI (Eng.) m. (var. of pare/pore) party
PARE m. (Eng., var. of pore) party
PARED: PARED VERDE (slang) f. Walgreen's drug store (national chain of stores)
PAREJO -JA: ESTAR or QUEDAR PAREJO -JA CON ALGUIEN to be even with someone, owe nothing to someone: "Aquí está lo último que te debo; quedamos parejos ahora"; to be tied, end up in a tie (with someone); SER PAREJO -JA to be honest, honorable
PARENTRO (var. of) para adentro 'inside'
PARIÁN m. large market; marketplace
PARIENTE (Ang.) m. (usually mpl.) parent(s)
PARNA (Eng.) m. partner (usually term of non-pej. address towards a U.S. black person)
PARPAREAR or PARPARIAR (vars. of) parpadear
PÁRPARO (var. of) párpado
PARQUE m. role of tape used as "ammunition" for cap guns; PARQUE DE ANIMALES zoo; PARQUE DE PELOTA (Ang.) baseball stadium, baseball park
PARQUEADERO or PARQUIADERO (Eng.) parking place; parking lot; act of parking a car
PARQUEADO -DA or PARQUIADO -DA (Eng.) parked (ref. to cars, or, hum. to persons, e.g., "parked" or seemingly immobile in a chair)
PARQUEAR or PARQUIAR (Eng.) va. to park; vr. (slang) to sit down, "park oneself in a chair; to remain seated at great length, thus overstaying one's welcome
PARQUETE (var. of) paquete m.
PARTE: PARTES (fpl.) DE CARRO auto parts
PARTIDO -DA m. SER BUEN PARTIDO to be a good partner (esp. in a sports competition); f. part (in one's hair); (vulg.) vagina
PARTO: SEGUNDO PARTO afterbirth (placenta and membranes)
PARRANDA group of drunken revelers
PARRANDEAR or PARRANDIAR vn. to go on a drunk, go on a drinking

spree
PARRIBA or PA' ARRIBA (vars. of) para arriba
PASADA: DE PASADA in passing: "Dale el libro de pasada" 'Give him the book as you go by'
PASADERO -RA or PASADOR -DORA adj. m., f. passable (ref. to a job accomplished, commitments fulfilled, the physical attributes of persons, etc.)
PASAR va. PASAR BRACA (Ang?) to give someone a break (opportunity); PASAR ALGO to be able to eat food without vomiting after an attack of stomach disorder: "El enfermo ya está pasando la comida"; vn. PASARLA to be getting along in a so-so fashion, just getting by: "¿Cómo le va? --Pasándola"; PASARLA BIEN to be doing well; PASARLA MAL to be doing poorly: PASAR UN BUEN TIEMPO (Ang.) to have a good time (Std. divertirse); PASÁRSELE A ALGUIEN LA MANO (var. of írsele a alguien la mano)
PASEADO -DA or PASIADO -DA f. ESTAR MUY PASEADA/PASIADA (ref. to women) to have a lot of mileage, to have indulged oneself freely in sexual relationships: "Esa mujer está muy pasiada"
PASEADOR -DORA or PASIADOR -DORA m., f. (said of someone fond of "doing the town," going out on a spree)
PASEANDO or PASIANDO (see s. ANDAR: ÁNDATE PASIANDO)
PASEÑO -ÑA person from El Paso, Texas
PASEO parade, procession
PASGUATO -TA idiot, numbskull
PASIAR (var. of) pasear
PASIÓN fpl. (slang) "¿QUÉ PASIONES?" 'What happened?' (deformation of ¿Qué pasó?)
PASITO adv. (said of rivers sufficiently empty of water to allow crossing without having to take one's clothes off)
PASO: EL PASO DEL ÁGUILA (Hispanization of) Eagle Pass, Texas
PASOTE (slang) m. handsome man, sexy male; sugar daddy; daddy-o; ¿QUÉ PASOTES (CON LOS ZAPATOTES)? (slang) What's wrong?, What happened? (deformation of ¿Qué pasó?, cf. PASIÓN)
PASTA hay, feed for livestock
PASTERO cowboy who rides the boundaries of a ranch to check whether everything is running smoothly
PASTILLA or PASTÍA (slang) money; money traditionally thrown to children by godparents at a baptism
PASTOR -TORA m., f. stupid; discourteous; countrified, hickish, farm-fresh (coll.)
PASTORELA traditional theatrical representation of the birth of Christ performed around Christmas time
PASTORES: LOS PASTORES traditional Christmas pastoral play which depicts the visit of the shephards to the stable at Bethleham
PASTURA (slang) tobacco
PATA: fpl. DE PATAS: ECHARLE A ALGUIEN DE PATAS to throw someone out feet first
PATADA (Ang.) kick (of a firearm), recoil; kick (obtained from alcohol or drugs), thrill; (see also AGARRAR PATADA, DAR LA PATADA, DAR PATADAS DE AHOGADO, ESTAR DE LA PATADA)
PATALEAR or PATALIAR: PATALEARLE LA OLLA A ALGUIEN (slang) to kick someone in the ass
PATERO -RA smuggler (esp. one using small rafts--patos--to smuggle goods across the Río Grande)
PATI (dim. of) Patricia
PATÍN m. wooden scooter used by children (see also A PATÍN)
PATITAS (see DE PATITAS)
PATO bedpan; small raft with canvas sails used in fording rivers (esp. the Río Grande/Río Bravo, by illegal immigrants from Mexico to the U.S.); (slang, vulg.) homosexual, faggot (slang); weakling, effeminate male
PATÓN (slang) m. policeman, "flatfoot" (slang)
PA' TRAS (var. of) para atrás 'again' (adv.): "¡Entra pa' tras!" 'Come on back in again!' (see also: DAR PATRÁS, HACERSE PATRÁS, IR PATRÁS, LLEVAR PATRÁS, PASAR PATRÁS, VENIR PATRÁS)
PAULEAR or PAULIAR (slang) va. to pay
PAVICO diaper
PAYAMA(S) (Eng.) m(pl.) pajamas
PEDAL: PEDAL DE GAS accelerator
PEDICHE or PEDICHI adj., mf. persistent, demanding, bothersome
PEDIDERA repeated asking, tiresomely constant requests for something
PEDIÓRICO (var. of) periódico

PEDIR: PEDIR EMPRESTADO -DA (var. of) pedir prestado -da; PEDIR LA ENTRADA (see ENTRADA); PEDIR UN OJO Y LA MITAD DEL OTRO to ask for an excessive amount of something

PEDO fight; uproar; drunkenness, inebriation; PEDO -DA adj. drunk; ECHARLE UN PEDO A ALGUIEN to scold, warn: "Le echó un pedo porque llegó tarde"; PARARLE A ALGUIEN LOS PEDOS to put a stop to someone's abusive behavior; to put someone in his/her place; ¡PURO PEDO! (slang, vulg.) Bull roar! (vulg.), The hell you say!; ¿QUÉ PEDO TE CARGAS? (slang) What are you trying to prove?, What are you up to?; TRAERLE A ALGUIEN AL PURO PEDO to harass someone; (see also ANDAR PEDO, HACER PEDO)

PEDORRA: CHINCHE PEDORRA stinkbug (any insect of the Pentatomidae family)

PEDORREAR or PEDORRIAR (slang) va. to scold, give a warning to; vr. (vulg.) to fart continuously

PEDORRERA (vulg.) continuous breaking of wind: "Le agarró una pedorrera de la fregada" 'He really farted up a storm' (slang)

PEDRADA innuendo, insinuation: "Esa pedrada no curvió" (lit.) 'That (intended) curve ball didn't curve' = 'Your attempted insinuation was actually a direct accusation'

PEGAR: ANDAR PEGANDO to get along well together (ref. to persons); PEGARLE (DE MÁS) (AL CUENTO / AL RELATO) to add something (usually a mendacious element) to a story or a narration; PEGARLE EL SUEÑO to get sleepy: "Al niño le pegó el sueño como a las doce"

PEGOISTIA or PEGOITES mf. pest (ref. to person who imposes his/her presence upon others against their wishes) (see also PEGOSTE)

PEGOSTE mf. pest (id. to PEGOISTIA)

PEGOSTEAR or PEGOSTIAR va. & vr. to smear with a sticky substance

PEINADOR m. vanity table (low table with a mirror, piece of bedroom or bathroom furniture also serving as a dressing table

PELADAJE m. crowd of pelados, group of lower-class people (who are usually acting in an "ill-bred" fashion)

PELADO -DA lower-class person; ruffian, bully

PELADORA gold digger (fig.), woman in search of a wealthy husband or boy friend

PELAR va. to give a haircut to; vr. to get a haircut; vr. to flee, leave in a great hurry; to peel off, flake; PELÁRSELA to pull back the foreskin of one's penis; PELAR GALLO (slang) to die; PELAR (EL) OJO to open one's eyes wide so as to stare fixedly at something; PELAR EL DIENTE / PELAR (LOS) DIENTES to smile mockingly; to bare one's teeth (as in anger)

PELEA boxing; boxing match

PELEONERO -RA or PELIONERO -RA pugnacious

PELERÍO pile of hair, great abundance of hair: "Barre ese pelerío que dejaste en el piso"

PELIAR (var. of) pelear

PELÍCOLA (var. of) película

PELITOS mpl. hair of the genital zone; soft hair on the human body

PELIZCADA (var. of) pellizcada

PELIZCAR (var. of) pellizcar

PELIZCO (var. of) pellizco

PELIZCÓN (var. of) pellizcón

PELMAS mfsg. slowpoke

PELO: stature, height (of person): "Juan y Jorge son del mismo pelo"; ALZÁRSELE A ALGUIEN EL PELO / ALZÁRSELE A ALGUIEN LOS PELOS to stand on end (said of one's hair): "Se le alzaron los pelos"; PELO CHINO curly hair; PELO DERECHO (Ang.) or PELO LISO straight hair (as opposed to kinky or curly hair); PELO PARADO hair standing on end, standing straight up (as in a crew-cut); PELO QUEBRADO naturally curly or wavy hair

PELÓN PELÓN PELACAS / PELÓN PELACAS, CUIDA LAS VACAS/ PELÓN PELACAS, CUIDA LAS VACAS, YO LAS ENGORDO Y TÚ LAS ENFLACAS (expressed used to poke fun at persons--usually boys--who wear crew cuts)

PELÓN -LONA skinhead, person with hair cut close to the scalp (as in a crewcut); difficult, hard to resolve; PELÓN -LONAS: NALGAS PELONAS (vulg.) (hum.) bare-assed: "Él anda con las nalgas pelonas" 'He's going around bare-assed'

PELOTA: CARGAR PELOTA POR / TRAER PELOTA POR (slang) to really have the hots for, be passionately in love with: "Se ve que ese bato carga pelota por su chava" 'You can see that that guy really has the hots for his chick'; EN PELOTAS (vulg.) naked
PELOTAZO m. (ref. to both men and women as adj.) astute, sly, sharp
PELUCA (hum.) hair; ANDAR or ESTAR PELUCAS (slang) to be cleaned out, broke (usually as a result of having lost one's money in a game of chance)
PELUCAR (slang) va. to clean someone out in a game of chance
PELUDO -DA physically mature; large in size
PELUQUERO -RA habitual winner in a game of chance
PELUSA riff-raff, ill-behaved lower-class types
PELLÍN m. buttocks
PENAR: ANDAR PENANDO (said of a soul clothed as a ghost which roams the earth, fulfilling an unfinished commitment or righting a wrong which circumstances did not permit it to right during its lifetime)
PENCO -CA child born out of wedlock
PENDEJADA foolish or stupid act
PENDEJIAR (var. of) pendejear
PENDEJO -JA: HACERSE (EL/LA) PENDEJO -JA to play dumb, pretend not to know or understand; HACER PENDEJO -JA A ALGUIEN to fool someone; to cheat, defraud
PENDEJÓN -JONA (pej.) stupid idiot, ignoramus
PENDIENTE: ESTAR CON EL PENDIENTE DE ALGUIEN to be worried about someone: "Estoy con el pendiente de María porque todavía no ha llegado"; TENERLE A ALGUIEN CON EL PENDIENTE to have someone worried (about someone): "¿Ya llegó María?--No, aún me tiene con el pendiente" 'Did María arrive? -- No, I'm worried about her'; TENER PENDIENTE DE ALGUIEN to be worried about someone: "Tengo pendiente de Jorge, porque llora tanto"
PENE or PENI (Eng.) m. penny, one-cent piece; f. (slang) penitentiary (reduction of penitenciaría)
PENITENCIA (var. of) penitenciaría
PENQUEQUE (Eng.) m. pancake (see also PANQUÉ et al.)
PEPA (slang) clitoris: "La pepa es donde la mujer siente más sensación sexual"
PEPE -PA m. (dim. of) José, f. (dim. of) Josefa and Josefina (see also Fina); ¡AY TÚ PEPE! (etc.--see AY)
PEPENAR: PEPENARLE A ALGUIEN UNOS GOLPES to hit someone
PEPETORIA or PEPITORIA (vars. of) pipitoria
PEPEYENDO breaking wind (ger.) (the ger. is the only form used of the consequently hypothetical verb pepeyer)
PERCURAR (var. of) procurar
PERDER: PERDER LA CAMISA (Ang.) to lose one's shirt (coll.), lose a considerable amount of money
PERFILADO unravelled sewing
PERICO -CA mf. talkative person, chatterbox (coll.), gossip; f. (slang) radio
PERIÓRICO (var. of) periódico
PERIQUEAR or PERIQUIAR (slang) vn. to talk incessantly, chatter
PERIQUERA (slang) upper gallery of a movie theater
PERLA (see IR DE PERLA)
PERSINAR (var. of) persignar
PERSONAL m. poll tax
PERRA (see HACER LA PERRA)
PERRILLA sty, inflamation on the eyelid
PERRO -RRA f.: LA PERRA DE CUATRO LLANTAS (hum.) greyhound bus; PERRO CALIENTE (Ang.) hot dog (type of sausage); PERRO CHATO bulldog; SER COMO EL PERRO / LA PERRA QUE NO TIENE NI DEJA TENER to have a dog-in-the-mangerish attitude (ref. to a selfish person); f. SUERTE PERRA very bad luck; TRABAJAR COMO PERRO to work quite hard
PERRODA (var. of) pedorra (also chinche pedorra)
PERRÓN -RRONA m., f. bully; malicious person
PERRUSQUILLO -LLA or PERRUSQUÍO -QUÍA drunk; lower-class person
PESADO -DA (Ang.) (slang) adj. (ref. to the very latest in extravagant and "far-out" popular music= Eng. slang expression heavy music); PONERSE PESADO -DA to get nasty (coll.), act in an unpleasant manner
PESAR: PESARLE A ALGUIEN LAS BOLAS / EL BUCHE/LAS PELOTAS (vulg.) to be (very) lazy

PESCADO fish in general (cf. Std. pez 'live, uncaught fish')
PESCAR: PESCAR A ALGUIEN EN LA MENTIRA / PESCAR A ALGUIEN EN LAS MORAS to catch red-handed (coll.), discover someone's involvement in a criminal act, in a falsehood, etc.; PESCARLE A ALGUIEN LA NOCHE to be overtaken by night fall
PESCUEZO: TENER EL PESCUEZO TORCIDO to have a crick in one's neck
PESCUEZÓN - ZONA or PESCUEZUDO -DA (vars. of) pescozudo -da
PESETA twenty-five cent piece; repugnant and repellent person (see also CAER PESETA)
PESETUDO -DA repugnant, repellent
PESTE: ECHAR PESTES to raise a stink (fig.), make trouble
PESUÑA: GRAN PESUÑA (slang) foot; toe-nail
PESO dollar (U.S. currency)
PESPUNTE (see A PESPUNTE)
PESTAÑA: TIRAR PESTAÑA (slang) to sleep
PESUDO -DA rich, well-to-do
PETACA automobile trunk
PETACONA large and shapely woman
PETATE m. small rug, mat
PETATEAR or PETATIAR (slang) vr. to die, kick the bucket (slang)
PETATERO -RA: EL MERO PETATERO/LA MERA PETATERA the boss, the big cheese (coll.)
PETATÓN -TONA EL MERO PETATÓN/ LA MERA PETATONA the boss, the big cheese
PETICOUT (Eng.) m. petticoat
PETRA (dim. of) Petrona
PEYER (var. of) peer vn.
PEZÓN: PEZÓN ENLECHADO engorged nipple, caked breast
PIATÓN -TONA (var. of) peatón -tona
PICADILLO confetti (see also HACER PICADILLO)
PICADO -DA adj. ready for more, stimulated, excited (ref. to person whose appetite has been whetted by something); DIENTE PICADO tooth with a cavity; ¡QUÉ PICADO! (fixed expression) You'd like that, wouldn't you? (used iron.)
PÍCAP (Eng.) m. (var. of) pícop
PICAR va. to provoke, incite, needle (fig.); to bug (slang), annoy, bother: "¿Qué te pica?" 'What's bugging you?; PA' QUE SE PIQUE(N) / PA' QUE TE PIQUES (slang) Eat your heart out! (slang), Put that in your pipe and smoke it (slang); PICARLE A ALGUIEN LOS OJOS to make a fool out of someone; vr. to become excited by something and to want more of it, get a taste of something and go to extremes to satisfy the appetite (cf. PICADO); to get angry; to inject oneself with drugs; to hurry, move quickly; ¡PÍCALE! Move it! Hurry up!;¡PÍCATE! interj. (an incitement to envy, approx.) Put that in your pipe and smoke it!
PICLE (Eng.) m. pickle
PICO: CERRAR EL PICO to keep silent; to become silent, shut up (coll.)
PICÓN -CONA m. act of provoking someone to anger; mpl. DAR PICONES to tease, make jealous needle (coll.); adj. mf. (ref. to instigator, i.e., person who enjoys needling or inciting to anger; ref. to person easily aroused to anger or otherwise incited)
PÍCOP (Eng.) m. pick-up truck (see also PÍCAP)
PICORETA child's toy metal trumpet
PICOSO -SA adj. spicy (ref. to food which "burns" the inside of the mouth)
PICOTE mf. chatterbox (coll.), excessive talker
PICUDO -DA card sharp (person expert and somewhat unscrupulous at playing cards)
PICHA (vulg.) penis; (Eng.) m. pitcher (baseball) (see also PÍCHAR); PICHA-QUECHA-NACA (composite ref. to game of baseball) (Eng.) (cf. QUECHA)
PICHADA (Eng.) pitch (in baseball)
PICHAR (Eng.) va. & vn. to pitch (baseball)
PICHEO (Eng.) act of pitching (baseball)
PÍCHER (Eng.) m. pitcher (baseball)
PICHICATO -TA stingy, miserly
PICHICUATE m. water snake (genus Natrix)
PICHÓN -CHONA m., f. born loser (coll.), person who always loses or comes out last; easy to defeat; easy to deceive; m. (vulg.) penis
PICHONEAR or PICHONIAR va. to effortlessly defeat a novice in a sports competition; vn. to engage in active sexual foreplay
PICHUDO (slang) cocksman (vulg., hum.) (ref. to man with a large penis)
PIDEMOS (var. of) pedimos (1st pers. pl. pres. indic. of pedir)

PIDICHE or PIDICHI (vars. of) pediche, pedichi
PIDIR (var. of) pedir
PILDORIENTO -TA (slang) user of narcotic pills
PIEDRA: fpl. gallstones; PIEDRAS EN LA VEJIGA gallstones; ESA PIEDRA NO CURVEÓ (id. to ESA PEDRADA NO CURVEÓ, q.v. supra); ESTAR TRES PIEDRAS (slang) to be tremendous, terrific, very nice (ref. to persons and things)
PIEDRADA (var. of) pedrada
PIEDRERÍA (var. of) pedrería
PIEDRIZA stoning, act of throwing stones
PIERDA (var. of) piedra f.
PIERDADA (var. of) pedrada
PIERNA: MÁS PUEDEN LAS PIERNAS QUE LOS BRAZOS (v.s. BRAZO)
PIERNUDO -DA large-legged; f. woman with attractive legs
PIESES mpl. (var. of) pies (mpl. of pie 'foot')
PIEZA: AGARRAR ALGO DE UNA PIEZA (v.s. AGARRAR); CAMBIAR LA PIEZA to stop harping on the same topic, cease to talk about the same thing: "Por fin cambió la pieza y comenzó a hablar de algo diferente"
PILDOREAR or PILDORIAR vr. to ingest narcotic pills: "Ese bato se pildorea" 'That guy is a pillpopper'
PÍLDORO -RA (slang) (person) high on narcotic pills
PILIAR (var. of) pelear
PILÍCULA (var. of) película
PILINGO -GA small child; child small for his/her age, pee-wee (slang) (see also PILINGUACHE et al., PIRRONGO -GA); f. (vulg.) penis
PILINGUACHE or PILINGUACHI or PILINGÜE mf. (vars. of) pilingo -ga
PILMAMA baby sitter
PILÓN m. additional amount, premium (a "little extra" given to someone who has made a purchase); DE PILÓN free, gratis
PILONGA (slang, vulg.) male sex organ, penis (cf. PILINGA)
PILOTEAR or PILOTIAR va. & vn. to drive a car
PILLIDO sharp cry
PIMIENTITO -TA (hum.) half-pint (coll.), person of very short stature
PIMPO (Eng.) pimp, whoremaster
PIMPÓN (Eng.) m. ping-pong, table tennis
PINCEL (see A PINCEL)
PINCHE adj. mean, base, despicable; m. punk, hoodlum; mpl. clothes pins
PINCHURRIENTO -TA weak-willed, easily swayed
PINGA (vulg.) penis (cf. PRINGA); mf. tricky person
PINGO mischievous person, little devil (coll.)
PINGUAS fpl. (usually pl.) narcotic pills; LLEVAR PINGUAS (slang) to behave mischievously
PINGUITO -TA malicious; mischievous
PININOS (usually mpl.) baby's first steps (when just learning to walk)
PINTA (slang) jail, penitentiary
PINTAR va. to dye one's hair; vr. escape, run off, leave rapidly
PINTERO -RA painter (Std. pintor m.)
PINTO -TA very dark-skinned though without negroid facial features; PINTO -TA VIEJO -JA jailbird (coll.), person often jailed; PONER PINTO A ALGUIEN to heap with insults, tear to pieces (fig.), tell someone off in no uncertain terms
PINTORREGEAR or PINTORREGIAR vr. to use cosmetics to excess
PINTOTE m. type of yellow catfish
PINTURA: PINTURA PA' LAS UñAS nail polish; NO PODER VER A ALGUIEN NI EN PINTURA not to be able to stand the sight of someone, hate someone intensely
PIOCHA pointed beard; (slang) nice-looking, attractive; swell, great, keen, excellent (etc.)
PIOJERO or PIOJERA swarm of lice
PIÓN, PIONA (var. of) peón, peona m.,f.
PIONILLO croton (Croton coresianus) (herb prepared as a tea and used in treating colic)
PIOR (var. of) peor
PIOSOL (Hispanization of) Pearsall, Texas
PIPA (Ang.) pipe for conducting gases or fluids (Std. tubo) (cf. PAIPA)
PIPI or PIPÍ (euph.) f. penis; HACER (LA) PIPI/PIPÍ (mildly euph.) to urinate, "go pee-pee" (euph., said esp. of and to children)
PIPIÁN (slang) m. food (in general)
PIPILÍN (var. of) pipirín m.
PIPILISCO -CA near-sighted
PÍPILO (slang) gigolo; effeminate man; male homosexual
PIPIRÍN (slang) m. food (in general) (cf. PIPILÍN)
PIPITORIA adj. (used only in the following fixed expression:) RAZA PIPITORIA (pej.) (ref. to

Mexicans or Mexican-Americans); f. type of candy made with brown sugar and pumpkin seeds
PIQUENIQUE (Eng.) m. picnic
PIQUETAZO (var. of) picotazo
PIQUETE provocation, insult; DARSE UN PIQUETE (slang) vr. to inject narcotic drugs; ECHAR PIQUETES to insult; ESTAR DE PIQUETE to be on unfriendly terms; PIQUETE DE AGUJA (hum.) fornication; SER DE PIQUETE to have a hot temper; to enjoy inciting others to anger; to be easily offended, quick to take offense; (slang) to be a drug addict
PIQUETEAR or PIQUETIAR (Eng.) va. to picket (as a factory, by workers on strike); to boycott
PIQUINIQUE (var. of) piquenique m.
PIQUITO kiss; small mouth
PIRATA (slang) drunk, soused; mf. thief
PIRATÓN -TONA (slang) very drunk, smashed (slang)
PIRFANTEAR or PIRFANTIAR va. & vr. to dress up, dress elegantly
PIRINOLA top (child's toy); penis
PIRUJO -JA sly, astute, clever
PIRULERO -RA vendor of pirulí (type of caramel candy); JUAN PIRULERO (type of children's game)
PIRRINGO -GA small child (see PILONGO et al.)
PISAR (slang) va. to fromp (slang), fornicate (with); (Ang?) to step on the gas (coll.), accelerate a car
PISÓN m. (var. of pisotón?=) step, heavy tread, heavy footstep
PISOTEADA or PISOTIADA trampling
PISPÍS: TENER PISPÍS to be afraid
PISPORRA or PISPORRIA bump on the head
PISTE m. alcohol
PISTEADERA or PISTIADERA act of drinking alcohol
PISTEAR or PISTIAR va. & vn. to drink alcohol
PISTO -TA drunk, inebriated; m. alcohol; ECHARSE UN PISTO to take a drink of alcohol; m. money; small quantity of anything
PISTÓN -TONA very drunk, ploughed (slang)
PISTUDO -DA wealthy
PITA dagger
PITAR va. & vn. to honk (the horn of a car); to blow on a whistle, blow on any wind instrument
PITAZO -ZA clever, shrewd; wise, intelligent
PITO -TA (id. to PITAZO -ZA)
PIZARRO asbestos siding (used in the construction of buildings)
PIZCA harvest (usually ref. to cotton crop harvest)
PIZCADOR -DORA m., f. cotton picker
PIZCAR va. to pick cotton; to pick up, collect, glean
PLANCHA JUGARSE PLANCHA to be slow to react (because of lack of preparation, laziness, etc.)
PLATA (see A PLATA LIMPIA)
PELOTAZO astute, clever, alert: "Juanita es un pelotazo; cuidado con ella"
PLACA false teeth, dental plate; plaque (clay-like substance that accumulates between teeth); (slang) police force, cops, "the badge"
PLACER: HACERLE PLACER A ALGUIEN to treat someone well, be very courteous toward someone; to humor someone
PLANCHA wallflower (fig.), shy and retiring person; person who fails to take advantage of opportunities; HACERSE PLANCHA to overstay one's welcome; TIRAR PLANCHA to be left holding the bag (fig.), be abandoned (as by one's boy- or girlfriend)
PLANCHADA fsg. (var. of) planchado msg. 'clothes to be ironed'
PLANCHAR: PLANCHAR OREJA (slang) to sleep
PLANIAR (var. of) planear
PLANTA: PLANTA DE HUEVOS (Ang.) eggplant
PLANTADO -DA stood up, jilted; dressed elegantly; f. hard slap on the face
PLÁNTANO (var. of) plátano
PLANTAR vr. to dress elegantly; to overstay one's welcome, visit for longer than one should; PLANTÁRSELA A ALGUIEN to hit someone with one's fist or with the palm of one's hand
PLANTÍA or PLANTILLA first baseman's glove (baseball)
PLASTA lazy person; slow-moving person; hair oil; adj. greasy
PLATICADA chat, conversation
PLATICADERA lively conversation
PLATICADOR -DORA chatterbox, excessive talker
PLATICAR va. to tell a story
PLATICÓN -CONA fond of talking
PLATO phonograph record; base (in baseball); COLMARLE A ALGUIEN EL PLATO to exhaust someone's

patience; ECHARSE AL PLATO to take advantage of someone; to seduce sexually; to kill
PLEBE f. mob of lower-class people; lower-class people in general; gang of children; children in general
PLEGÓN: ECHARLE A ALGUIEN UN PLEGÓN to tell someone off
PLEIT (Eng.) m. home plate (baseball)
PLEITO boxing; boxing match
PLIT (Eng.) m. (usually mpl. PLITS) pleat
PLOCHA (var. of) piocha
PLOGA f. or PLOGUE m. (Eng.) plug (e.g., electric plug); (vulg.) mistress, kept woman
PLOGUE f. (Eng.) (vulg.) mistress, kept woman, bed-mate
PLOGUEAR or PLOGUIAR (Eng.) va. to plug, plug in (Std. enchufar); (Eng.) (vulg.) va. to fornicate
PLOMAZO pistol shot
PLOMEAR or PLOMIAR (slang) va. & vn. to shoot with a pistol
PLOMO -MA gray (color); m.,f. slow-moving person who dislikes work; SER (MUY) PLOMO -MA to be (very) slow to react to a given situation
PLUJEAR or PLUJIAR (Eng.) va. & vn. to plunge
PLUMA prostitute; woman of easy virtue, run-around (coll.)
POBRAR (var. of) probar va.
POCA or PÓCAR (Eng.) m. poker (card game) (see also PÓQUER)
POCITO (hum.) vagina
POCO: ¡A POCO! (fixed expression of surprise: You don't say!, Really?!; (expression of doubt): "¡A poco crees que me vas a engañar!" 'So you think you're going to cheat me!'; POCO A POQUITO (var. of) poco a poco
POCHISMO Spanish word or construction reflecting English influence (cf. POCHO -CHA)
POCHO -CHA (pej.) "gringoized" Mexican; (pej.) Mexican-American, Chicano
PODER: PODERLAS to be influential; to be a favorite (e.g., in political circles, among members of the opposite sex, etc.): "Él es de los que las puede"; PODERLE A ALGUIEN to wound, hurt; to displease, annoy: "Le pudo lo que le dije" 'What I said hurt him'; PUEDE QUE perhaps, maybe
PODO (slang) marihuana
POETA (slang, ant.) jitterbug (person who enjoys dancing the jitterbug, a popular dance of the 1940's)
POLECÍA (var. of) policía
POLI f. police
POLICÍA: HIJO DE POLICÍA (v.s. HIJO)
POLIS f. insurance policy
POLÍS (Eng.) m. policeman; f. police force
POLITIQUIAR (var. of) politiquear
PÓLIZA (Ang.) policy, course of action
POLO -LA (dims of) Hipolito, Apolonio, Leopoldo -da
POLQUEAR or POLQUIAR (var. of) polcar
POLQUERO -RA person who enjoys polkas
POLVADERA (var. of) polvareda 'dust cloud'
POLVEADO -DA or POLVIADO -DA all powdered up, covered with powder
POLVEAR or POLVIAR vr. to powder oneself, cover oneself with powder (e.g., to powder one's nose)
POLVERO -RA (vars. of) polvareda; f. powder puff
POLVITO: ECHAR POLVITOS to hex, bewitch (see also POLVO)
POLVO: ECHAR POLVOS to hex, bewitch
POLVOSO -SA (var. of) polvoroso -sa
POLLITO: POLLITO DE ESTAÇA (=pollo -lla q.v. infra)
POLLO spit, phlegm
POLLO -LLA or POLLÓN -LLONA person entering a subsequent stage in his/her life, e.g., an adolescent about to become an adult; can also ref. to someone whose physique is advanced for his/her chronological age, e.g., an adolescent with a body that is already adult
POMPA (Eng.) faucet; pump (Std. bomba)
POMPAÑERO -RA (rus.) (var. of) compañero -ra
POMPE or POMPI (dims. of) Pomposa
POMPEADOR -DORA or POMPIADOR -DORA (slang) swinger (person who enjoys a very active and adventuresome sex life) (cf. POMPEAR)
POMPEAR or POMPIAR (Eng.) va. to pump; (vulg.) to fornicate
POMPIADO -DA (slang) tired, exhausted
PONCHAR (Eng.) va. to puncture; to punch; vr. to go flat (said of

an aut. tire)
PONCHE: ESTAR PONCHE (slang, Eng.) to be punchy, punch-drunk (analogy with behavior of a groggy boxer); (slang) to be crazy
PONCHE or PONCHI (Eng.) m. punch, blow with the fist
PONCHI (var. of) ponche adj.
PONE (Eng.) m. pony (see also PONI)
PONER vr. (var. of) oponerse
PONER: va. to supply, provide, furnish: "El padrino va a poner el salón" 'The best man is going to furnish the dance hall' ESTAR PONIÉNDOSELA A ALGUIEN (see ESTAR); PON (var. of) supon (< suponer); PONER DE PATITAS EN LA CALLE to fire, dismiss (from a job) in short order; to run off, tell to leave (usually ref. to the manner in which one common law partner tells the other to depart); PONER EL CARRO EN REVERSA to shift into reverse gear; PONER CUIDADO to pay attention; PONER A ALGUIEN AL ALBA (slang) to alert someone, put someone on guard; PONER A ALGUIEN DEL ASCO to heap insults upon someone: "Pobrecito, lo pusieron del asco"; PONER A ALGUIEN EN MAL to speak ill of someone, discredit, run down (fig.); PONER A ALGUIEN PINTO to heap insults on someone; PONER COLA (slang) to "tail" someone (coll.), have someone followed; PONER DE LA BASURA to heap with insults, shout insults at: "Se metió a la casa porque la estaban poniendo de la basura"; PONER (EL) DEDO to accuse, point the finger at; PONER GORRO to harass; PONERLE EL OJO MORADO A ALGUIEN to give someone a black eye; PONER NOMBRE to name, give a name to: "¿Cómo le pusieron?" 'What name did they give him?'; PONER PA' TRAS (Ang.) to put back, fail to promote (as a child in school); to put back, return to a place (as a glass to a cupboard); PONER UN HASTA AQUÍ to draw the line (fig.), indicate the limits beyond which a particular form of behavior is unacceptable; vr. PONERSE ÁGUILA (slang) to become alert, be on the alert; PONERSE CABALLÓN -LLONA (slang) to get high on alcohol or narcotic drugs; PONERSE (CON) to challenge, mess around with: "No te pongas con él" 'Don't mess around with him'; PONERSE CON UNO DEL TAMAÑO DE UNO to pick on someone one's own size; PONERSE CUETE to get drunk; PONERSE CHANGO to become alert; PONERSE DEL ASCO to get extremely dirty; PONERSE EL AIRE PESADO for a situation to become tense; PONERSE EN EL AVISPERO to become alert; PONERSE EN LA LÍNEA/LINIA to get drunk; PONÉRSELA A ALGUIEN to hit someone (fig.), succeed in obtaining money through pressure or artful persuasion: "Si no te cuidas, te la van a poner"; PONÉRSELAS to get drunk: "Anoche se las puso, por eso todavía no se levanta"; PONERSE LAS BOTAS to have a ball (fig.), have a good time; PONERSE PESADO -DA to get tough with, act insultingly towards: "Hórale, no te pongas tan pesado" 'Don't get so tough'; PONERSE TRUCHA / PONERSE TRUCHE (slang) to become alert, get wise (slang)
PONI (Eng.) m. pony
PONÍ, PONISTE(S), PONIÓ, PONIMOS, PONIERON (vars. of) puse, pusiste, etc. (pret. conj. of poner)
¡PÓNELE!, ¡PÓNGA(N)LE! interj. Get to work!, Get busy!, Get with it!, Hurry up! (etc.); ¡PÓNELE JORGE AL NIÑO! interj. Get to work, Get busy! (etc.)
POPE (Eng.) m. puppy, infant dog
POPULACIÓN (Ang.) f. population, number of inhabitants within a given area
POQUEAR or POQUIAR (Eng.) vn. to play poker
PÓQUER (Eng.) m. poker (card game) (see also POCA et al.)
POR: DE POR SÍ It's bad enough as it is (without your making it worse): "De por sí que hace frío y tú dejas la puerta abierta" 'It's cold enough as it is, and you have to go and leave the door open'; POR LA BUENA willingly; POR LA MALA by force; POR MIENTRAS meanwhile; POR SÍ LAS MOSCAS just in case; POR SÍ O POR NO just in case: "Vamos a cerrar la puerta por sí o por no" 'We're going to shut the door, just in case'
PORA m. man encharged with maintaining sheep-shearing equipment
PORAZO (Eng., cf. PORE) blow-out

(slang), large noisy party
PORE (Eng.) m. party
PORO (var. of) pero conj.
PORTABLE (Eng.) adj. portable (Std. portátil)
PORTAMONEDA fsg. (var. of) portamonedas fpl.
POS (var. of) pues conj.
POSTA ball bearing; pellet; railroad tie
POSTE tall; skinny; (vulg.) m. rod (slang,vulg.), large penis
POSTEMILLA abscess in the mouth
POSTERO -RA (pej.) cedar chopper (lower- or working-class central Texas Anglo-Saxon); poor white (in general)
POSTOTES (Eng.) mpl. Post Toasties (brand name of type of breakfast cereal); dry breakfast cereal (in general)
POZO (slang) solitary confinement cell in a jail
POZOL(E) m. drink made from corn and sugar
PRAI: LA PRAI (Hispanization of) La Pryor, Texas
PRACTICIAR (Eng?) (var. of?) practicar 'to practice'
PRÁTICA (var. of) práctica
PREBA (var. of) prueba
PREBAR (var. of) probar
PRECINCTO or PRECINTO (Eng.) precinct (electoral)
PRECULA (Eng.) pre-cooling system in vegetable cannery, used to keep vegetables fresh and unspoiled
PRECUPAR (var. of) preocupar
PRECURAR (var. of) procurar
PREGUNTAR: PREGUNTAR UNA PREGUNTA or PREGUNTAR UNA CUESTIÓN (Ang.) to ask a question (Std. hacer una pregunta)
PRENCEPAL (var. of) principal
PRENCIPIO (var. of) principio
PRENDER va. to hook on (=cause to be addicted to) narcotic drugs
PRENDIDO -DA hooked on (addicted to) narcotic drugs
PREVILEGIO (var. of) privilegio
PRICULA (Eng.) (var. of) precula
PRICULERO -RA (Eng.--see PRECULA/PRICULA) worker in the pre-cooling section of a vegetable processing plant
PRIETO -TA (term of endearment)
PRIMERO: DE PRIMERO at the beginning
PRINCIPAL (Ang.) m. principal of a school (Std. director de escuela)
PROBE or PROBRE (var. of) pobre 'poor'
PROCURAR va. to look after, watch over: "Juan la procura mucho a su hermanita"; to make a play for, seek to gain the affections of: "Jorge anda procurando a esa chavala"; to seek out the company of, go look for
PRODUCÍ, PRODUCISTE, etc. (vars. of) produje, produjiste, etc. (pret. forms of producir)
PROFESIONISTA (var. of) profesional
PRONTA adj. f. (sole ref. to women) (said of a very young adolescent girl who begins to "run around with" men)
PRONTO: AHORA PRONTO recently
PRONUNCIAR (Ang.) va. to declare that something is so (Std. declarar): "Yo los pronuncio casados" 'I now pronounce you man and wife'
PROPETARIO -RIA (var. of) propietario -ria
PROTESTANTE -TA m., f. Protestant (Std. protestante mf.)
PROVISIÓN fsg. groceries
PUCHA: ¡LA PUCHA! interj. Oh yeah?! (simultaneous indication of doubt and defiance)
PUCHAR (Eng.) va. to push, shove
PUCHE (Eng.) m. push, shove
PUCHI interj. Whew! (expresses distaste towards an awful smell)
PUEBLO downtown, business section of a city
PUELA frying pan
PUERTA (interj., vulg.) (used to indicate that a woman is revealing, whether intentionally or not, those parts of her body which, should not be shown, esp. the vaginal region); DAR PUERTA to show off something new; (said of women) to show (uncover) the vaginal region, whether intentionally or not; DE PUERTA nice, good, super (expression of approval)
PUERTAZO (var. of) portazo
PUERTERO -RA (var. of) portero -ra
PUERTÓN (var. of) portón m.
PUJAR vn. to grunt
PUJIDO grunt
PUL (Eng.) m. pool, billiards; (Eng.) pull, influence (usually political)
PULGA fpl.: ¡ÚJULE, PA' MIS PULGAS! (fixed expression of annoyance:) 'That's the last thing I needed!'
PULGIENTO -TA flea-ridden, lousy (in the literal sense)
PULIAR (Eng.) va. to pull
PULMAN (Eng.) m. pullman

PUNTADA very appropriate joke or story; fpl. ¡QUÉ PUNTADAS! What crazy ideas!

PUNTÍA (var. of) puntilla

PUNTO -TA: SER PUNTO -TA to be cooperative, accommodating; to to be game, willing to try something; mpl. ANDAR DE PUNTOS (v.s. ANDAR)

PUÑETA: HACERSE LA PUÑETA (vulg.) to masturbate; f. masturbation

PUÑETEADA or PUÑETIADA (vulg.) masturbation

PUÑETEAR or PUÑETIAR (vulg.) va. to masturbate

PUÑETERO -RA (vulg.) fond of masturbation

PURGACIÓN f. gonorrhea, clap (slang)

PURO -RA utter, absolutely; only, nothing but (e.g.,: "Pura perica!" 'Nothing but talk!')

PUTEAR or PUTIAR vn. to solicit customers (said of prostitutes)

PUTO (slang) male homosexual, fag (slang)

Q

QUÉ: ¡QUÉ ESPERANZA(S)! interj. (used to express strong doubt as to whether something will take place:) That'll be the day!; ¡QUÉ BONITO!, ¿NO? (iron.) That's a fine howdy do!; ¡QUÉ GRACIA! (iron.) Why, that's nothing!; ¿QUÉ HÚBOLE? or ¿QUIÚBOLE? (slang) What's up?, What's happening? (phrases often used in greeting); ¿QUÉ LE HACE? What's the difference? What does it matter? So what? (fixed expressions); QUE NI QUÉ for sure, certainly, without doubt: "Ese niño se va a enfermar, que ni qué"; ¿QUE QUÉ? Huh? Whatcha say? (discourteous); ¡QUÉ SI! (stress on qué) I should say so!, Absolutely!: "¿La besó el novio? --¡Qué si!"; ¿QUÉ TAL? (indication of pleasant surprise upon hearing good news) How about that?, Imagine that!; ¿QUÉ TANTO? How much? (Std. ¿Cuanto?); SER QUÉ DE: ¿QUÉ ES UD. DE MARÍA? How are you related to María?; YO QUE TÚ (YO QUE ÉL, etc.) If I were you (If I were him, etc.)

QUEBRADO -DA (Ang.) broke, penniless; (Ang.) f. break, opportunity; first shot in a game of pool; DAR QUEBRADA to give someone an opportunity: "¡Dame una quebrada nomás!" 'Just give me a break!'

QUEBRANZAS fpl. (hum.) taxes

QUEBRAR: SER DE ESOS QUE NO QUIEBRAN NI UNA TAZA/NI UN PLATO not to be able to hurt a fly (coll.), be extremely gentle

QUECHA (Eng.) m. catcher (baseball) (see also QUECHE et al.)

QUECHAR (Eng.) va. to catch (a ball, in baseball); vn. to play the position of catcher (in baseball)

QUECHE or QUÉCHER (Eng.) m. catcher (in baseball) (see also QUECHA)

QUEDAR va. to fit, match, harmonize with, go well with: "Este traje le queda bien" 'This suit fits him well'; vn. to match, harmonize: "¿Le queda ese pantalón a ese saco?" 'Do those pants match that coat?'; to matter, concern, involve: "¿A mí qué me queda de eso?" 'What's that to me?/ How does that involve me?'; vn. to die: "Allá quedó" 'He died then and there' 'That was the end of him'; vr. to end, terminate: "La vista se quedó donde se besaron" 'The movie ended where they kissed each other'; AY QUE QUEDE let it rest, let it be (etc.): QUEDAR A LA MEDIDA (for clothes) to fit to a T: "El sombrero le quedó a la medida" 'The hat fit him to a T'; QUEDAR AL PELO to fit to a T: "La chaqueta le quedó al pelo" 'The coat fit him to a T'; QUEDAR EN DONDE MISMO to make no progress, make little headway; to not better oneself, not improve; QUEDAR EN NADA to amount to nothing, turn out to be a failure; to fail to reach an agreement or solution; to be abandoned: "¡Qué pasó con el programa? --Quedó en nada"; QUEDAR HECHO PEDAZOS / QUEDAR COMO TRAPO MOJADO to be dead tired, end up dead tired (as after vigorous activity); QUEDAR PAREJOS to be tied, end up in a tie; QUEDARLE A ALGUIEN vn. to be someone's business, be of interest to someone: "¿A ti qué te queda eso?" 'What business is that of yours?'; vr. QUEDARSE SÚPITO -TA to fall fast asleep as soon as one lies down; vr. QUEDAR(SE) TIESO -SA to die; vr. QUEDARSE LIMPIO -PIA to become broke (penniless), get cleaned out (slang); QUEDARSE TAMAÑITO -TA to be left on pins and needles, become nervous in anticipation of; QUEDÁRSELE to retain (a thought): "Eso no se me queda a mí, por más que lo estudie" 'I can never remember that, no matter how much I study it'; SIN QUE ME QUEDE NADA (SIN QUE TE etc. QUEDE NADA) all modesty aside, if I say so myself: "¡Qué bien escribí esta carta!, sin que me quede nada"; vr. TÚ ¿DÓNDE TE QUEDAS? You're no better, You're just as bad

QUEDRÉ, QUEDRÁS, etc. (vars. of) querré, querrás, etc. (future conj. of querer)

QUEDRÍA, QUEDRÍAS, etc. (vars. of) querría etc. (cond. conjugation of querer)

QUEHACEROSA or QUIHACEROSA adj. & f. woman who enjoys doing housework

QUEJÓN -JONA plaintive, complaining; querulous

QUELA (dim. of) Ángela or Micaela

QUEMADO -DA suntanned; f. burn, scald

QUEMADORA incinerator

QUEMAR vr. to be close to the solution of, be near to a hidden object one is seeking (usually in a game); to get a sun tan; TRAER QUE QUEMAR (slang) to have cigarettes in one's possession

QUEMAZÓN m. fire (Std. incendio); an object that has been burned; VENTA DE QUEMAZÓN fire sale (sale of merchandise minimally damaged by a fire in the store)

QUEMÓN m. burn; (fig.) burn, insult; DAR QUEMONES (slang) to attempt to anger, to taunt, to needle (coll.)

QUÉMPAR or QUÉMPER (Eng.) m. camper (recreational vehicle)

QUEN (rus.) (var. of) quien

QUENEDE (Hispanization of) Kenedy, Texas

QUENO -NA (dims. resp. of) Eugenio, Eugenia

QUENQUE adv. piggyback; m. piggyback ride; SUBIR AL QUENQUE to climb on (someone's back) for a piggyback ride

QUEQUE or QUEIQUE (Eng.) m. cake; ¡AIRE AL QUEQUE! interj. Beat it!, Scram!, Get out of here!

QUEQUITO (Eng.) cupcake

QUERENDÓN -DONA loving, affectionate; (ref. to person who forms close attachments easily)

QUERMES (var. of) quermés or quermese m. 'church bazaar'

QUERO, QUERES, etc. (vars. of) quiero, quieres, etc. (pres. indic. conj. of querer)

QUESO (slang) smegma that collects around the lower part of the head of an uncircumcised child's penis

QUETA (dim. of) Enriqueta

QUIEN: ¿A QUIÉN Y A CUÁNTOS? What concern is that of anyone's?; ¿QUIÉN TE LO MANDA? I told you so!

QUIHACER (var. of) quehacer m.

QUIMONA (var. of) quimono

QUINCEAÑERA or QUINCIAÑERA girl who is just turning fifteen and in whose honor a "coming-out" party is traditionally given

QUINDA or QUINDER (Eng. < German) m. kindergarten

QUINESVIL (Hispanization of) Kingsville, Texas

QUINIPA (Hispanization of) Knippa, Texas

QUINO (dim. of) Joaquín

QUINTA small park-like area containing a gazebo, a band platform, etc., in the center, which is used for meetings or recreational purposes

QUIQUE (dim. of) Enrique

QUIRE (Eng.) mf. kitty, kitten

QUIRO -RA (Eng.) kiddo, bud, bub (slang) (terms of endearment, also vocatives)

QUIT (Eng.) Kid (used, at times maliciously, as a prefix to a series of sobriquets denoting physical attributes, e.g., QUIT JOROBAS [said to a hunchback])

QUITAR va. QUITAR LA LINDA (slang) to deflower (euph.), cause to lose one's virginity (said of women): "Si no te cuidas te van a quitar la linda"; vr. to stop, cease, subside (esp. with ref. to weather phenomena): "Ya se quitó l'agua" 'It's stopped raining now'; QUIEN QUITE Y perhaps: "Quien quite y vengan temprano" 'Perhaps they'll come early'; NO SE LE QUITA You can't take that away from him (fig.), You've got to give him his due: "No se le quita, de veras sabe sus cosas" 'You've got to hand it to him, he really knows his stuff'

R

RABO: VIEJO RABO VERDE (see VERDE)
RABÓN -BONA (hum.) short-statured; overly short (ref. to articles of clothing shorter than is appropriate): "Ese vestido le queda muy rabón" 'That dress is too short for you'; PANTALONES RABONES highwater pants (hum.) pants not reaching the ankle
RACHAR (Eng.) va. to rush, crowd up upon (esp. in sports)
RADIODERÍA (var. of) radiador (aut.)
RAFA or RAFE or RAFEL (dims. of) Rafael
RAID (Eng.) m. ride (in a car)
RAIHUOT (Hispanization of) Redwood, Texas
RAITAR or RAITEAR or RAITIAR (Eng.) vn. to ride (in a car), go for a ride, go riding
RAITÓN (Eng.) m. ride (in a car)
RAIZ (var. of) raíz f.
RAJADA (vulg.) vulva
RAJADA (var. of) rajadura
RAJAR vr. RAJARSE CON to denounce, squeal (slang), betray to: "Ya no tengo nada que ver con él porque se rajó con la policía" 'I don't have anything to do with him anymore because he squealed to the cops'
RAJETA(S) mfsg. (mfpl.) (most often used as an adjective) tattletale, betrayer, denouncer, squealer (slang); breaker of promises: "Todo el mundo sabe que ella es muy rajetas"
RAJOLEAR or RAJOLIAR vr. to back down, take back (a promise)
RAJÓN -JONA coward; tattle-tale, betrayer, stool pigeon (slang); breaker of promises
RALEA bunch of disorderly and ill-bred persons
RALO -LA weak, flavorless (commonly ref. to coffee or other beverage)
RAMAS fpl. bushes
RAMFLA (slang) jalopy, old battered-up car
RANCHERO -RA adj. shy, bashful, "countrified"; country; regional: MÚSICA RANCHERA country music (the Mexican and Chicano equivalent of the Anglo-American "country and western" music)
RANCHO small rural farming community; (Eng.) ranch (Std. hacienda); HACER RANCHO to overstay one's welcome, continue to visit for too long; adj. DE RANCHO countrified, cornfed (coll.), farm-fresh, hickish, from the sticks: "Tu primo es muy de rancho" 'Your cousin is quite farm-fresh'; SER PURO RANCHO to be very countrified, straight from the farm (fig.), a hick from the sticks (coll.)
RANFLA (orthog. var. of) ramfla
RANQUEAR or RANQUIAR (Eng.) va. to rank, arrange, classify
RAPTAR (Ang.) va. to rape (Std. violar)
RAPTO (Ang.) rape
RAQUETA (Eng?) racket, illegal business operation
RASCADA or RASCADERA act or effect of scratching
RASCARRABIAS mfsg. irritable and easily annoyed person
RASCÓN m. (id. to RASCADA supra)
RASCUACHE mf. punk, worthless person
RASGUÑADA (id. to RASCADA supra)
RASGUÑÓN m. scratch
RASPA adj. & f. riff-raff, ill-bred person: "Había mucha gente raspa ahí"; stingy, parsimonious; f. snow cone (shaved ice, to which is added a sweet fruit flavoring)
RASPADA act and effect of scraping
RASPADORA apparatus used to make scraped ice (esp. for snow cones --see RASPA)
RASPOSO -SA scratchy, uneven (ref. to surfaces), bumpy
RASQUERA itching sensation
RASTRILLAZO blow delivered with a rake
RASTRILLO (slang) comb
RASURADA act or effect of shaving
RATO: A POCO RATO shortly, soon thereafter; MÁS AL RATO (pleonasm) (var. of) al rato
RATÓN: SER RATÓN DE UN AGUJERO to be a one-woman man or a one-man woman (i.e., to be completely uninterested in any member of the opposite sex except one's spouse)
RATONERA (fig.) old and decrepit

house, squalid or depressing dwelling; swarm of mice or rats; den of thieves, hang-out for criminal or other low-life elements
RATONERO (var. of) ratonera 'mouse hole', rat hole' (also fig. 'old house')
RAUN(D) (Eng.) m. round (period of time into which a boxing match is divided); DAR UN RAUND to go for a whole round, be able to last for a whole round (boxing)
RAYA pay, wages, paycheck; penny-pitching (game won by person who pitches a penny closest to a designated line)
RAYADO -DA (said of person carrying large sums of money or various other valuable possessions); scratched: "Ese disco está rayado" 'That record is scratched'
RAYAR (rus.) va. to write; to pay wages; vr. to come into money or property; to hit a streak of good luck; RAYARSE EL DISCO to sound like a broken record (said of any conversation in which the speaker wears out the listeners by harping on the same subject): "¡Cállate, ese disco ya se rayó!'
RAZA (collective ref. to persons of Hispanic background in general; also ref. esp. to Mexican-Americans; note: the word may have negative or pej. connotations to older Mexican-Americans): "En esa escuela había pura raza" 'There were nothing but Mexican-Americans in that school'
REAJUSTE m. period of adjustment
REAL m. unit of currency equal to twelve and a half cents, hence only used in multiples of two or more, with ref. to U.S. currency; thus DOS REALES= $.25, CUATRO REALES= $.50, OCHO REALES= $1.00
REALIZAR (Ang.) va. to realize, become aware of (Std. darse cuenta de)
REATA or RIATA (vulg.) penis; interj. Pow! (accompanies the administration or simulation of a blow, usually with the fist); SER BUENA REATA/RIATA (coll.) to be a good Joe (coll.), be considered a good fellow by others; (see also PANCHO RIATA)
REATAL or RIATAL m. large quantity of something
REATAZO or RIATAZO blow with the fist; mpl. severe beating, whipping, thrashing (see also DAR REATAZOS)
REATIZA or RIATIZA severe beating (see also DARSE UNA REATIZA)
REBAJAR va. to belittle, disparage; humiliate; to reduce in price; (also REBAJAR DE PESO) to lose weight, reduce
REBAJE or REBAJO reduction of price, discount
REBALOSO -SA (rus.) (var. of) resbaloso -sa
REBATAR (var. of) arrebatar
REBORUJO noise; confusion, commotion, melee
REBOTAZO big bounce
REBUSTO -TA (vars. of) robusto -ta
RECA (Eng.) wrecker (Std. camión grúa)
RECAR (Eng.) va. to wreck (usually a car); vr. to have a wreck
RECARGADO -DA arrogant, presumptious

RECARGAR vr. to brag, boast; RECARGÁRSELAS to brag, boast
RECARGUISTA mf. braggart
RECAR (Eng.) va. to wreck
RECEBIR (var. of) recibir
RECLAMAR va. to confront (i.e., to confront someone with the truth): "Voy a reclamarle la verdad"; "No dijo nada cuando se lo reclamé"
RECLE: AL RECLE (slang) in a while
RECOGIDO -DA adopted child; foster child
RECONOCIENCIA recognition; acknowledgment; gratitude, appreciation
RECORTADO -DA low on funds (see also ANDAR RECORTADO -DA DE DINERO)
RECORTAR va. to denigrate, put down (a person), speak ill of; to trim a small amount (of hair); to lay off, disemploy
RECORTE m. newspaper clipping; slight hair trim
RECRECIÓN (var. of) recreación f.
RECULÓN m. sudden jerk made by a car when the accelerator is depressed rapidly
RECHANCHO -CHA selfish, egocentric
RECHINAR vr. RECHINÁRSELE A ALGUIEN EL CUERPO to get goose pimples (goose bumps)
RECHINCHE stingy, parsimonious (cf. CHINCHE)
REDEPENTE (var. of) de repente
REDETIR or REDITIR (var. of) derretir
REDICULEZA or RIDICULEZA (vars. of) ridiculez f.
REDÍCULO (var. of) ridículo
RÉFERI (Eng.) m. referee
REFERIR va. to recall a favor one

has done (for someone): "A mí no me gusta que refieran nada" 'I don't like for people to recall the favors they've done me'
REFÍN (slang) m. food
REFINAR (slang) va. to eat
REFUEGA wild and volatile woman
REGADERA shower-bath; (ref. to any messy room full of misplaced objects)
REGANCHAR (var. of) reenganchar va. to contract for work (often for agricultural work, field work, etc.)
REGANCHE (var. of) reenganche m. (used with the following variant meanings:) bonus given to a (farm) worker in advance of the start of the job
REGANCHISTA mf. payer of the reganche (q.v.) bonus
REGAÑADA bawling out, scolding
REGAR: REGARLA to make a mess of things, foul things up, do a poor job; to create problems; to be foolish; REGÁRSELA to make trouble
REGRESAR va. to return an object to its owner
REGÜELTO -TA (var. of) revuelto -ta
REIMUNDO (var. of) Raimundo
REIR (var. of) reír
REJA (slang) jail
RELACIÓN f. buried treasure
RELAJAR va. to ridicule, make a fool of; vr. to ridicule oneself
RELAJE m. trick, joke; cruel teasing, humiliation
RELATIVO -VA (Ang.) relative (person one is related to by blood or other kinship ties)
RELÍS m. sharp cliff, precipice; (Eng.) m. release (from a job, from prison, from responsibility, etc.)
RELÓ (var. of) reloj m.
RELOJ DE ALARMA (Ang.) m. alarm clock
REMODELACIÓN f. remodeling (of a house or other edifice)
REMOVER(SE)LE A ALGUIEN LA CONSCIENCIA to be bothered by one's conscience: "Se le removió la consciencia"
REMPLE (slang) m. car, automobile
REMUDA herd of horses
REMUDERA lead horse, horse which wears a bell in a herd of horses
REMUDERO cowboy in charge of watching the horses at night
REMUEQUES mpl. excessive and tasteless adornments
RENDIR vn. to suffice, be enough (usually used in the negative): "Veinte tortillas no rinden aquí; debes hacer más"
RENEGAR vn. to protest, complain, grumble
RENEGÓN -GONA m., f. constant complainer
RENTAR (Ang?) va. to lease, rent, offer for rent: "Voy a rentar esta casa el mes que viene porque me hace falta el dinero"
RENTERO -RA (Ang?) renter, person who pays money for the privilege of using or occupying)
REPELAR vn. to complain, grumble
REPELIDO act of complaining, grumbling
REPELÓN -LONA complainer, grumbler
REPETIR vn. to belch, burp (esp. said of babies)
REPIOCHA adj. mf. extremely beautiful; terrific, swell (coll.)
REPITIR (var. of) repetir
REPUÑOSO -SA selfish
REQUE (Eng.) m. wreck (of an automobile)
REQUEAR or REQUIAR (Eng.) va. to wreck (a car); vr. to have a wreck (see also RECAR)
RÉQUER (Eng.) m. wrecker (Std. camión grúa)
REQUINTADO -DA (var. of) arrequintado -da
RES f. numbskull; CAER LA RES (ref. to someone who has been fooled, taken in, deceived): "¿Sabes que Samuel se casó con ésa de quien te hablé antes? -- ¡Uh, pues cayó la res!"
RESACA artificial lake or reservoir
RESBALÓN m. affair (amorous); ANDAR EN EL RESBALÓN to be having an affair; RESBALÓN -LONA shrewd, clever, slippery (fig.); teasing
RESEDÁ (var. of) reseda
RESEQUEDAD f. dryness
RESONGAR to talk back rudely (esp. to one's elders)
RESORTES mpl. suspenders (for trousers)
RESPINGAR vn. to complain; to kick (as a burro); to blow one's top (slang), get angry
RESPINGÓN -GONA m., f. habitual complainer
RESPONSABLIDAD f. (var. of) responsabilidad
RESPONSALIDAD f. (var. of) responsabilidad
RESTA (slang) restaurant
RESURADA (var. of) rasurada (cf. resurar)

RESURAR (Eng?, combination of 'razor' with Std. rasurar?) va. to shave; vr. to shave oneself
RESVIL (Hispanization of) Reedville, Texas
RETACAR va. to fill a container tightly up to the very top; vr. to stuff oneself (said of someone who overeats)
RETEJILADO -DA very rapid: "La chota lo paró porque iba retejilado"; in quick succession: "Perdieron cinco juegos retejilados" 'They lost five games in quick succession'
RETESUAVE (slang) adj. mf. great, super, keen, tremendous
RETINTO -TA very dark-skinned (though without other specifically Negroid features)
RETOBAR or RETOBEAR or RETOBIAR vn. to talk back impudently (esp. to older persons, to one's parents, etc.)
RETOBÓN -BONA m., f. sassy back-talker (ref., esp., to young person who consistently talks back to older people)
RETRA (slang) m. (var. of) retrato
REVERSA (Ang.) reverse gear (vehicle); DARLE DE REVERSA (A UN VEHÍCULO) to back up (reverse) (a vehicle); (fig.) to back up (backtrack) when one has made a mistake
REVOLVER va. to confuse, muddle; vr. to become confused, muddled: "No digas nada ahorita; me voy a revolver si no te callas"; REVOLVÉRSELE A ALGUIEN EL ESTÓMAGO to get an upset stomach
REVUELTO -TA upset (said of stomach)
REZUMBAR: REZUMBARLE A ALGUIEN (EL APARATO / EL MANGO) PARA HACER ALGO to excel at doing something: "A Chente le rezumba (el mango) para jugar al pimpón"
RIACLO (slang) AL RIACLO in a while
RIAL (var. of) real
RIATA (var. of) reata
RIATAZO (var. of) reatazo
RIATIZA (see REATIZA, DAR UNA REATIZA)
RICÉS (Eng.) m. recess (play period during the school day)
RICHE (Eng.) (dim. of) Richard
RIDETIR or RIDITIR (vars. of) derretir (see also DIRRETIR, REDETIR et al.)
RIDÍCOLO -LA (var. of) ridículo -la
RIELES (slang) mpl. woman's legs (hum.)
RIELOTES (slang, hum.) mpl. woman's legs
RIFA card reading (form of fortune telling); ECHAR RIFAS to read the cards
RIFAR vr. to excel at something
RIFLE m. ESTAR COMO RIFLE to be in superb physical condition for any undertaking (esp. for the sex act)
RILEY or RÍLEY (Eng.) m. relay (race)
RILLO (var. of) río 'river'
RIN (Eng.) m. ring; rim
RINCONAR (var. of) arrinconar
RINCONERA quack midwife
RINCHE (Eng.) m. Texas Ranger (paramilitary state police corps member)
RING (Eng.) m. ring (boxing, Std. cuadrilático)
RINGUEAR or RINGUIAR (Eng.) va. to ring (a bell)
RIR (var. of) reír (see also REIR)
RISIÓN -SIONA m., f. ridiculous; brunt of jokes
RISIONADA anything that provokes laughter
RITMO rhythm method (of birth control)
RIUMA (var. of) reúma
RIUMÁTICO (var. of) reumático
RIUMATISMO (var. of) reumatismo
RIYO ,RIYES, RIYE, RIYEMOS/REYIMOS, RIYEN (vars. of) río, ríes, etc. (pres. ind. of reír)
ROBÓN -BONA m., f. thief; adj. thieving, larcenous
ROCHE or ROCHO m. (Eng. < roach < Sp. cucaracha) roach, cockroach (see also RUCHO)
RODIADO -DA (var. of) rodeado -da
RODIAR (var. of) rodear
ROGÓN -GONA m., f. person who constantly begs for favors; person who enjoys being coaxed to do things; f. brazen hussy (coll.), woman who does not hesitate to make advances at men
ROGAR: HACERSE DEL ROGAR (var. of) hacerse de rogar 'to want to be coaxed'
ROL (Eng.) m. bread roll; hair roll, hair roller
ROL m or ROLA f. (slang) automobile
ROLA (slang) phonograph record; song
ROLADO -DA (slang) asleep; lying down
ROLANTE (slang) m. automobile
ROLAR (slang) vn. to sleep; vr. to go to bed, go to sleep
ROLE (slang) (Eng?) m. hair roller; automobile (see also ROL, ROLA); sleep (state or act of sleeping)
ROLETA (var. of) ruleta
ROLIAR (slang) (Eng.) va. to roll

someone (slang), steal from someone while he/she is asleep or drunk
ROMANCE (Eng.) m. romance, love
ROMO -MA short-statured
ROMPER va. to tear (Note: verb does not mean 'to break' as in Std.; for the "Texas" equivalent of 'to break' see QUEBRAR); vr. ROMPERSE LA CABEZA to hurt oneself in the head
ROMPIDO -DA (var. of) roto -ta (ppart. of romper)
RONCADERA loud snoring; combined snoring of many persons
RONCÓN -CONA person who snores frequently
RONCHA: HACER RONCHA to run up one's winnings in a game of chance after starting out with very little money
ROPA: ROPA DE ABAJO underwear, underclothes; ROPA DE SALIR dress clothes, "Sunday best" (coll.)
ROQUIROL (Eng.) m. Rock 'n' Roll (the music; the dancing appropriate thereunto)
ROSA: ROSA DE CASTILLA herb rose (Rosa sp.) (its petals are prepared as a tea and taken as a mild purge)
ROSADO -DA irritated (skin); chapped (lips): "Traigo la piel rosada aquí en el pescuezo"; ANDAR ROSADO -DA to have a skin irritation in a "certain place" (euph. --when the irritated part of the body in not mentioned it is assumed to be the anal region)
ROSAR (var. of) dorsal m.
ROSAS (var. of rosetas?) fpl. popcorn
ROSQUITA (var. of rosquilla?) ring-shaped pastry
ROST (Eng.) m. roast (roasted meat); roasting pan
ROSTICERÍA (Eng., roast) place where roast meat is sold; restaurant which specializes in roast meat
ROTADO -DA (ppart. of rotar, q.v. infra) ruptured (with a hernia)
ROTADURA rupture (with a hernia) (see also ROTURA)
ROTAR va. & vr. ("var." of romper, apparently a back formation from the Std. ppart. of romper, i.e., roto) (Note: rotar is used in all the expected tenses and modes and is fully regular in its conjugation: Uds. rotan, rotaron, rotaban, rotarán, rotarían, que roten, que rotaran, etc.)
ROTURA rupture (with a hernia)
ROYER (var. of) roer va.
ROZAR vr. to chap one's skin (esp. the lips)
ROZÓN m. slight scratch, break, or irritation of the skin; flaying of the skin
RUBE (dim. of) Rubén
RUCAIBA (slang) mother, ole lady (slang)
RUCAILO -LA old person
RUCO -CA (slang) m. old man; husband; boy friend; boy (in general); f. old woman; wife; girl friend; girl
RUCHO (Eng. <roach, <Sp. cucaracha) roach, cockroach (see also ROCHE, ROCHO)
RUFIANO -NA overly-familiar, overbearing
RUEDA: RUEDA DE LA FORTUNA Ferris wheel; RUEDA DE SAN MIGUEL type of children's game
RUIDO: BUSCARLE RUIDO AL CHICHARRÓN (see CHICHARRÓN)
RULA (Eng.) ruler (measuring instrument)
RUMALDO (var. of) Romualdo
RUMBADO -DA strewn, scattered (often with ref. to possessions such as toys, clothes, etc., left every whichwhere in a room)
RUMBAR va. to carelessly strew or scatter things about
RUNRÚN m. gossip
RUÑIR va. to gnaw; to eat away at
RURE or RURI (Eng.) Rudy (dim. of Rudolph)
RUSCO -CA stingy, parsimonious
RÚSTICO -CA lusterless, dull, uninteresting (ref. to persons)
RUTERO -RA newspaper deliverer, m. paperboy

S

SABER: NO SABER DAR SANTO Y SEÑA DE ALGUIEN to be unable to tell where someone is; NO SABER EN DONDE ESTÁ UNO not to know whether one is coming or going (fig.), to be highly confused; PARA QUE SEPAS (SEPAN, etc.) (set expression of defiance) So there!; QUE QUIÉN SABE QUÉ very, extremely, _____-er than a ____ (used in comparative expressions:) "Está más loco que quién sabe qué" 'He's crazier than a loon'; SABER A QUE ATENERSE to know the score (slang), know in advance what the situation is; SABER LO QUE ES AMAR A DIOS EN TIERRA AJENA to know firsthand what trouble really is; SABER LOS SECRETOS DE ALGUIEN (said, hum., when drinking from someone else's glass); SEPA DIOS or SEPA EL BURRO DE LOS MECATES (expressions indicating incredulity) God only knows!, Who can say?!

SABO (rus.) (var. of) <u>sé</u> (1st pers. indic. of <u>saber</u>)

SABROSO -SA superior to others, hot stuff (slang): "Él se cree muy sabroso" 'He thinks he's really something'

SACAR va. to throw in someone's face (fig.) the favors one has done for that person: "Vete, a mí no me gusta que me saquen los favores que me hacen"; to inherit (as physical or personal traits): "María sacó la nariz de su mamá" 'María inherited her mother's nose; to make (money), earn: "Con esta chamba no vamos a sacar ni para pagar por los frijoles" 'With this job we're not even going to make enough to pay for the beans'; vr. to get (what one deserves): "Eso es lo que se sacan por andar molestando gente" 'That's what they get for going around bothering people'; vr. to weasel out (slang), cleverly find a way out of a responsibility or commitment; to move quickly aside to avoid a blow; DE AHÍ NO TE SACAN (DE AHÍ NO LO etc. SACAN) (set expression) No one can make you yield on that point (ref. to stubborn person unwilling to be convinced); SACAR AIRE to burp (a baby); SACAR DAGA CON to show off something new (esp. an article of clothing); SACAR LA GARRA to gossip; SACAR LUMBRE to harp on the same subject, talk incessantly about the same topic; SACARLE A ALGUIEN LA COLORADA to give someone a bloody nose (see also COLORADA); SACARLE (LA VUELTA) A ALGO/ALGUIEN to dodge, avoid something/someone: "El jefe siempre nos da mucho trabajo y por eso le sacamos (la vuelta) cuando lo vemos venir"; SACARLE A ALGUIEN LOS TRAPOS/TRAPITOS AL SOL / SACARLE A ALGUIEN LOS TRAPOS/TRAPITOS A REMOJAR to hang out someone's dirty linen (fig.), bring the skeleton(s) out of someone's closet (fig.); SACARLE CANAS A ALGUIEN to give someone gray hairs; SACAR PATADA (Ang.) (slang) to get a kick out of (something): "Él es de los que sacan su patada de las drogas" 'He get his kicks from drugs'; ¡SÁCATE! interj. Pow!; ¡SÁCATE LA DAGA! Get to work!; Get with it!; Your turn to pay!

SACATE (orthog. var. of) <u>zacate</u> m.

SACATEADA or SACATIADA evasive act, avoidance

SACATEAR or SACATIAR va. to avoid, evade, side-step, duck, dodge

SACATÓN -TONA (coll.) m.,f. freeloader

SACÓN -CONA m.,f. shirker, avoider of responsibilities

¡SÁCOTE! (var. of) ¡SÓCATE! (q.v.)

SACUDIR vr. to try to shake off the blame from oneself, attempt to exculpate oneself

SAFADO -DA (orthog. var. of) <u>zafado -da</u>

SAFAR (orthog. var. of) <u>zafar</u>

SAFO(S) (orthog. var. of) <u>zafo(s)</u>

SAIN (Eng.) m. sign, placard, poster

SAINAR or SAINEAR or SAINIAR (Eng.) va. to sign (Std. <u>firmar</u>)

SAL: ECHARLE A ALGUIEN LA SAL to jinx, bring bad luck to

SALADO -DA jinxed, cursed with bad luck

SALAMANQUEZCO salamander

SALAMÓNICOS (slang) San Marcos, Texas

SALARETE m. bicarbonate of soda; baking powder

SALIDA: SALIDA DE LOS DIENTES teething; VENIR DE ENTRADA Y SALIDA to call on someone briefly, stop by for a brief visit

SALIDERA Y ENTRADERA constant leaving and entering, coming and going

SALIDERO -RA gad-about, person who is always "out on the town"

SALIDOR -DORA m., f. person who enjoys going out on the town (coll.), frequent seeker of night-life entertainment

SALIR: SALIR A LUZ (Ang?) to come to light, become apparent;

SALIR A MANOS to break even in a game of chance; SALIR CANUTO to attempt to defer payment on merchandise or services after these have been delivered or performed: "Le corté el sacate y me salió canuto" 'I cut his grass and then he promised to pay me some other day'; SALIR DE SU CUIDADO to give birth: "Tu tía ya salió de su cuidado"; SALIR DIOQUIS (see DE HOQUIS, DIOQUIS); SALIR GORDA to get pregnant; SALIR PA' FUERA (euph.) to go to the bathroom (euph.= to urinate or defecate) (see also IR PA' FUERA); SALIR POR DEBAJO DE LA MESA to always come out on the short end of the stick, always fail in whatever one attempts; SALIR SOBRANDO to be superflous, redundant; to be academic; to be useless or of little or no importance (often said with ref. to help offered after a problem has been solved); SALIRSE to spill one's seed (coll.), for the man to withdraw the penis before ejaculation so as to avoid pregnancy

SALUBIDAD f. (var. of) salubridad

SALVAR (Ang.) va. to save (money)

SANABABICHE or SANABABICHI (Eng.) (vulg.) m. son-of-a-bitch

SAN ANTON (slang) San Antonio, Texas

SAN ANTOÑO (var. of) San Antonio, Texas

SAN CUILMAS (hum.) San Antonio, Texas; (hum.) (any town one wishes to burlesque)

SANAR (euph.) vn. to give birth, deliver

SANCHAR va. to cheat on one's spouse, commit adultery

SÁNCHEZ m. the "third person" in an amorous triangle (ref. to the male lover of the other man's wife)

SANCHO -CHA adj. adulterous; m. adulteror; f. adultress; mf. animal raised as bottle-fed (in the absence of or rejection by the animal's mother)

SAN FELIPE DEL RÍO (original Spanish name of) Del Rio, Texas

SANGRE (slang) adv. no (negative response); SANGRE DÉBIL anemia (coll.) SANGRE DE CHANGO mercurochrome; SANGRE DE CHINCHE unpleasant, repulsive (ref. to persons); SANGRE POBRE anemia; TENER LA SANGRE LIVIANA to be pleasant, agreeable, well-liked

SANGRIAR (var. of) sangrar

SANGRÓN -GRONA disagreeable, repugnant (ref. to persons); conceited

SÁNGÜICH(E) or SÁNGÜICHI or SÁNHUICH (E) (Eng.) m. sandwich

SANTA CLOS (Eng.) m. Santa Claus (Std. Padre Noel)

SANTO mpl. DARSE UNO DE SANTOS to be grateful, to thank one's lucky stars; NO SABER DAR SANTO Y SEÑA DE ALGUIEN to be unable to say what became of someone who is unaccountably absent)

SAPO frog; (orthog. var. of) zapo

SAPOLTURA (var. of) sepultura

SARAMPIÓN: SARAMPIÓN DE TRES DÍAS German measles, rubella

SARDERA camp-follower (prostitute who establishes herself near a military base); woman very fond of soldiers

SARDINA (fig.) low man on the totem pole, person whose job is of minimal importance

SARDO (slang) soldier; sergeant

SARSA (var. of) salsa

SARTÉN m. (var. in gender of sartén f.)

SARRUCHAR (var. of) serruchar

SARRUCHE m. (var. of) serrucho

SARRUCHO (var. of) serrucho

SASTRERÍA dry-cleaners (Std. tintorería)

SASTRERO -RA tailor (Std. sastre)

SATÍN m. (var. of) satén 'satin'

SÁTIRO -RA senile old person

SAURINO -NA (var. of) zahorí 'fortune teller, soothsayer'

SAXOFÓN (var. of) saxófono m.

SECADOR m. napkin

SECIÓN (var. of) sección f.

SECO: VENIRSE EN SECO to engage in coitus interruptus, have an ejaculation elsewhere than inside the woman's vagina

SECONDARIA (var. of) secundaria (most typically escuela secondaria)

SECTIEMBRE (var. of) septiembre

SEDAL m. type of strong string (used in fishing line, for flying kites, etc.)

SEDAZO screen door; window screen

SEGUIDA: EN SEGUIDA (DE) alongside, next door (to): "Vive en la casa de en seguida" 'He lives in the house next door'

SEGUIDO adv. frequently, often

SEGUNDO (see DE SEGUNDO 'second hand')

SEGURANZA insurance

SEGURO safety pin (Std. imperdible):

SEGURO QUE SÍ of course, naturally (see also DE SEGURO 'for sure'); SEGURO QUE NO of course not, by no means

SEGUROLA interj. (slang) Yessir, Yes indeed

SEMÁFARO (var. of) semáforo

SEMÁSFORO (var. of) semáforo

SEMBRAR (slang) va. to bury a corpse

SEMÍA (var. of) semilla

SEMOS (var. of) somos (1st pers. pl. pres. ind. of ser)

SENCÍO -CÍA (var. of) sencillo -cilla

SENSE or SENSÉN m. game of marbles; the ring in that game (played in essentially the same fashion as the game of "marbles," i.e., the object is to knock out marbles from the center of the ring)

SENTADERAS (var. of) asentaderas fpl.

SENTADOR -DORA (Ang.) baby sitter

SENTENCIA (Ang.) sentence, combination of words constituting a complete utterance (Std. oración, frase)

SENTENCIADA: TENÉRSELA SENTENCIADA A ALGUIEN to place someone under warning, indicating that revenge will be carried out at some future time: "Mira, Concha, cuídate que ya te la tengo sentenciada" 'Watch out, Concha. The day you're least expecting it I'm going to get my revenge on you'

SENTENCIAR: SENTENCIÁRSELA A ALGUIEN (id. to tenérsela sentenciada, see s. SENTENCIADA)

SENTIDO outer ear (Std. oreja)

SENTIR: SENTIR BASCAS to gag, feel nauseated

SENTÓN m. hard flop experienced when one sits down abruptly

SEÑORITA virgin: "Ella todavía es señorita, gracias a Dios"

SEPO (var. of) sé (1st pers. sg. pres. ind. of saber) (see also SABO)

SEPULGRO (var. of) sepulcro

SER: ¡NO VAYA A SER (TAN DE REPENTE)! That'll be the day! (general expression of incredultiy); SER ALGO DE ALGUIEN to be related to someone: "¿Qué es Carlos de Jorge?" 'How is Carlos related to Jorge?'; SER DE AGUA (v.s. AGUA); SER DE DULCE (v.s. DULCE); SER DE LOS OTROS (v.s. OTRO); SER DE ORILLA (v.s. ORILLA); SER DE PALO (v.s. PALO); SER LUMBRE (v.s. LUMBRE); SER POR DE MÁS to be useless, be in vain: "Es por de más tratar de darle consejos" 'It's useless to try to give him advice'; SEA POR DIOS so be it (fixed expression indicating resignation); SI ES DE QUE if: "Iremos si es de que viene temprano" 'We'll go if he comes early'; TÚ LO SERÁS (UD. LO SERÁ, etc.) The same to you! (expression used to return an insult)

SERENATEAR or SERENATIAR va. to serenade

SERENATERO -RA serenador, person who serenades

SERVICIO (euph.) chamber-pot

SERVIENTE m. -TA f. (var. of) sirvienta

SÉSGALE (interj.) Stop that!; Cut it out!, Stop bothering me!

SESO mpl. TENER (BUENOS) SESOS to be intelligent

SESONAR (slang) to sniff glue (for a mildly narcotic effect)

SETEAR or SETIAR (Eng.) va. to set (esp. with ref. to hair)

SEYA, SEYAS, etc. (vars. of) sea, seas, etc. (pres. subj. of ser)

SHAINEAR or SHAINIAR (Eng.) (var. of) chainear or chainiar (Note: digraph "sh" pronounced as palatal sibilant [š])

SHO (Eng.) (var. of) cho (Eng.)

SÍ: (NO) DAR DE SÍ (used more in the negative) (not) to be reasonable, yield, be compromising, easy to convince; DE POR SÍ QUE as it is, as things (now) stand: "No hables de él; de por sí que no quiere venir a la fiesta" 'Don't talk about him; as things now stand he surely won't want to come to the party'; TRAER DE POR SÍ to be born with: "Ese talento lo trae de por sí" 'He was born with that talent'; Y TÚ SI (Y ELLA etc. SI) (iron.) Yeah, I'll bet, That'll be the day: "Me voy a casar mañana.-- Y tú sí"

SÍA (var. of) silla

SIEMPRE after all, anyway, still: "¿Siempre te vas?" 'Are you still going to go?'/'Are you going, after all?'

SIETECUEROS msg. watery blister on the sole of the foot (caused, according to popular tradition, by stepping barefoot in horse urine)

SIGUIR (var. of) seguir

SILABARIO (slang) (expansion-disguise of sí) adv. yes

(affirmative response)
SILENCITO -TA quiet; taciturn
SILINDRO (slang) (expansion-disguise of sí) adv. yes (affirmative response)
SÍMBULO (var. of) símbolo
SIMÓN or SÍMON, LEÓN or SIMONACHO (all slang) (expansion-disguises of sí) adv. yes (affirmative response)
SIMPLE adj. (euph.) mentally retarded (cf. INOCENTE)
SIMPLETÓN -TONA (Eng?) m., f. simpleton, idiot, fool
SINC (Eng.) m. sink, washbasin (see also sinque)
SINGLISTA mf. player of a singles match in tennis
SINÓ (var. of) sino 'but, but rather'
SIÑOR -ÑORA (rus.) (var. of) señor, señora
SINQUE (Eng.) m. sink, washbasin (see also SINC)
SINSONCLE or SINSONTLE or SINSONTE m. mockingbird (see also CENZONCLE et al.)
SINTAR (var. of) sentar
SINTARAZOS (slang) (expansion-disguise of sí) adv. yes (affirmative response)
SINTEMOS (var. of) sentimos (1st pers. pl. pres. ind. of sentir)
SINTIR (var. of) sentir
SINVERGÜENZO (var. of) sinvergüenza
SÍQUELE (Eng.) (interj.) Sic 'em! (expression of encouragement said to dogs)
SIRANDA "spanking" (neologism used as a pseudo-noun solely within a specific context: "Bueno, si quiere siranda" 'Well, if you want a spanking...') (derived from the phrase "Bueno, si quieres ir, anda," said to a child who asks permission to go somewhere knowing in advance that his/her parents have already denied that permission; in a sense siranda is a form of disguised speech to prevent the child from losing face in front of a playmate)
SIROL or SIROL SIROLACHO (slang) (expansion-disguise of sí) adv. yes (affirmative response)
SIRVIR (var. of) servir
SIRRE m. (var. of) sirle or sirria 'dung, manure' (esp. of cows, sheep, goats)
SISOTE m. boil (skin inflamation); sore; ringworm
SISTA (Eng.) sister (female sibling); Sister (nun)
SO (rus.) (var. of) soy (1st pers. sg. pres. ind. of ser)
SO (Eng.) conj. so 'therefore' (Std. así que)
SOBADOR -DORA m. masseur; f. masseuse
SOBAJAR va. to humiliate, shame
SOBITA mf. son-of-a-bitch (Eng. < S.O.B. plus -ita)
SOBRANDO (see SALIR SOBRANDO)
SOBRES (usually mpl.) overshoes; (slang) adv. yes (affirmative response)
SOCA: NI SOCA (slang) not a bit, not at all; (Eng.) f. sucker, all-day sucker (type of hard candy mounted on a stick and ingested through sucking)
SOCADO -DA (Eng.) soaked, cleaned out (in a game of chance) (cf. SOCAR); (see also ANDAR SOCADO -DA)
SOCAR (Eng.) va. to soak (slang), clean out (slang), win all of someone's money in a game of chance
SOCAS (see ANDAR SOCAS)
¡SÓCATE! (interj.) Wham!, Pow!
SOCROSO -SA dirty, filthy
SODERÍA soft-drink bottling plant
SODERO -RA person who bottles soda (soft drinks) in a bottling plant; person who sells or delivers soft drinks; person fond of consuming soft drinks
SODONGA (slang) soda water, soft drink
SOFACEAR or SOFACIAR vn. to lie on a sofa
SOFBOL or SÓFBOL (Eng.) m. softball (baseball played with a larger, softer ball); f. softball (the ball itself)
SOFLAMERO -RA finicky; oversensitive, touchy
SOFOQUE mf. heckler
SOLANO -NA (slang) alone, unaccompanied
SOLAR m. patio; yard (either front or back yard or else both considered as a single space)
SOLDADERA camp-follower
SOLECITAR (var. of) solicitar
SOLECITO intense heat
SOLIMAS (slang) (expansion-disguise of sólo or a solas) alone
SOLOLOY m. (var. of) celuloide
SOLTAR va. to let out, expand (the size of clothes); vn. to fade (clothes), come off (color on utensils)
SOLTURA diarrhea, loose bowels
SOMBREAR or SOMBRIAR vr. to move into or stay in the shade
SOMBRERÓN -RONA or SOMBRERUDO -DA

person (usually male) who habitually wears a large hat
SOMBRÍA (var. of) sombrilla
SONADO -DA (slang) turned on (slang), under the influence of narcotic drugs
SONAJEAR or SONAJIAR va. to spank or whip a child
SONAR va. to spank: "Le sonaron fuerte" 'They gave him a sound spanking'; to pay; vr. to beat up; to spank: "Al niño se lo sonaron"
SONCEAR or SONCIAR (orthog. vars. of zoncear or zonciar
SONCERA (orthog. var. of) zoncera
SONGA (Eng.) (slang) song
SONSERA (orthog. var. of) zoncera
SONSEAR or SONSIAR (orthog. vars. of) zoncear or zonciar
SONSO -SA (orthog. var. of) zonzo -za
SOÑALIENTO -TA (var. of) soñoliento -ta
SOÑAR (slang) vr. to put oneself under the influence of marihuana
SOPA mf. convict, jailbird (coll.); ¡SOPA! interj. Pow!, Wham!; SOPAS adv. yes (affirmative response) (slang)
SOPEAR or SOPIAR vn. to use tortillas or pieces of bread (rather than forks and spoons) as eating utensils
SOPERA soup bowl; bowl for any purpose
SOPETÓN (see DE UN SOPETÓN 'in one gulp')
SOPITAS fpl. pieces of cornmeal tortillas mixed with scrambled eggs and bits of onion
SOPLADO -DA bloated; heavy, fat
SOPLAR va. to punish with a whipping or with blows
SOPLETE m. harsh scolding
SOPLETÓN or SOPLÓN m. punishment through a severe beating or whipping
SOPLO heart murmur
SOPONCIO uneasiness; despair
SOPORA (Eng.) mf. supporter (Std. partidario -ria)
SOPORTAR (Ang.) to support, back up, be a partisan of (Std. apoyar); to sustain, maintain; to finance
SOPORTE (Ang.) m. support, backing, partisanship (Std. apoyo)
SOPRESA (var. of) sorpresa
SOQUEADO -DA or SOQUIADO -DA (Eng.) (vars. of) socado -da; (see also ANDAR SOQUEADO -DA et al.)
SOQUEAR or SOQUIAR (Eng.) (vars. of) socar (Eng.)
SOQUETE (orthog. var. of) zoquete m.
SORDEQUE m., SORDECA f. (slang) (disguise of sordo) deaf person
SORPRENDIENTE (var. of) sorprendente
SORRASTRO -TRA dissipated; degenerate
SOSPIRAR (var. of) suspirar
SOSPRESA (var. of) sorpresa
SPICH (Eng.) m. speech, discourse, oration (see also ESPICHE)
STAR (var. of) estar 'to be' (resultant conjugation:) stoy, stas, sta, etc. (pres. ind.) and ste, stes, ste, etc. (pres. subj.) (see also TAR)
STEPIAR (Eng.) vn. to step (Std. plantar el pie)
STIMROLA (Eng.) steamroller
STORIA (rus.)(var. of) historia
STRAIQUE (Eng.) m. (var. of) estraique (Eng.)
STRAIQUIAR (Eng.) (var. of) estraiquear, estraiquiar
SUADERO (var. of) sudadero
SUATO -TA foolish, stupid
SUAVE (slang) easy, unconcernedly (see AGARRARLA SUAVE); (slang) nice, cool (slang), okay: "(Es) tá suave, bato" 'Cool, man'; DARLE A ALGUIEN LA SUAVE to humor someone; to flatter someone; ¡QUE SUAVE (LE HACES/ HACE/HACEN)! Nice going! (iron.), That's a fine howdy do!
SUAVIZAR vr. to regain one's composure, to "cool it" (slang)
SUBAJAR va. to discredit, run someone down (coll.)
SUBE Y BAJA or SUBEIBAJA m. teeter-totter
SUBIR: SUBIR PA(RA) ARRIBA (pleonasm) to go up, ascend; SUBÍRSELE A ALGUIEN EL/LO INDIO to lose one's temper; to get very angry; SUBÍRSELE LA TOMADA A ALGUIEN to get tipsy, high on alcohol
SUDADA act and effect of sweating
SUDAR: SUDAR LA GOTA GRUESA (var. of) sudar la gota gorda to sweat blood, overtax oneself
SUDÓN -DONA m., f. person who sweats easily, profusely, and often; m. act and effect of sweating
SUEÑO: LLENAR DE SUEÑO to have enough sleep
SUEÑAL m. considerable tiredness or sleepiness
SUERA (Eng.) sweater (see also SUÉTER)
SUERTE fpl. magic tricks; HACER SUERTES to do magic tricks; SUERTE CHAPARRA / SUERTE PERRA very bad luck; SUERTE LOCA good luck

SUERTERO -RA lucky, fortunate
SUERTUDO -DA lucky, fortunate
SUICH or SUICHE (Eng.) (elec.) switch
SUICHE or SUICHI (Eng.) m. switch (electric) (Std. interruptor m.)
SUIDADANÍA (var. of) ciudadanía
SUIDADANO -NA (var. of) ciudadano -na
SUIMEAR or SUIMIAR (Eng.) vn. to swim
SUIMIMPUL (Eng.) m. swimming pool
SUMBAR (orthog. var. of) zumbar
SUMIR vr. to get into debt
SUPCIO -CIA (var. of) sucio -cia
SUPRENTENDENTE or SUPRINTENDENTE mf. (vars. of) superintendente mf.
SURA quarter, twenty-five cent piece; CAERLE SURA A ALGUIEN not to be liked by, be disagreeable or distasteful to (said of persons): "Ese tipo me cae sura" 'I can't stand that guy'
SURE (Eng.) m. sewer
SUROTO -TA (slang) unpleasant, annoying; f. petty thief
SUR(R)UMATO -TA (orthog. vars. of) zurumbato -ta (see also ZURUMBÁTICO -CA)
SUSIRIO (var. of) susidio
SUSTITUIGO (var. of) sustituyo (1st pers. sg. pres. ind. of sustituir)
SUSTITUYIR (var. of) sustituir
SUSTO (an illness which, according to popular belief, is caused by a traumatic experience, resulting in symptoms of nervous tension, loss of appetite, etc.); CURAR DE SUSTO to cure (by sorcery) the after-effects of susto or any frightening experience; ESTAR CURADO -DA DE SUSTO (said of a person who doesn't scare easily)
SUT (Eng.) m. suit (Std. traje)
SWINGUEAR or SWINGUIAR (Eng.) to swing (slang), enjoy oneself as the jet set does (frequent connotation: to participate actively in sex of an often exotic variety)
SUIDAD f. (var. of) ciudad
SÚPITO -TA fast-asleep

T

TA, TAMOS, TAN (see s. TOY)
TABACEADO -DA or TABACIADO -DA weak; tired, played-out (see also TABAQUIADO -DA)
TABAQUIADO -DA (slang) weak etc. (id. to TABACEADO -DA)
TABIQUE (slang) m. jail
TABIRO (slang) jail
TABLA: TABLA MARINA surfboard; ESTAR / QUEDAR / SALIR TABLAS to be tied (e.g. in a sports competition); to be even, break even
TABLITA shoe with a pointed toe
TACOTILLO tumor; boil (skin irritation)
TACUACHE m.(var. of) tlacuache; adj. mf. drunk, inebriated
TACAUCHITA or TACUACHITO (type of polka)
TACUCHE m. suit of clothes; clothes (in general), wardrobe; (slang) worthless bum, good-for-nothing person
TACUCHO (var. of) tacuche 'suit of clothes'
TACHO -CHA (dim. of) Anastasio -sia
TADRE (var. of) tarde (adv. and f.)
TAFETÁN m. adhesive tape
TAIPEAR or TAIPIAR (Eng.) to type, typewrite va.
TAIPIADOR -DORA (Eng., cf. TAIPEAR) m., f. typist; f. typewriter
TAIPISTA (Eng.) mf. typist
TALACHE m. (var. of) talacho 'pickaxe'
TAL: TAL POR CUAL mf. so-and-so (oblique ref. to person one does not wish to name): "Nunca me ha gustado ese tal por cual"
TALARAÑA (var. of) telaraña
TALÓN -LONA m. f. (slang) thief, hustler (coll.); m. fifty-cent piece, half-dollar
TALONEAR or TALONIAR (slang) va. to steal; to hustle (slang)
TALTASCUÁN m. cockroach (see also JUAN, TAPAJUÁN, TAPASCUÁN, TASCALCUÁN et al.)
TALLADOR m. washboard
TALLA joke, witty anecdote; (Eng.) tire (aut.); (Eng.) tie, necktie; (Eng.) railroad tie
TALLAR va. to scrub, wash (e.g.

clothes); TALLARSE LOS OJOS to rub one's eyes
TALLARÍN -RINA (Eng.? <tired?) tired
TALLE (slang) m. work; job
TALLUDO -DA stubborn; tough, resistant; old, aged; flexible as regards the truth, moderately mendacious
TAMALADA tamale bake (social event at which tamales are the main dish)
TAMALES mpl.: HACERLE A ALGUIEN LOS TAMALES DE CHIVO to deceive one's spouse in an adulterous affair
TAMAÑITO -TA (see ESTAR TAMAÑITO -TA, QUEDARSE TAMAÑITO -TA)
TAMBO (slang) jail
TAMBORERO -RA (var. of) tamborilero -ra drummer
TAMBORETEADO -DA or TAMBORETIADO -DA tired, worn-out; beaten up (in a fight)
TAMBORETEAR or TAMBORETIAR va. to beat up (in a fight)
TAMBORIZA: DARLE A ALGUIEN UNA TAMBORIZA to beat someone to a pulp in a fight
TAMIÉN (var. of) también
TANATES mfsg. strong-willed person
TANDO (slang) hat
TANQUE mf. (fig.) fat person; m. (slang) jail
TAN-TAN (onomatopoeic) knock-knock (sound made when knocking at a door)
TANTEADA or TANTIADA estimate, calculation
TANTITO -TA (dim. of) tanto -ta: "Échale tantita sal" 'Just throw in a little bit of salt'; a moment, a second: "Espérate tantito" 'Wait a second'
TANTO -TA: EN TANTO QUE NADA in the twinkling of an eye: "Lo hizo en tanto que nada"; ¿QUÉ TANTO? How much? (Std. ¿cuánto?); UN TANTO a little bit, a fixed amount: "Le podemos dar un tanto ahora y mañana lo demás"
TAPA (slang) hat; (see also VOLARSE LA TAPA)
TAPADO -DA constipated; narrow-minded; unyielding, uncompromising; naive
TAPAJUÁN m. cockroach (see TALTASCUÁN et al.)
TAPAR va. to constipate: "El pan me tapó" 'The bread constipated me'; vr. to become constipated
TAPASCUÁN m. cockroach (see TALTASCUÁN et al.)
TAPÓN -PONA m., f. short, stocky person; m. ECHARLE A ALGUIEN UN TAPON to tell someone off
TAQUERO -RA person who prepares and sells tacos
TAR (var. of) estar (see also STAR)
TARÁNTULA (fig.) mf. hairy person
TARDEADA or TARDIADA late afternoon party (usually held out-of-doors)
TARDECITO -TA adv. a little bit late; very late (iron.)
TARECUA (slang) shoe
TARIS (slang) m. jail
TARLANGO (slang) hat
TARTANA old car, jalopy
TARUGADA foolish action
TARUGO -GA fool, idiot
¡TAS! or ¡TAS TAS! interj. Pow!, Wham!, Bang! (imitation of sound of bullets)
TASAJEAR or TASAJIAR va. to slice (esp. meat)
TASAJILLO or TASAJÍO type of cactus plant with very prickly leaves
TASCALCUÁN m. cockroach (see TALTASCUÁN et al.)
TASINQUE m. sheep-shearer (person who shears sheep for a living)
TATAJUÁN m. cockroach (see TALTASCUÁN et al.)
TATEMA meat roasted in the hot embers of a fire (esp. ref. to heads of animals cooked in this fashion)
TAUN (Eng.) m. town; downtown, city center
TAÚR m. (var. of) ataúd
TAURERÍA funeral home
TAVÍA (var. of) todavía
TAXA (Eng.) tax (esp. income tax)
TAXACIÓN (Eng.) f. taxation
TAYA (orthog. var. of) talla (Eng.)
TÉ (slang) m. marihuana
TECATO -TA (slang) junkie, heroin user
TECLA (slang) cigarette butt
TECOL (slang) (abbrev. of) tecolote m.
TECOLOTA (slang) cigarette butt
TECOLOTE (slang) m. policeman; owl; night watchman
TECORUCHO old tumble-down-house
TECURUCHO (var. of) tecorucho
TEIP (Eng.) m. tape
TEIPIAR (Eng.) va. to tape
TEJABÁN m.or TEJABANA small old house, often in disrepair, covered with a tile roof
TEJÓN -JONA m., f. (hum.) short-statured; (euph.) TEJONES SI NO HAY LIEBRES (untranslatable --tejones is euph. for "Te jodes ...", thus the last four words constitute nonsense syllables; the literal translation is 'Badgers if there are

no hares')
TELA (dim. of) Estela
TELE (abbrev.) f. television; woman's breast; baby bottle, nursing bottle
TELEFÓN (Eng.) m. telephone (Std. teléfono)
TELEFONAZO: ECHAR UN TELEFONAZO to make a telephone call, to phone someone
TELEFONEADA or TELEFONIADA telephone call
TELEFONIAR (var. of) telefonear
TELEVÍ f. (abbrev. of) televisión
TELEVIGENTE m. (var. of) televidente
TEMBELEQUE (var. of) tembleque mf. adj.
TEMOLOTE m. (var. of) tejolote 'stone pestle'
TEMPLETE m. badly-built construction armature (scaffolding)
TEMPONEAR or TEMPONIAR va. to be accustomed to
TENCHA (dim. of) Hortensia, Cresencia
TENDAJERO -RA storekeeper (esp. ref. to owner of a grocery store)
TENDAJO small store (esp. small grocery store)
TENDEDERO or TENDERADA act of hanging out clothes to dry on a clothesline
TENDIDO -DA: ESTAR TENDIDO -DA to be lying in state (said of a dead person in a funeral parlor)
TENDIDA act of hanging out clothes to dry on a clothesline (cf. TENDEDERO ET AL.); clothes hung out to dry
TENDER: TENDER LA CAMA (Std. hacer la cama)
TENER: NO TENER EN QUÉ CAERSE MUERTO -TA to be destitute, dirt-poor; TENER BOCA CHICA to be taciturn, speak infrequently; TENER (UN) BUEN TIEMPO (Ang.) to have a good time, enjoy oneself; TENER CARRITO to harp on the same subject, talk constantly about the same thing; TENER CUERPO DE TENTACIÓN Y CARA DE ARREPENTIMIENTO to have a beautiful body and a homely face (ref. to women); TENER EL ALMA EN EL CUERPO to wear one's heart on one's sleeve (fig.), allow one's emotional state to be very noticeable; TENER FON / TENER UN FONAZO (Eng.) to have fun, have a good time; TENER HUEVOS (vulg.) to have a lot of guts (coll.), have sufficient bravery for; TENER LA CARA DE HACER ALGO to have (sufficient) audacity to do something; TENER LA SANGRE DE CHINCHE to be repugnant to, be repellent to; TENER MALA LA TOMADA: "Tiene mala la tomada" 'When he drinks he really gets his Irish up' (ref. to person--Irish or not--who habitually becomes belligerent or pugnacious after having had a few alcoholic drinks); TENERLA HECHA (Ang?) to have it made (to have achieved a level of accomplishment sufficient to insure future success); TENER A ALGUIEN DE SU CUENTA to have someone on a string (fig.), have someone in a position of dependency: "Ya déjalo, ya lo tuviste bastante de tu cuenta"; TENER LENGUA SUELTA to be garrolous, speak frequently; TENER (UN) MAL TIEMPO (Ang.) to have a bad time, not to enjoy oneself; TENER MUCHA LENGUA to be very talkative; TENER QUE DARLE A ALGUIEN EN EL CODO to have to make someone pay for something (ref. to difficulties in getting a stingy person to pay; cf. CODO); TENER UN TORNILLO SUELTO (Ang?) to have a screw loose, to be slightly crazy
TENIS mpl. (Eng?<tennies--slang for tennis shoes?) tennis shoes; COLGAR LOS TENIS (slang) to die
TENTADERA repeated act of touching, feeling, pawing (excessive handling by one person of another)
TENTÓN -TONA m., f. person given to excessive and repeated touching, feeling, fondling, etc. (cf. TENTADERA)
TEÓRICA (slang) talk, chatter
TEORICAR (slang) va. & vn. to talk, chatter, jabber
TEPALCATES mpl. odds and ends of little value
TEPASCUÁN m. cockroach (see TALTASCUÁN et al.)
TEPOCATE m. (coll.) kid, runt (small child of unprepossessing appearance)
TEQUILERO -RA seller of tequila
TERALAÑA (var. of) telaraña
TERE (dim. of) Teresa
TERREGAL m. dust cloud
TERRERO dust cloud
TERROSO -SA dusty

TESÓN: AGARRAR TESÓN CON to harp on (a subject); to use or wear (repeatedly): "Agarró tesón con la corbata nueva" 'He kept on wearing the new tie'
TESTAL m. round ball of dough constituting the proper amount of masa (q.v.) needed to make a single tortilla
TESTEAR or TESTIAR (Eng.) va. to test, examine
TESTO -TA full, stuffed
TETERA (var. of) tetero 'baby bottle'; sinecure; act of drinking alcohol; AGARRAR LA TETERA to talk to the bottle (coll.), become an alcoholic
TIATRO (var. of) teatro
TIBÓN m. (Eng.) T-bone steak
TICHA (var. of) tícher (Eng.) mf.
TICHAR (Eng.) va. & vn. to teach
TÍCHER (Eng.) mf. teacher
TIEMPAL m. long period of time, coon's age (slang): "Hace un tiempal que no lo veo" 'I haven't seen you in a coon's age'
TIEMPECITO bad weather; plenty of time, time to spare
TIEMPO (Ang.) time, clock time (Std. hora): "Ya es tiempo de ir" 'Ya es la hora de ir'; (see also BUEN TIEMPO, MAL TIEMPO)
TICURUCHO (var. of) tecorucho
TIENDA fly (of trousers); TRAER LA TIENDA ABIERTA to have one's fly open
TIENDERO -RA (var. of) tendero -ra
TIERNÍSIMO -MA (var. of) terníisimo -ma
TIERRA: CAERLE TIERRA A ALGUIEN to be taken by surprise: "Estaban jugando a los dados cuando les cayó tierra. Fue la policía" 'They were playing dice when they were taken by surprise. It was the cops'; SABER LO QUE ES AMAR A DIOS EN TIERRA AJENA (see s. SABER)
TIERRAL m. large cloud of dust; large amount of dust
TIERROSO -SA (var. of) terroso -sa
TIESO -SA: (fig.) QUEDAR(SE) TIESO -SA to die
TÍGUERE -RA m., f. (var. of) tigre mf.
TIJERA: SER CORTADAS POR LA MISMA TIJERA (said of persons having the same characteristics) to be cut from the same cloth (fig.)
TILA (dim. of) Otilia
TILICHES mpl. stuff, junk, old bits of odds and ends
TIMBA (slang) capsule of heroin
TINA pail (usually one of galvanized iron)
TINACO large elevated tank for the storage of drinking water (often the water supply for an entire municipality)
TINIADO -DA (Eng.) (slang) high from sniffing paint thinner (which produces a slightly narcotic effect)
TINTO -TA (slang) U.S. black person
TÍO: TÍO SAMUEL (Eng.) Uncle Sam (symbolic representation of the United States); TÍO TACO (pej.) Mexican-American who has "sold out" (slang) to Anglo society, accepts its values, and generally opposes militant Chicano politics
TIPAZO Adonis, extremely handsome man
TIPO -PA adj. elegantly dressed; ANDAR (MUY) TIPO -PA to be elegantly dressed
TÍQUETE (Eng.) m. ticket (entrance pass), receipt, etc.; ticket (list of political candidates); traffic ticket
TIQUETERÍA (Eng., cf. TÍQUETE) large number of tickets (defs. 1 & 3)
TIQUETERO -RA ticket-seller
TIRACHO -CHA (slang) U.S. black person
TIRADERO disorderly collection of items left scattered about a room
TIRADO -DA disorderly, helter-skelter, unkempt; f. hunting (with a firearm); (vulg.) fornication, sexual intercourse; DAR UNA TIRADA (vulg.) to fornicate; ESTAR TIRADO -DA to be abed, lying in bed (usual ref. to sick or lazy person)
TIRANTE adj. mf. stiff (slang), dead
TIRANTITAS fpl: LLEVÁRSELAS TIRANTITAS to keep a tight rein on someone: "A sus hijos se las lleva tirantitas"
TIRAR: va. (slang) to use, come out with (coll.): "Está tirando mucho totacho" 'He's using a lot of English'; TIRAR A LEÓN / LIÓN to pay no attention to, ignore; TIRAR AL LOCO (slang) to ignore; TIRAR A LUCAS (slang) to ignore; to ditch (slang), leave unaccompanied; TIRAR ALTO to aspire to a lucrative or prestigious position or career, to shoot for the stars (fig.);

TIRAR BESOS to throw kisses (usually at an audience or at children, as along a parade route); TIRAR FLORES to compliment; TIRAR LÍNEA (Ang?) to feed someone a line, tell someone an embellished version of the truth; vn. TIRAR (LA) BASURA (mildly euph., slang) to defecate; TIRAR BONQUE (slang) to sleep; TIRAR CHANCLA/TIRAR CHANCLE (slang) to dance; TIRAR (EL) AGUA (slang) to urinate; TIRAR GARRA (slang) to dress well; TIRAR GRITOS to shout, yell; TIRAR PESTAÑA (slang) to sleep; TIRAR PLANCHA (slang) to be left holding the bag (slang), be abandoned (e.g., a woman waiting in vain for her fiancé at the church on their putative wedding day); TIRAR ZOQUETE (mildly euph., slang) to defecate; TIRARLA PA' (slang) to head for, go toward a destination: "Ése, ¿pa' onde la tira?" 'Hey you, where ya goin'?"; TIRARLE A TODO to try one's hand at everything; TIRARLE A TODO Y NO DARLE A NADA to be Jack of all trades and master of none (coll.), be able to do many things but none well; TIRAR MOCO (slang) to cry; TIRAR NAILON (slang) to dance; TIRAR PLAYA (slang) to take a bath; to take a showerbath; TIRAR SALIVA (hum.) to talk; vr. TIRARSE A LA CALLE / TIRARSE A LA PERDICIÓN to go wrong, take the road to perdition; to become a prostitute; TIRARSE LA MANTECA (slang) to let the cat out of the bag (coll.), tell a secret; TIRARSE UN PEDO (vulg.) to expel anal gas

TIRICIA sadness

TIRILÍ (slang) juvenile delinquent (see also TIRILÓN, TIRILONGO)

TIRILÓN -LONA (slang) juvenile delinquent

TIRILONGO -GA (slang) (id. to TIRILÍ, TIRILÓN -LONA)

TIRO shooting marble used in the game of marbles; cue ball (in pool or billiards); (see also A TIRO DE QUE, A TODOS TIROS, DE A TIRO/DEL TIRO)

TIRÓN: VIVIR A(L) TIRÓN to have a hard time making ends meet, barely eke out a living

TIRONEAR or TIRONIAR (slang) to make love; to pull at each other's limbs and clothes in a fight or in fun

TIS f. (var. of) tisis (q.v.)

TÍSICO: NARICES DE TÍSICO extra-keen sense of smell

TISIS adj. (var. of) tísico -ca 'tubercular'

TITIRITEAR or TITIRITIAR (vars. of) tiritar

TIVÍ (Eng.) m. television. T.V. (abbrev.)

TIZÓN -ZONA dark-complexioned person

TLACHICHINOLE m. type of herb (Kohleria deppeana) prepared in solution and used as a vaginal douche

TO or TOO (vars. of) todo 'all'

TOALLA napkin, table napkin

TOALLITA protective cover for furniture surfaces (tables, chests of drawers, etc.)

TOAVÍA (var. of) todavía

TOCADOR m. large cloth draped over chest of drawer for decorative effect

TOCAR: YA LE TOCABA His number was up, He was destined to die

TOCINO ham

TOCHAR (Eng.) va. to touch

TOCHDAUN or TOUCHDÁUN (Eng.) m. touchdown (in football)

TODO (see TIRARLE A TODO Y NO DARLE A NADA); (see also ESTAR EN TODO)

TOFUDO -DA (Eng.) (slang) tough, rough, (ref. to aggressive persons)

TOÍTO -TA (var. of) todito -ta

TOLACO or TOLECO (slang) fifty-cent piece, half-dollar

TOLIDO or TOLIRO (slang) toilet

TOLOLOCHE m. string bass, bass viol (Std. contrabajo)

TOLÓN (slang) m. fifty-cent piece, half-dollar

TOMADA or TOMADERA act of drinking alcohol; TENER MALA LA TOMADA: "Tiene mala la tomada" 'When he drinks he really gets his Irish up' (ref. to person--Irish or not--who habitually becomes belligerent or pugnacious after having had a few alcoholic drinks)

TOMADOR -DORA m., f. habitual drinker; alcoholic

TOMAR va. & vn. to drink alcoholic beverages; TOMAR AL CABO to carry out, execute (Std. llevar a cabo); TOMARLE SABOR A ALGO to enjoy something

TOMATE (slang) m. eye, eyeball; TOMATE DE FRESADILLA small-

sized tomato which remains green when ripe
TOMATEAR or TOMATIAR (slang) va. & vn. to see; to look
TOMATERA tomato-packing factory
TONADITA singsong intonation
TONCES (var. of) entonces
TONE (Eng.<Tony?) (dim. of) Antonio -nia
TONTARREAJE or TONTARRAIJE m. bunch of idiots, aggrupation of foolish persons
TONTIAR (var. of) tontear 'to talk nonsense, act foolishly'
TONINO -NA heavy-set person
TOÑO -ÑA (dims. of) Antonio -nia
TOPE mpl. DARSE TOPES to bump heads; to try to outdo each other (said of two persons)
TOPILLO or TOPIO: HACER TOPILLO (slang) to make a fool of someone
TOQUE (slang) m. puff on a cigarette (esp. on a marihuana cigarette)
TORCADISCOS (var. of) tocadiscos
TORCER va. (slang) to draft into the army; (slang) to jail, put in jail; TORCERLE LA CARA A ALGUIEN to snub someone; vn. (slang) to die; TORCER MUY FEO or TORCER MUY GACHO to die a horrible death; vr. to have a falling out with someone: "Jorge y Julio se torcieron, pero ya se conformaron"; TORCERSE EL PESCUEZO vr. to twist one's neck; to sprain one's neck
TORCIDO -DA angry; (slang) jailed
TORCHA (var. of antorcha?) (slang) match (for lighting fire to an object)
TOREAR or TORIAR: TOREARLA (slang) to defy the law; (slang) to do the town, go out on a spree; vr. to make the attempt
TÓRICA (var. of) teórica
TORITO: TORITO DE LA VIRGEN horned toad
TORNILLO or TORNIO: ANDAR DE TORNILLO to be in a bad mood; TENER UN TORNILLO SUELTO (Ang?) to have a screw loose (slang), be slightly crazy
TORQUE or TORQUI (Eng.) m. turkey
TORTA: TORTA DE PAN loaf of bread
TORTEAR or TORTIAR va. to applaud; vn. to slap one's hands back and forth while making tortillas
TORTILLA: TORTILLA DE AZÚCAR flour tortilla prepared with sugar and cinnamon; TORTILLA DE HARINA flour tortilla; TORTILLA DE MAÍZ/MAIZ corn-meal tortilla; TORTILLA DE MASA corn-meal tortilla; (see also HACER TORTILLA)
TORTILLERÍA place where tortillas are made and sold
TORÓN -RONA m., f. adj. strong and heavy-set, bull-like (usually applied to male persons)
TORZÓN m. sharp internal pains (in person's intestine, etc.)
TORRE: DARLE A ALGUIEN EN LA TORRE (slang) to hit someone where it hurts (coll.); to beat someone up in a fight
TOSTA (slang) fifty-cent piece, half-dollar
TOSTÓN (slang) fifty-cent piece, half-dollar; CAERLE TOSTÓN A ALGUIEN not to be liked by, to be repugnant to: "Ese bato me cae tostón" 'I don't like that guy'
TOTACHA (slang) the English language; Pachuco speech style (the Spanish typically spoken by Pachucos); Chicano slang (in general)
TOTACHAR (slang) vn. to speak using Chicano slang (cf. TOTACHA); to switch codes, speak in a "mixture" of Spanish and English, alternate between Spanish and English
TOTACHO (var. of) totacha
TOTORUSCO -CA awkward, graceless; coarse-featured
TOVIERON (var. of) tuvieron (3rd pers. pl. pret. of tener)
TOXIDO (Eng.) tuxedo
TOY, TAS, TA, TAMOS, TAN (vars. of) estoy, estás, está, etc. (pres. indic. forms of estar)
TOY (var. of) todo y '___ and all': "Se lo comió con toy todo" 'He ate it, ___ and all' (___=whichever item of food)
TRABAJANTA babysitter
TRABAJAR va. to bewitch, hex: "Parece que te están trabajando desde que volviste del viaje, pues te estás portando muy mal"
TRABAJO: TRABAJO COCHINO (Ang?) (slang) dirty work (slang), criminal undertaking
TRÁCALA debt
TRACALADA uproar, din
TRACALERO -RA person frequently in debt
TRACO shoe
TRADUCÍ, TRADUCISTE, etc. (vars. of)

traduje, tradujiste, etc. (pret. conjugation of traducir)

TRAER va. to have (ref. to physical condition or part of the body): "Traes los ojos chinitos" 'You have sleepy eyes'; TRAER CARGA (slang) to be carrying narcotic drugs; TRAER (MUCHO) EMPALME to be (heavily) bundled up, be wearing (a considerable amount of) heavy clothing; TRAER DE POR SÍ to be born with: "Ese talento lo trae de por sí" 'He was born with that talent'; "Es malo de por sí" 'He was born bad'; TRAER ENTRE OJOS to have one's eye on someone (fig.) keep a watch out for someone, observe someone with interest; TRAER LA EDUCACIÓN EN LAS PATAS / TRAER LA EDUCACIÓN EN LOS PIES not to behave like an educated person (said of any ill-mannered recipient of a higher academic degree); TRAER A ALGUIEN AL PURO PEDO (slang) to harass, annoy someone; TRAER PELOTA (vulg.) to be passionately in love with someone, have the "hots" for someone; to be carrying the torch for someone; TRAER PURO CLAVO (slang) to be loaded with money, be in the money; TRAER QUE QUEMAR (slang) to have cigarettes in one's possession; TRAER TIEMPO (see s. TIEMPO); TRAER TRAGO to have a few drinks under one's belt (slang), to have been drinking alcohol for quite a while: "Ese ya trae trago" 'He's already had a few'; TRAER TROTE (coll.) to have something up one's sleeve, be up to something: "¿Qué trote traes?" 'What are you up to?'; TRAERLA to be "it" in the game of tag; vr. ¿QUÉ TRAES? (fixed expression) What's with you?, What are you up to ? (coll.); TRAÉRSELA A ALGUIEN MUY CERQUITA to keep a tight rein on someone, keep someone on a short leash (fig.)

TRAGADERO -RA act of eating heavily

TRAGANTE m. esophagus

TRAGAR: TRAGARSE LOS AÑOS to look younger than one's years

TRAGO alcohol in general

TRAIBA, TRAIBAS, etc. (vars. of) traía, traías, etc. (imperfect conjugation of traer)

TRAIDO -DA (var. of) traído -da (ppart. of traer)

TRAIDRÉ, TRAIDRÁS, etc. (vars. of) traeré, traerás, etc. (future conjugation of traer)

TRAIDRÍA, TRAIDRÍAS, etc. (vars. of) traería, traerías, etc. (conditional conjugation of traer)

TRAILA (Eng.) trailer (Std. remolque)

TRAIR (var. of) traer

TRAJEADO -DA or TRAJIADO -DA elegantly dressed

TRAJIAR (var. of) trajear

TRAJIERA, TRAJIERAS, etc. (vars. of) trajera, trajeras, etc. (past subj. conjugation of traer)

TRAMA wheat flour bread

TRAMADOS mpl. (slang) pants, trousers

TRAMOS: mpl. (slang) pants; TRAMO FREGÓN (slang) zoot suit (type of clothing affected by hoodlum elements in the 1930's and 1940's)

TRAMPA or TRAMPE (Eng.) m. tramp, bum; villain in a movie

TRAMPAR OREJA (slang) to sleep

TRAMPEAR or TRAMPIAR va. to hunt animals; to trap animals; vn. to enter without paying (as into a movie theater)

TRANCA: ECHAR LA TRANCA (see s. ECHAR)

TRANCALERO -RA (var. of) tracalero -ra

TRANVÍ m. (var. of) tranvía

TRAPEADA or TRAPIADA sponge bath

TRAPEAR or TRAPIAR (Eng.) va. to trap (see also TREPEAR); va. to give a spong bath; vr. to take a sponge bath

TRAQUE (Eng.) m. railroad track

TRAS interj. Bang!, Crash!

TRAS(H)AMBRIDO -DA undernourished

TRASCULCAR (var. of) esculcar to search (a person), search through (boxes, etc.)

TRASTEAR or TRASTIAR va. to wash dishes, "do" the dishes

TRASTERÍO pile of dirty dishes (waiting to be washed)

TRASTERO closet; storage room; attic

TRAVESÍA shortcut; ECHAR/HACER/ TOMAR UNA TRAVESÍA to take a shortcut

TRAYER (var. of) traer

TREATO (var. of) teatro

TREILA f. or TRÉILER m. (Eng.) trailer (Std. remolque)

TREILÓN (Eng.) m. large tractor trailer attached to a truck

TREILONA (Eng.) truck

TREINTATREINTA m. thirty-thirty

(type of firearm)
TREMPRANO (rus.) (var. of) tempra-no
TREN (see A TODO TREN)
TRER (var. of) traer
TRES: LAS TRES three puffs (on a cigarette); ¡DAME LAS TRES! 'Let me have a puff!'; TRES PIEDRAS (slang) keen, excellent, great, super (etc.); "El cho estuvo tres piedras" 'The show was terrific'
TRES RÍOS (Hispanization of) Three Rivers, Texas
TREÚNFO (var. of) triunfo
TRIATO or TRIATRO (var. of) teatro
TRIBO m. (var. of) tribu f.
TRILAZO (Eng.) thrill
TRIMIADA (Eng.) trimming (of hair)
TRIMIAR (Eng.) va. to trim (hair)
TRINE or TRINI (dims. of) Trinidad mf.
TRIPA water hose; (hum.) thin person; AMARRARSE LA TRIPA to tighten one's belt (fig.), economize; to endure hunger; TRIPA IDA blocked intestine; (folk medicine) belief that fear can serve to lock or block intestines
TRIPÓN -PONA small child under the age of ten
TRIQUI-TRIQUI interj. (Eng.) m. trick-or-treat! (said by children on Halloween as they go from house to house begging for candy or other treats)
TRISTE fpl. LAS TRISTES (slang) three puffs on a cigarette (cf. TRES)
TRITIAR (Eng.) va. to treat, entertain at one's own expense
TROCA (Eng.) truck (see also TROQUE); TROCA DE DOMPE dump truck
TROCÓN (Eng.) m. large truck
TROCONA (Eng.) large truck
TROCHEMOCHE: HACER ALGO A(L) TROCHEMOCHE to do a half-assed job (coll.), do something poorly
TROLA (slang) match (for igniting); cigarette
TROLE (slang) mf. crazy; drunk
TROMPA (slang) mouth; fpl. thick-lipped person; mfpl. sour puss (coll.), person having a grouchy disposition often accompanied by an unhappy facial expression; HACER TROMPAS / PONER TROMPAS to put on a sad facial expression; to be grouchy; (see also DARSE TROMPA)
TROMPADAS fpl. fist fight
TROMPAZOS (see DARSE TROMPAZOS)
TROMPEZAR (var. of) tropezar
TROMPEZÓN (var. of) tropezón m. trip, stumble
TROMPÓN -PONA thick-lipped
TRONADERA thunderstorm; repeated cracks of thunder; volley of shots from a firearm; volley of bangs from firecrackers
TRONADO -DA drunk
TRONADOR m. (vulg.) male fond of engaging with frequency in amorous activities
TRONAR va. to smoke (esp. marihuana); vn. TRONAR LOS HUESOS to crack (ref. to bones): "Al sentarse le truenan los huesos" 'When he sits down his bones crack'; vr. to kill: "Se tronaron a González" 'They killed González'; (vulg.) to copulate; to spank; to beat up (in a fight); to shoot
TRONCO (fig. & vulg.) male sexual organ (esp. one of larger than average dimensions); (fig.) short and chubby person; CAER COMO UN TRONCO to drop off to sleep, fall asleep rapidly; DORMIR COMO UN TRONCO (Ang?) to sleep like a log
TROQUE (Eng.) m. truck
TROQUERO -RA truck driver
TROSTEAR or TROSTIAR (Eng.) va. to trust
TROTE: AGARRAR TROTE CON to keep harping on (a theme); to wear or do (something) unceasingly (i.e., to fail to change one's clothes): "Ya agarraste trote con esa camisa"; ANDAR AL TROTE CON to be all wrapped up in (fig.), completely involved with: "El niño anda al trote con el juguete que le compramos"; HACERLE TROTE A ALGUIEN to make advances at someone; TRAER TROTE (coll.) to have something up one's sleeve, be up to something: "¿Qué trote traes?" 'What are you up to?'
TRUENAR (var. of) tronar
TRUJE, TRUJISTE, TRUJO, TRUJIMOS, TRUJ(I)ERON (vars. of) traje, trajiste, etc. (pret. conjugation of traer)
TRUNCO -CA (Eng.) drunk
TRUNQUIS (Eng.) adj. mf. drunk
TUALLA (var. of) toalla
TUBO (slang) sock, stocking; inner tube; TUBO DE PLÁSTICO interuterine device, coil, loop (contraceptive device)
TUERCA: (LLAVE DE) TUERCA monkey wrench

TUÉTARO (var. of) tuétano
TUNA (Eng.) tunafish (Std. atún m.)
TUPIDO -DA abundant; dense; filled to the brim DE BARBA TUPIDA heavy-bearded
TURRON m. block, bar: "Cómprame un turrón de magnesia" 'Buy me a bar of magnesia'

U

UJU or ÚJULE (expression of disappointment, varying in intensity according to intonation, emphasis, etc.)
UGENIO -NIA (var. of) Eugenio -nia
ULALIO -LIA (var. of) Eulalio -lia
ULTIMADAMENTE (var. of) últimamente
ÚLTIMO: AL ÚLTIMO finally, at last (Std. por fin, al fin)
UMBLIGO (var. of) ombligo
UNDE (var. of) donde
UNIÓN (Ang.) f. (labor) union; fpl. long underwear (Eng? cf. union suit)
UNO: UNO TRAS OTRO (slang) (euph.) sausage: "Le dieron uno tras otro pal refín" 'They gave him sausages for dinner'
UNQUE (var. of) aunque
UNTADA (var. of) untadura
UÑA: UÑA DE GATO type of prickly shrub
UÑERA (var. of) uñero 'ingrown toenail' (also 'hangnail')
¡ÚPALE! (interj. used when lifting up a child) Up you go!
UROPA (var. of) Europa
URUTAR (var. of) eructar
URZUELA split hair (tip of hair which has split in two)
ÚRZULA (var. of) úlcera
URRACA (fig.) (pej.) non-negroid person with a very dark complexion
USEBIO -BIA (var. of) Eusebio -bia

V

VACA (fig.) adj. stupid, unintelligent (said of persons); HACER VACA to run up one's winnings in a game of chance after starting with a very small amount of money
VACILADA (slang) kidding, joking; fooling around, having a good time; VACILARSE A ALGUIEN to make a fool of someone; to play a joke on someone; to kid or tease someone; ANDAR EN LA VACILADA to have a good time, fool around; to flirt; A VACILAR A CA CHAPA (< a vacilar en acas de Chapa): "Vete a vacilar a ca Chapa" 'Go tell it to the marines' (=Std. a otro perro con ese hueso) (Note: this saying may be peculiar to San Antonio, Texas, as it involves a local ref. to a well-known drugstore on the west side of that city; the store was torn down in the 1960's)
VACIAR vr. to bleed to death
VACIL m. fun, amusement (cf. VACILADA); act of flirting
VACILADOR -DORA m., f. joker, kidder; flirt
VACILÓN -LONA m., f. flirt, person who flirts; person who serves as comic relief, joker; movie cartoon
VACOTA (fig.) clumsy, awkward
VAGONERO man who loads railroad cars
VAISA (orthog. var. of) baisa
VALA, VALAS, etc. (vars. of) valga, valgas, etc. (pres. subj. of valer)
VALER: NO VALER CACA (vulg.) not to be worth XXXX, be very worthless; VALER MADRE to be worthless
VALSEAR or VALSIAR (vars. of) valsar
VAMPIRO -RA bloodthirsty person (fig.), mercenary
VANELA (var. of) vainilla
VARAÑA (orthog. var. of) baraña
VARO dollar (U.S. currency); peso (Mexican currency et alibi)

VÃRVULA (var. of) válvula
VASIJA set of dishes
VEDERA (var. of) vereda
VEGETABLE (Eng.) m. vegetable (Std. verdura
VEJARANO -NA or VEJERANO -NA (blend of viejo and veterano?) (pej.) old person
VEJIGA balloon
VELADORA large votive light
VELIZ (orthog. var. of) velís m.
VENADO -DA square, person not atuned to the latest fads. slang, etc.
VENDIDO -DA (pej.) Uncle Tom, race traitor (very pej. ref. to Mexican-American who has "sold out" to Anglo interests or who always sides with Anglos in ethnic conflicts)
VENIR va. VENIRLE A ALGUIEN MUY AGUADO to be no match for someone: "Ese tipo me viene muy aguado" 'That guy is no match for me'; VENIR A LA MEDIDA to fit to a T: "El sombrero le vino a la medida" 'The hat fit him to a T; VENIR AL PELO (for clothes) to fit to a T: "La chaqueta le quedó al pelo" 'The coat fit him to a T'; VENIR DE ENTRADA Y SALIDA to visit or call upon someone briefly; vn. VENIR PA' TRAS (Ang.) to return, come back (Std. volver); vr. (vulg.) to have an orgasm; VENIRSE EN SECO (vulg.) to have an orgasm outside the woman's vagina; ¿A QUÉ VIENE (TODO) ESO? What are you implying?, Why are you bringing that matter up?; VIENE SALIENDO LA MISMA GATA It's all the same in the end, It comes to the same thing, Same difference; YA VENGO I'll be back soon, I'll see you shortly
VENTA: VENTA DE GARAJE (Ang.) garage sale, sale of miscellaneous objects; VENTA DE QUEMAZÓN fire sale, sale of merchandise minimumly damaged by a fire in the store
VENTAJOSO -SA opportunistic
VENTO (dim. of) Ventura
VENTOSA (folk medicine) cure for pains in the side of the abdomen supposedly caused by contack with cold air; the cure consists in placing the mouth of a glass over the affected region; the cold air is then supposed to be sucked out by the glass and the patient is cured
VER va. to opine, think about: "¿Cómo la ve?" 'What do you think (about it)?'; AHORA VERÁS (AHORA VERÁN etc.) Now you're in for it, Now you're going to get it (phrases of warning); ESTAR DE VERSE to be acceptable; NO PODER VER A ALGUIEN NI EN PINTURA not to be able to stand the sight of someone, hate someone with extreme intensity; VERLE LA CARA A ALGUIEN to seek out humbly, to ask for forgiveness or reconciliation, to eat crow (fig.); to face someone reluctantly to ask for a favor (expression most often used in the negative); VERLE LA CARA DE PENDEJO A ALGUIEN (slang) to see someone approaching; YA LO VERÁS (YA LO VERÁ etc.) Now you're in for it, Now you're going to get it (phrases of warning): "Te dije que limpiaras el carro y no lo hiciste. Ya lo verás" 'I told you to clean the car and you didn't do it. Now you're in for it'
VERDAD: ¿PA(RA) QUÉ MÁS QUE LA VERDAD? Let's tell it like it is, Why tell anything but the truth?
VERDE mf. greenhorn, inexperienced person
VERDELAGAS(S) or VERDOLAGA (slang) mf. greenhorn, inexperienced person
VERGÜENZOSO -SA (var. of) vergonzoso -sa
VERIGUATA (var. of) averiguata 'dispute, argument, din, noise'
VERIJÓN -JONA m., f. wide-hipped; clumsy; f. adverse to doing housework
VERNE (Hispanization of) Vernon, Texas
VESITAR (var. of) visitar
VEVA (dim. of) Genoveva
VEVIR (var. of) vivir
VEYA, VEYAS, etc. (vars. of) vea, veas, etc. (pres. subj. conjugation of ver)
VEYO (var. of) veo (lst pers. sg. pres. ind. of ver)
VÍA, VÍAS, etc. (vars. of) veía, veías, etc. (imperfect conjugation of ver)
VIAJEAR or VIAJIAR (vars. of) viajar
VIANCICO (var. of) villancico
VÍBORA (slang) penis; PICAR LA VÍBORA (slang): "Cuídate, no te vaya a picar la víbora" 'Watch out, don't let them get into your pants' (euph.) (said to a girl about to go out on a date,

warning her not to let the male persuade her to become engaged in copulative activities)
VICA (orthog. var. of) bica
VICEPRINCIPAL (Eng.) m. vice principal, assistant director of a school
VÍCERAS (slang) fpl. sunglasses
VICI- (var. of) vice- (prefix indicating subordinate position, e.g., vici-presidente = vice-presidente
VICOCA (orthog. var. of) bicoca
VICTROLA (Eng.) (var. of) vitrola (Eng.)
VIDE (var. of) vi (1st pers. sg. pret. of ver)
VIDO (var. of) vio (3rd pers. pret. of ver)
VIDRIERA (DE CARRO) windshield (of a car)
VIDRIOS mpl. (slang) eyeglasses; AY NOS VIDRIOS (slang) Catch ya later (slang), See you later; ¡POR VIDRIOS! interj. (euph.) (var. of) ¡Por vida de Dios!
VIEJERO -RA m. woman who chases around after men; f. man who chases around after women
VIEJEZ (var. of) vejez f.
VIEJITA (slang) cigarette butt
VIEJO -JA (slang) m. husband; father; f. wife; mother; whore; attractive woman (in general); cigarette butt (see also VIEJITA); VIEJO -JA RABO VERDE (var. of viejo -ja verde)
VIEN (orthog. var. of) bien
VIERNES: CUCHARA DE VIERNES meddler, meddlesome person
VÍGORA or VÍGURA (var. of) víbora
VINAGRÓN m. scorpion (Scorpionida)
VINIR (var. of) venir
VIRDIO (var. of) vidrio
VIRGÜELA (var. of) viruela
VIROL (slang) m. bean (usually mpl.)
VIRONGUEAR or VIRONGUIAR (orthog. vars. of) bironguear, bironguiar
VIRONGUERO -RA (orthog. var. of) bironguero -ra
VIRUELA: VIRUELA LOCA chicken pox
VIRUL mf. or VIRULO -LA one-eyed
VIRULA bicycle
VIS- (var. of) vice- (id. to VICI-, q.v.)
VISITA: EN VISITAS on a visit, visiting (Std. de visita); VISITA DE DOCTOR (var. of visita de médico 'very brief visit')
VISTA (slang) film, movie; fpl. (more frequent than fsg.) motion-picture show, movies: "Anoche fuimos a las vistas" 'Last night we went to the movies'
VISTERO -RA movie fan, avid moviegoer, cinéaste
VISTIR (var. of) vestir
VÍTOR (var. of) Víctor
VITORIA (var. of) Victoria
VITORIANO (var. of) Victoriano
VITROLA (Eng.) victrola, phonograph, record-player
VIVIDOR -DORA m., f. opportunist
VIVIR: VIVIR A(L) TIRÓN to have a hard time making ends meet, barely eke out a living
VODEVILES (Eng.) mpl. vaudeville
VOLADO -DA (said of a person who reacts quickly and positively to advances or flattery); very much in love; ANDAR VOLADO -DA CON ALGUIEN to be very much in love with someone
VOLADA: DE A VOLADA or DIAVOLADA fast, rapidly, quickly
VOLANDO right away, right this minute; "Traime el papel volando"
VOLANTÍN m. merry-go-round
VOLAR va. (slang) to steal; vr. to fall in love; to blow one's brains out, shoot oneself in the head; vr. to become giddy; to become infatuated; VOLARLE A ALGUIEN LA CABEZA to give someone a swell head (fig.), an exaggerated sense of importance; to make someone feel dizzy, light-headed, giddy; VOLÁRSELA or VOLARSE LA TAPADA DE LOS SESOS to blow one's brains out, shoot oneself in the head (see also LEVANTARSE or SALTARSE LA TAPA DE LOS SESOS); VOLÁRSELE A ALGUIEN LA CABEZA to become dizzy, giddy, light-headed; to get dizzy spells; to become confused; VOLÁRSELE A ALGUIEN LA TAPA to blow one's top, get angry: "A Rubén se le voló la tapa de deveras" 'Rubén really blew his top'; (see also A VOLAR)
VOLCÁNICO -CA vulcanized; m. patent medicine, in liquid form, applied to sore muscles
VOLCANIZAR va. to vulcanize
VOLCANO (Ang.) volcano (Std. volcán)
VOLER (var. of) oler
VOLTEADO -DA or VOLTIADO -DA m., f. homosexual
VOLTEAR or VOLTIAR: VOLTEAR EL ESTÓMAGO A ALGUIEN to turn one's stomach (fig.), be repugnant to; VOLTEARLE A ALGUIEN LA CABEZA to give someone a swell head

(fig.), cause someone to assume an exaggerated sense of importance

VOLVER: vn. VOLVER PA' TRAS (Ang.) to return, go back (Std. volver); va. VOLVERLE A ALGUIEN EL ALMA AL CUERPO to regain one's composure after being scared; YA VUELVO I'll be right back, I'll see you shortly

VOLVIDO -DA (var. of) vuelto -ta (ppart. of volver)

VOMITADERA vomiting spell, serial regurgitation

VORRADO (orthog. var. of) borrado

VOZ f. (Ang.) voice (lessons): "Estoy estudiando voz" 'I'm taking voice lessons'

VRIGEN (var. of) virgen f.

VUELO: AGARRAR VUELO to get a running start; (see DE TODO VUELO)

VUELTA: DAR LA VUELTA to drop by (a place), drop over (for a visit): "Mañana no dejes de dar la vuelta" 'Don't forget to come by tomorrow for a visit'; DE VUELTA again; after returning

VUEVO (var. of) huevo

W

WAXEAR or WAXIAR (Eng.) va. to wax (a floor)

Y

Y: ¿Y DIAY (QUÉ)? or ¿Y DE AHÍ (QUÉ)? So? So what?; Y ¿QUÉ HAY CON ESO? So what about it? (coll.)

YA: YA ESTA or YA ESTUVO That's it!, Consider it done (consider the job finished); YA ESTUVO I've got it made, There's no way I can fail; YA LO HUBO or YA LUVO (id. to YA ESTÁ); YA NI YO (YA NI ELLA, etc.) (expression used to shame someone into doing something that another person of lesser ability can do): "¿No puedes hacer esto? ¡Qué vergüenza! Ya ni Linda que es tan joven" 'Can't you do this? That's absurd! Linda can do it and she's much younger than you'; ¿YA SI NO? Well after all, what did you expect (would happen)?; YA TE LO HAIGA or YA TE LO HAYA You will be sorry!; YA, YA (expression of sympathy usually directed at children) There, there, that's all right

YANITORIA (Eng.) janitorial service

YAQUE (Eng.) m. jack (aut.) (Std. gato)

YARDA (Ang.) yard, lawn, plot of grass in front of or behind a house; YARDA DE MADERA (Eng.) lumberyard

YAYO (dim. of) Eduardo (see also HUAYO)

YEC (Eng.) m. jack (Std. gato) (see also YAQUE)

YEDO (slang) marihuana

YEQUEAR or YEQUIAR (Eng.) va. to jack up (a car, a structure, etc.)

YERSE (Eng.) m. jersey, sweater

YES (Eng.) m. jazz

YESCO -CA (slang) marihuana smoker; drug addict; f. marihuana

YET (Eng.) m. jet, jet airplane

YIDO (var. of) ido (ppart. of ir)

YIN (Eng.) m. gin (alcohol); YIN DE ALGODÓN cotton gin

YIP(E) (Eng.) m. jeep

YIR (var. of) ir 'to go'

YIRA or YIRI (Eng.) mf. jitterbug (dance); jitterbugger (person fond of dancing the jitterbug)

YOCHE (Eng., dim. of) George; (Hispanization of) George West (city in south Texas)

YOGA f. or YOGUE m. (Eng.) jug (see also YOQUE)

YOGAS or YOGAS EL CANTINERO (slang) I (1st pers. sg. pron.) (disguise-expansion of Std. yo)

YOLE (dim. of) Yolanda

YOLI (dim. of) Yolanda

YOMPA (Eng?) jumper (type of hunting jacket worn by men)

YÓMPER (Eng?) m. jumper (type of single-piece combination blouse and skirt worn by women)

YONCA (Eng., < junker?) bicycle

YONQUE (Eng.) m. junk; junkyard

YONQUEAR or YONQUIAR (Eng.) va. to junk

YOQUE (Eng.) m. jug (see also YOGA et al.)

YOYO (Eng.) yoyo, type of toy top

which is raised or lowered by being spun from a string
YUDAR (rus.) (var. of) ayudar
YULA (Hispanization of) Beulah, Texas
YÚNIER or YÚNIOR (Eng.) m. younger; youngest of several; Junior (e.g., "Éste es Juan yúnier" 'This is Juan Jr.', said by a father in ref. to his identically-named son)
YUTA (Hispanization of) Utah (U.S. state)
YUYO (dim. of) Jesús (see also CHUY)

Z

ZACATAL m. tall dense grass in great abundance
ZACATE (slang) m. low-grade marihuana
ZACATEADA or ZACATIADA (orthog. vars. of) sacateada or sacatiada
ZACATEAR or ZACATIAR (orthog. vars. of) sacatear or sacatiar
ZAFAR: ZAFARSE UN HUESO to dislocate a bone from the socket or the joint
ZAFO: CON ZAFOS (slang) The same to you!, Take your words and eat them (fig., said to take revenge for any derogatory remarks initially directed toward you by someone else)
ZAMBO -BA bow-legged
ZAMBUTIR (var. of) zambullir
ZANCUDERÍO or ZANCUDERÍA or ZANCUDERO swarm of mosquitos
ZANORIA (var. of) zanahoria
ZAPETA diaper
ZAPO (slang) shoe (disguise or var. of zapato)
ZARABANDA spanking
ZARAPE (orthog. var. of) sarape m.
ZIGZAQUEAR or ZIGZAQUIAR (vars. of) zigzaguear or zigzaguiar
ZÍPER (Eng.) m. zipper
ZONCEAR or ZONCIAR vn. to fool around; to joke
ZONCERA foolishness
ZOPILOTE (slang, pej.) m. policeman
ZOQUETAL m. mudhole
ZOQUETE m. mud; (fig.) good-for-nothing, worthless person
ZOQUETERA mud-guard (aut.); mudhole
ZOQUETOSO -SA muddy
ZUCA (rus.) (var. of) azúcar
ZUCADERO -RA (vars. of) azucarero -ra
ZUCARERO -RA (vars. of) azucarero -ra
ZUMBAR va. to win; to conquer; (slang) to eat up; ZUMBARLE A ALGUIEN EL APARATO/EL MANGO to excel in something (esp. in sports); ZUMBARLE A ALGUIEN EL COCO to be daffy, screwy, slightly crazy
ZUMBIDO gossip, wagging of tongues; running around (usually in search of sexual adventures)
ZURUMBÁTICO -CA daffy, screwy, slightly crazy; dumb, stupid, ignorant
ZURUMBÁS adj. (var. of) zurumbático -ca
ZURUM(B)ATO -TA (var. of) zurumbático -ca
ZURRAR vr. to get angry, become infuriated

Apéndice A: Proverbios y refranes
Appendix A: Proverbs and Sayings

A

¡A BUENA HORA! (iron.) High time!: "¡A buenahora vas llegando!" 'A fine time to be arriving!'
A BUEN ENTENDEDOR, POCAS PALABRAS A word to the wise is sufficient
A BUEN HAMBRE NO HAY MAL PAN Hunger is the best sauce
A BUEN SANTO TE ENCOMIENDAS The blind are leading the blind (A fine choice of a guide you've made)
A CABALLO DADO NO HAY QUE MIRARLE EL COLMILLO / LOS DIENTES One should never look a gift horse in the mouth (also: A CABALLO REGALADO NO HAY QUE MIRARLE EL DIENTE id.)
A CADA SANTO SE LE LLEGA SU DÍA Every dog has his day (Everyone gets his reward sooner or later)
A GUSTOS SE ROMPEN PANZAS Every man to his own taste (Arguments on likes and dislikes often provoke fights)
A HUEVO NI LOS ZAPATOS ENTRAN You can lead a horse to water but you cannot make him drink
A LO DADO NO SE LE BUSCA LADO Don't look a gift horse in the mouth
A MAL TIEMPO BUENA CARA Keep a stiff upper lip
A OTRO PERRO CON ESE HUESO Go tell it to the marines
A QUIEN LE VENGA EL GUANTE, QUE SE LO PLANTE If the shoe fits, wear it
A QUIEN MADRUGA, DIOS LE AYUDA The early bird gets the worm / God helps him who helps himself
A TODO LE TIRA, Y A NADA LE DA Jack of all trades, master of none
A VER SI COMO RONCAN DUERMEN Talk is cheap / Let's see if they can deliver the goods
AL FLOJO LO AYUDA DIOS/AL FLOJO DIOS LO AYUDA/AL PEREZOSO LO AYUDA DIOS/AL PEREZOSO DIOS LO AYUDA Some people have all the luck (comment directed to a lazy person who has had a much easier time with a chore than was expected)
AL OJO DEL AMO ENGORDA EL MACHO A watched pot does boil / If you want it done right, do it yourself
AL QUE LE APRIETA EL ZAPATO QUE SE LO AFLOJE/AL QUE LE APRIETE EL ZAPATO QUE SE LO AFLOJE God helps those who help themselves
AL QUE LE DÉ COMEZÓN QUE SE RASQUE God helps those who help themselves
AL QUE LE DUELA LA MUELA QUE SE LA SAQUE/AL QUE LE DUELE LA MUELA QUE SE LA SAQUE God helps those who help themselves
AL QUE LE QUEDE EL ZAPATO, QUE SE LO PONGA If the shoe fits, wear it
AL QUE MADRUGA, DIOS LE AYUDA The early bird gets the worm / God helps him who helps himself
AL QUE NO HABLA, DIOS NO LO OYE Faint heart never won fair lady
ABEJA: s. ESTAR COMO . . .
ABRAZAN: s. DE FAVOR TE . . .
ABRIR EL CORAZÓN To bare one's heart
ABUELA: s. CUÉNTASELO A TU . . .
ACÁ LA MADRE DE LOS BORREGOS Far, far away / Way down yonder / East of the twelfth of never
ACABA: s. LA MUERTE LO ACABA TODO
ACABA: s. QUIEN MAL ANDA, MAL . . .
ACOSTARSE CON LAS GALLINAS (Y LEVANTARSE CON LOS GALLOS) Early to bed and early to rise / To go to bed with the chickens and wake up with the roosters
ACUERDO: s. NO LLORO, PERO ME . . .
AGUANTE: s. NO HAY MAL QUE DURE CIEN AÑOS . . .
AHORA ES CUANDO, YERBABUENA, LE HAS DE DAR SABOR AL CALDO Strike while the iron is hot / Now is the time to make one's move
AHORA QUE ENTIERRAN DIOQUIS Get it while the getting's good
AHORA SI BAILA MI HIJA CON EL DOCTOR /CON EL SEÑOR Now you're talking! (indicates complete accord between speaker and listener)
AHORA SÍ CHISPAS, QUÉMENME Strike while the iron is hot / Now is the time to make the move
AHORA VA LA MÍA / LA TUYA / LA SUYA (etc.) Now it's my turn / your turn (etc.)
AJENA: s. CUIDA TU VIDA Y DEJA . . .
AMIGO: s. EL QUE PRESTA A UN AMIGO . . .
AMOLAR: s. PARA ACABARLA DE . . .
AMOR CON AMOR SE PAGA By love is love repaid / As you sow, so shall you reap
AMOR DE LEJOS, AMOR DE PENDEJOS Out of sight, out of mind

AMORES: s. NI BESOS NI APACHURRONES. . .
AMOS: s. ES POR DEMÁS, NADIE PUEDE SERVIR A DOS . . .
ANDA: s. QUIEN MAL ANDA . . .
ANDAR VUELTA Y VUELTA to pace the floor
ANDAS: s. DIME CON QUIEN . . .
ANTES DE HABLAR ES BUENO PENSAR Think before you act / Look before you leap
ANTES QUE TE CASES, MIRA LO QUE HACES Look twice before you leap
APAREZCA: s. DE LO PERDIDO . . .
APRIETA: s. EL QUE MUCHO . . . / QUIEN MUCHO ABARCA . . .
ÁRBOL: s. EL ÁRBOL SE CONOCE POR SU FRUTA
ARRIBA: s. BUSCAR ALGO DE . . .
ARRIEROS SOMOS Y EN EL CAMINO ANDAMOS We are all the children of God (expression used to admonish someone who is criticizing deficiencies he himself will inevitably come to possess)
ARRIESGA: s. EL QUE NO
ASTILLA: s. DE TAL PALO TAL . . .
ATIENDA/ATIENDE: s. QUIEN TIENE TIENDA . . .
ATOLE: s. CORRERLE A ALGUIEN . . .
AUNQUE LA MONA SE VISTA DE SEDA, MONA SE QUEDA You can't make a silk purse from a sow's ear / Clothes do not make the man
AVENTAR: s. HAY HASTA PARA . . .
AYUDA: s. AL FLOJO LO AYUDA DIOS
AYÚDATE, QUE DIOS TE AYUDARÁ God helps those who help themselves
AZUL: s. EL QUE QUIERE . . .

B

BAILA: s. POR DINERO BAILA EL PERRO . . .
BAJÁRSELE A ALGUIEN LA SANGRE A LOS PIES To be scared stiff
BARRIO AJENO: s. ESTAR COMO PERRO EN . . .
BIEN: s. EL QUE MAL HAGA, . . .
BITOQUE: s. LA JERINGA . . .
BOCA: s. EL QUE TIENE . . .
BORREGOS: s. ACÁ LA MADRE DE LOS...
BOTICA: s. HAY DE TODO COMO EN . . .
BRINCOS: s. ¿PARA QUE DAR TANTOS . . . ?
BROCHE: s. CERRAR CON . . .
BUEN: s. A BUEN ENTENDEDOR . . .
BUENA: s. A MAL TIEMPO BUENA CARA
BUENOS: s. CUMPLIR COMO LOS MEROS . . .
BURRA: s. CUANDO DIGO QUE . . .
BURRADA: s. HACER UNA . . .
BUSCAR ALGO DE ARRIBA A ABAJO To look high and low for something
BUSCARLE TRES PATAS AL GATO To complicate matters

C

CABEZA: s. ECHARLE A ALGUIEN POR . . .
CADA CHANGO A SU MECATE Y A DARSE VUELO Let each one mind his own business and get on with it / Keep your nose to yourself
CADA OVEJA CON SU PAREJA Birds of a feather flock together
CADA POBRETE LO QUE TIENE METE (general meaning: The poor must use all the resources at their disposal)
CADA UNO ES COMO DIOS LO HIZO We are all as God made us
CAE MÁS PRONTO UN HABLADOR QUE UN COJO A liar is more likely to slip up than a lame person
CALZÓN: s. PON, PON, PON UN NICLE PA' JABÓN
CAMARÓN QUE SE DUERME SE LO LLEVA LA CORRIENTE Opportunity only knocks once
CAMINO: s. ARRIEROS SOMOS Y EN EL . . .
CAMPOSANTO: s. VALE MÁS SUCIO EN CASA . . .
CANASTA: s. QUITARLE A ALGUIEN LA . . .
CANDIL DE LA CALLE, OSCURIDAD DE LA CASA A saint abroad and a devil at home
CANTA Y CANTA Y NADA DE ÓPERA Much ado about nothing
CÁNTARO: s. TANTO VA EL . . .
CAPITÁN: s. DONDE MANDA . . .
CARA: s. A MAL TIEMPO BUENA CARA
CARO: s. LO BARATO ES . . .
CASA: s. VALE MÁS SUCIO EN CASA ...
CASCARÓN: s. NO SALIR DEL . . .
CASES: s. EL MARTES NI TE . . .
CERRAR CON BROCHE DE ORO To end a program or event with a bang / with a grand finale
CIEGO: s. EL AMOR ES . . .
CIEN: s. MÁS VALE UNA TOMA . . .

CIENCIA: s. LA EXPERIENCIA ES LA MADRE DE . . .
COCHINOS: s. EL QUE NO QUIERA RUIDOS . . .
COLA DE RANA: s. SANA, SANA, . . .
COLMARLE A ALGUIEN LA PACIENCIA To cause someone to run out of patience
COLMILLO: s. A CABALLO DADO NO HAY QUE MIRARLE . . .
COMER FRIJOLES Y REPETIR POLLO Weak to perform though mighty to pretend (ref. to person who tries to give the impression that he is better off than he really is)
COMER: s. NO HAY QUE MORDER LA MANO . . .
COMER: s. NO MUERDAS LA MANO . . .
COMEZÓN: s. AL QUE LE DÉ COMEZÓN...
COMO: s. CADA UNO ES COMO DIOS LO HIZO
CON EL TIEMPO Y UN GANCHITO HASTA LAS VERDES SE ALCANZAN All things come to him who waits
CON LA VARA QUE MIDAS SERÁS MEDIDO As you sow, so shall you reap
CONOCE: s. EL ÁRBOL SE CONOCE POR SU FRUTA
CONOCER: s. MÁS VALE LO MALO CONOCIDO QUE LO BUENO POR . . .
CONSEJO: s. DAR EL . . .
CONSUELO: s. MAL DE MUCHOS, . . .
CORAZÓN: s. ABRIR EL . . .
CORAZÓN: s. OJOS QUE NO VEN, . . .
CORAZÓN: s. PANZA LLENA, . . .
CORAZONES: s. POR LAS ACCIONES SE JUZGAN LOS . . .
CORRERLE A ALGUIEN ATOLE POR LAS VENAS To be extremely patient / To be slow as molasses
CORRIENTE: s. CAMARÓN QUE SE DUERME
CORTITO -TA: s. TRAERLE A ALGUIEN MUY . . .
COSA MALA NUNCA MUERE A bad penny always turns up
COSA: s. DECIR UNA . . .
COSTA: s. HAY MOROS EN . . .
CREER: s. VER ES . . .
CRIE: s. EL QUE NO QUIERA RUIDOS...
CUAL MÁS CUAL MENOS Six of one, half dozen of the other
CUANDO DIGO QUE LA BURRA ES PARDA, ES PORQUE TRAIGO LOS PELOS EN LA MANO When I say it's so, it's because I have the proof right here in my hand
CUANDO MÁS SE TIENE, MÁS SE QUIERE The more one has, the more one wants
CUANDO UNA PUERTA SE CIERRA, OTRA SE ABRE There are other fish in the sea
CUANDO UNO ANDA DE MALAS HASTA LOS PERROS LO MEAN When it rains, it pours
CUANDO YO TENÍA DINERO ME LLAMABAN DON TOMÁS, Y AHORA QUE NO TENGO ME LLAMAN TOMÁS NOMÁS Wealth makes worship / A rich man has many friends
CUENTAS: s. EN RESUMIDAS . . .
CUÉNTASELO A TU ABUELA Tell it to the marines
CUENTO CHINO tall tale, fish story
CUIDA TU VIDA Y DEJA LA AJENA / LA DEL PRÓJIMO / LA DEL VECINO Go mind your own business
CUIDADO: s. SI QUIERES VIVIR SIN . . .
CULECAS: s. SON MÁS LAS . . .
CUMPLIR COMO LOS MERO BUENOS To live up to one's word / To fulfill one's commitments to the letter
CURA: s. LA CURA ES PEOR . . .

CH

CHÁVEZ: s. TÚ SABES QUIEN TRAE LAS LLAVES, . . .
CHINGUES: s. NO ME CHINGUES ...
CHINO: s. CUENTO ...
CHISPAS: s. AHORA SÍ ...

D

DAN: s. POR DINERO BAILA EL PERRO ...
DAÑO: s. HASTA LO QUE NO COMES TE HACE ...
DAR EL CONSEJO Y QUEDARSE SIN ÉL Not to practice what one preaches
DAR GATO POR LIEBRE to deceive someone, to give someone a song and a dance
DARÉ: s. MÁS VALE UN TOMA ...
DÉ: s. AL QUE LE DÉ COMEZÓN...
DE FAVOR TE ABRAZAN, Y QUIERES QUE TE APRIETEN They give you an inch and you want a mile
¡DE LA QUE ME ESCAPÉ! That was a close shave / close call!
DE LO PERDIDO A LO QUE APAREZCA Something is better than nothing (lit. 'From having lost it to

whatever may appear')
DE MÚSICO, POETA Y LOCO, TODOS TENEMOS UN POCO Everyone is a little bit crazy
DE TAL PALO TAL ASTILLA Like father like son
DE UNA MENTIRA NACEN MUCHAS One lie leads to a thousand
DE UN DÍA PARA OTRO any day now, any time soon
DE UN MOMENTO PARA OTRO any minute now, any time soon
DEBE: s. EL QUE NADA ...
DEJES: s. NO DEJES PARA MAÑANA ...
DEL ÁRBOL CAÍDO TODOS HACEN LEÑA Everyone kicks a man when he's down
DEL DICHO AL HECHO HAY MUCHO TRECHO Sooner said than done
DECIR POR DERECHO To call a spade a spade / To tell it like it is
DECIR UNA COSA Y HACER OTRA To say one thing and do another
DEJARSE TRATAR CON LA PUNTA DEL PIE to let someone walk all over you
DERECHITO: s. SANGRE DE PERRITO ...
DERECHO: s. DECIR POR ...
DESEA: s. LA SUERTE DE LA FEA ...
DESHONRA: s. EL SER POBRE NO ES ...
DÍA: s. A CADA SANTO SE LE LLEGA ...
DÍA: s. DE UN ...
DIENTE: s. A CABALLO DADO NO HAY QUE MIRARLE ...
DIFERENTE: s. LA JERINGA ...
DIGO: s. HAZ LO QUE YO DIGO ...
DIME CON QUIEN ANDAS Y TE DIRÉ QUIEN ERES A man is known by the company he keeps
DINERO: s. EL QUE PRESTA A UN AMIGO ...
DINERO: s. POR DINERO BAILA EL PERRO ...
DINERO LLAMA DINERO Money begets money / The rich get rich (and the poor get poorer)
DINERO TRAE DINERO (id. to DINERO LLAMA DINERO)
DIOS: s. A QUIEN MADRUGA, ...
DIOS: s. AL FLOJO LO AYUDA DIOS
DIOS: s. AL QUE MADRUGA, ...
DIOS: s. AL QUE NO HABLA, ...
DIOS: s. AYÚDATE , QUE ...
DIOS: s. CADA UNO ES COMO DIOS LO HIZO
DIOS: s. DONDE ...
DIOS: s. EL HOMBRE PROPONE Y ...
DIOS: s. EL QUE NO HABLA ...
DIRÉ: s. DIME CON QUIEN ANDAS ...
DONDE COMEN DOS , COMEN TRES There's always room for one more / Two can live as cheaply as one
DONDE DIOS ES SERVIDO On the other side of nowhere / Beyond the twelfth of never
DONDE MANDA CAPITÁN , NO MANDA MARINERO Too many cooks spoil the broth (There can be only one boss)
DOS: s. MÁS VALE QUE HAIGA ...
DUELA/DUELE: s. AL QUE LE DUELA LA MUELA ...

E

ECHAR EL GATO A RETOZAR to steal
ECHAR LA CASA POR LA VENTANA to go for broke, to shoot the works
ECHARLE A ALGUIEN POR LA CABEZA To let the cat out of the bag (give someone away, betray someone)
ECHAR MENTIRAS PARA SACAR VERDADES To tell a lie and learn the truth
EL AMOR ES CIEGO Love is blind
EL ÁRBOL SE CONOCE POR SU FRUTA By their fruits ye shall know them
EL BURRO POR DELANTE PARA QUE NO SE ESPANTE "Me first" (said to a person who always mentions his/her name before the names of others, e.g., 'Yo y mis amigos lo hicimos')
EL COMAL LE DIJO A LA OLLA: QUÉ COLA TAN PRIETA TIENES The pot is calling the kettle black
EL HÁBITO (NO) HACE AL MONJE Clothes (don't) make the man
EL HOMBRE PROPONE Y DIOS DISPONE Man proposes, (but) God disposes
EL MARTES NI TE CASES NI TE EMBARQUES (folk wisdom:) Don't marry or set sail on Tuesdays
EL MUERTO AL POZO Y EL VIVO AL NEGOCIO Let the dead bury the dead / Life must go on
EL SER POBRE NO ES DESHONRA Poverty is no sin
EL TIEMPO ES ORO Time is money
EL QUE CANTA, SUS MALES ESPANTA He who sings chases away his blues
EL QUE LA HACE LA PAGA As you sow so shall you reap
EL QUE MAL HAGA, BIEN ESPERE As you sow so shall you reap
EL QUE MUCHO APRIETA, POCO ABARCA Don't bite off more than you can chew

EL QUE NADA DEBE NADA TEME If your hands are clean you have nothing to fear
EL QUE NO ARRIESGA, NO GANA Nothing ventured, nothing gained
EL QUE NO HABLA DIOS NO LO OYE God helps those who help themselves
EL QUE NO LLORA NO MAMA One must speak up to be heard, God helps those who help themselves
EL QUE NO QUIERA RUIDOS QUE NO CRÍE COCHINOS/EL QUE NO QUIERE RUIDOS QUE NO CRÍE COCHINOS If you can't stand the heat, stay out of the kitchen (lit. 'He who wants no noise should not raise hogs')
EL QUE PRESTA A UN AMIGO, PIERDE EL DINERO Y PIERDE EL AMIGO Neither a borrower nor a lender be (lit. 'He who lends money to a friend loses both money and friend')
EL QUE QUIERA AZUL QUE LE CUESTE One must pay for what one wants (='Take what you want and pay for it, says God'--Spanish proverb)
EL QUE RÍE ÚLTIMO, RÍE MEJOR He who laughs last, laughs best
EL QUE TIENE BOCA A ROMA VA Speak up loud and you'll draw a crowd (he who speaks up is heard / is listened to)
EN BOCA CERRADA NO ENTRAN MOSCAS Silence is golden
EN LA UNIÓN HAY FUERZA In unity there is strength, United we stand, divided we fall
EN RESUMIDAS CUENTAS when all is said and done
EN TIERRA DE CIEGOS EL TUERTO ES REY In the land of the blind the one-eyed is king
ENCUERAS: s. ¿QUÉ ESPERAS QUE NO...
ENFERMEDAD: s. LA CURA ES PEOR ...
ENGAÑAN: s. LAS APARIENCIAS ...
ENSEÑAR LA OREJA to show one's ignorance
ENTENDEDOR: s. A BUEN ENTENDEDOR ...
ENTIENDES: s. ¿ME ENTIENDES, ...
ENTIERRAN: s. AHORA QUE ...
ENTRARLE PAREJO To go for broke (to go all out for something)
ERES: s. DIME CON QUIEN ANDAS ...
ES MEJOR ANDAR SOLO QUE MAL ACOMPAÑADO better to travel alone than to keep bad company
ES MEJOR QUE HAYA UN TONTO Y NO DOS You've made enough of a fool of yourself already (and you'll make more of one of yourself if you keep doing what you are doing)
ES POR DEMÁS, NADIE PUEDE SERVIR A DOS AMOS No one can serve two masters
ESCAPE: s. ¡DE LA QUE ME ... !
ESPANTA: s. EL QUE CANTA, SUS MALES ...
ESPANTE: s. EL BURRO POR DELANTE ...
ESPERAS: s. ¿QUÉ ESPERAS QUE NO ...
ESTAR COMO LA ABEJA, QUE VOLANDO PICA (ref. to the person who enjoys malicious insinuation)
ESTAR COMO PERRO EN BARRIO AJENO To be like a fish out of the water
ESTAR TAMAÑITO to have one's heart in one's mouth, to feel "just so big"
EXPERIENCIA: s. LA EXPERIENCIA ES MADRE ...
EXPLICO: s. ¿ME ENTIENDES, ...

F

FALTA: s. NUNCA FALTA ...
FAROL DE LA CALLE, OSCURIDAD DE LA CASA A saint abroad and a sinner at home
FEA: s. LA SUERTE DE LA FEA ...
FEDERICO: s. ¿ME ENTIENDES, ...
FLOJO: s. AL FLOJO LO AYUDA DIOS
FREGASTE: s. TE CASASTE, TE ...
FUERZA: s. EN LA UNIÓN HAY FUERZA
FUERZA: s. MÁS VALE MAÑA QUE ...

G

GALVÁN: s. NO LO ENTENDERÁ ...
GALLINAS: s. ACOSTARSE CON LAS ...
GALLO: s. MÁS CLARO NO CANTA ...
GANCHITO: s. CON EL TIEMPO Y ...
GANSO: s. ME CANSO DIJO UN ...
GARROTE: s. LIMOSNERO ...
GATO: s. BUSCARLE TRES PATAS ...
GATO: s. HAY ...
GUANTE: s. A QUIEN LE VENGA ...
GUATEMALA: IR DE GUATEMALA A GUATEPEOR/SALIR DE GUATEMALA PARA IR A GUATEPEOR to go from bad to worse
GUSTOS: s. A GUSTOS SE ROMPEN PANZAS

H

HABLA: s. EL QUE NO HABLA ...
HABLADOR: s. CAE MÁS PRONTO UN ...
HABLAR: s. ANTES DE ...
HACER ALGO A COMO DÉ LUGAR to do something by hook or by crook
HACER DE LAS SUYAS to be up to one's tricks
HACER UNA BURRADA to pull a real boner
HACER: s. NO ES LO MISMO DECIR QUE ...
HAGO: s. HAZ LO QUE YO DIGO ...
HAIGA: s. MÁS VALE QUE HAIGA ...
HAMBRE: s. A BUEN HAMBRE ...
¡HASTA LO QUE NO COMES TE HACE DAÑO! Busybodies never lack a bad day/ If you look for trouble you will find it
HAY DE TODO COMO EN BOTICA (Here) there's a little bit of everything
HAY GATO ENCERRADO There's something rotten in Denmark / There's something fishy going on
HAY HASTA PARA AVENTAR PA' ARRIBA There is enough (here) to take care of an army
HAY MOROS EN LA COSTA The walls have ears
HAY MUERTOS QUE NO HACEN RUIDOS Y SON MAYORES SUS PENAS Silent rivers run deep
HAY: s. NO HAY MAL QUE ...
HAZ BIEN Y NO MIRES A QUIEN Charity is its own reward
HAZ LO QUE YO DIGO, Y NO LO QUE YO HAGO Do as I say, not as I do
HERMOSA: s. LA SUERTE DE LA FEA ...
HERMOSO: s. QUIEN A FEO AMA, ...
HIJA: s. AHORA SÍ BAILA MI ...
HINCAN: s. VEN LA TEMPESTAD Y NO SE ...
HIZO: s. CADA UNO ES COMO DIOS LO HIZO
HOCICO: s. PERRERO HUEVERO AUNQUE LE QUEMEN ...
HOMBRE: s. NO SÓLO DE PAN VIVE ...
HORA: s. A BUENA HORA ...
HOY: s. NO DEJES PARA MAÑANA LO QUE PUEDES HACER...
HUESO: s. A OTRO PERRO CON ESE ...

I

IMPORTA: s. NO IMPORTA QUE NAZCAN CHATOS ...
INCOMODA: s. LA VERDAD NO MATA, PERO ...
IR POR LANA Y SALIR TRASQUILADO (lit. 'To go to buy wool and to come back sheared'; the sense is that one has gone with the intent of winning but returns a complete loser)

J

JICOTERA: s. MOVER LA ...
JUAN DOMÍNGUEZ: s. NO ME CHINGUES ...
JUSTOS PAGAN POR PECADORES The just pay for the sins of the guilty

L

LA CURA ES PEOR QUE LA ENFERMEDAD The cure is worse than the disease
LA ENEMA: s. LA JERINGA ...
LA EXPERIENCIA ES LA MADRE DE LA CIENCIA Experience is the mother of wisdom
LA GRACIA ES ANDAR ENTRE LAS LLAMAS Y NO QUEMARSE The real trick is to emerge unscathed from flame and fire
LA JERINGA/LA LAVATIVA/LA ENEMA ES LA MISMA, SÓLO EL BITOQUE ES DIFERENTE (mildly vulg.) Plus ça change, plus c'est la même chose
LA MALA YERBA NUNCA MUERE The bad penny keeps coming back
LA MENTIRA DURA HASTA QUE LA VERDAD LLEGA The truth will always come out in the end

LA MUERTE A NADIE PERDONA Death pardons no man
LA MUERTE LO ACABA TODO Death puts an end to everything
LA SUERTE DE LA FEA LA HERMOSA LA DESEA The grass is always greener on the other side (lit. 'The beautiful woman envies the good fortune of the ugly one')
LA VERDAD NO MATA, PERO INCOMODA The truth sometimes hurts
LAS APARIENCIAS ENGAÑAN You can't judge a book by its cover
LADO: s. A LO DADO NO SE LE BUSCA ...
LADO: s. SANGRE DE VENADO ...
LADRE: s. NO TENER NI PADRE ...
LADRÓN: s. MÁS PECA LA VÍCTIMA ...
LANA: s. IR POR LANA Y SALIR TRASQUILADO
LAVATIVA: s. LA JERINGA ...
LEJOS: s. POCO A POCO SE VA ...
LEÑA: s. DEL ÁRBOL CAÍDO TODOS HACEN ...
LIEBRE: s. DAR GATO POR ...
LIMOSNERO Y CON GARROTE Beggars can't be choosers
LIMPIO: s. VALE MÁS SUCIO EN CASA ...
LO BARATO CUESTA CARO / LO BARATO ES CARO Cheap goods cost dear in the long run
LO CORTÉS NO QUITA LO VALIENTE Civility never detracted from valor
LO QUE PASÓ VOLÓ Let bygones be bygones, No use crying over spilled milk
LOCO: s. DE MÚSICO, POETA Y ...
LOCOS: s. LOS NIÑOS Y LOS ...
LOS NIÑOS Y LOS LOCOS DICEN LA VERDAD Children and crazy people always tell the truth / Words from the mouth of babes
LUGAR: s. HACER (ALGO) A COMO DÉ ...

LL

LLAMAS: s. LA GRACIA ES ANDAR ENTRE ...
LLORA: s. EL QUE NO LLORA ...

M

MACHO: s. AL OJO DEL AMO ENGORDA ...
MACHO: s. TAPARLE EL OJO AL ...
MADRE: s. LA EXPERIENCIA ES MADRE ...
MADRE: s. NO TENER NI PADRE ...
MAL: s. A MAL TIEMPO BUENA CARA
MAL: s. NO HAY MAL QUE ...
MAL: s. QUIEN MAL ANDA ...
MAL ACOMPAÑADO: s. ES MEJOR ANDAR SOLO QUE .../ MÁS VALE ANDAR SOLO QUE ...
MAL DE MUCHOS, CONSUELO DE TONTOS Misery loves company / Fools are comforted by the misfortunes of others
MALES: s. PARA ALIVIO DE MIS ...
MAMA: s. EL QUE NO LLORA ...
MAÑANA: s. NO DEJES PARA MAÑANA ...
MANDADOS: s. UNOS NACIERON PARA MANDAR ...
MANDAR: s. UNOS NACIERON PARA MANDAR ...
MANO: s. NO HAY QUE MORDER LA ...
MANO: s. NO MUERDAS LA ...
MÁS CLARO NO CANTA UN GALLO As clear as the nose on your face
MÁS PECA LA VÍCTIMA QUE EL LADRÓN (roughly equivalent to 'The coward dies a thousand deaths, the valiant only one', though the literal meaning shows a variation on that theme: 'The victim sins more than the thief--because the victim suspects and blames everyone whereas the thief only sinned during the single act of thievery')
MÁS VALE ALGO QUE NADA Every little bit helps
MÁS VALE ANDAR SOLO QUE MAL ACOMPAÑADO It is better to be alone than in bad company
MÁS VALE LO MALO CONOCIDO QUE LO BUENO POR CONOCER Better safe than sorry / Better a lean agreement than a fat sentence
MÁS VALE MAÑA QUE FUERZA The pen is mightier than the sword
MÁS VALE PÁJARO EN MANO QUE CIEN VOLANDO A bird in the hand is worth two in the bush
MÁS VALE QUE HAIGA UN TONTO Y NO DOS (roughly equivalent to:) Two wrongs do not make a right

(though lit. 'Better for there to be just one fool than two')
MÁS VALE TARDE QUE NUNCA Better late than never
MÁS VALE UN TOMA QUE CIEN TE DARÉ A bird in hand is worth two in the bush
MATANCEROS: s. NADIE QUIERE SER CHIVO; TODOS QUIEREN SER ...
ME CANSO / ME CANSO, DIJO UN GANSO / ME CANSO, DIJO UN GANSO, CUANDO VOLAR NO PUDO (ritualistic response given--usually by a child--to someone ordering him/her to cease any particularly taxing form of behavior; the sense of the refrain is "I'll do what I'm doing as long as I feel like doing it")
¿ME ENTIENDES, MÉNDEZ, O TE EXPLICO, FEDERICO? (expression used to emphasize the speaker's desire to be understood; rough Eng. equivalent would be 'Ya see what I mean, Gene, or must I tell it all, Paul?')
MECATE: s. CADA CHANGO A SU ...
MÉNDEZ: s. ¿ME ENTIENDES, ...
MENOS: s. CUAL MÁS CUAL ...
MENTIRA: s. DE UNA ...
METE: s. CADA POBRETE LO QUE TIENE METE
MIRA: s. ANTES QUE TE CASES, ...
MIRES: s. HAZ BIEN Y NO ...
MISMA: s. LA JERINGA ...
MISMA: s. SER PÁJAROS DE LA MISMA PLUMA
MOMENTO: s. DE UN ...
MONA: s. AUNQUE LA ...
MONJE: s. EL HÁBITO (NO) HACE ...
MOSCAS: s. EN BOCA CERRADA NO ENTRAN ...
MOSCO: s. YA TE CONOZCO ...
MOVER LA JICOTERA to stir things up, to start a commotion
MUELA: s. AL QUE LE DUELA LA MUELA ...
MUERDE: s. PERRO QUE LADRA NO ...
MUERE: s. COSA MALA NUNCA ...
MUERE: s. YERBA MALA NUNCA ...

N

NACIERON: s. UNOS NACIERON PARA MANDAR ...
NADA: s. MÁS VALE ALGO QUE ...
NADIE QUIERE SER CHIVO; TODOS QUIEREN SER MATANCEROS Everyone wants to be a chief and no one an Indian
NAZCAN: s. NO IMPORTA QUE NAZCAN CHATOS ...
NI BESOS NI APACHURRONES SON AMORES Actions speak louder than words
NO DEJES PARA MAÑANA LO QUE PUEDES HACER HOY Don't leave for tomorrow what you can do today
NO ES EL LEÓN COMO LO PINTAN / NO ES LA LEONA COMO LA PINTAN Things are seldom what they seem
NO ES LO MISMO DECIR QUE HACER Actions speak louder than words
NO ES ORO TODO LO QUE RELUCE All that glitters is not gold
NO HAY COSA / NO HAY PERSONA TAN MALA QUE PARA ALGO NO SIRVA There's a little bit of gold in every mine / There's some good in everyone
NO HAY MAL QUE DURE CIEN AÑOS NI ENFERMO QUE LOS AGUANTE Nothing can last forever / Everything must have an end
NO HAY MAL QUE POR BIEN NO VENGA Every cloud has a silver lining/ It's a blessing in disguise
NO HAY QUE MORDER LA MANO QUE NOS DA DE COMER Don't bite the hand that feeds you
NO IMPORTA QUE NAZCAN CHATOS CON TAL QUE TENGAN RESUELLO Handsome is as handsome does, You can't judge a book by its cover (lit. 'It doesn't matter if they're born flat-nosed just as long as they can breathe through it')
NO LE ENTENDERÁ GALVÁN If he doesn't know, nobody will
NO LLORO, PERO ME ACUERDO I may not be crying, but I can remember the pain
NO ME CHINGUES, JUAN DOMÍNGUEZ (rough Eng. equivalent:) Don't try to cheat, Pete (=Don't try to get the better of me)

NO MUERDAS LA MANO QUE TE DA DE COMER Don't bite the hand that feeds you
NO SALIR DEL CASCARÓN (TODAVÍA) To be (still) wet behind the ears
NO SÓLO DE PAN VIVE EL HOMBRE Man does not live by bread alone
NO TENER NI PADRE NI MADRE NI PERRITO QUE LE LADRE to be all alone in this world
NO VENGO A VER SI PUEDO SINO PORQUE PUEDO VENGO (literally: I haven't come to see if I am able but because I know I'm able, I'm here)
NUNCA: NUNCA FALTA UN YOLOVÍ There's always going to be someone watching, There will always be a witness
NUNCA: s. MÁS VALE TARDE QUE ...

O

OJOS QUE NO VEN, CORAZÓN QUE NO SIENTE Out of sight, out of mind
OJOS: s. PELAR TAMAÑOS ...
OLLA: s. EL COMAL LE DIJO A ...
ÓPERA: s. CANTA Y CANTA Y NADA DE ...
OREJA: s. ENSEÑAR ...
ORO: s. EL TIEMPO ES ...
OSCURIDAD: s. CANDIL DE LA CALLE .../FAROL DE LA CALLE...
OTROS: s. UNOS NACIERON PARA MANDAR ...
OYE: s. EL QUE NO HABLA ...

P

PACIENCIA: s. COLMARLE A ALGUIEN ...
PAGA: s. AMOR CON AMOR SE ...
PAGA: s. EL QUE LA HACE ...
PÁJAROS: s. SER PÁJAROS DE LA MISMA PLUMA
PALABRAS: s. A BUEN ENTENDEDOR...
PAN: s. POR DINERO BAILA EL PERRO ...
PANZA LLENA, CORAZÓN CONTENTO A full stomach makes a happy heart / <u>Man ist was man isst</u> (German proverb)
PANZAS: s. A GUSTOS SE ROMPEN ...
PARA ACABARLA DE AMOLAR On top of everything else / To top it all off
PARA ALIVIO DE MIS MALES To make matters worse / On top of everything else
¡¿PARA QUÉ DAR TANTOS BRINCOS ESTANDO EL SUELO TAN PAREJO?! (ref. to the folly of excessive pride, egotism, etc.)
PAREJA: s. CADA OVEJA CON SU ...
PAREJO: s. ENTRARLE ...
PAREJO: s. ¡¿PARA QUÉ DAR TANTOS BRINCOS ...?!
PASÓ: s. LO QUE PASÓ VOLÓ
PECA: s. MÁS PECA LA VÍCTIMA ...
PECADORES: s. JUSTOS PAGAN POR ...
PEDITO: s. SANA, SANA, COLA DE RANA ...
PELAR TAMAÑOS OJOS to open one's eyes very wide (as in astonishment)
PENAS: s. HAY MUERTOS QUE NO HACEN RUIDOS ...
PENDEJOS: s. AMOR DE LEJOS ...
PEOR: s. LA CURA ES PEOR ...
PERDIDO: s. DE LO PERDIDO ...
PERDONA: s. LA MUERTE A NADIE ...
PERRERO HUEVERO AUNQUE LE QUEMEN EL HOCICO Once a _____ always a ________
PERRITO: s. NO TENER NI PADRE ...
PERRITO: s. SANGRE DE PERRITO ...
PERRO: s. POR DINERO BAILA EL PERRO ...
PERRO: PERRO QUE LADRA NO MUERDE A barking dog never bites
PERROS: s. CUANDO UNO ANDA DE MALAS ...
PIE: s. DEJARSE TRATAR CON LA PUNTA ...
PIE: s. TE DAN LA MANO Y QUIERES ...
PIERDE: s. EL QUE PRESTA A UN AMIGO ...
PINTAN: s. NO ES EL LEÓN ...
PLUMA: s. SER PÁJAROS DE LA MISMA PLUMA
POBRETE: s. CADA POBRETE LO QUE TIENE METE
POCAS: s. A BUEN ENTENDEDOR ...
POCO A POCO SE VA LEJOS Rome wasn't built in a day / Little by little one goes a long way
PODER: s. QUERER ES ...
POLLO: s. COMER FRIJOLES Y REPETIR ...
PON, PON, PON UN NICLE PA' JABÓN, PA' LAVAR TU CALZÓN Every

little bit helps (expression hopefully encouraging contributions into a general fund, as at a church bazaar, etc.)
POR DINERO BAILA EL PERRO/POR DINERO BAILA EL PERRO Y POR PAN SÍ SE LO DAN Money talks
POR LAS ACCIONES SE JUZGAN LOS CORAZONES Actions speak louder than words
POR UN OÍDO LE ENTRA Y POR OTRO LE SALE In one ear, out the other
POZO: s. EL MUERTO AL ...
PRESTA: s. EL QUE PRESTA A UN AMIGO ...
PRESTADO: s. SI QUIERES VIVIR SIN CUIDADO, NO PIDAS NUNCA ...
PUERTA: s. CUANDO UNA ...

Q

¿QUÉ ESPERAS QUE NO TE ENCUERAS? (vulg.) What are you waiting for, doomsday?
QUERER ES PODER Where there's a will there's a way
QUIEBRA: s. TANTO VA EL CÁNTARO AL AGUA HASTA ...
QUIEN: s. DIME CON QUIEN ANDAS ...
QUIEN A FEO AMA, HERMOSO LE PARECE Love makes even the ugly look beautiful
QUIEN BIEN SIEMBRA, BIEN RECOGE As you sow, so shall you reap
QUIEN MAL ANDA, MAL ACABA He who lives by the sword shall die by the sword; As you sow so shall you reap
QUIEN MÁS TIENE, MÁS QUIERE The more you have the more you want
QUIEN MUCHO ABARCA, POCO APRIETA Your eyes are bigger than your stomach
QUIEN NO OYE CONSEJOS NO LLEGA A VIEJO Heed my advice or pay the price
QUIEN TIENE TIENDA Y NO LA ATIENDA, QUE LA VENDA/QUIEN TIENE TIENDA Y NO LA ATIENDE, QUE LA VENDA (lit. 'He who has a store and doesn't attend to business should sell the store')
QUIERE: s. QUIEN MÁS TIENE,...
QUITARLE A ALGUIEN LA CANASTA To cut the umbilical cord (=to withdraw financial or other type of support)
QUITARSE ALGUIEN LA VENDA DE LOS OJOS To see things the way they really are

R

RASQUE: s. AL QUE LE DÉ COMEZÓN ...
RECOGE: s. QUIEN BIEN SIEMBRA ...
RELUCE: s. NO ES ORO TODO LO QUE ...
RESUELLO: s. NO IMPORTA QUE NAZCAN CHATOS ...
RETOZAR: s. ECHAR EL GATO ...
RÍE: s. EL QUE ...
ROMPEN: s. A GUSTOS SE ROMPEN PANZAS
RONCAN: s. A VER SI COMO ...
RUIDOS: s. EL QUE NO QUIERA RUIDOS ...
RUIDOS: s. HAY MUERTOS QUE NO HACEN ...

S

SALE: s. POR UN OÍDO LE ENTRA Y POR OTRO LE ...
SALIR: s. IR POR LANA Y SALIR TRASQUILADO
SALIR DE GUATEMALA PARA IR A GUATEPEOR To go from bad to worse
SANA, SANA, COLA DE RANA, TIRA UN PEDITO PARA AHORA Y MAÑANA (expression said to children when one applies medicine to their cuts and bruises or when one simply kisses the wound to "make it better")
SANGRE: s. BAJÁRSELE A ALGUIEN ...
SANGRE DE PERRITO QUE SE VAYA DERECHITO (said to or by a person trying to hit the target he is shooting at)
SANGRE DE VENADO QUE SE VAYA POR UN LADO (said to someone to cause him to miss a target he is shooting at)
SANTO: s. A BUEN SANTO ...
SAQUE: s. AL QUE LE DUELA LA MUELA ...
SER PÁJAROS DE LA MISMA PLUMA To be birds of a feather

¡SI FUERA VÍBORA TE MORDIERA! It's staring at you right in the face! (said of a sought object)
SI QUIERES VIVIR SIN CUIDADO, NO PIDAS NUNCA PRESTADO Neither a borrower nor a lender be
SIRVA: s. NO HAY COSA TAN MALA QUE PARA ALGO NO ...
SÓLO: s. LA JERINGA ...
SÓLO EL TIEMPO DIRÁ Only time will tell
SON MÁS LAS CULECAS QUE LAS QUE ESTÁN PONIENDO There are more birds in the barn than eggs in the nest (expression used to criticize pretense, exaggerated claims, etc.)
SUCIO: s. VALE MÁS SUCIO EN CASA ...

T

TANTO VA EL CÁNTARO AL AGUA HASTA QUE SE QUIEBRA The pitcher went to the well once too often/ You'll get yours (=your just deserts) sooner or later
TAPARLE EL OJO AL MACHO to keep up appearances
TARDE: s. MÁS VALE TARDE QUE NUNCA
TE CASASTE, TE FREGASTE A man's troubles begin when he gets married
TE DAN LA MANO Y QUIERES EL PIE They give you an inch and you want a mile
TEMPESTAD: s. VEN LA TEMPESTAD ...
TENER: s. NO TENER NI PADRE ...
TIEMPO: s. A MAL TIEMPO BUENA CARA
TIEMPO: s. SÓLO EL ...
TIENDA: s. QUIEN TIENE TIENDA ...
TIENE: s. CUANDO MÁS SE ...
TIRA: s. A TODO LE ...
TODO: s. LA MUERTE LO ACABA TODO
TOMA: s. MÁS VALE UN TOMA ...
TOMÁS: s. CUANDO YO TENÍA DINERO ME LLAMABAN ...
TONTO: s. ES MEJOR QUE HAYA ...
TONTO: s. MÁS VALE QUE HAIGA ...
TRABAJA: s. UNO NUNCA SABE POR QUIEN ...
TRAERLE A ALGUIEN MUY CORTITO -TA to keep a tight rein on someone/ to keep someone on a short leash
TRASQUILADO: s. IR POR LANA Y SALIR TRASQUILADO
TRECHO: s. DEL DICHO AL HECHO ...
TRES: s. DONDE COMEN DOS ...
TÚ SABES QUIEN TRAE LAS LLAVES, CHÁVEZ You know who runs the show around here / You know who's boss, Hoss
TUERTO: s. EN TIERRA DE CIEGOS, ...

U

UNIÓN: s. EN LA UNIÓN HAY FUERZA
UNO NUNCA SABE POR QUIEN TRABAJA One never knows who will reap the rewards of one's labor
UNOS NACIERON PARA MANDAR Y OTROS PARA SER MANDADOS Some were born to command, others to be commanded, Some were born to be chiefs and other Indians

V

VALE: s. MÁS VALE QUE HAIGA ...
VALE: s. MÁS VALE TARDE QUE NUNCA
VALE: s. MÁS VALE UN TOMA ...
VALE MÁS SUCIO EN CASA Y NO LIMPIO EN EL CAMPOSANTO (approx. equivalent:) Better a messy house than an early death (lit. 'It's better to be dirty at home than clean in the cemetery')
VALIENTE: s. LO CORTÉS NO QUITA LO ...
VARA: s. CON LA ...
VAYA: s. SANGRE DE PERRITO ...
VAYA: s. SANGRE DE VENADO ...
VEN LA TEMPESTAD Y NO SE HINCAN They don't know enough to come in out of the rain
VENADO: s. SANGRE DE VENADO ...
VENDA: s. QUIEN TIENE TIENDA ...
VENDA: QUITARSE UNO LA ...
VENGA: s. NO HAY MAL QUE POR BIEN ...
VENTANA: s. ECHAR LA CASA POR ...
VER ES CREER Seeing is believing
VERDAD: s. LA MENTIRA DURA HASTA QUE ...
VERDADES: s. ECHAR MENTIRAS PARA ...
VÍBORA: s. ¡SI FUERA ... !

VÍCTIMA: s. MÁS PECA LA VÍCTIMA ...
VIEJO: s. QUIEN NO OYE CONSEJOS ...
VOLANDO: s. MÁS VALE PÁJARO EN MANO ...
VOLÓ: s. LO QUE PASÓ VOLÓ
VUELTA: s. ANDAR ...

Y

YA TE CONOZCO MOSCO I've seen through you
YERBA MALA NUNCA MUERE A bad penny always shows up
YERBA: s. LA MALA ...
YERBABUENA: s. AHORA ES CUANDO, ...
YOLOVÍ: s. NUNCA FALTA ...

Z

ZAPATO: s. AL QUE LE QUEDE ...
ZAPATOS: s. A HUEVO NI ...

Apéndice B: Verbos en -EAR/-IAR
Appendix B: Verbs in -EAR/-IAR

Uno de los cambios fonéticos de mayor difusión social que se halla en el español de Tejas se relaciona con la terminación verbal -<u>ear</u>. Las dos vocales "fuertes" (bajas) se diptongan por un proceso de simplificación que convierte la <u>e</u> en <u>i</u>. Dicha transformación se realiza en el infinitivo y en los participios pasivos y presentes, así como en muchas formas de los tiempos sencillos. Conjugamos a continuación el verbo <u>desear</u> como ejemplo:

One of the most widespread phonetic variations observable in Texas Spanish (and one which affects the speech of all social levels) concerns verbs whose infinitives end in -<u>ear</u> and -<u>iar</u> in "standard" Spanish. The two "strong" (low) vowels are diphthongized and thereby simplified in a process which converts <u>e</u> into <u>i</u>. This trajectory is observed in the infinitive and in the past and present participles as well as in most forms of the simple tenses. There follows the partial conjugation of the verb <u>desear</u> as an example:

INFINITIVO/INFINITIVE: desiar

PARTICIPIO PASIVO/PAST PARTICIPLE: desiado

GERUNDIO (PARTICIPIO PRESENTE)/PRESENT PARTICIPLE: desiando

PRESENTE DE INDICATIVO/PRESENT INDICATIVE:

deseo
deseas
desea
desiamos
desean

PRESENTE DE SUBJUNTIVO/PRESENT SUBJUNCTIVE:

desee
desees
desee
desiemos / desiamos (la segunda forma se usa más, a pesar de no marcarse morfológicamente como subjuntivo / the second form is used more, even though it is morphologically unmarked as a subjunctive)
deseen

FUTURO DE INDICATIVO/FUTURE INDICATIVE:

desiaré, desiarás, etc.

POTENCIAL/CONDITIONAL:

desiaría, desiarías, etc.

PRETÉRITO/PRETERITE:

desié, desiaste, desió, desiamos, desiaron

IMPERFECTO DE SUBJUNTIVO/PAST SUBJUNCTIVE:

desiara, desiaras, etc.

IMPERFECTO/IMPERFECT: desiaba, desiabas, etc.

En el polo opuesto encontramos la "descomposición" del diptongo de <u>i</u> mas <u>a</u>, <u>e</u> u <u>o</u> que se halla en los verbos que terminan en -<u>iar</u> en el español "estándar," v. gr. <u>copiar</u>. La ultracorrección convierte la <u>i</u> a <u>e</u> en los tiempos sencillos:

On the other hand we observe the "decomposition" of diphthongs occuring in verbs whose infinitives end in -<u>iar</u> in "standard" Spanish, e.g., <u>copiar</u>. Ultracorrection variously converts <u>i</u> to <u>e</u> in simple tenses:

PRESENTE DE INDICATIVO/PRESENT INDICATIVE:

copeo, copeas, copea, <u>copiamos</u>, copean

PRESENTE DE SUBJUNTIVO/PRESENT SUBJUNCTIVE:

copee, copees, copee, <u>copiemos</u>/<u>copiamos</u>, copeen

Parece, por lo tanto, reflejarse en la casilla a la izquierda de la designación de número y persona, una resistencia de parte de ambas conjugaciones variantes hacia toda vocal que no sea la alta _i_, a menos que se coloque el énfasis en la casilla a la izquierda; en este caso tiene que aparecer la vocal no alta. Así que la distinción entre los verbos -_ear_ e -_iar_ parece haberse eliminado.

In effect, both variant conjugations appear to reflect a resistance in the slot immediately to the left of the designation of number and person towards all but high vowel _i_ unless stress falls on the leftward slot, in which case a non-high vowel must occur. The distinction, then, between -_ear_ and -_iar_ verbs appears to have been eliminated.

Apéndice C: Bibliografía
Appendix C: Bibliography

Cada una de las siguientes obras de consulta se encuentra anotada (la mayor parte de manera crítica) en: Richard V. Teschner, Garland D. Bills and Jerry R. Craddock, Spanish and English of United States Hispanos: A Critical, Annotated, Linguistic Bibliography, Arlington, Va.: Center for Applied Linguistics, 1975, xxii, 352 pp. Al lector se le recomienda encarecidamente la consulta de esa fuente bibliográfica para más informes tocante las obras aquí citadas tanto como más de 600 libros, artículos, monografías, tesinas, etc. adicionales que versan sobre el español de Tejas, el Sudoeste estadounidense y demás regiones de los Estados Unidos también.

Each of the following secondary sources is annotated (for the most part critically) in: Richard V. Teschner, Garland D. Bills and Jerry R. Craddock, Spanish and English of United States Hispanos: A Critical, Annotated, Linguistic Bibliography, Arlington, Va.: Center for Applied Linguistics, 1975, xxii, 352 pp. The user is urged to consult that source for information on these and more than 600 other books, articles, monographs, dissertations, theses, etc., pertinent to the Spanish of Texas, the Southwest and other regions of the United States as well.

Atwood, E. Bagby. The Regional Vocabulary of Texas. Austin: Univ. of Texas Press, 1962. 273 pp.

Baugh, Lila. "A Study of Pre-School Vocabulary of Spanish-Speaking Children." MA Thesis, Univ. of Texas, Austin, 1933. 129 pp.

Braddy, Haldeen. "Narcotic Argot Along the Mexican Border." American Speech 30.84-90 (1955).

__________. "Smugglers' Argot in the Southwest." American Speech 31.96-101 (1956).

__________. "The Pachucos and Their Argot." Southern Folklore Quarterly 24.255-271 (1960).

Carrow(-Woolfolk), Elizabeth (Sister Mary Arthur). "Comprehension of English and Spanish by Preschool Mexican-American Children." Modern Language Journal 55.299-306 (1971).

__________. "Auditory Comprehension of English by Monolingual and Bilingual Preschool Children." Journal of Speech and Hearing Research 15.407-412 (1972).

Castillo Nájera, Francisco. "Breves consideraciones sobre el español que se habla en Méjico." Revista Hispánica Moderna 2.157-169 (1936).

Cerda, Gilberto, Berta Cabaza and Julia Farias. Vocabulario español de Texas. Univ. of Texas Hispanic Studies, Vol. 5 (Austin: Univ. of Texas Press, 1953). 347 pp. (Reprinted unrevised, Austin: Univ. of Texas Press, 1970.)

Cervantes, Alfonso. "A Selected Vocabulary of Anglicisms Used by First Grade Students of Elementary Schools of Del Rio, Texas." MA Thesis, Southwest Texas State Univ., San Marcos, 1973. vi, 68 pp.

Coltharp, Lurline. "The Influence of English on the 'Language' of the Tirilones." PhD Diss., Univ. of Texas, Austin, 1964. (Subsequently published with occasional revisions as: The Tongue of the Tirilones. University, Alabama: Univ. of Alabama Press, 1965. 186 pp.)

__________. "Some Additions: Lexicon of 'Tongue of the Tirilones.'" In Ralph W. Ewton, Jr. and Jacob Ornstein, eds., Studies in Language and Linguistics 1969-70, El Paso: Texas Western Press, 1970, pp. 69-78.

__________. "'Invitation to the Dance': Spanish in the El Paso Underworld." In Glenn G. Gilbert, ed., Texas Studies in Bilingualism, Berlin: Walter de Gruyter Co., 1969, pp. 18-41.

Cornejo, Ricardo Jesús. "Bilingualism: Study of the Lexicon of the Five-Year-Old Spanish-Speaking Children of Texas." PhD Diss., Univ. of Texas, Austin, 1969. 228 pp.

Elías Olivares, Lucía E. "Study of the Oral Vocabulary of Ten High-School Mexican-American Students in Austin, Texas." MA Thesis, Univ. of Texas, Austin, 1970. 100 pp.

Fody, Michael III. "A Glossary of Non-Standard Spanish Words and Idioms Found in Selected Newspapers of South Texas During 1968." MA Thesis, Southern Illinois Univ., Carbondale, 1969. 154 pp.

Frausto, Manuel. "Vocabulario español de San Marcos, Texas." MA Thesis, Southwest Texas State Univ., San Marcos, 1969. 55 pp.

Galván, Roberto A. "Un estudio geográfico de algunos vocablos usados por los habitantes de habla española de San Antonio, Texas." MA Thesis, Univ. of Texas, Austin, 1949. 142 pp.

__________. "El dialecto español de San Antonio, Texas." PhD Diss., Tulane Univ., New Orleans, 1955. 315 pp.

__________. "Más observaciones sobre el argot de Baranquilla." Hispania 49.483-485 (1966).

__________. "'Chichecano', neologismo jergal." Hispania 53.86-88 (1970).

__________. "More on 'Frito' as an English Loan-Word in Mexican Spanish." Hispania 54.511-514 (1971).

García, Anita H. "Identification and Classification of Types of Common Deviations from

Standard Spanish Made by Representative Native Speakers in South Texas." MA Thesis, Texas A & I Univ., Kingsville, 1969. 110 pp.
García, Lucy. "Vocabulario selecto del español de Brownsville, Texas." MA Thesis, Southwest Texas State Univ., San Marcos, 1972. 64 pp.
González, Gustavo. "A Linguistic Profile of the Spanish-Speaking First-Grader in Corpus Christi, Texas." MA Thesis, Univ. of Texas, Austin, 1968. 83 pp.
______. "The Acquisition of Spanish Grammar by Native Spanish Speakers." PhD Diss., Univ. of Texas, Austin, 1970. 178 pp.
Harrison, Helene. "A Methodological Study in Eliciting Linguistic Data from Mexican-American Bilinguals." PhD Diss., Univ. of Texas, Austin, 1967. 119 pp.
Ivey, Alfred Joe. "A Study of the Vocabulary of Newspapers Printed in the Spanish Language in Texas." MA Thesis, Univ. of Texas, Austin, 1927. iii, 137 pp.
January, William Spence, Jr. "The Chicano Dialect of the Mexican-American Communities of Dallas and Fort Worth." MA Thesis, Texas Christian Univ., 1971. 242 pp.
Keever, Mary, Alfredo Vásquez and Anna Padilla. Glossary of Words and Expressions, Irregular in Form or Meaning, Encountered in the Examination of Spanish Mail on the Mexican Border. El Paso, Texas: El Paso Office of the United States Office of Censorship, 1945. vii, 46 pp. mimeographed. (Location: Library of Congress, PC 4832 .U5.)
Kelly, Rex Robert. "Vocabulary as Used on the Mexican Border." MA Thesis, Baylor Univ., Waco, Texas, 1938. 39 pp.
______ and George W. Kelly. Farm and Ranch Spanish. N. place: Authors, 1961. xv, 241 pp.
Kercheville, Francis M. "A Preliminary Glossary of Southwestern and Rio Grande Spanish Including Semantic and Philological Peculiarities." Unpublished ms., Kingsville: Texas A & I Univ., 1967. 71 pp.
Lance, Donald M., ed. and chief contributor. A Brief Study of Spanish-English Bilingualism. Bethesda, Maryland: U.S. Dept. of Health, Education and Welfare, 1969. 104 pp. (ERIC System No. ED 032 529.)
León, Aurelio de. Barbarismos comunes en México. 2 vols. México D.F.: Imprenta Mundial, (1: 1936, 2: 1937). 80 +/92 pp.
Luna, Juanita J. "A Selected Vocabulary of the Spanish Spoken in Sabinal, Texas." MA Thesis, Southwest Texas State Univ., San Marcos, 1970. 101 pp.
Marambio, Juan. "Vocabulario español de Temple, Texas." MA Thesis, Southwest Texas State Univ., San Marcos, 1970. 110 pp.
Marrocco, Mary Anne W. "The Spanish of Corpus Christi, Texas." PhD Diss., Univ. of Illinois, Champaign-Urbana, 1972. 502 pp.
McKee, Okla Markham. "Five-Hundred Non-Dictionary Words Found in the El Paso-Juárez Press." MA Thesis, Univ. of Texas-El Paso, 1955. 75 pp.
Montemayor, Elsa Diana. "A Study of the Spanish Spoken by Certain Bilingual Students of Laredo, Texas." MA Thesis, Texas Women's Univ., Denton, 1966. 106 pp.
Ornstein, Jacob S. "Sociolinguistics and New Perspectives in the Study of Southwest Spanish." In Ralph W. Ewton, Jr. and Jacob Ornstein, eds., Studies in Language and Linguistics 1969-70, El Paso: Texas Western Press, 1970, pp. 127-184.
______. "Language Varieties Along the U.S.-Mexican Border." In Applications of Linguistics: Selected Papers of the Second International Congress of Applied Linguistics, edited by G.E. Perren and J.L.M. Trim, New York et alibi: Cambridge Univ. Press, 1971, pp. 349-362.
Patterson, Maurine. "Some Dialectal Tendencies in Popular Spanish in San Antonio." MA Thesis, Texas Women's Univ., Denton, 1946. 120 pp.
Ramírez, Carina (Karen). "Lexical Usage of and Attitude Toward Southwest Spanish in the Ysleta, Texas, Area." Graduate Paper, Univ. of Texas-El Paso, 1971. 84 pp. (Circulates through Library, Univ. of Texas-El Paso.)
______. "Lexical Usage of and Attitude Toward Southwest Spanish in the Ysleta, Texas, Area." Hispania 56.308-315 (1973).
Ramón, René Simón. "Vocabulario selecto del español regional de Del Río, Texas." MA Thesis, Southwest Texas State Univ., San Marcos, 1974. vii, 70 pp.
Reséndez, Víctor. "Vocabulario español de Seguín, Texas." MA Thesis, Southwest Texas State Univ., San Marcos, 1970. 81 pp.
Reynolds, Selma Fay. "Some Aspects of Spanish as Spoken and Written by Spanish-Speaking Students of a Junior High School in (Corpus Christi,) Texas." MA Thesis, Texas Women's Univ., Denton, 1945. 105 pp.
Romano-V., Octavio I. "Donship in a Mexican-American Community in Texas." American Anthropologist 62.966-976 (1960).
Rubel, Arthur J. Across the Tracks: Mexican-Americans in a Texas City. Austin: Univ. of Texas Press, 1966. xxvii, 266 pp.
Said, Sally Eugenia Sneed. "A Descriptive Model of Austin Spanish Syntax." MA Thesis, Univ. of Texas, Austin 1970. 62 pp.
Sawyer, Janet Beck. "A Dialect Study of San Antonio, Texas: A Bilingual Community." PhD Diss., Univ. of Texas, Austin, 1957. 325 pp.
Sharp, John M. "Some El Paso Spanish Etymologies." In Ralph W. Ewton, Jr. and Jacob Ornstein, eds. Studies in Language and Linguistics 1969-70, El Paso: Texas Western

Press, 1970, pp. 207-232.
Simón, Alphonse, O.M.I. Pastoral Spanish. San Antonio: Standard Printing Co., 1945. xxii, 511 pp.
Vásquez, Librado Keno and María Enriqueta Vásquez. Regional Dictionary of Chicano Slang. Austin, Texas: Jenkins Publishing Co./The Pemberton Press, 1975. 111 pp.
Wagner, Max Leopold. "Ein mexikanisch-amerikanischer Argot: Das Pachuco." Romanistisches Jahrbuch 6.237-266 (1953-54).
Ward, Hortense Warner. "Ear Marks." Texas Folklore Society. Publications 19.106-116 (1944).
Wesley, Howard D. "Ranchero Sayings of the Border." Texas Folklore Society. Publications 12.211-220 (1935).